THE GREAT
RAILROAD
REVOLUTION

CHRISTIAN WOLMAR

THE GREAT RAILROAD REVOLUTION

The History of
TRAINS IN AMERICA

PUBLICAFFAIRS
New York

Published in the United States by PublicAffairs™, a Member of the Perseus Books Group

Printed in the United States of America.

First published in Great Britain in hardback in 2012 by Atlantic Books, an imprint of Atlantic Books Ltd.

PublicAffairs books are available at special discounts for bulk purchases in the US by corporations, institutions, and other organizations. For more information, please contact the Special Markets Department at the Perseus Books Group, 2300 Chestnut Street, Suite 200, Philadelphia, PA 19103, call (800) 810-4145, ext. 5000, or e-mail special.markets@perseusbooks.com.

Designed by Trish Wilkinson
Text set in 11 point Minion Pro

Maps by Jeff Edwards

Library of Congress Cataloging-in-Publication Data
Wolmar, Christian.
    The great railroad revolution : the history of trains in America / Christian Wolmar.
— 1st ed.
        p.   cm.
    Includes bibliographical references and index.
    ISBN 978-1-61039-179-5 (hbk. : alk. paper) — ISBN 978-1-61039-180-1 (e-book)
1. Railroads—United States—History—Juvenile literature. 2. Transportation—United States—History—Juvenile literature. I. Title.
HE2751.W73 2012
385.0973—dc23   2012020987

First US Edition

10 9 8 7 6 5 4 3 2 1

Contents

Maps and Illustrations

MAPS

ILLUSTRATIONS

THE GREAT
RAILROAD
REVOLUTION

N

CANADA

Seattle

Spokane

Portland

Helena

Bismarck

Salt Lake City

San Francisco

Denver

Los Angeles

Santa Fe

El Paso

Dallas

PACIFIC OCEAN

MEXICO

0   150   300 miles

0   250   500 km

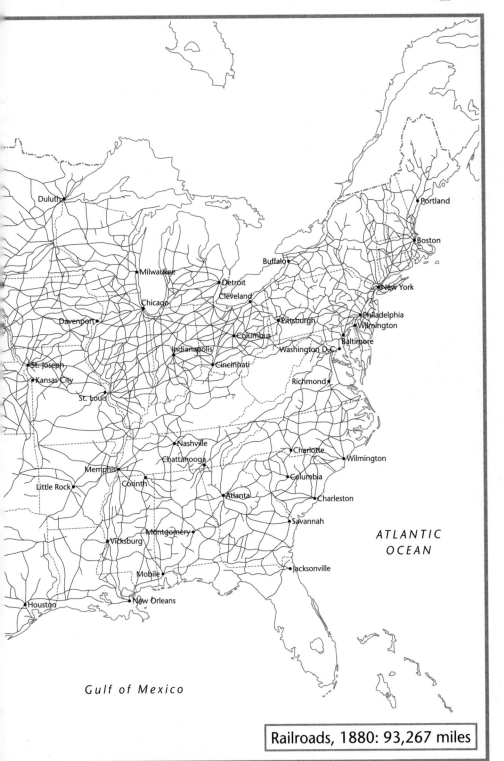

Duluth

Portland

Boston

Buffalo

Milwaukee

Detroit

New York

Chicago

Cleveland

Philadelphia

Pittsburgh

Wilmington

Davenport

Columbus

Baltimore

Indianapolis

Washington D.C.

St. Joseph

Cincinnati

Kansas City

Richmond

St. Louis

Nashville

Charlotte

Wilmington

Chattanooga

Columbia

Memphis

Little Rock

Corinth

Atlanta

Charleston

Savannah

Montgomery

Vicksburg

Jacksonville

Mobile

Houston

New Orleans

ATLANTIC
OCEAN

Gulf of Mexico

Railroads, 1880: 93,267 miles

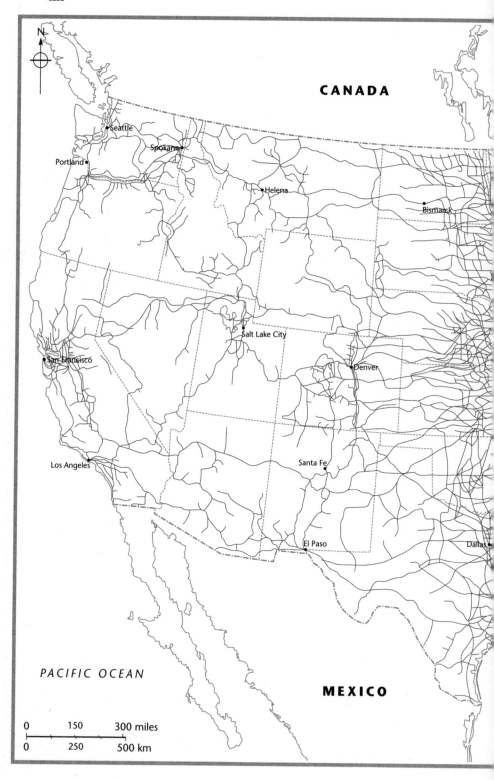

CANADA

Seattle
Spokane
Portland

Helena

Bismarck

Salt Lake City

San Francisco

Denver

Los Angeles

Santa Fe

El Paso

Dallas

PACIFIC OCEAN

MEXICO

| 0 | 150 | 300 miles |
| 0 | 250 | 500 km |

Railroads, 1916: 254,037 miles

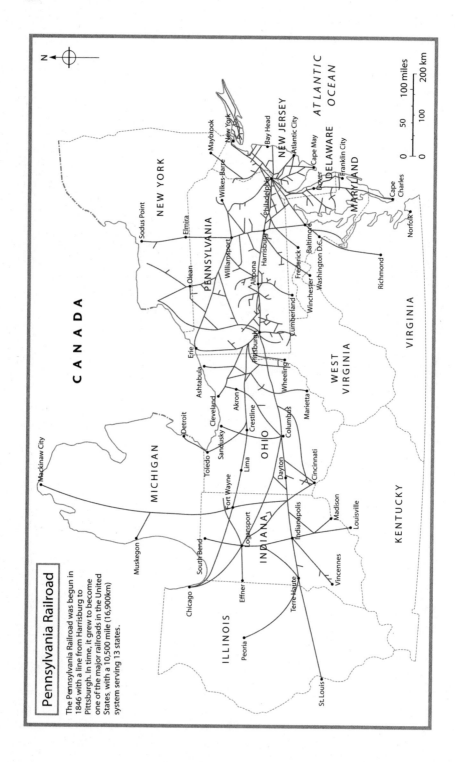

Pennsylvania Railroad

The Pennsylvania Railroad was begun in 1846 with a line from Harrisburg to Pittsburgh. In time, it grew to become one of the major railroads in the United States, with a 10,500 mile (16,900km) system serving 13 states.

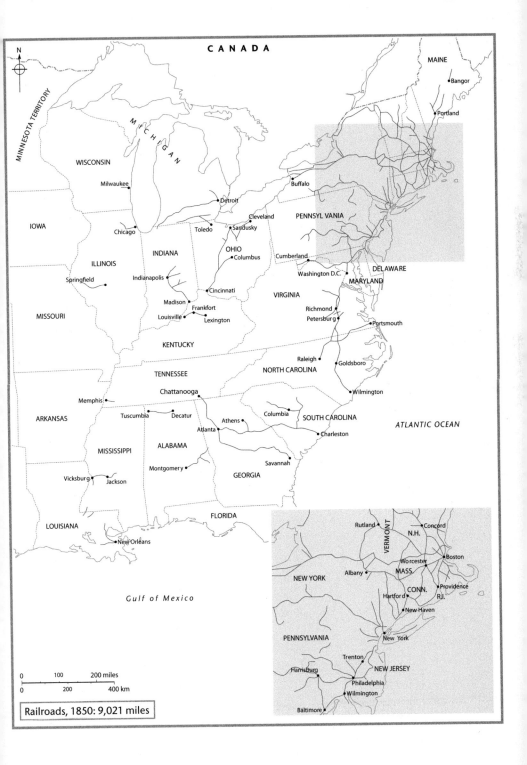

Railroads, 1850: 9,021 miles

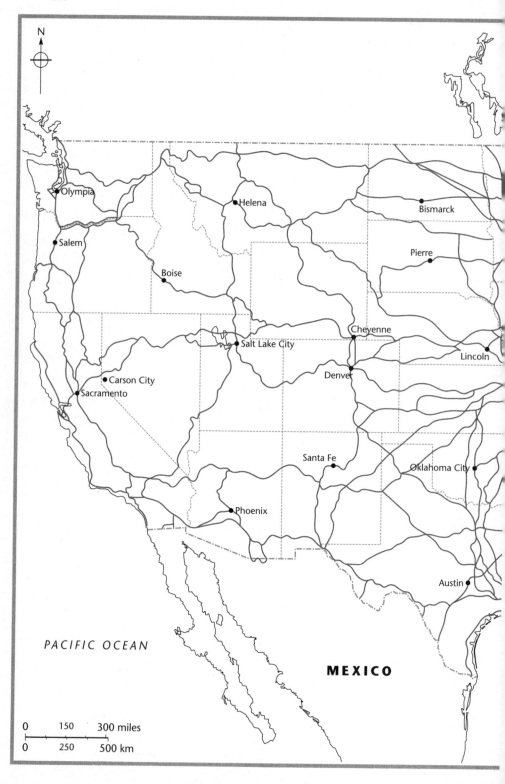

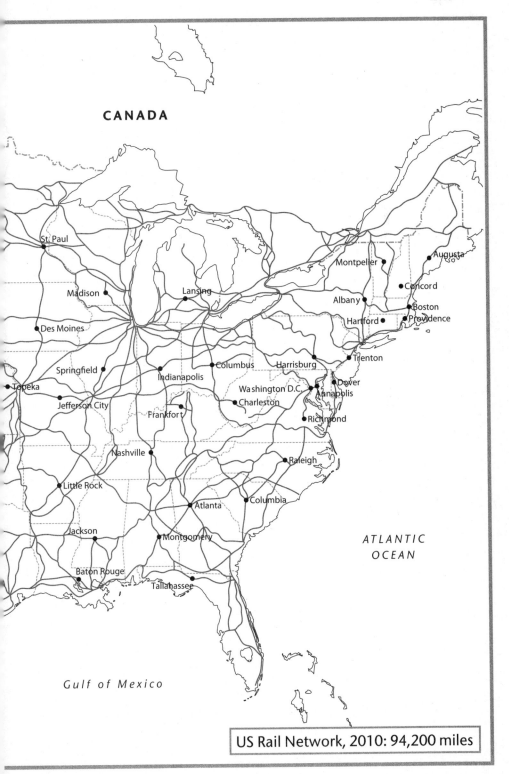

CANADA

St. Paul

Madison

Des Moines

Springfield

Topeka

Jefferson City

Frankfort

Nashville

Little Rock

Jackson

Baton Rouge

Lansing

Indianapolis

Columbus

Charleston

Atlanta

Montgomery

Tallahassee

Montpelier

Albany

Hartford

Harrisburg

Washington D.C.
Annapolis

Richmond

Raleigh

Columbia

Augusta

Concord

Boston
Providence

Trenton

Dover

ATLANTIC
OCEAN

Gulf of Mexico

US Rail Network, 2010: 94,200 miles

Introduction

America was made by the railroads. They united the country and then stimulated the economic development that enabled the country to become the world's richest nation. The railroads also transformed American society, changing it from a primarily agrarian economy to an industrial powerhouse in the space of a few decades of the nineteenth century. Quite simply, without the railroads, the United States would not have become the United States.

The extraordinary growth of the railroads changed the very nature of America. From modest beginnings in the 1830s, the mileage grew to cover nearly two hundred thousand miles by the turn of the century, more than in any other country in the world. Yet the epic tale of the growth of the railroads and their influence on the development of the nation is now largely forgotten and ignored. By the middle of the twentieth century, as the automobile and the airplane continued their relentless march toward domination of the US domestic transportation network, the historical importance of the railroads was being written out of the nation's consciousness. Passenger railroads were reduced to a loss-making irrelevance. Mention the American railroads to most people, and they will talk about them as a spent force. Yet railroads still flourish in the United States and are a vital part of the infrastructure. The tracks are still there, but even when the huge freight trains run through town centers, they somehow remain invisible to the American public. It is a surprising fact that America's railroad network remains the world's largest and is the bedrock of the country's freight transportation system. There are, too, signs of a revival in passenger railroads, with money available from the federal government thanks to President Obama's welcome, if flawed, stimulus package of 2009 and a rise in passenger numbers on Amtrak services. America may have gradually disowned its railroad heritage—but now is the time to reclaim and reinstate it. This book attempts to do just that.

Although there are countless tomes on railroad history, few have tried to tell the story of the American railroads and their impact in one concise narrative. That has meant taking a very selective approach, and inevitably many facets of the rich story of America's railroads have been left out. Inevitably, it has been impossible to be comprehensive, and I have had to be selective on what aspects to cover in detail. I have, for example, chosen particular railroads to look at in some depth as examples, since there is no way that any book of a reasonable length could adequately cover the history of 250,000 miles of track, which was America's route mileage at the railroads' height. Obviously, most of the prominent companies are mentioned in the book, but there are numerous omissions for reasons of space or repetition.

As with several of my other books, I have focused more on the nineteenth century than the twentieth. That is deliberate. It was in the nineteenth that the railroads were being built, and they reached their zenith soon after the turn of the century. The story of the twentieth is one largely of decline and waning influence, a time when railroads were losing their importance and where opportunities to make the best use of this historic legacy were missed. Although this period is covered in less detail than the earlier times, I try to explain why what started out as a love affair between the American people and their railroads has turned out so badly and why an industry that makes such a positive contribution to America's economy today is largely ignored or even reviled.

I have highlighted for particular attention the role of a few of the individuals who created or ran the railroads, but again for reasons of space I have left out many other great characters who have contributed to the making of American railroads during its near two centuries of existence. I make no apology, but hope the reader will understand how difficult this selection has been.

The first chapter looks at how railroads emerged and why they developed as opposed to other forms of technology. Each aspect of what constituted a railroad had to be conceived, developed, and refined: track beds, rails, cars, and locomotives. Railroads brought together the most complex

set of technologies developed since the dawn of civilization. And
was a pioneer, joining the railroad age just after the first modern
had been opened in the United Kingdom. America was a young c
ripe for the railroad revolution, and within a few years of the first line opening, there were already a thousand miles in short separate lines laid principally on the Eastern Seaboard. Quite clearly, the railroad's moment had
arrived. It soon became obvious to its early promoters that—on grounds of
efficiency and cheapness—locomotives rather than horses must be used to
pull the carriages and railroad trucks. The first significant railroad had been
developed in Britain in 1830, and several European countries had quickly
followed suit. The United States fast caught up and was soon leading the
world in railroad mileage. The railroad age had arrived, and nothing could
stop it.

The second chapter shows how America's relationship with the railroads soon became a passionate affair. They grew symbiotically, rapidly
spreading across the more economically advanced states. From harboring
doubts about the railroads, suddenly everyone wanted to be connected to
the railroad. The burgeoning United States adopted railroad technology
faster and with more enthusiasm than any other nation, embracing the
new invention that seemed to reflect the pioneering spirit of the age. Up
and down the East Coast, railroad lines sprang up with amazing speed,
stimulating economic growth that would change the way people lived and
eventually make America the most powerful nation on earth. Of the
twenty-six states that constituted the Union in 1840, only four—Arkansas,
Missouri, Tennessee, and Vermont—had not completed their first mile of
track. The beginnings of what would become the major railroad companies were established during the 1840s with the opening of the New York
Central & Hudson River and Pennsylvania lines. However, for the most
part in the 1830s and 1840s, the development of the railroads was a local
affair. People wanted to have easy access to the local town, or possibly to
the other end of the state, rather than across the nation. These early railroad companies were a true ragbag of outfits, ranging from, literally, one-
horse companies carrying coal out of a mine to longer lines stretching
into the outback and carrying thousands of passengers a week.

The third chapter shows how the railroads took off as an industry in the
years running up to the Civil War. The 1850s saw a massive increase in

the pace of track development, and the mileage more than tripled during the decade. This was a period of strong economic performance, both driven by the railroads and speeded up by their construction. Although most of the railroads were built by the private sector, little of this remarkable growth would have been possible without government support through various mechanisms, such as allowing companies to run lotteries, the granting of monopolistic rights, tax exemptions, and land grants. It was the start of a difficult relationship between government and the railroads.

The American railroads were bigger in every sense than those in Europe. They covered longer distances, used larger locomotives, and hauled longer trains. The railroads seemed to be tailor-made for the huge American landmass and for the indomitable spirit of its people. European countries were constrained by reactionary governments slow to recognize the social and economic benefits of the railroads and by old-fashioned customs that those with vested interests worked hard to protect. Americans, however—free from the shackles of tradition and unencumbered by obstructive government—took to the new method of transportation with far more gusto and enthusiasm than their European peers.

The Civil War, covered in Chapter 4, was the first true railroad war and was particularly lengthy and bloody as a result. Key battles were fought around railroad junctions, railroad sabotage became a key tactic of the war, and troops were transported huge distances in a way that would have been impossible even a decade previously. The North, industrially stronger than its rival, was lent a key advantage by its superior railroads, which, crucially, were far better managed during the war than those of the South. The Unionists quickly realized that the operation of the railroads could not be left to chance and placed them under military control early in the conflict. By contrast, the secessionists never established government rule over their railroads, with the result that they operated far less efficiently. The war would also witness remarkable examples of derring-do on the railroads: the Andrews Raid (or Great Locomotive Chase) in April 1862—in which Union volunteers commandeered a locomotive on the Western & Atlantic line, deep in Confederate territory, and created mayhem as they drove it north—has entered American folklore but somewhat obscured the true story of the railroads in this conflict.

The fifth chapter tells the story of the construction of the first transcontinental railroad in the United States. The dream of a coast-to-coast line had first been mooted as early as 1820, but it was not until the 1850s that the idea was seriously considered; its start was delayed by the Civil War, although ironically it was the absence of the Southern politicians that allowed the legislation to be passed by Congress. It was by far the most ambitious railroad project of this period in the world—to be surpassed thirty years later only by the Trans-Siberian, the subject of my next book—but its exact purpose was somewhat unclear. To reach the Pacific Ocean, three thousand miles away, was an obvious ambition for the federal government in Washington seeking to unify the new nation, but it was never going to be a commercial proposition. Thanks to lobbying by a remarkable young dreamer, Theodore Judah, who gained the political backing of Abraham Lincoln, Congress passed the act to build the line in 1862. The law also allowed for massive subsidies in the form of both cash and land grants to the two companies building the line, the Union Pacific and the Central Pacific.

Like much of the story of the US railroads, the building of the transcontinental encompassed both the best and the worst aspects of pioneering American culture. On the one hand, there was the extraordinary achievement of building nearly two thousand miles of line through two mountain ranges and a long stretch of desert, making it by far the longest railroad in the world up to that point; on the other, there was the shameless corruption that allowed the directors of both companies to make extraordinary riches through the simple expedient of contracting the work through dummy construction companies. Crédit Mobilier of America, established in 1864 by Dr. Thomas Durant, was at the center of the scandal that broke in 1872, when it was revealed that a number of congressmen had received cash bribes or shares in the company. There was, too, the excess of competitive zeal that saw, at one point, the ridiculous phenomenon of the two railroad companies grading parallel lines in order to maximize the land grants paid by the government. Nevertheless, the celebration to mark the completion of the transcontinental railroad at Promontory Point, Utah Territory, in 1869 must be seen as one of the turning points of US history.

In Chapters 6 and 7, the amazing exponential growth of the railroads during the rest of the nineteenth century is explored against the backdrop of their growing unpopularity. No community of any size in the United States could afford to be out of range of a locomotive's whistle, and, by the end of the century, with a network encompassing more than two hundred thousand miles, very few were. The transcontinental had prompted growth in the West, and the railroad was beginning to knit the nation together. The 1880s saw the biggest increase in rail mileage of any period of US history: seventy-one thousand miles of track were built during this decade, most of it in the states west of the Mississippi. The construction boom was greatly stimulated by the federal government's continuing program of offering land grants to the railroad companies constructing these lines. The grants were controversial, as they benefited a relatively small number of companies, but they undoubtedly played a critical role in bringing the eastern and western parts of the United States together. Without them, the widespread settlement of the West by newly arrived immigrants might not have been possible.

For passengers, technical improvements were making their journeys better. Significant improvements to the quality of the tracks allowed faster speeds, while better locomotive technology enabled the railroads to carry heavier loads at a cheaper rate. Introduction of better brakes, steel rails, and improved couplers enhanced the performance of an industry that had been widely criticized for delays and accidents. The needs of passengers were catered to by such innovations as dining and sleeping cars promoted by inventor and industrialist George Pullman. In addition, the railroads began to standardize equipment and operating procedures, further reducing costs and making it easier for trains to run on the lines of other companies.

During this period of rapid growth, the very nature of the rail system changed in fundamental and highly visible ways: for instance, towns with two or more stations often built one consolidated "union" station, and lines that had hitherto been separate were linked for the first time. In November 1883, time was standardized into four zones to help the railroads keep a schedule. A truly national rail network was taking shape.

Despite these many positive developments for the railroads, services remained basic on many lines, adding to the unpopularity of the railroads with some members of the public. The postbellum period was also the age of "bare knuckles," as the major companies began to slug it out for increased market share. Powerful and unscrupulous railroad magnates—

men like Cornelius Vanderbilt, Daniel Drew, and banker Jay Gould—became a feature of the industrial landscape of America's "Gilded Age," and they exacerbated the railroads' unpopularity, as did their response to the increasing labor unrest. The resentment engendered by several railroad strikes would be a significant factor in the birth of labor unions in the United States. The farmers became an especially strong force opposed to the monopoly of the railroads, and even though many of their accusations were unfair, they were a potent and influential opposition. Over the course of barely a generation, the railroads became, first, disliked, and then widely resented. It was partly a natural cycle. At first the railroads had been the plucky innovator, the new kid on the block bringing prosperity and opening new horizons, then they became the established but respected business, and eventually they turned into the rapacious monopolist, reviled by almost everyone.

Chapter 8, taking a breather from the chronological narrative, looks at how, despite the increasing hostility toward them, the railroads had changed America. Few aspects of American life remained unaffected. Most of the changes brought about by the railroad were beneficial: economic growth, creation of jobs, more efficient markets, opportunities to travel, easier distribution of goods, and so on. There were numerous others ways in which trains and stations stimulated local economic activity. The trains brought in mail-order goods from department stores in the city, fresh produce for the local shops, mail, packages, and newspapers. Even the station clock was a useful public amenity, providing what was probably the best local estimate of the time. The station, or depot, however modest, would become a key part of the town's amenities, the start or end of most people's visits or of journeys by local inhabitants to far-distant lands. The relationship between the town and the station would be symbiotic, and as with much of this story, it is difficult to disentangle the causation.

There were, though, negatives too. Because the poor could not afford to travel, it could be argued that the railroads exacerbated the differences between the haves and the have-nots. The big towns prospered thanks to these crowds who boosted their economies as they shopped, ate in restaurants, and stayed in hotels. The consequent rapid and unplanned growth of the cities, stimulated by the railroads, was not necessarily a welcome change. Railroads, as with all transportation improvements, benefit the areas where people want to go, and although there may have been the occasional rural excursion, for the most part it was the cities that profited from the ability of people to travel more easily. Central business districts sprang up near railroad stations, and, in order to maintain as much density as possible, the notion of the office block, and later the skyscraper, was born. These buildings full of white-collar staff were the new factories of the age, housing hundreds, if not thousands, of office workers in the way that the manufacturing industry had done earlier.

The ninth chapter looks at the effect of the restrictive legislation, born of the increasing mistrust of the railroads, which was to do them great harm in the twentieth century when their stranglehold over the transportation industry was lost. By the early years of the new century, the railroads had consolidated into seven major groupings (although many other smaller companies remained independent), a process that both increased their efficiency and allowed them to invest more in improvements. New lines were no longer the priority, since virtually every community was now connected to the network, but there was a need for massive investment in the system. Whereas many improvements were made in the pre–First World War period, the strictness of the control by the new regulator, the Interstate Commerce Commission, reduced the railroads' profits and therefore their ability to invest. The key question was whether the railroads would actually have used any extra profits to good effect, or would they have simply paid out more money to their shareholders?

Consequently, the railroads entered the First World War in a relatively poor state. The neglected railroads were now called upon to provide for unprecedented levels of demand and were found wanting. They were short of every type of capital asset, from new rails to functioning locomotives, and the lack of coordination between them meant services were inefficient and slow. As a result, the government was forced to take over control of the railroads during the war, an unprecedented and largely unwelcome situation, which also posed the dilemma of what to do with them when the fighting ceased.

Chapter 10 covers the interwar years when, to arrest the decline in passenger numbers, the railroads invested heavily in new equipment and, after prevaricating, began to move over to the new technology of diesel that offered cheaper and faster services. This was the period when the rail companies provided the most exciting trains that ever ran on the American rail network, although sadly only for a relatively brief period, as competition from roads and later aviation killed off these services. This time, in 1941, the railroads entered the war better equipped and ready to cooperate with each other in order to ensure there was no repeat of government takeover.

And, finally, the last two chapters show how the performance of the railroads in the Second World War was their last heyday, preceding a remarkably rapid decline, first in passengers, and then in freight, which actually could have resulted in the closure of much of the network. In the event, the railroads were rescued by the government and by changes in legislation. The freight railroads are now flourishing and passenger rail growing, amid much discussion about increased investment and, in particular, high-speed rail. Towns and cities across the country see rail as a way of reducing the burden on the roads, and, despite opposition, many new schemes are being put forward. The railroad, a nineteenth-century invention that struggled in the latter part of the twentieth, undoubtedly has a great future in the twenty-first.

I dislike the expression *road*, shortened from *railroad* and used very widely in America, because of the confusion it might have caused among readers little versed in railroad history, and therefore have rarely used it. I have, too, eschewed initials. The Baltimore & Ohio remains just that, rather than the B&O, because the proliferation of initials makes for difficult reading. This style, too, imposed on me a discipline not to use the names too often.

There are a few passages that are based on my earlier book *Blood, Iron, and Gold,* which, although covering the world's railroads, detailed the US story, and therefore inevitably I have drawn upon some parts of the narrative but expanded them. Similarly, a few events described in *Fire and Steam,* my book on the history of Britain's railroads, have inevitably been repeated in the first chapter, which recounts the prehistory of the railroads, and the chapter on the Civil War relies in part from the equivalent chapter in *Engines of War.*

I have ignored the Canadian and Mexican railroads, although they are in many ways part of the same interconnected system, not least through shared ownership. That is particularly true of the transcontinentals—like the United States, Canada built far too many too quickly, ending up with three to serve a tiny population—but I have left them out for reasons of simplicity and brevity. Recounting those stories is for another book.

I realize that it is somewhat cheeky of me, a Brit, to try to write a concise history of American railroads. My justification is that it sometimes takes an outsider to understand the importance of what local people take for granted or simply ignore out of familiarity. It has been a fantastic and hugely enjoyable task. I traveled twice extensively on the US rail network and met numerous people with an interest in rail who helped formulate my ideas. Nevertheless, I am sure there are mistakes, and errors in interpretation. They are, of course, all my own. I hope, though, that they do not detract from the thrust of the book, which is to show the railroads in context and to explain how they helped to create the America of today, even though that has been largely forgotten. Please do point out any mistakes by e-mailing me via my website, www.christianwolmar.co.uk. This has proved very useful in the past, and any corrections will find their way into future editions.

Special thanks are due to the hardy individuals who read the full draft and provided detailed corrections and suggestions: Clyde Williams, Gerald Rawling, John Fowler, Andrew Dow, and John Sears. I cannot thank them enough. Some of the mistakes they uncovered required a level of attention to detail and knowledge that astonishes me. Many other people provided support, advice, corrections, or information. In no particular order: Robert Lester Porter, Fritz Plous and the people on his e-mail list, Diana Bailey Harris, Teresa Glynn (for office support), Xavier Bryce, Rupert Brennan Brown, Andrew Adonis, Deborah Reddig, Craig Haberle and all at the Pennsylvania Railroad Museum, Kelly Ohler, Mike Forter, Ed Burkhardt, Nigel Harris, Mark Sullivan, Pip Dunn, and Tony Streeter.

Because of a hard-drive failure at just the wrong time, I may have omitted several people, to whom I am deeply apologetic. I would, too, like to thank Amtrak, which did provide me with free travel—though not sleeper accommodation—for my tour around the country in the autumn of 2010. I may be a bit hard on the company, but at least it is still there celebrating its fortieth anniversary, which many thought it would never reach.

My agent, Andrew Lownie, steers me through the confusing world of publishing, and the team at PublicAffairs is ever supportive. Special thanks are due to my editor, Richard Milbank, at my British publisher, Atlantic Books, who did so much to improve the book with amazingly detailed and thorough work, and to Toby Mundy, Atlantic's chief executive, who always believes in my ability to pull off these projects. Thank you also to Annette Wenda, copy editor of the American edition, for her excellent work. And special thanks to my partner, Deborah Maby, who is always there for me.

Dedicated to all my children and stepchildren—
Molly, Pascoe, Misha, Harriet, and Robyn—
and in memory of
Tony Telford (1942–2011),
who sadly died
in the summer of 2011 and
had helped me greatly
with several of my earlier history books.

1

THE RAILROADS
WIN OUT

It was a particularly prescient remark. Indeed, so prescient that it has subsequently become the stuff of legend.[1] The speaker was an old man, Charles Carroll, the last surviving signatory of the Declaration of Independence. The event was the ceremonial turning of the first sod of earth to begin work on the Baltimore & Ohio, America's pioneering railroad. The date, inevitably, was Independence Day, July 4, 1828, just over a half century after the declaration that resulted in the creation of the new nation. The words were simple: "I consider what I have just now done to be among the most important acts of my life, second only to my signing the Declaration of Independence, if indeed, it be even second to that."

And so it proved. If the Declaration of Independence in 1776 marked the birth of a nation, the advent of the railroads enabled America to become the most prosperous nation on earth within a few decades of Carroll's spadework, turning a preindustrial society into an economic powerhouse. America and the railroads were to be a perfect fit, their joint growth intertwined so intimately that countless historians have been unable to determine whether it was the growth of the American economy that sparked the expansion of the railroads or vice versa. The Baltimore & Ohio was not the first entity in America to call itself a railroad, and, as we shall see, its reputation as the first modern railroad in the United States rests on shaky ground, but there is no doubting the importance of its inauguration as a stimulus in creating America's most important industry of the nineteenth century.

Railroads had, in fact, been a long time coming. The first American railroads were the product of a disparate series of inventions stretching back centuries, but which were mostly spawned by the Industrial Revolution in Britain that began in the first half of the eighteenth century. The long gestation period of the railroads can be explained by the fact that it became possible to construct them only once the various aspects of technology that prefigured their birth had been developed and subsequently improved through application. A railroad was a far more sophisticated concept than any previous invention, requiring several elements to come together: the technology, both for the traction and the track; the financing to pay for it; the permission of the state to build it; the creation of an appropriate legal framework; and, of course, the labor for construction. Such a coordination of different agencies, technologies, and resources had been effected only for military purposes and required vision and ambition, as well as the cooperation of the various entities involved. It is hardly surprising, therefore, that the emergence of the railroads was a stuttering process, conducted in fits and starts with numerous failures and dead ends along the way. Once they had been established, however, the railroads would spread far faster than any of their pioneers could have imagined.

The precursor to railroads, normally called wagonways[2] or tramways, which consisted of wagons pushed or hauled along tracks by animal or human power, was actually quite an old invention. There are some suggestions that the ancient Greeks used tracks built into the road to drag boats across the Isthmus of Corinth. Traces of heavy, flat-topped stone blocks placed along a Roman road, the Fosse Way, near Leicester in the English Midlands—possible evidence of an early form of wagonway—can be found in the local museum. It was not until the middle of the seventeenth century, however, that the increase in demand for coal prompted the invention of more sophisticated wagonways. The replacement of stone blocks with wooden tracks to support the wagons provided a better all-weather surface that could be used in conditions that turned conventional roads into mud. Soon there were extensive networks of these tracked wagonways, all with the same purpose, namely, hauling heavy material such as coal or slate out of the mines and, usually, to the nearest waterway. Wagonways also appeared in Germany and France, but it was in Britain, the cradle of the Industrial Revolution, that their number grew fastest. Although these early lines were crude and mostly quite short, several were substantial operations whose scale reflected the increased demand for coal. The Tanfield Way in County Durham, in northeastern England, opened in 1725 and soon built up to an astonishing traffic of 450,000 tons annually (or, as has been calculated, "one fully loaded wagon every 45 seconds on working days")[3] and necessitated the construction of the Causey Arch, the world's oldest stone railroad bridge.

As loads became heavier, the simple wooden timbers laid on earth were quickly worn away. To counter this problem, the wood was covered with a layer of iron to protect the rails, a practice that was first recorded as early as 1738. This innovation led to a rapid spread in wagonways. Until the introduction of iron-covered rails, the total extent of the network was limited to a few hundred miles, with the longest wagonway stretching about a dozen miles, but the greater durability of the new rails encouraged the building of thousands of miles of iron ways. By the middle of the eighteenth century, some longer tracks had been built to connect different mines, although sometimes less cooperative mine owners would ban their neighbors and rivals from transporting coal across their land, thus blocking the easiest access to waterways.

The next requirement was to stop the wagons from slipping off the rails. Various ideas were tried, such as sinking the rails into the ground, as with some streetcar lines today, and L-shaped rails to keep the wheels aligned, but the crucial idea of putting a flange all around the wheel began to be developed only in the late eighteenth century. There were two ways of ensuring the wheels stayed on the track: either the edge of the rails could be turned up, making an L shape to guide the wheel along the track, or the wheel could be fitted with a flange—a projecting rim—with similar results. The L-shaped rail was first tried out in 1776 at the Duke of Norfolk's colliery in Yorkshire.

Not for the first or last time, a technological development proved unpopular with those affected by its introduction. In this instance, it was the colliers, who, on finding that the new type of rail required the use of fewer horses and men to haul the coal, broke up the rails—called plates—and chased the terrified plate layer, one John Curr, into the forest, where he hid for three days. L-shaped rails, though, proved cumbersome and inefficient, and various inventors tried putting the guiding flange on the wheel instead of the track. The pioneer of this method seems[4] to have been William Jessop, who used flanged wheels on a wagonway in Loughborough, in the English Midlands, in 1789, a design that, of course, became the norm on all railroads. Jessop is also credited with another crucial improvement: the laying of transverse ties (or sleepers, as they are known in Britain) on which to lay and fix the rails, greatly improving the stability of the track.

There was fun to be had with these innovations, too. A century before Jessop, the idea of coaches running on tracks had appealed to King Louis XIV of France. The Sun King used to entertain his guests by giving them rides on the Roulette, a kind of roller coaster built in the gardens of his château at Marly, near Versailles, in 1691. It was a carved and gilded carriage on wheels that thundered down an eight-hundred-foot wooden track into a valley and, thanks to its momentum, up the other side—much to the amusement of the king's bewigged guests.

None of these early lines, whether for hauling coal or entertaining French aristocrats, which were operated by human or animal power supplemented at times by gravity, could truly be said to resemble a "railroad" in the modern sense of the word. A convenient definition for a true railroad might be a trackborne transportation system powered by mechanical means—though horses were used in some early systems—able to carry freight or passengers in both directions and intended for public use. This latter point was a crucial step forward. Railroads would not have had their transformative effect if their use had been confined to the owner's personal needs or to a single purpose such as hauling minerals. The next logical stage in their development was to become common carriers—that is, not just to provide the facility for the owner, but to make it available to all comers. These new lines tended to be run by canal companies, using the railroads as feeders for their own networks. In July 1803, however, the nine-mile Surrey Iron Railway—in what is now suburban South London—was completed and was the first public railroad open to anyone prepared to pay the toll. Numerous similar enterprises followed, connecting mines and waterways within their localities and allowing a wider range of potential customers, including mills and factories, to transport their goods along the tracks.

With long-lasting track now available, the other requirement for a railroad was the development of a power source other than the wretched animals that would never be suitable for anything beyond hauling relatively light loads for short distances. Steam power was the obvious answer, but, again, there were numerous technical and practical obstacles to overcome. The first engines driven by steam were probably devised by Thomas Newcomen, an ironmaster from Devon, early in the eighteenth century. His work was based on the pioneering efforts of a seventeenth-century French scientist, Denis Papin, who had recognized that a piston contained within a cylinder was a potential way of exploiting the power of steam. Newcomen, using a recently improved version of smelting iron, developed the idea into working engines that could be used to pump water from mines. His invention proved to be crucial in keeping the tin and copper-ore industry viable in Cornwall, since all the mines had reached a depth where they were permanently flooded and existing waterpower pumps were insufficient to drain them. By 1733, when Newcomen's patents ran out, around sixty of his engines had been produced.

Working in the second half of the eighteenth century, Scottish inventor and engineer James Watt made steam commercially viable by improving the efficiency of engines and adapting them for a wide variety of purposes. Boulton & Watt, his partnership with Birmingham manufacturer Matthew Boulton, became the most important builder of steam engines in the world, cornering the market by registering a patent that effectively gave them a monopoly on all steam-engine development in the UK until the end of the eighteenth century. Steam power quickly became commonplace in the early nineteenth century, and it was Boulton & Watt that provided the engine for the world's first "practical" steamboat, the *Charlotte Dundas*, which made its short maiden voyage on a Glasgow canal in 1803. Various attempts to propel boats by steam power had been made in both Europe and America since the mid-eighteenth century, but they had proved short-lived as a result of technical failure or other factors, notably fear of explosions. The most successful experiment had been the steamboat built by the US inventor John Fitch, who in 1788 operated a regular commercial service on the Delaware River between Philadelphia, Pennsylvania, and Burlington, New Jersey, carrying up to thirty passengers. Fitch's steamboat traveled more than two thousand miles during its short period of service, but competition from the roads meant that it was not a commercial success.

Boulton & Watt's much-improved engines led to the construction of numerous steamboats that were to prove particularly useful in America, with its vast distances and long stretches of navigable waterways. Steam power, therefore, was to be the catalyst for the early opening up of America—but on water rather than on rails. As George Rogers Taylor, author of the standard work on early transportation systems in the United States, suggests, right from its birth as a nation, the United States was "peculiarly dependent upon river transportation."[5] River courses determined the location and size of settlements, as, for a generation and more, waterways were the only way to reach much of the huge landmass eventually occupied by the United States.

The rivers, however, were obstacles as well as pathways, and navigating up them was an arduous and perilous task. On the lower reaches of the bigger rivers like the Mississippi or the Hudson, it was possible for seagoing sailing ships to tack upriver for a few miles, but elsewhere swift currents and shallow waters made even such limited progress impossible. Produce from inland was, therefore, floated down on crude rafts and flatboats that were too unwieldy to make the return journey and were broken up for lumber. According to Taylor, "Transportation up the rivers proved extremely time consuming and costly." Labor costs to operate the narrow keelboats that were able to travel upriver were so high that these boats carried only the most essential items. The farther west, the greater the difficulty of river transportation. Pittsburgh could be reached from New Orleans only by a journey of nearly two thousand miles that took four months "and required a crew of strong men prepared to utilize every known method in overcoming the difficulties of upriver navigation."[6] Sometimes these tireless men rowed or towed, or even, occasionally, "bushwhacked," pulling themselves along with whatever overhanging vegetation might be available.

Steamships, therefore, transformed the scope of travel by river and the economies of the inland towns and villages. Once Watt's engines had been refined by a series of inventors on both sides of the Atlantic, the feasibility of regular steamboat travel was demonstrated on northeastern waterways such as the Delaware and Hudson Rivers in the first decade of the nineteenth century. *The North River Steamboat*, designed by the distinguished inventor and entrepreneur Robert Fulton, plied the New York to Albany stretch of the Hudson River from September 1807, becoming the first commercially successful paddle steamer. In the winter of 1811–12, another Fulton venture, a vessel optimistically named *New Orleans,* steamed down the Ohio and Mississippi Rivers to New Orleans and thereby became the first steamship to navigate the western waters of the United States. Going back upriver, however, proved too tough, and the *New Orleans* never made the return journey. It was not until 1815 that a steamship, the *Enterprise,* successfully made the journey in both directions, confirming the potential of steamboats to navigate long distances both up- and downriver. This epoch-making journey ushered in the heyday of the steamship. Although New York City quickly became the center of the steamboat industry, rivers and bays along the whole Eastern Seaboard from Maine to Florida were soon filled with steamers. On the Great Lakes, steamships took longer to displace the sailing boats that were well suited to local conditions and cheaper to operate, but they eventually did so. From their first appearance on the Great Lakes around 1816–17, steamships grew steadily in size and number.

Farther west, the advent of the steamship changed the whole economy of the region: "In the great valley of the Mississippi, steam-driven vessels proved the most important factor in the great industrial development of that region from 1815 to the eve of the civil war." By 1820, 69 steamships were navigating the western rivers, and the total peaked at 727 in 1855, demonstrating why it took some time for the railroads to establish their complete domination of inland travel. The mileage of the river system, with the Mississippi as its spine, was impressive: "One of the great pioneers of western expansion, Senator Thomas Hart Benton (1782–1858) of Missouri—which in 1821 had been admitted as the first state wholly west of the Mississippi—reckoned that some 50,000 miles of water in the Mississippi river system were navigable by some kind of boat; in any case some 16,000 miles of steamboat routes are recorded."[7] It would take until the mid-1850s for the mileage of railroads to exceed even the latter figure. Indeed, at first, railroads and steamships complemented each other since many of the great rivers had not been forded, and it was not until the completion of continuous rail routes through the construction of bridges that the decline of the waterways became inevitable.

Ships, of course, were limited to where they could go by the course of the rivers, and it was not really until the advent of the steamship that the notion of changing the features of the landscape to suit the mode of transportation, rather than the other way around, was born. The resulting canal boom came late to America. Whereas in Europe the heyday of canal building was already well under way by the turn of the century, following the opening of the Bridgewater Canal in northwestern England in 1761, there were still fewer than 100 miles of canal in the United States a half century later, and only two of these man-made waterways were more than a couple of miles long. There was no shortage of ambitious projects being put forward by entrepreneurs, but few canals were actually built. As with the turnpikes, the nascent road network, it was the difficulty of finding capital, together with the failure of early ventures, that underlay this lack of interest. America's belated canal mania was triggered by the brave decision to build the Erie Canal, an astonishingly ambitious project, which stretched 363 miles across New York State between the lower Hudson River at Albany and Buffalo, on the shores of Lake Erie. First proposed in 1807, it was built remarkably quickly between 1817 and 1825, becoming, by far, the longest man-made waterway in the world. Despite the difficulties of operation—there was only one towpath, and every time two boats met, one had to drop its towline into the water to allow the other to pass—its economic impact was immediate. Even before the canal's completion, traffic crowded onto the finished sections, and there was soon talk of overcrowding and expansion.

The wider economic impact of the canals demonstrated the same pattern that would later be seen in the railroad boom. Transportation costs to the interior were reduced dramatically, by as much as 95 percent according to some assessments, and trade between the East Coast and the Midwest expanded dramatically. The Erie Canal stimulated early westward migration and enabled farm produce from the interior to be transported east, beginning the process of uniting America. From Maine to Virginia, the success of the Erie set off a nationwide enthusiasm for canal building with the expectation that similar ambitious projects would be equally profitable. Projects that had been put forward before the construction of the Erie were quickly dusted off and now found ready investors, though for the most part this was through bonds sold and guaranteed by state governments. Even when canals were built privately, they often relied on some form of financial support from the states. These canals were mostly designed to improve connections between the Atlantic ports and inland communities and waterways, and, in the West, to connect the Ohio-Mississippi river system with the Great Lakes. Despite the fact that many of the projects did not, ultimately, see the light of day, there were more than 3,300 miles of canal in the United States by 1840.

The canals, however, struggled. The biggest failure of the period was the 365-mile Pennsylvania Main Line between Philadelphia, Pennsylvania, and Columbus, Ohio, an attempt to marry railroad and canal technology. It consisted of canals for most of its length except on the steep gradients through the mountains, where there were inclined planes on which a cable system hauled canal boats over the brow and then eased them down on the other side. The inclined-plane railroad sections proved to be a bottleneck, as they had less capacity than the rest of the system, and the scheme never became a true competitor to the far more successful Erie, not least because it had 174 locks, more than twice the number of its rival. Indeed, most of the canal projects never made money for their investors, and the brief canal boom came to an end by the late 1830s because of two financial crises and a general lack of confidence in the idea. The failure of the canals stemmed from several internal factors: they were expensive to build, had severe capacity limitations (which meant that even at times of maximum usage, many remained unprofitable), and were vulnerable to severe weather conditions (most crucially, they had to close in winter when they froze over and were also susceptible to floods—which made towpaths unusable—and droughts). On top of all this, the canal companies were bedeviled by management failures, reflected in poor maintenance of the water in the canals and the encroachment of vegetation.

However, they might have survived all these difficulties had it not been for the arrival of the railroads, which proved to be their undoing. Whereas Taylor is keen to avoid the suggestion that the history of the canals was wholly lacking in success ("The student of the canal era will do well not to dismiss the canals as obvious 'failures,'" he advises), they had mostly been built after the emergence of the railroads and consequently faced immediate competition. As Taylor concludes, the canal-building mania came too late to give them even a brief period of monopoly, as they had enjoyed in

Europe: "It was the misfortune of most canals to become obsolescent even before they were opened for traffic. The advantages of the railroads were so great that even the strongest canals could not long retain a profitable share of the business."[8] He suggests, rather regretfully, that such projects as the Main Line of Pennsylvania and the Chesapeake & Ohio Canal would be remembered today as great monuments of the age had not the railroads usurped their position as the most efficient mode of transportation. As with the railroads, however, profits should not be the only criterion by which to judge the success of America's now largely forgotten canal network. The hidden benefits that arose from the availability of improved and cheaper transportation—what economists call "externalities"—far outstripped the purely monetary profits that could be earned through the payment of tolls or fares, but these gains ended up in the hands of third parties who did not contribute toward the cost of providing these expensive schemes.

The success of steamships and the brief flourishing of canals invites the question of why roads did not become a more successful mode of transportation earlier, given that boats were obviously limited to watercourses and the cost of digging lengthy canals was prohibitive. In the early nineteenth century, there were, indeed, numerous roads crisscrossing rural areas, but they were crude affairs that were little more than tracks. Taylor remarks that in 1815, the roads were "unbelievably poor by [modern] standards, . . . hardly more than broad paths through the forest."[9] When it rained, they turned into a series of muddy ruts, and when too dry, they became a powdery dust bowl. For the most part, they consisted of mere cleared paths, but in swampy or marshy land, logs were laid at right angles to the direction of the road to form what were known as "corduroy roads." Given the impossibility of traveling far on these terrible roads, villages were generally built close to waterways.

The condition of the roads was a result of the way they were managed. Their upkeep was the responsibility of the local "community," which, as in Britain, was supposed to provide labor to build and maintain them. In reality, it was a haphazard process: local farmers were press-ganged into providing their labor for a few days, normally in winter. This arrangement was fine for the farmers, as they had little else to do during the cold season, but it was hardly conducive to effective road improvement, since winter was the worst time of the year to prepare a stable surface. The farmers were understandably unenthusiastic about working on roads other than those that led to the nearest village, market, or waterway. Nor did they have the requisite skills for making and maintaining a decent road surface. Despite these limitations, some local roads were joined together to form through routes. By 1816 there was a highway of sorts running north-south between Maine and Georgia, but it had few tentacles stretching westward.

More significant was the development, beginning in the 1790s, of a series of turnpikes—roads on which tolls were payable. Turnpikes were typically built by private companies given permission in the form of charters by local state governments. The private toll-road movement had been boosted by the success of a number of early turnpikes, notably the Lancaster Turnpike, connecting Philadelphia and Lancaster, Pennsylvania, which was completed in 1794. Its profitability stimulated several imitators, with the result that by 1815, the main commercial centers between eastern Pennsylvania, New York, New Jersey, and southern New England were blessed with good roads, several of which were well constructed with a solid stone foundation topped with a gravel dressing.

As more states joined the Union, and settlers sought to move west, the logic would have been to create a network of these roads. However, this would have required federal funding, which was regarded with great suspicion in Washington and in many states. Furthermore, the idea of encouraging centralized national projects was seen as contrary to the Constitution, but Taylor sees a more prosaic reason behind the reluctance to spend money on these schemes: "The real obstacle which defeated a national system of internal improvements is to be found in the bitter state and sectional jealousies which were wracking the new nation."[10] In particular, the more-developed New England states felt that federal support for road schemes would undermine their hard-earned competitive advantage and encourage western migration to their detriment. In the South, too, there was widespread opposition to the construction of roads and a lack of capital to build them.

The turnpike boom of the first quarter of the nineteenth century was largely funded by private local investors, which greatly limited both their

extent and their quality. States did, on occasion, provide additional financial support, and they were ready to grant charters to all manner of road-
building schemes, many of which never saw the light of day or survived
only a few years. The most ambitious scheme was the National Road, one
of the rare roads to be supported by funding from the federal government.
Construction of the road began at Cumberland, Maryland, in 1811, and it
reached Wheeling, West Virginia,[11] on the Ohio River—which would also
be the intended destination of the Baltimore & Ohio Railroad—by 1818. It
was extended to Columbus, Ohio, in 1833 and finally to Vandalia, Illinois,[12]
by the middle of the century, but by then the railroad was emerging as the
preferred mode of transportation for most people and freight carriers.

For the most part, however, turnpikes were, like the canals, a failure:
"Though a boon to travelers, turnpikes generally did not cheapen and
stimulate land transportation sufficiently to provide satisfactory earnings
from tolls." Many turnpike companies were not even able to collect sufficient tolls to provide for the maintenance and operation of the road, let
alone make a contribution to capital for the investors who had put up the
money: "Even in New England, where they were relatively most successful,
only five or six out of 230 turnpikes paid barely satisfactory returns to investors."[13] They were not helped by "shunpikes," detours around tollbooths
built by mischievous locals, or long-distance travelers' habit of waiting until nightfall, when toll collectors went off duty, to use the road. A scarcity of
honest tollbooth operators was another obstacle to profitability, and some
companies simply sold the right to run the tollbooth for a fixed sum,
knowing they could never collect the true income. The turnpikes could
not, crucially, tap into the most significant market, the long-distance transportation of agricultural goods such as wheat, corn, or pork, because the
tolls were simply too high in relation to the value of the produce. As railroad historian Albro Martin sums it up, "Road haulage could only be had
at rates per ton that exceeded by several times the market value of such
commodities at eastern points." Consequently, many roads deteriorated for
want of money to maintain them. As early as 1819, turnpikes were abandoned by owners unable to make a profit while paying for the operating
costs. It was not, therefore, the competition of canals and railroads that did
in the turnpikes, but their own shortcomings: "Many turnpike companies

had failed even before this [railroad and canal] competition appeared and those which lasted after about 1830 [the advent of the railroads] had for the most part already demonstrated their financial unprofitability."[14]

Moreover, railroads would have the advantage of a technology that ultimately proved to be their most effective weapon. Whereas steam engines were quickly adapted to operate on rails, they could not function on roads because they were too heavy and appropriate steering mechanisms had not yet been devised. A road carriage had to be light enough to spare the road surface while having to carry all the paraphernalia of its own heavy and hot machinery in addition to the payload of passengers or freight, all crammed into a single vehicle and perhaps, at most, one trailer. As a study into the rival technologies of the period puts it, steam road carriages "were lacking in a number of technical respects," despite all the efforts to develop them.[15] There were a few hardy inventors in Europe who tried to develop "road carriages," but as it became clear, by around 1840, that railroads would become dominant, they gave up for a generation or so, leaving the field open to the iron road.

Thus, at the start of the railroad age, in 1830, neither turnpikes nor canals had proved sufficiently profitable to maintain a sustained boom in their construction and continued operation. Railroads, therefore, held all the trump cards in relation to their rivals, but they still needed the technology of steam locomotives to ensure their success. The engines in steamships may have been precursors of those used in locomotives, but they were different in several respects: most notably, they could be far bigger, since they did not have to drag their weight along on land, and they could be less efficient, since ships had the capacity to carry vast quantities of fuel. Nevertheless, thanks to the steamships, by the time serious thought was being given to railroads, the key requirements for locomotive technology were in place. However, it was one thing to fit a large steam engine into a ship, where space was not at a premium, and quite another getting it down to a size small enough to move itself under its own power.

To progress from the production of steam power to the development of a railroad required two significant steps. First, the engine had to be put on wheels to make it mobile, and then the wheels had to be placed on rails. As we have seen, this second step was essential because of both the primitive nature of the roads and the absence of any steering mechanism. Provided sufficiently sophisticated and small engines could be developed, the railroads offered a neat solution to both these limitations.

The first attempt to create a self-propelled locomotive had taken place as early as 1769 in Paris, when Nicolas Cugnot's Fardier[16]—which rather fancifully is mentioned in some automotive histories as the world's first automobile—took to the streets but was declared a danger to the public when it hit a wall and overturned. Various other similar patents were taken out, even one by Watt, and several devices intended to run on roads were built in the late eighteenth century. None, however, met with any success, owing to their technical limitations or to the inability of the poorly built roads to support their weight.

The answer was to use rails to support the locomotives. It was a Cornishman, Richard Trevithick, who first thought of the idea and therefore has the best claim to the much-disputed accolade of "father of the steam locomotive." At the turn of the century, Trevithick had tried to run an engine on a road, but the lack of a steering mechanism inevitably resulted in a crash. In 1803, however, a locomotive placed by Trevithick on a track consisting of L-shaped rails laid on stone-block ties at the Pen-y-Darren ironworks in Wales managed to haul wagons weighing nine tons at a speed of five miles an hour. The feat was undoubtedly a world first, but the locomotive proved too heavy for the rails and was soon converted into a stationary engine hauling wagons by means of cables. Five years later, Trevithick demonstrated a steam locomotive playfully named Catch Me Who Can on a small circular track in a field close to what is now London's Euston Station, but once again the rails proved to be insufficiently robust for the engine that ran on them. The locomotive attracted little public interest and would be his last such effort, as he emigrated to South America to develop stationary steam machines that were used in mines to haul up wagons and died in Britain in 1833, a forgotten figure.

Trevithick's efforts, however, had not been in vain. Others soon followed in his footsteps on both sides of the Atlantic. The early development of the railroad, though, took place in the Northeast of England, the Silicon Valley of its time. The main spur to its development was to harness steam power to improve the exploitation of mines. In 1812 mining engineer John Blenkinsop designed an engine, the Salamanca, the first steam locomotive to run on a commercial basis, whose cogs meshed with a toothed rail, the rack-and-pinion system that later became a feature of mountain railroads, for the Middleton colliery in Yorkshire, the first steam locomotive to run on a commercial basis.

George Stephenson, a gruff, self-educated genius from the Northeast, picked up on the idea and became the most famous of these early pioneers, pushing the concept of steam locomotives far further than any of his predecessors, thanks to his talent of being able to develop and improve on other people's ideas. In 1812 Stephenson was appointed as the "enginewright" at Killingworth colliery, just north of Newcastle upon Tyne. Within a couple of years he had produced the Blücher, named after a Prussian general who helped the British defeat Napoléon at Waterloo, which could pull thirty tons up a slight gradient at five miles per hour. It was just the beginning. If Trevithick was the father of the steam locomotive, Stephenson was its midwife, building a series of engines for collieries in England's Northeast. Each new invention proved better than the last. In November 1822, on the eight-mile line connecting Hetton colliery, near Sunderland, with the River Wear, Stephenson's "iron horses," as they came to be known, began to regularly haul seventeen wagons weighing a total of sixty-four tons, more than double the performance of the Blücher. Nevertheless, all these engines were still primitive beasts that frequently broke down, lost steam through every join, and battered the tracks, which could barely withstand their weight.

It was Stephenson who was chosen to lay out the Stockton & Darlington Railway. Although it is best characterized as the last of the wagonways, rather than the first modern railroad, the Stockton & Darlington represented a significant advancement over its predecessors. Opened in September 1825, it was the first common-carrier railroad to use locomotive power, as well as horses, and was designed for use by both passengers and freight. Nevertheless, it still lacked several of the necessary requirements to call itself a fully fledged railroad. Initially just twelve miles long, it was designed, like all the early wagonways, to transport minerals—in this case coal— from mines to a waterway. Although Stephenson built locomotives to run on the Stockton & Darlington, in its early years it was largely operated by horses pulling the wagons and the converted stagecoaches that were used for the few passengers who ventured onto the line. The railroad was crude in other respects, too. At its opening, only one steam locomotive, Stephenson's Locomotion, was available. The track was single throughout, with limited passing points, which meant the engineers or horsemen sometimes argued over who should have the right-of-way when their trains met on the line, reputedly coming to blows on occasion. The Stockton & Darlington struggled financially in its early years, but eventually became highly profitable once steam locomotives became universally used. Despite its limitations, however, it demonstrated what proved to be the spur to the construction of so many railroads across the world: it brought down the price of the goods it carried, most notably coal.

Stephenson kept producing improved locomotives for the Stockton & Darlington, but soon turned his attention to the Liverpool & Manchester, which, when it opened in September 1830, was the world's first fully fledged railroad. Thirty-seven miles long, linking two major towns[17] with a double-track railroad, and open to all comers for the carriage of both freight and passengers, this was a genuine precursor to all the world's future iron roads. George Stephenson again had overall charge of both the construction of the track and the production of the locomotives, aided by his son Robert, who built far more reliable engines than those on the Stockton & Darlington. Several improvements, notably the multitube boiler, were incorporated into the prototype "premium engine," which was given the name that is famous throughout the world, the Rocket.[18] In 1829 the promoters of the Liverpool & Manchester Railway organized a competition, the Rainhill Trials, to find the best locomotive, and the Rocket easily won. Thanks to the Rocket and the quality of the route designed by George Stephenson, the Liverpool & Manchester was a triumph that was to usher in the railroad age. Both commercially and technically successful, it soon spawned imitators not just across Britain but throughout the world.

Indeed, even the ramshackle Stockton & Darlington had attracted attention across the Atlantic, and promoters were beginning to come forward. America was at the time a couple of decades behind Britain in terms of industrial development, but was fast catching up, a process that would be greatly accelerated by its rapid adoption of the iron road. America might have been lagging behind Britain in technology, but not in initiative and ideas. As in Britain, there had been proposals for railroads long before they were technically possible. In 1815 there had been calls by a railroad pioneer, John Stevens, for a double-track railroad to connect the Great Lakes with the Atlantic, an idea that at the time must have seemed to many as far-fetched as sending a rocket to the moon. But Stevens was not alone in proposing such ambitious schemes. That same year a charter was actually granted to the New Jersey Railroad Company, the first railroad charter in the United States, for a long line linking the Delaware River near Trenton with the Raritan River in New Jersey, but no investors came forward to back the plan. Railroads continued to be promoted in various parts of the East Coast during the early 1820s, but there was both a lack of capital to undertake such investment and widespread doubts that the technology was sufficiently developed to see these schemes realized.

While the more ambitious ideas for railroads foundered, a few short lines serving mines or wharves did get built in the 1820s, using either standing engines or horsepower. The most sophisticated was the Granite Railroad in Quincy, Massachusetts, completed in 1826 and thought to be the first commercial railroad in America, since it was used by more than one company. Trains of three wagons, hauled by horses, took stone from a quarry to a dock at Boston Harbor three miles away on wooden rails protected by a layer of iron. It was an innovative railroad that included rudimentary switches (called points in Britain) and an inclined section where the track was carved into the granite. By the end of the decade, two much longer streetcar lines had been built at anthracite mines in northeastern Pennsylvania: a nine-mile line at Mauch Chunk[19] and a sixteen-mile one at Carbondale, using contrasting traction methods. At Mauch Chunk, cars were hauled up a gradual incline by horses and mules, which then were given a ride in the empty wagons back to the bottom of the hill. Initially, there was a similar arrangement at Carbondale on the line built by the Delaware & Hudson Canal Company. However, the engineer of the line, Horatio Allen, had grander ideas. He had been to England to attend the Rainhill Trials and was so impressed that he arranged to import a British-built engine, the Stourbridge Lion, named after the town in the Midlands in which it was built. It had to be stripped down for the voyage and rebuilt, but its arrival in America aroused much fanfare, as it was the first locomotive to be operated in the country. Since he did not want anyone else to risk his life, Allen, the future president of the Erie Railroad, himself drove the Lion on its maiden journey, a six-mile run that included crossing a thirty-foot-high trestle bridge, in August 1829. The timbers of the track, which had been built for the far-lighter coal wagons, creaked threateningly beneath the seven-ton Lion, and the experiment proved to be a failure. The Lion never roared again: it was left in a shed and subsequently ignominiously broken up for parts. But it had shown the way, as Allen later recalled: "At the end of two or three miles, I reversed the valves and returned without accident to the place of starting, having thus made the first railroad trip by locomotive in the Western Hemisphere."[20]

These early lines, though, were in truth just slightly more complex versions of the wagonways whose history stretched back into the mists of time. The burgeoning cities of the Eastern Seaboard needed something rather more sophisticated to boost trade, and it was competition between them that spurred Baltimore into sponsoring the pioneering Baltimore & Ohio Railroad.

The initiative to build the Baltimore & Ohio was very much a stab in the dark. Its origins lay in the formation of the inelegantly named Pennsylvania Society for the Promotion of Internal Improvements, which sent one William Strickland across the Atlantic to learn about Britain's burgeoning railroads. Strickland's subsequent glowing report about the Stockton & Darlington, presented to the society in 1826, suggested that railroads, rather than canals, were the answer to the need for better transportation links. Two other farsighted Baltimore citizens, Philip E. Thomas and George Brown, also visited the Stockton & Darlington and other railroad projects in Britain in 1826. Back in Baltimore, they set about raising money. They organized a meeting of local merchants, an echo of a similar gathering that had been the genesis of Britain's first major railroad, the Liverpool & Manchester, to galvanize support for a 380-mile double-track line linking Baltimore, Maryland, with the Ohio River at Wheeling, West Virginia.

It was one thing to have such a grand idea, but quite another to see it to fruition in the face of the many financial and technical obstacles. However, a key factor in persuading the local merchants of the need for a railroad was the fear that Baltimore would be left behind by the other three major eastern seaports, New York, Philadelphia, and Washington, as the main conduit between the interior of the United States and the Old World. All four cities were jostling for primacy and realized that communications with the interior were key to their development. Given that the other three cities chose canals or, in the case of Philadelphia, the ill-fated mixed canal and railroad Main Line, Baltimore's decision to opt for a railroad was a farsighted one.

This fierce intercity rivalry was the key stimulus to the demand for better transportation links. A particular concern for the citizens of Baltimore was that the Erie Canal gave New York a huge competitive advantage. Proposals to construct a Chesapeake and Ohio canal that would run parallel with the Potomac River also threatened the viability of Baltimore's port, and consequently the railroad was quickly granted a charter by the Maryland legislature in February 1827. It was a courageous decision: the economics of building such a long railroad line were unknown, and the capital required was the then enormous sum of $5 million. It was courageous, too, from a technological point of view, since it was unclear whether British know-how, which had been developed for a milder climate and shorter distances, could be adapted to the harsher weather of the United States. In the event, the burghers of Baltimore needed little persuasion to be convinced of the need for the railroad. As Sarah H. Gordon, a chronicler of the impact of the development of the US railroads, suggests, "The merchants of Baltimore, anxious to establish a connection between their port city and the Ohio River, organized a railroad company in 1827, before they even knew whether a railroad would accomplish their goal."[21] Ultimately, the Baltimore & Ohio did not achieve its commercial aim, as New York, with its far-superior natural harbor and easy river access, won out, becoming the port of choice for European traffic, but that should not detract from the importance of the pioneering railroad.

Construction of the Baltimore & Ohio Railroad began in 1828, but by then another ambitious project was already taking shape in South Carolina. This was the Charleston & Hamburg Railroad,[22] which is less well known than the Baltimore & Ohio but has a good claim as the more impressive innovator of the two. Although it did not obtain its charter until after the Baltimore & Ohio, the Charleston & Hamburg completed its line in 1833, far more quickly than its northern counterpart, which did not reach Wheeling, its planned destination, until 1852—twenty-four years after Carroll had turned the first sod. Moreover, whereas the first trains on the Baltimore & Ohio were horse drawn, the Charleston & Hamburg quickly adopted locomotive technology, and homegrown at that. It was Horatio Allen, the engineer of the Delaware & Hudson, who had moved down south as engineer for the Charleston and commissioned the building of the first American locomotive, the rather quaintly named Best Friend of Charleston. He had persuaded the promoters of the line to adopt steam power, pointing out with great foresight that "there is no reason to expect any material improvement in the breed of horses in the future while, in my judgment, the man is not living who knows what the breed of locomotive is to place at command." As rail historian Stewart H. Holbrook concludes, "While the Baltimore & Ohio was fooling around with sail cars and with horse-treadmill locomotives, the Charleston & Hamburg . . . had the first American-built steam locomotive."[23]

The engine had been built at the West Point Foundry in New York and was delivered by steamer to Charleston, where it was assembled and tested. In December 1830 the Best Friend pulled its first train, carrying some two hundred shareholders and local notables and the following year was in regular use, hauling passengers at speeds of up to thirty-five miles per hour. The locomotive met an unfortunate end, however, when, as the possibly apocryphal story goes, a fireman,[24] annoyed at the sound made by the escape of steam from the safety valve, sat on the offending piece of machinery, which, after a few minutes of quiet, resulted in the boiler exploding, killing him and scalding the engineer.

In Britain there had been worries right from the start that steam locomotives would wreak havoc, turning sheep black, stopping cows milking, and even causing asphyxiation, as their speed would prevent travelers from breathing. In America such fears were compounded by the country's relative unfamiliarity with the new technology. The United States was much less industrialized than Britain and had far fewer factories that employed steam technology: "The steam, the smoke, the sparks emitted from the belly of the monster were quite sufficient to invoke anxiety, if not downright terror, in timid souls who drew nigh the early demonstration trains."[25] Explosions, though, had always been the main concern, and to allay these fears, when traffic on the Charleston & Hamburg resumed, the trains ran with a flat "barrier" car loaded with cotton to protect the now understandably nervous passengers from similar mishaps.

The motive for building the Charleston & Hamburg, as with the other pioneering lines, had been narrowly and nakedly commercial. Charleston's foreign exports had gone into decline, and its merchants looked inland to restore their fortune. They hoped to secure the trade of the rich cotton-growing area both in their own state of South Carolina and in Georgia by building the line northwest from Charleston to the bank of the Savannah River at Hamburg,[26] just across the water from Augusta, Georgia. By adopting the new technology right away, these southern pioneers proved more farsighted than their peers at the Baltimore & Ohio, who remained unconvinced of the need for the newfangled devices called steam locomotives. This attitude was not unusual at the time. In several European countries, notably Austria, long lines were still being built in the early 1830s with the idea of using horses, rather than locomotives, to haul the trains. Although the Stourbridge Lion had demonstrated the feasibility of locomotive technology, provided the track was sufficiently robust, the promoters of the Baltimore & Ohio insisted on a trial between horses and locomotives to determine the best means of traction, although in truth they probably knew that horses would never be suitable, given the hilly terrain the railroad was intended to cross.

The railroad's construction standards, with their sharp curves and light rails, precluded the use of locomotives imported from Britain. The promoters therefore called upon a notable inventor, Peter Cooper, to build a suitable locomotive. He produced a tiny engine, later nicknamed Tom Thumb, which had just four small wheels and was described by one onlooker as having a boiler "not as large as the kitchen boiler attached to many a modern mansion."[27]

Nevertheless, on a test run along the first thirteen miles of track, the unprepossessing engine reached an exhilarating eighteen miles per hour, impressing the assorted investors and VIPs who had come along for the ride. On the way back, Cooper foolishly agreed to race his locomotive against a horse to prove that it was superior. The powerful gray initially took the lead, thanks to its faster acceleration, but once the little engine had gained purchase on the track and Cooper opened its safety valve to provide extra power, Tom Thumb glided past the galloping steed. Cooper's machine was a quarter of a mile ahead when disaster struck. Just as the horse rider was ready to give up, the belt that drove the pulley on the locomotive snapped, and the engine eased to a halt. Cooper managed to effect a repair, burning his hands badly in the process, but he finished the course well behind his rival. The equine victory, though, proved Pyrrhic, as the engine had done enough to convince the investors that steam haulage, rather than horsepower, was the only way to make the line viable. Although some horse traction was used early on, locomotives were dominant, and the line was soon operated exclusively with engines.

History is harsh on losers, which is perhaps why, in most accounts of the early railroads, the Charleston & Hamburg gets such scant attention. It was, in fact, initially a far more significant achievement than the Baltimore & Ohio, but as it was in the South and was soon subsumed into another railroad, the South Carolina Railroad Company, its role as a pioneer has been largely forgotten. Nor did it have a charismatic wordsmith like Charles Carroll to inscribe its place in history. Thus, the Baltimore & Ohio, which survived as an independent company until long after the Second World War, was free to promote the myth that it was America's first proper railroad. In fact, Holbrook, like other impartial historians, is unequivocal about which came first: "The Charleston & Hamburg, six miles long, may be said to have been the first American railroad as the term is generally understood."[28] It was soon 136 miles long, the longest in the world for a few short years, as it was completed remarkably quickly and fully operational by 1833. The rapidity of construction was helped by the ability of the railroad to call on slave labor, which, as we will see in the next chapter, was an important factor in southern railroad construction (and may also account for the Charleston & Hamburg being written out of history). Ultimately, the Baltimore & Ohio became more important because the railroads in the North developed in a far more sophisticated way than their southern counterparts. In particular, they were prepared to go over state boundaries to provide long-distance services, unlike in the South, where the railroads largely stayed within individual state borders.

These two railroads were part of a wider spurt of railroad activity, a mini version of the "railroad manias" that characterized future developments not just in the United States but across the world. In addition to the two longer coal railroads in Pennsylvania, New York State's first railroad, the Mohawk & Hudson, which provided a shortcut to a circuitous section of the Erie Canal, had been chartered in 1826. However, financial and political difficulties meant that work did not start until the summer of 1830, and a 16-mile route between Albany and Schenectady opened a year later. Then there was the New York & Harlem, chartered in 1831, which ran initially from the Bowery to Fourteenth Street and within a couple of years along Fourth Avenue to Harlem, making it one of the world's first street railroads. Unlike the steam-hauled Mohawk & Hudson, the New York & Harlem initially used animal power, as did the Chesterfield Railroad in Virginia, a 13-mile mining line that connected the Midlothian coal mines with wharves on the James River. By the early 1830s, numerous other projects, with evocative names such as the Tuscumbia, Courtland & Decatur, the Rensselaer & Saratoga, and the Little Schuylkill Navigation, Railroad, and Coal Company, received charters and were being built. More significantly in 1832, a seminal year in US railroad history, services began on the Camden & Amboy between Trenton and New Brunswick in New Jersey, a response to the obvious need to improve transportation links between the two biggest cities of the day, New York and Philadelphia. By 1835, remarkably, there were nearly 1,000[29] miles of completed railroad on thirty-nine lines in the United States. The railroad age had arrived, and nothing could stop it from transforming America.

2

A PASSIONATE
AFFAIR

These early lines represented an impressive start and marked the beginnings of the love affair between ordinary Americans and the railroads, but it would take a few years before the right conditions were in place to spark a prolonged railroad boom and begin the establishment of a nationwide network.

Although rapid improvements to the technology were being made, it was still primitive and crude, and there were several other respects in which America was still not geared up for railroads. Obtaining the requisite financing, a problem for railroads the world over, was a major obstacle for the nascent industry. Labor, too, was not always available, which, as mentioned in the previous chapter, meant that in the South there was widespread recourse to slaves. The legal status of the railroads was overdependent on the whim of local state legislators, since, initially, there was no clear understanding of how to treat these new and potentially monopolistic enterprises. During the first two decades of the railroad age, much effort was expended in overcoming these hurdles.

The railroads were a novel concept that would cross state boundaries and require large swaths of land, and there was no real precedent for coping with such an intrusive invention. They needed a sympathetic environment in which to flourish and to overcome any doubt and hostility that they were bound to engender. In Britain, railroad promoters were required to obtain an act passed in Parliament that enabled them to force landowners to cede their land to the company and made provision for all the other various requirements of the railroad. This was by no means a perfect arrangement, as it made the fate of the railroad dependent on the whims of parliamentarians who not infrequently had their own agendas that were likely to prejudice them either for or against the project. Powerful landowners were able to pressure railroads into paying significantly more for the land than it was worth. However, by and large the British system was sufficiently adaptable to encourage promoters to come forward with schemes and to ensure lines were built.

In the United States the procedure was different, and, perhaps inevitably in a nation that had only come into being in 1776, no clear system had been devised by the time the first railroads were being debated in the 1820s. Consequently, aspiring railroad entrepreneurs faced a battle to persuade legislatures to allow them to build their lines. The power to grant the necessary charters belonged to the states rather than the federal government, and the inadequate legal system had to grow quickly with the railroads in order to meet their needs. Anyone seeking to start a business and form a corporation had to obtain a charter, which placed certain obligations on the new company. In the case of the railroads, these related to such matters as fares, the nature of the services, the location of the track, and even the speed of the trains. The states, too, had rights over any company to which they granted a charter, including the assumption that they could ultimately revoke the charter and run the company directly. It was only later, as the railroad companies grew and became more powerful, that this right was challenged and eventually set aside.

While obtaining a charter was a difficult and expensive process, the crucial legal requirement for the railroads was to obtain "eminent domain," which was the right to take over whatever property was needed in return for fair compensation. This put the US railroads in a much stronger position than their British counterparts, since it gave them a general power to take over any land rather than only particular plots specified in the acts obtained by British promoters. The right of eminent domain in US law had a long history, born of the necessities of a new and expanding nation. It started with mill owners who flooded land upstream by building dams but were granted the right to do so, despite the damage caused to landowners, because they created wider benefits for the general public. Once established, this principle was extended to turnpike promoters and canal owners on the same basis—that the public advantage outweighed the drawbacks for the few unlucky proprietors whose land happened to be in the wrong place.

The railroads faced an uphill struggle to persuade the courts to give them this power because, initially, they were by no means universally welcomed. They faced opposition from canal owners and turnpike operators, who rightly saw them as major competition, and there were other vested interests lined up against them as well. Tavern owners and stagecoach drivers were two such groups, but many farmers resented the incursion of tracks across their land. Moreover, there was a debate about whether the railroads were really for public use and were of sufficient benefit to justify the granting of such a widespread power as "eminent domain." The early railroads were crude affairs, covering only short distances at slow speeds, and with no guarantee of trains reaching their destination. The canals and turnpikes had more obviously widespread benefits and, significantly, were open to all comers to travel on their own conveyances, whereas the railroads not only provided the cars and locomotives but also insisted on rigid schedules. These early-nineteenth-century objections to the granting of legal powers to the railroads offer an interesting parallel to the reluctance of twenty-first-century Americans to leave their much-loved automobiles at home and take the bus or train. American suspicion of the railroads' intentions, therefore, started early in their history, and such feelings are at the root of much of the antagonism toward them documented in later chapters of this book.

Nonetheless, the railroads were granted eminent domain in various court cases, notably in New York, which established the principle thereafter. The courts recognized the early railroads as a major technological breakthrough, promising immense economic benefits in opening new territories and allowing the rapid transportation of goods, people, mail, and, of course, troops in time of war. One crucial New York case, in 1837, captures the mood of the era and reveals the arguments put forward for the development of railroads generally:

> Railroads are not only of great public use in the ordinary business transactions of the citizen, but they may be more advantageously used than turnpike roads for national purposes; . . . they tend to annihilate

distance, bringing in effect places that are distant near to each other: tending in their magic influence to the extension of personal acquaintance, the enlargement of business relations, and cementing more firmly the bond of fellowship and union between the inhabitants of the States. Next to the moral lever power of the press should be ranked the beneficial influence of railroads in their effects upon the vast and increasing business relations of the nation, and promoting, sustaining and perpetuating the happiness, prosperity and liberty of the people.[1]

This sort of rationale was followed in other US state supreme courts that considered the grants of eminent domain to the early railroads, which were thus spared the British experience of negotiating for rights-of-way with each individual owner. In the United States, it was simply a matter of selecting a route, assessing the damage caused to private owners, and paying them. This process, which amounted to the legal confiscation of land, was a much cheaper method of acquiring for railroad development than in Europe, where land had to be purchased at considerable expense from the owner, representing a significant proportion of the cost of building a railroad line. This was one of the reasons US railroads were less expensive to build than those on the other side of the Atlantic and was a key factor in their remarkably rapid growth.

The legal arrangements were part of a complex relationship between the state and the nascent railroads that was to prove troublesome for both sides, particularly when it came to money. Ostensibly, the railroads were supposed to be private businesses, as befitted the American ethos. But, in fact, the idea that they were an entirely private enterprise is one of the great myths of railroad history. The railroads couldn't be funded by purely private means. The economics and practicalities of railroad development made that impossible, and the reality was very different. The desire to make the railroads a privately owned enterprise, given the already-established American suspicion of government involvement, was always a vain hope. The railroads were such a large and complex enterprise and so capital-hungry that, almost invariably, they were forced to seek various types of support and, in many cases, funding from either local or the federal government.

Raising capital was a perpetual struggle for the railroad promoters. Unlike in Europe, where railroads usually connected existing settlements, even ones that were quite far apart, in America the railroads were often being built from, as an English wit put it, "nowhere-in-particular to nowhere-at-all." Unsurprisingly, there was little capital available from parsimonious bankers in New York or Boston to fund such enterprises: "A banker might be more than willing to foot the bill for a railroad between Boston and Worcester or between New York and Philadelphia, but a railroad between two log cabin villages in Indiana was something altogether different."[2] Furthermore, the banking system in Europe was more developed and was expanding swiftly to cater to the needs of the railroads, which were fast becoming the biggest industry. In America, mostly still agrarian and mercantile, there was a shortage of capital for the building of new lines.

Therefore, while the promoters may, mostly, have been private individuals, the role of the state—and, particularly, of the individual states—was absolutely crucial for the majority of early railroads. Notionally, the government was not supposed to become involved in the business of providing what were known as "internal improvements," infrastructure projects such as new turnpikes, canals, and railroads. In practice, neither the federal government nor the states could avoid becoming embroiled, and most of the early railroad schemes had some sort of government support. In many cases, states recognized that the local railroads were so important to their economy and their development that the railroad companies had to be supported. This meant that, far from being an example of raw capitalism in which investors were risking all their money, the railroads were a hybrid, a mix of private and public interests. It was, in modern parlance, a public-private partnership, where both the capital outlay and the risks were shared.

In what has been called "a typical manifestation of shifty American pragmatism," a host of devices, ranging from the entirely legal to the distinctly dubious, were developed to fund the construction of railroads. State support for the construction of canals had been widespread, and therefore the pattern had already been set. The railroad companies, however, were given privileges through their charters that were far more favorable than those granted to any other corporations. Not only did they acquire rights over land through eminent domain, but they were also given unprecedented tax exemptions and money-raising opportunities. Freedom from taxation was the most obvious advantage, but railroad companies were also permitted to hold lotteries and create special banks to tap into the savings of even modestly affluent citizens. Crucially, too, many states granted monopolies that prevented rivals from building parallel lines. Although this idea was put forward as a way to prevent the inefficiency and waste of duplication, in practice it put the beneficiary in a very strong position to exploit both local businesses and people. Most notoriously, the Camden & Amboy, stretching across New Jersey, was given the monopoly for rail transportation over the whole of the state, described by one rail historian as "a very foolish action of the New Jersey legislature."[3]

The spectrum of railroad funding covered a wide range of approaches, from state subsidy to wholly private financing. At the subsidized end of the spectrum was Pennsylvania, a state that adopted an interventionist role vis-à-vis its railroads—almost in the mold of a European government—unlike some of the other states, which adopted a more hands-off approach. Pennsylvania appointed an "internal improvements commission" that was originally established to oversee canal traffic but then played a key part in the state's development of the railroads. The commission determined the route of all the early railroad lines in the state, sold the bonds to fund construction, and then oversaw the construction of the lines. According to historian Sarah H. Gordon, in the early days, "the state controlled such matters as the speed of the trains, tolls to be charged for the use of the track, safety considerations such as the need to enclose all lamp and lantern flames, and the order of priority of different types of trains using the track."[4]

Support for the railroads was offered even by states in the Northeast, where—unlike in many midwestern and southern states—private capital was plentifully available. For example, in 1833 Massachusetts provided the bulk of the cost of constructing the Western Railroad, providing a vital link between two other railroads, with a $4 million loan and direct investment of $600,000. This kind of support was commonplace, but it often came at a price. The state lawmakers in New York, which loaned the Erie Railroad $3 million, forced the railroad to go through a sparsely populated region, the southern tier, along the border with Pennsylvania, hoping that it would stimulate economic growth there. New York was, in fact, a serial supporter of the railroads, and by 1846 had advanced $9 million to ten different railroad companies.

In the Midwest the perceived need for railroads, together with a lack of private capital, stimulated states—such as Michigan and Illinois—into building railroads themselves. In the absence of a developed banking sector, railroad promoters in these states did not have any access to capital, and therefore the state was the principal source of funds. In Michigan, even before the state was formally constituted, its lawmakers were agitating for building lines. After Michigan entered the Union in 1837, work started on three state railroads, but they lost money and were eventually privatized in 1846 on, inevitably, unfavorable terms for the state. Having spent $3.5 million on the construction of 150 miles of railroad, the State of Michigan sold the lines for half that sum to a group of Massachusetts and New York money investors.

Illinois, prompted by Stephen A. Douglas, later a senator, who, like many early promoters, was both forward looking and self-serving, drew up a grandiose plan envisaging the construction of 1,300 miles of line together with canals and turnpikes, all to be funded by the state. This was a remarkably ambitious scheme given that at the time, Illinois's population consisted of a few thousand people living in villages and farms, with no settlement worthy of being called a city. Rather fortuitously, the plan was delayed by the financial panic of 1837, but nevertheless ended up costing the state a fortune. Railroad construction became a moneymaking venture for numerous state employees who found there were rich pickings to be had from setting themselves up as "surveyors," "land buyers," and "estimators" and thereby obtaining lucrative contracts from the state. Illinois thus found itself with a few miles of railroad but a big debt. By the late 1840s, however, much of the state's plan for railroad construction had been completed by private companies. These privatizations were not without their critics. For example, Lorenzo Sherwood, a prominent Texas lawyer and politician, was furious about the takeover of lines by private corporations intent only on making a profit and argued that publicly owned railroads carried more tonnage at less cost. These sentiments would be echoed far more widely in later years, as mergers made the railroad companies more and more powerful.

In the South, the pattern of railroad development was very different, as lines were deliberately prevented from crossing state boundaries in order to ensure that each state could retain control of its own railroads. The South's railroads were therefore mostly short and built to a lower standard than elsewhere. For the most part, they ran from cotton plantations to ports with little provision for passengers. Because of the lack of private capital, the southern states, according to one railroad historian, "lavished their funds on railroads in a positively shameless manner."[5] Some, such as Georgia, even raised money through lotteries. The states seemed to be always at hand to ensure key projects were realized. Whereas the pioneering Charleston & Hamburg was built with a minimum of state aid, a mere $100,000 loan, its branches required far more substantial support, amounting to several million dollars, from the State of South Carolina. As in the Midwest, the states of the South were not averse to building lines themselves if they were seen as economically vital. In the 1840s, the State of Georgia built the 137-mile Western & Atlantic Railroad between Atlanta and Chattanooga and ran it successfully, whereas in Virginia the state constructed a line through the Blue Ridge Mountains and leased it to the Virginia Central Railroad. Indeed, Virginia had a policy of taking 60 percent of the share capital of all railroads in its area, whereas Louisiana, adopting a similar policy, took only 20 percent. Even the pioneering Baltimore & Ohio had been dependent on government funds, having obtained money from both the State of Maryland and the City of Baltimore, and only in 1896 did the railroad become entirely controlled by private interests.

There was considerable public pressure on the federal administration to support at least some of the myriad of railroad schemes popping up in every state, but the government's hands were tied by the Constitution, which seemed to preclude the provision of direct funding for improvements in the infrastructure. Even if, in apparent defiance of the Constitution, a bill seeking funding for a railroad project reached Congress, it was invariably blocked by the southern states, whose desire for transportation improvements was not strong enough to overcome their fears of interference from the North. Nevertheless, the strength of the public's support for railroad expansion persuaded the federal government to devise various indirect means of providing help—if not straight cash—that did not transgress the law. Initially, many early railroads, including both the Baltimore

& Ohio and the Charleston & Hamburg, benefited from having surveys carried out by army engineers. This was a valuable form of covert subsidy for the railroads, but given the lack of capital and the high cost of lines, further substantial federal assistance was needed. The obvious answer was land. In 1835, Congress endorsed the first railroad land grant, giving the Tallahassee Railroad Company in Florida the right-of-way thirty feet on each side of the line, as well as considerable amounts of timber and ten acres for a terminal. It was a modest start to what would be the key method of supporting railroads across the West, but it was not until the passage of the Land Grant Act of 1851 that the procedure was formalized and recognized as a vital component of railroad funding.

A rather more direct form of subsidy, the remission of duties on imported iron, also proved essential to the early railroads. When the railroad revolution took hold in the 1830s, America had not yet developed the capacity to produce iron on an industrial scale. As a result, the early American railroads relied on importing iron from Britain. In July 1832, Congress passed an act providing for the refund of all duties on iron used for building new lines, the first but by no means the last time that the railroad industry would receive preferential treatment from federal lawmakers. It was a generous deal worth several hundred thousand dollars to the larger railroad companies. Eventually, as American iron became available, its manufacturers pressed for repeal of the law, even though their produce remained more expensive than British iron until after the Civil War. Nevertheless, they succeeded in getting the law scrapped in 1843, by which time it had been worth $6 million to the railroads, a considerable sum given the relatively low costs of railroad construction.[6]

At the other end of the funding spectrum from the state-supported railroads, there were those railroads built entirely with private capital. The sponsors were usually local people, eager to connect with the neighboring town or facilitate the transportation of local produce or minerals to the coast. Even those with state support had to find local money to help bring about their dream, and invariably self-interest was a great motivator. The Baltimore businessmen who promoted the partly state-funded Baltimore & Ohio Railroad readily put their hands in their pockets to kick-start the scheme. So did the members of the Chamber of Commerce of Charleston, who hoped to take local trade away from their rivals in Savannah by building the Charleston & Hamburg, whereas in Boston the funds for the Boston & Lowell came largely from the cotton textile manufacturers of Lowell.

The key to successful promotion was the selling of the railroad, a task at which railroad sponsors became increasingly adept, given the need to persuade local people to invest. They stressed not only the physical advantages of the railroad, but also the much more exciting idea of opening up new frontiers, which dovetailed perfectly with the burgeoning optimism that was rapidly establishing itself at the heart of the national mood. Like all good marketing people, they instilled in the public's mind the perception of a need where there had never been one before, one that only they could satisfy. The dream they sold was a simple one. The entertaining historian Stewart H. Holbrook captures the mood brilliantly in his account of a group of promoters trying to persuade the residents of a mythical town, "Brownsville," of the need for a railroad to the neighboring settlement. A local notable would develop the notion that "what Brownsville needed if it were to share in America's great destiny, was a steam railroad." A meeting would be held, an application for a charter made, and the "virus of the fever" would begin to circulate, persuading the local citizenry of the importance of having a railroad. Then the hard sell to obtain funds would begin: "Some local practitioner of letters was engaged to write a splendid pamphlet outlining the opportunity offered in the stock of the Brownsville & Western Railroad. . . . [W]idows and old men, and guardians of fools and minors were told how a thousand dollars would not only help to make Brownsville a leading city of the nation, but would also return a multitude of rich dividends, now and forever." The promoters would call upon publicists who wrote skillfully worded prospectuses and powerful orators who would give rousing speeches at the public meetings held to galvanize support. They even resorted to calling on the Almighty: "Needy pastors were hurriedly converted to steam, and they presently could see God's hand on the throttle."[7]

In fact, much of this effort was probably unnecessary. The American people needed little persuasion, as the growth of the nation and the spread of the iron road so patently went hand in hand. As it became clear that the railroad was an invention whose time had come, Americans began to define themselves in its terms. They liked the idea that the spread of the railroad needed a population of entrepreneurial and forward-looking people to make best use of such an important technological development: "Promoters used the steam engine as a metaphor for what they thought Americans were and what they were becoming. They frequently discussed parallels between the locomotive and national character, pointing out that both possessed youth, power, speed, single-mindedness, and bright prospects."[8]

According to the promoters, there was no end to the improvements that railroads would bring about. They would liberate the city dwellers from the terrible housing conditions by allowing them to move into the countryside—the suburban sprawl that would be created by these very railroads had not yet begun—or at least to visit it for a day out to get away from the urban stench. Remarkably, as early as 1832, when hardly three hundred miles of rail had been laid across the United States, and Florida was hardly more than a mosquito-infested wasteland of swamps populated by the Creek and Seminole peoples, Charles Caldwell, a contemporary writer on railroad matters, envisaged that the new invention would soon be "enabling and inducing invalids, and people of feeble constitutions, to migrate from the south to the north, in summer, and from the north to the south, in winter."[9] These were prescient words indeed, though it would take a couple of generations and the efforts of the equally farsighted Henry Morrison Flagler before the dream of developing Florida's east coast would be realized (see Chapter 8).

The railroad was seen as an answer to virtually all society's ills, from poverty to illiteracy. Education would be improved through the spread of knowledge. People's health, argued the prospectus for the Long Island Rail Road in 1834, would be improved because they would have easy access to the joys of sun, sand, and sea in the summer, thanks to the railroad. The railroads were seen as democratic, a way of improving the lives of all those who traveled on them: "Equality of opportunity as a national goal was everywhere in the air and accorded very neatly with Americans' hopes for national unity." The hope was that they could afford easy access to one and all. For example, as early as the mid-1830s, the Boston & Worcester Railroad in Massachusetts ran Fourth of July specials, carrying fifteen hundred passengers on four trains—not a bad figure at a time when many railroads transported only a few dozen passengers each day. The resulting intermingling of the classes would, it was argued, improve the manners of the poor, who would see the example of the genteel better off and seek to imitate them. In fact, when it came to the issue of class, the railroad prose-lytizers were treading a thin line. They knew that to have any hope of being profitable, the railroads needed to attract the masses, but they were aware, too, that the investors, particularly the richer ones, might not entirely welcome the notion of having to travel with the great unwashed. While some promoters actively stressed the democratic idea that the railroads offered the poor an unprecedented freedom to travel, others were more reticent and, instead, emphasized the advantages that the new invention could offer the more affluent traveler, suggesting, for example, that the rich might hitch their own carriages to the trains. In the main, though, "enthusiasts promised that their projects would go far to narrow the social and income gaps that tended to pit Americans against Americans." The railroads were to be the great unifier, the building bricks of the Union: "Observers everywhere argued that the best antidote to political schism was the spread of common ideas; the continuation of the federal experiment was predicated upon the existence of a mass of like-thinking, but disputatious individuals with free and easy access to useful ideas and precepts." Railroads, they maintained, were to be the catalyst for ensuring this could take place, creating the very notion of a "national" sense of identity, as otherwise knowledge, culture, and ideas would be confined to small areas based on the coastal towns. In a rather tautologous argument, the enthusiasts suggested that "the *idea* that railroads were a positive good and always in the nation's interest was itself a powerful unifying force."[10]

The cause and effect of the changes brought about by the railroad are hard to disentangle, and whether the railroads formed America's character or vice versa is a classic chicken-and-egg conundrum. As James A. Ward notes, "The notion that railways were both physical manifestations of a new intellectual world and the means for making that world available to all citizens and, in the process, elevating the national character was one of the major reasons for the era's optimism." It was precisely the depth of this understanding between the public and the railroads that would heighten the sense of betrayal when that relationship soured so badly. Remarkably, it is evident that many of the early supporters, particularly the more affluent ones, were not investing in the railroads for immediate personal gain. They were driven by the genuinely altruistic motives of furthering the national, state, or municipal good, and any profit they could make was regarded as something of a bonus. Perhaps, more accurately, one could say they were taking a long view, realizing that they were likely to benefit from the general increase in prosperity that the railroads would bring about. More prosaically, there were numerous ways in which the building of a railroad could bring immediate benefit to local people, most significantly through the increase in land values that rose for several reasons after the arrival of the railroad. First, it became easier for farmers to send their produce to market as the cost of transportation and the time taken to deliver it were reduced. Agricultural land thus became more profitable to farm and accordingly more attractive—and expensive—to acquire. Second, the ease of connection between different locations afforded by the railroads encouraged people to settle in towns served by the railroads. This led to an increase in demand for land for housing and, later, for shops and light industry. And, third, this very process of growth stimulated further development. There seemed to be no downside. Everyone was a winner, not only local people but the local authorities, too, as their tax base was enhanced. Land that had hitherto been regarded as worthless—except, of course, by its original Native American inhabitants, from whom it was often simply stolen—became highly prized, offering as it did the possibility that it could earn rent for the landowner. The promise of rising land prices became a central tenet in the railroad promoters' prospectuses: "The promoters were appealing to a deeply ingrained American image embedded in a belief in the primacy of land and of the men who owned and worked it. Land was the great national treasure and promoters' promises to give remote land value, real value, for the first time, to enable enterprising individuals to reap the mineral, timber and crop harvests for their own good and for the welfare of the nation were simply practical steps towards strengthening national unity."[11]

Above all, the arrival of a railroad line satisfied what has been called the "booster spirit," a manifestation of the "can-do" culture that was at the heart of the frontier mentality.[12] It didn't really matter if you lived in a two-bit town that consisted of a few houses and a church; a railroad connection opened up all sorts of possibilities for commerce and development. Those who did not own land at least had the prospect of being more likely to find a job, initially in construction but later in working on the railroad or for employers attracted by the transportation improvement.

However, all these advantages had to be won at a price, and one that was not just financial. Railroad construction in the early days was extremely primitive and labor intensive. Most of the work was carried out with picks, hand drills, and shovels, as steam shovels had not yet been invented and pile drivers were little used. Gunpowder, whose effectiveness was limited, was the only available explosive for breaking through rocks and creating tunnels, which was an arduous process. Once the route had been surveyed and selected, the labor gangs would first have to clear the trees and other vegetation and then grade the ground to ensure it was flat enough to take the tracks. Since the early locomotives could not climb any substantial gradient—though American engines were more powerful, and therefore steeper gradients were allowed than in Europe[13]—this involved creating cuttings and embankments or, more commonly in the early railroads, following the contours of the landscape.

There is remarkably little written in US railroad histories on the labor used to build the railroads, especially about the early days. Whereas in Britain the railroads were carved out by specialist gangs of "navvies," who traveled from site to site and were famous for their prodigious feats of both laboring and drinking, in America local labor was used whenever it was available, supported, at times, by teams of immigrants.[14] In the South, railroad construction was carried out mostly by slaves before the Civil War and by convict labor after emancipation. The usual arrangement was to appoint a construction company—a total misnomer since it did no actual construction—that acted as a buffer between the railroad promoters and the contractors who actually built the line. The construction company, which would usually have some or all of the railroad's directors on its board, would remain a separate legal entity, taking the risk and the financial responsibility for ensuring that the line was completed. Therefore if, as often happened, costs exceeded original estimates and the construction company failed, the original railroad company would not face bankruptcy. The construction company was usually paid partly in cash, which was needed to cover the cost of the work, and partly in securities on which it could raise loans. The arrangement of channeling work through a construction company was, as we shall see in Chapter 6, which describes the building of the first transcontinental railroad, open to widespread abuse and corruption.

The first American railroads were built largely by local people, with little or no experience of construction techniques. The planned route would be broken up into short sections, typically one mile long, and parceled out to contractors. In the early days, these were mostly partnerships formed by people in the area, relying on idle farm labor and any other available source of unemployed men. At first many of these contractors were the notables of the neighborhood, with social and political connections that could prove especially useful when the enterprise needed support from the local state government. Later, though, as the railroads headed farther west, where there were few inhabitants, immigrants would be called upon to make up the numbers. As in Britain, many of the early railroad builders were Irish, with canny foremen at times recruiting labor straight off the ships on which they had just arrived. New railroads would occasionally offer inducements to attract workers. In the 1840s, the Illinois Central advertised in the East for "3,000 laborers," offering wages of $1.25 per day and a cheap fare of just $4.95 on the train from New York to Chicago.

Usually, the basic contract for a new railroad would be solely for the grading and establishment of the roadbed. American standards were lower than those in Europe. To avoid building expensive tunnels and embankments, American railroad tracks followed the contours of the land, using steeper gradients and sharper curves than were found in Europe. This meant that the basic contract could be undertaken by the available—mostly unskilled—labor. The more complicated tasks, such as river crossings and even laying and spiking the rails down, were generally contracted separately to experienced bridge builders and tracklayers—the latter sometimes the railroad's own skilled employees. America did not initially have large contractors such as Thomas Brassey or Samuel Peto, who flourished as civil-engineering contractors in mid-nineteenth-century Britain, but soon larger firms emerged that were able to take on the construction of a whole line, though invariably with the use of subcontractors.

In the South, the arrangements for building railroads were rather different because of their use of cheap or free labor, provided by slaves before the Civil War and afterward through the subterfuge of convicts contracted out by the states. Few railroad histories address the shameful history of how the southern railroads were built in this way. However, according to Theodore Kornweibel Jr., author of the seminal study of the African

American people and the railroads, their use of unpaid black labor was extensive and universal: "Slaves constructed most of the antebellum South's 8,784 mile (by 1861) network."[15]

Because contractors found southern white farmers to be uninterested in taking up railroad construction, and "Irish and German immigrants were stereotyped as being prone to walk off the job and riot over pay disputes," presumably as a result of the wretched conditions, slaves were the principal source of labor for the early southern railroads, along with a few free blacks who could be paid less than their white counterparts.[16] At the outbreak of the war in 1861, fifteen thousand slaves were working for the southern railroads.

For the most part, these slaves were hired from their original owners, the plantation farmers or miners, on fixed-term contracts of a year or two to provide a flexible and elastic source of labor. Many did not survive the length of the contract. Railroad construction was dangerous enough for wage laborers, but for the slaves the mortality rate was far higher. According to Kornweibel, slaves working on the railroads endured even worse conditions than their peers who were left behind on the plantations. Not only were the health risks of working in untamed countryside, which included attacks by animals and snake bites, compounded by the meager rations provided, but the regime imposed by overseers was often far worse than anything they had previously experienced. Housing often consisted of little more than a tent, and diseases such as scarlet fever, cholera, and malaria were rife. Kornweibel cites a particularly egregious case where a contractor on the Atlantic & North Carolina Railroad kept slaves "in a square pen, made of pine poles, through which one might thrust his double fists, [with] no shutter on the door . . . no chimney and no floor, no bed clothing and no cooking utensils." The conditions were, routinely, so bad that many owners refused to hire out their slaves to the railroad companies, knowing that they might lose their valuable asset. It was, in fact, not only the slaves who died in the difficult working conditions of the South but also their paid colleagues, as, according to the *Encyclopedia of North American Railroads*, "free Irish laborers died like flies in the Southern swamps."[17]

With labor becoming more available, through immigration and slavery, and the requisite capital more readily accessible, it was improvements in technology that constituted the third element in stimulating the growth of the railroads. Had Peter Cooper's Tom Thumb remained the apogee of locomotive development, the railroads would have been confined to a small part of the Eastern Seaboard. Instead, there was progress on every front, from tracks and sleepers to locomotives and cars. The rapid improvements in technology were essential to underpin the equally rapid spread of the railroad. The history of this technological development is often complicated by the fact that simultaneous progress was being made on both sides of the Atlantic. It can be difficult to determine precisely who deserves the credit for a particular invention, with sources at times contradicting one another as to whether a specific advance should be attributed to America or to Britain. But it was essential for America to harness railroad technology to its own environment, to develop its own methods, and thereby to ensure that it was no longer dependent on British know-how.

The needs of the US railroads were very different from those in Britain, given the longer distances, steeper gradients, and sharper curves of the American lines. Locomotive construction was therefore a priority. But first the railroad owners, who in the 1830s continued to build railroads with the intention of using horsepower, had to be persuaded that the steam locomotive was the future. Peter Cooper had paved the way, but it was on the Camden & Amboy that the crucial breakthrough was made. In 1831, a young engineer named Isaac Dripps, who was just twenty-one—many of the early locomotive designers, like today's software wizards, were barely out of their teens when they started building engines—put together the John Bull, a Robert Stephenson locomotive that had been imported in parts from Britain. Although Dripps had never seen a locomotive before and there were no drawings accompanying the pieces, he managed the task in just a few weeks, and his reward was to be appointed as the Camden & Amboy's chief engineer, a post he would hold for twenty-two years. Dripps was adept at improvisation. The locomotive had no tender for carrying the wood and water, so he built a small flatcar on which he fitted an old whiskey cask adapted as a water tank.

Dripps made further improvements to the original John Bull and then produced a batch of similar engines, the first time a series of locomotives, rather than just one-offs, was manufactured in America. Dripps is also credited with creating the most distinctive feature of American locomotives, the cowcatcher, or rather the cow killer. Right from the start, US railroads had been built without protective fences, which was good for keeping costs down, but rather bad for safety, as cattle would seek out tasty morsels on the tracks, and hitting a cow at full speed could easily derail a train. The risk was increased by the American habit of building railroads on the cheap, which resulted in a large number of level crossings on both main roads and farm tracks.[18]

The Camden & Amboy was plagued with a series of such incidents involving farm animals, and Dripps hit upon the idea of attaching a low truck to the front of the engine equipped with pointed bars of wrought iron to impale any hapless animal and ensure it did not fall under the engine wheels. The initial design of the truck was not perfect. One of the first locomotives to be equipped with it did indeed hit a huge bull, but the poor beast was impaled so deeply on the bars that it took block and tackle to dislodge him. Dripps decided that rather than impaling the animals, the cowcatcher should, instead, knock them out of the way. He therefore fitted the snowplowlike device on the front of the locomotive that would remain a familiar sight throughout the steam era known inaccurately as "cowcatchers."

At almost the same time, Matthias Baldwin, the foremost American locomotive builder, whose company would eventually become the world's biggest producer of engines, entered the scene. Baldwin was by then in his thirties and had already enjoyed a successful career as a jewelry manufacturer, having built up his own company in his hometown, Philadelphia. He expanded into bookbinding and engraving and in 1827, by way of a hobby, had produced a stationary engine. A few years later, this encouraged a local museum owner, Franklin Peale, to ask Baldwin to manufacture a small locomotive, just large enough to pull a couple of cars around a circular track to be set up in the museum. Baldwin was by no means unique in coming to locomotive production in this haphazard way. According to historian Dee Brown, "In the 1830s, it seemed that every blacksmith, tinker, and ironworker, every wagonwright, carriagesmith and boilermaker—all the craftsmen of America—wanted to build a better locomotive." It just so happened that Baldwin, after an uncertain start, proved to be better at it than his competitors. He was also in the right place to attract attention: "All Philadelphia felt an urge to ride behind the tiny iron horse that made its own power as it moved."[19] Crucially, Baldwin's miniature museum ride was seen by the promoters of the Philadelphia, Germantown, and Normantown Railroad, who asked him to produce a locomotive for them. Baldwin had visited the Camden & Amboy workshop and based his locomotive design on the John Bull, but his Old Ironsides, completed in 1832, proved at first to be no world beater, as befitted its rather mundane name. It made an inauspicious start, averaging one mile per hour on the six miles between Philadelphia and Germantown, the five-ton engine requiring a great deal of coaxing, and even some pushing, to reach its destination. The railroad retained its horses for the time being, but Baldwin made improvements to his locomotive, and within a few months the animals could be put out to pasture—except on rainy days when the track was greasy and locomotives struggled to gain purchase (Old Ironsides regularly reached thirty miles per hour and occasionally more). Baldwin's future was ensured, and by the time of his death in 1866, his company was producing more than a hundred annually. Despite the progress in locomotive development during the 1830s, horses remained the main motive power for many lines, and even when steam engines had been adopted, the animals were frequently called upon to help trains up sections with steep gradients.

In some respects, American locomotives were better than their British counterparts right from the outset. For example, they were always fitted with cabs for the crew, a necessity given that the journeys were longer and the weather more extreme than in Britain. They were also equipped, for the most part, with four front bogie wheels. These were required—because of the poor condition of much of the track in the United States—to minimize the risk of derailment, as they guided the engines around the sharply curved lines. Another visual characteristic of US locomotives, necessitated by the widespread use of wood rather than coal as fuel, was the bulbous chimney, the sparkcatcher to go with the cowcatcher, that was designed to reduce the number of sparks flying from the chimney, which, in the early days, set off numerous fires beside the tracks.

The resulting quintessentially American locomotives became objects of great fascination, affection even, among the American public. They looked like no other engines anywhere in the world, and to meet the onerous physical demands of the US railroads, they quickly grew to become the biggest in the world. Although the majority of US railroads chose four feet and eight and a half inches as the distance between the two rails, the same as in most of Europe, their locomotives could be designed to larger specifications. This was because the US railroads adopted a bigger "loading gauge"—the size of the overall envelope required by trains to fit into tunnels and under bridges—which enabled trains to be both wider and higher than their European counterparts. By the early 1830s, Dripps had already developed on the Camden & Amboy a locomotive appropriately named Monster, which weighed forty tons and had driving wheels four feet in diameter. As Ward puts it, "When locomotives became longer, more graceful, with attractively curved smokestacks, ornate wooden cabs, outsized headlights, fine brasswork, and painted detail, they became American works of art."[20]

If the first locomotives were crude, the cars were worse. As in Europe, most early cars (or carriages, as they were known there) were based on stagecoach designs and coupled together with chains that jolted ferociously as the trains slowed or accelerated. On the first run of the Mohawk & Hudson in September 1831, a Philadelphia lawyer traveling on the train reported that the passengers in the cars, which were stagecoach bodies attached to flat trucks coupled with chains with "two to three feet slack," were consequently buffeted by jolts that had "sufficient force to jerk the passengers, who sat on seats across the tops of the coaches, out from under their hats." All these notables, unaware of the realities of train travel, carried umbrellas to protect themselves against the all-pervasive black smoke and sparks. But it was to no avail, as a scene that would have done justice to a silent-film comedy ensued: "In the first mile, the last umbrella went overboard, all having their covers burnt off from the frames, when a general mêlée took place . . . each passenger whipping his neighbor to put out the fire."[21]

American cars were different from European coaches in one crucial respect—right from the start they were open inside, without compartments or class distinctions, described by one historian as "a democratic palace instead of a nest of aristocratic closets."[22] Actually, this approach to coach interior design was probably born more of necessity than of any great democratic principle, since traveling long distances in a cramped compartment in very hot or cold weather, without access to a toilet—which was fitted far earlier to US than European cars—would have been unbearable. This was, too, a nation where black people, even in the North, where they were supposedly free, were made to travel in separate accommodation on many railroads. Nor was the open-plan arrangement always welcome. Many early passengers, confined to the relatively small cars, complained of the habits of their fellow travelers, such as spitting and chewing tobacco.

Many improvements came through serendipity rather than research. The sandbox, essential for ensuring that the wheels could grip on slippery rails, was invented, bizarrely, as a result of a biblical-scale plague of grasshoppers in Pennsylvania in 1836, which caused the trains of the Camden & Amboy to slip on their squashed bodies. Crews of men armed with brooms swept the rails in front of the trains, but their efforts were insufficient. Then some bright spark hit upon the idea of filling a box with sand and feeding it down gently in front of the driving wheels: "It worked wonderfully well and since then no American locomotive has been without a sandbox."[23] The sandbox seems to have been one of those inventions that was developed simultaneously on both sides of the Atlantic, since many European railroads adopted them at the same time.

If the locomotives were improving rapidly, so were the rails and the track bed. The early tracks, designed for light coaches pulled by horses, were inadequate for the weight of the iron horses that were rapidly taking over from their equine equivalents and had to undergo rapid improvement. The early "strap-iron" rails, which were wooden and covered by a thin sheet of metal, could not withstand the pressure of heavy trains. Rather disturbingly, passengers could find themselves confronted by a swirling piece of metal as the iron broke loose, forming "snakeheads" that were, on occasion, long enough to break through the floors of passing coaches, unsurprisingly causing panic. The solution was the all-iron T-rail, initially imported from Britain but later produced locally, though, remarkably, some of the smaller railroads operating light locomotives, notably in the South, used strap-iron rails until the Civil War. According to American legend, it was John Stevens's son Robert, the president of the Camden & Amboy, who first thought of developing the T-shaped rail that is now universal on railroads across the world, but in all likelihood he was probably merely copying the example of Britain, where such rails had already been in use. Indeed, Stevens ordered a supply of these rails from

Britain, which were laid on the Camden & Amboy in 1832. The early T-rails were remarkably light and weak by modern standards, their weight per foot being perhaps a quarter of that normally used today and consequently prone to cracks and breaks.

The track bed, too, required innovative thinking. Granite was tried because of its stability and hardness, but this very lack of resilience made for a rough ride, which harmed the rolling stock, and it also proved susceptible to damage from frost. A number of early lines were mounted on piles, but this method, too, was found to be unsatisfactory because of the lack of stability. As we will see in the next chapter, the ever-struggling Erie Railroad wasted more than $1 million (perhaps thirty times that amount in today's money) on a failed experiment with piling. Instead, all railroads gradually turned to the method of track-bed construction that has largely survived, with remarkably little change, through to this day. First, after the route is prepared through grading, ballast—chunky gravel—is laid to absorb the impact of the passing trains, and then ties (sleepers in Britain) are placed at right angles to the direction of the train and used as a base for the rails. Remarkably, modern track laid for high-speed rail lines today still uses ballast and consequently would be quite recognizable in appearance to the railroad builders of the mid-nineteenth century, the only obvious difference being the electrification equipment.

Despite their initial reliance on British imports, American railroads were, right from the start, very different in style and technology from their European counterparts—not only in the design of the locomotives but also in the way the railroads themselves were built. As previously mentioned, keeping costs down was paramount. Wherever possible, expensive digging and tunneling were avoided, and station buildings were minimal, being constructed of freely available timber. Ballast, which was expensive to quarry and transport, was used sparingly, and bridges were put up in the characteristic perilous-looking trestle style. The philosophy was simple—and very different from the approach that prevailed in Europe: get the track laid and the locomotives built, and start running trains as quickly as possible to start generating income, even if that means cutting corners that push up operating costs. Improvements could be made later, once the line started making a profit. In the event, this placed a great burden on many railroads toward the end of the nineteenth century because of the need to improve the infrastructure on heavily used routes. Crucially, the lower initial expense ensured that railroads could be built for around the same price as canals, though comparisons are difficult, as the costs of both varied quite dramatically. For example, according to George Rogers Taylor, the early lines in New York that later formed the New York Central cost around $30,000 per mile, whereas the more solidly built Boston & Lowell in Massachusetts came out at $71,000. At the other end of the scale, there was the Georgia Railroad at just $17,000 per mile (thanks, of course, to slave labor). Canals showed similarly wide variations in construction costs, ranging from $20,000 per mile to as much as $80,000.[24]

The price difference between US and European railroads was significant, helped by the far lower land and labor costs and the advantage of "eminent domain" granted to the railroads. One statistic illustrating this is particularly telling. By 1850, the United States had built an impressive twenty-six thousand miles of railroad but just eleven miles of tunnel, whereas the UK, with just one-third as many miles of track, had built nearly eighty miles of tunnel, seven times the length in America. And that in a country that is by no means as mountainous or hilly as America.

This remarkable difference did not go unnoticed. European visitors to the United States tended to be either impressed or horrified by the ability of the Americans to build their railroads so cheaply and still make a profit given the sparse traffic. A Captain Douglas Galton of the Royal Engineers, who made a comparison between British and American railroads after a trip across the Atlantic in 1856, concluded, "In a rapidly developing new country, capital is dear. Hence a rough and ready cheap railway although it entails increased cost for maintenance is preferable to a more finished and expensive line." Given that there were fewer trains on the US railroads, this was a trade-off that the early promoters were happy to make, given their perennial shortage of capital. As traffic increased, they were able to generate more capital to improve the railroads, making them more similar to their European counterparts, but they still remained distinctive. Galton highlighted other ways in which the US railroads kept costs down, noting that although American railroads ran fewer trains, this ensured that they were better filled and therefore earned more revenue per mile. The paucity of traffic meant that there was no need for sophisticated signaling equipment and that the numerous level crossings could be left ungated and unmanned, keeping labor costs lower. Overall, fewer workers were employed per mile of railroad in the United States than in the UK. Galton concluded that the American system was in general "well adapted to the wants of the country."[25]

Cheapness of construction may have had much to recommend it in these early days, but there would be a heavy price to pay later in terms of passenger safety, which would, in turn, contribute to the American people's disillusionment with their railroads. In the short term, however, the low costs encouraged a railroad boom during which, until it was briefly cut short by the panic of 1837, "some two hundred lines had been chartered, taking the savings of thousands of investors, many of whom had never seen a railroad track or a steam locomotive."[26] Of course, not all of these charters resulted in the construction of any track, but by the end of the railroad age's first full decade, there was a total of more than twenty-seven hundred miles of line.[27] Virtually all these early railroads were single track, and many still used horses for all or part of their traction. However, in view of the primitive nature of the available technology and the arduous nature of the construction methods, the rapid spread of the iron road represented an astonishing achievement.

Having built a railroad, the question then was how best to run it. One of the early decisions made in Britain was that the railroad should be a vertically integrated operation—in other words, the railroad company would control the line that it had built by not only providing the locomotives and the track, but also determining the timetable and regulating the operations. There had been some initial moves to operate lines in the same manner as canals or turnpikes. For instance, the Stockton & Darlington allowed anyone to use the railroad provided they had the right equipment. But there were compelling reasons *not* to use that approach. Unlike a turnpike, a railroad has only a limited capacity, determined by factors such as the speed of the trains, the length of the single track, the signaling arrangements, the power of the locomotives, and so on. Allowing all comers onto the tracks inevitably resulted in problems and inefficiencies. The lessons of the Stockton & Darlington, with its occasional fisticuffs between drivers of trains facing each other on the single track, had been learned. A free-for-all was clearly no way to run a railroad, and in Britain no other railroad followed the example of the Stockton & Darlington. Consequently, virtually every American railroad also adopted the system of operating its own trains and providing the locomotives, though private wagons and cars were normally allowed.

All this represented progress, but the railroads remained crude in many respects. Early US railroads were simple in layout but faced considerable operational difficulties over long distances with single tracks and no telegraph, combined with unreliable machinery. Brakes were fitted only to the cars and had to be applied by conductors or brakemen in each one. The chains linking the cars meant they crashed into each other when the train braked and were wont to break if acceleration was too rough. Signaling was for the most part nonexistent, until the lines became busier and accidents forced a change of policy, as we will see later. Solutions were basic. The Georgia Railroad, for instance, solved the problem of the clash of signaling by running trains in each direction on alternate days.

The railroad companies were a true ragbag of outfits, ranging from, literally, one-horse companies carrying coal out of a mine to longer lines stretching into the backcountry, though only three, all interestingly in the South—the Wilmington & Raleigh Railroad in North Carolina and two in Georgia, the Georgia Railroad & Banking Company and the Central Railroad & Banking Company—could boast more than a hundred miles of track in 1840. The names of these pioneering lines embraced the prosaically ambitious, such as the Western Railroad of Massachusetts and the Central Railroad of Michigan; the romantically parochial two-and-a-half-mile Mine Hill & Schuylkill Haven and the slightly longer Palmyra & Jacksonburgh; and the formidable-sounding Tuscarora & Cold Run Tunnel & Railroad Company. America's early railroads were a hodgepodge of disconnected lines serving a few major towns or specific mines and in no way represented a network. Some did have ambitions, invariably unrealistic ones, which they often demonstrated by adding the words *& Western* to their company name—and later, as they progressed west, *& Pacific*[28]—to signal their intent. However, for the most part the early promoters did not have a vision of a national rail network, or even one that extended very far beyond their immediate locality: "This technology [of railroads] was more or less in place by the end of the 1830s but the psychology wasn't. Most early promoters looked upon the railroad as a feeder to waterways or a means of serving the needs of a local community."[29]

Locally, though, the railroads were welcomed by one and all. The arrival of the iron road was a cause for celebration, and the railroad companies would invariably try to build on that goodwill by outfitting a special train for the local notables and throwing a party for the residents. Brass bands, fireworks, and lavish banquets were held for their benefit, an early example of public relations, which could be said to have been invented by the railroads. There was no shortage of attempts to capitalize on the event. Local potters and glass blowers would hastily produce commemorative china and glassware, often, to save themselves the services of a designer, using the same much-copied pattern showing a basic engine of the early teapot design hauling a single car and with the singularly unoriginal motto "God Speed Thee." In what would turn out to be presciently accurate reporting, local newspapers would print laudatory articles representing the event as epoch making. There was negative coverage too, often focusing on the potential dangers of the railroad, since many of these early lines went down the main street, already full of horses, carts, and pedestrians, many of whom were utterly unaware of the perils posed by even a slow-moving locomotive. But the railroad was greeted by most people with open arms: "Generally, though, when the iron horse made its first appearance, the reception was one of breathless expectation and delight. The backers and planners of all the early railroads saw to it that their first demonstration runs were occasions of festivity."[30]

In general, these early railroads did not change the American way of life. They might allow travel to the nearest big town and allow some produce to be taken farther, but they were in no sense a national network. The next couple of decades, however, would change all that, as the beast of the iron road was finally unleashed—with extraordinary consequences for America.

3

ΤΗΕ RAILROADS
TAKE HOLD

In the twenty years running up to the outbreak of the Civil War in 1861, the railroads became an unstoppable force, conquering the whole of the Eastern Seaboard and making major inroads westward. From an experimental technology with a precarious base, railroads became mainstream and ubiquitous, sweeping through the country with the support of the population. The love affair was becoming a marriage, a symbiotic relationship that was to last almost a century. In the words of Ralph Waldo Emerson, "Americans take to this contrivance, the railroad, as if it were the cradle in which they were born."[1]

The impact of such a major invention took time to sink in. At the beginning, the railroad was "mostly an object of awe, excitement and mild trepidation."[2] It was unclear whether the railroads were merely a novel form of amusement, a grandiose fairground ride, or an invention that would change people's way of life. By the start of the 1840s, everything needed to build railroads quickly and cheaply was coming together—the technology, the labor, the financing, and the legal framework. Galvanized by its promotion funded by a combination of private and public money, and now supported by just about everybody apart from those whose vested interests were directly threatened by the spread of the new technology, railroad fever spread dramatically across America. The brief financial downturn caused by the panic of 1837 proved to be barely a hiccup in the onward march of the iron horse. Although the subsequent downturn following the panic finished off dozens of putative rail schemes, some of which would never have been viable anyway, and delayed many others, the railroads recovered far more quickly than the rest of the economy, and indeed helped to stimulate the subsequent boom. The panic, though, caused rather longer-term damage in terms of the creditworthiness of both states and railroads, since several states, notably Pennsylvania, Indiana, and Michigan, defaulted on their debts as a result of the panic, making it more difficult for future railroads to raise funds for investment. Manufacturers suffered, too, with several bankruptcies, a list that would have included Baldwin but for the leniency of his creditors and his foresight in entering into partnership with several other manufacturers to spread the risk in what was a difficult business.

Initially, "few Americans thought of the railroad as being a harbinger of an industrial revolution or of any drastic change in the social order." Quite the opposite. The Boston & Lowell, for example, was "built because people in Lowell wanted ready access to Boston [and] the same kind of need had given birth to the Camden & Amboy, the Philadelphia, Germantown & Norristown, the New York & Harlem, the Pearson & Hudson River Railroad . . . and so on."[3] The early railroad promoters, like the inventors of the World Wide Web, could not have had any notion of the dramatic changes that their conception would bring about. Their initial philosophy was parochial, but, by the mid-1840s, as the number and extent of the railroads spread, and the notion of the iron road as a unifying national force took hold, they developed a wider, more ambitious vision of its potential. There was no central plan. In contrast to the growth of the railroads in a number of European countries, where governments dictated the shape of the network in accordance with a central plan, in America there was no such scheme. In the United States, the emphasis on states' rights—the assumption that power resides primarily with the states rather than the federal government—would never have allowed that, but several states that funded or supported railroads strongly influenced their routes. Indeed, government of all levels by and large made a point of keeping out of the railroads, which was to have implications for safety and passenger comfort.

New England enjoyed much of the postpanic growth. Indeed, for a brief period, its capital, Boston, could boast of being the best-connected city in America. By 1850, it was possible to travel from Boston to most of the cities of Massachusetts, as well as north to Portland, Maine, and even to Montreal in Canada and west to Albany, in New York State, and down to New York City itself. The majority of railroad lines, however, were still relatively short. Longer journeys required a complex series of interchanges and—since stations belonging to different companies were invariably and, at times deliberately, built well apart—the occasional trudge or carriage ride through towns.

Even America's first truly long-distance railroad,[4] the Erie, had its origins as much in local interests as regional or national considerations. The line, conceived as a link between the Hudson River and Lake Erie, or in other words, like the Erie Canal, as a connection between the Atlantic Ocean and the Great Lakes, was inevitably opposed by canal owners. Support from local people, however, enabled the promoters to overcome these narrow interests. According to railroad historian George Douglas, "Numerous communities along the way, communities that had no transportation at all, created such an uproar that the canal interests had to back down and allow the Erie Railroad to be chartered." It was to be a direct rival to the highly profitable Erie Canal, whose owners did manage to ensure that several restrictions were placed on the railroad to protect the canal's interests.

Despite its parochial roots, the Erie was a different kind of railroad from anything that had been envisaged before. It was a *grand projet* of its day, a line stretching nearly 450 miles to link Lake Erie with the ports of the Atlantic. Its origins stretched back to 1829, when the idea of linking the ocean with the lakes had been first touted by a farsighted pamphleteer, William Redfield, who later became the inaugural president of the American Association for the Advancement of Science. He published a map of a proposed railroad from New York to the Great Lakes, and his pamphlet led to the granting of a charter to the New York & Erie Railroad, as it was initially called, by the governor of New York in April 1832, but it would take nearly two decades to bear fruit.

Right from the start, the Erie, which would eventually suffer no fewer than five bankruptcies, struggled. Construction of such an ambitious line, which would, briefly, be the longest in the world, had inevitable difficulties. It might have been broadly welcomed by people in the communities through which it passed, but there was no shortage of smallholders directly on its path who saw the opportunity to make a fast buck by demanding excessive amounts for small parcels of land. These were frontiersmen and hillbillies, early settlers who had migrated westward in a haphazard way to carve out a subsistence living from the relatively poor land and who had no truck with the railroad. Cannily, they would wait until the railroad's workforce was all ready to cross into their field and then suddenly up their demand for cash. Even the local Native Americans got in on the act. One oft-reported tale describes how, when the Erie sought to cross the Seneca reservation in Cattaraugus County, in western New York State, the local chief demanded ten thousand dollars for the right-of-way. Appalled at this demand, the railroad manager blustered that the land was no good for anything else, such as growing corn or potatoes, and that it had no good timber on it. The sage paused and then said, "It pretty good for railroad."[5] His tribe got the money.

The construction of the Erie is an epic story that has been largely forgotten in American railroad folklore, having been overshadowed by the much-recounted tale of the transcontinentals a couple of decades later (see Chapter 5).[6] In fact, the Erie merits an equally prominent place in railroad history, as the line was built at a time when the railroad pioneers were still feeling their way with the technology, and fully deserved its appellation as "the work of the age." The Erie's reputation, too, has suffered because of the numerous mistakes made during its construction and its later role as the plaything of the railroad barons (see Chapter 8), but the building of the line was the greatest achievement of the early railroad entrepreneurs, as the scale of the construction dwarfed all other contemporary schemes.

To support the construction of the Erie, the State of New York put up a loan of $3 million, and the company tried to raise $1 million, but faced immediate difficulties when, a few weeks after the ceremonial turning of the first sod in 1836, New York's financial district was razed to the ground in a catastrophic fire that bankrupted many of the putative investors in the railroad. This was just the start of a string of financial problems that would not only delay the construction of the Erie but call its very existence into question. Work proceeded in fits and starts, as money was made available by pressuring stockholders and persuading local rich residents to commit themselves to the scheme, but there were long periods when the work camps were quiet. Following the company's default on its interest payments in 1842, construction ceased altogether and would not recommence for three long years. Remarkably, the citizens of Middletown, New York, succeeded in persuading the promoters to complete a nine-mile stretch of line from the neighboring town of Goshen before construction ceased to ensure they would enjoy the benefits of being the Erie's western terminus until work could resume. At this stage the Erie stretched barely forty miles from the Hudson, less than one-tenth of its planned length, and there were doubts as to whether it could ever be completed. The stoppage proved especially damaging, since stockpiles of material, such as ties and stone, left on uncompleted sections of the track, were purloined, often by the very farmers who had supplied the material but not been paid for it. Many local farmhouses would subsequently boast solid timber frames hewn from wood originally intended to support the railroad rather than their roofs.

Somehow, though, New York State was prevailed upon not only to cancel the original $3 million debt, but also to allow the railroad to issue new stock to raise a further $3 million to ensure work could recommence. This time, there was a new powerful president at the helm of the railroad, Benjamin Loder, who had made his fortune out of dry goods. Though having no knowledge of the railroads, he was just the sort of man the Erie needed, because he had the ability and strength of character to drive through construction of the line despite all the obstacles, financial and practical, in its path. He made the Erie into an unstoppable force, helped by thousands of Irish laborers who fled their native country during the long potato famine that started in 1845 and who consequently were grateful even for the low wages offered. The Irish were not, though, always a happy bunch, given the perilous nature of their work. It was remarkably similar to that of the laborers building India's first major railroad through the Western Ghats outside Bombay at around the same time, who were forced to hang down from the tops of cliffs in flimsy baskets to drill holes in which they placed gunpowder.[7] An almost identically risky technique was used in the hilly region around Port Jervis, on the Delaware, where the cliffs rose almost straight up from the river. The brave fellow in the basket with the task of setting the charge would signal to be rapidly hoisted to safety before the fuse burned down. Inevitably, at times ropes got snagged or instructions misheard, and the consequent explosion would send the hapless man to his doom. Many of the dislodged rocks plunged into the neighboring Delaware & Hudson Canal, leading to a series of lawsuits between the two companies.

The Irish were prone to fighting, and at one stage something akin to a war broke out between two factions, the Corkonians, from the Southwest, and the Fardowners, who confusingly mostly came from Connaught in the West of Ireland.[8] The men were working for contractors who had been charged with cutting through a wall of solid rock to create a mile-long embankment in a hilly region called Shin Hollow. It was slow work, necessitating the establishment of semipermanent work camps that provided very basic housing for the laborers, usually consisting of big barns where food was served downstairs and the dormitories above were reached by outside ladders. Others lived in simple outlying huts, mostly without heating or ventilation. Both gangs had arrived recently off the boat and wanted to establish themselves as the dominant force. The Fardowners, who back in Ireland usually fared worse in these disputes, decided to attack one of the barns occupied by the Corkonians with the aim of chasing them off the work site. The row may have started because the Cork men had accepted the low daily rate of seventy-five cents rather than the usual dollar. Several days of battles and skirmishes ensued, including one incident in which, after a whole barn housing the hapless Corkonians had been brought down by sawing through the timbers, each man was made to swear that he would not work on the railroad again. There was, more by luck than design, no loss of life. The Fardowners then set about attacking a group of Germans who proved to be far better organized than either Irish group and, despite their small number, saw off the men from the Emerald Isle. It took the intervention of the local militia, called in by the contractors and, oddly, sporting full-dress uniforms as they had no other, to confront the men and quell the riot. There were other, more minor, disturbances too, but, according to railroad historian Stewart H. Holbrook, it was not the hillbillies, the difficult terrain, or the aggressive Irish laborers that were the major delaying factor for the railroad but "the tremendous snows that blanketed New York State [that] . . . piled onto the tracks four, five, six feet deep on the levels with drifts up to thirty feet and more in the cuts."[9]

There were other major natural obstacles, too. The Erie could boast that it had built the most impressive railroad structure to date on the American railroad system, the Starrucca Viaduct, a stone-arch bridge spanning a creek near Lanesboro, Pennsylvania. The valley was wide, and the twelve-hundred-foot, sixteen-arch bridge was built in stone with concrete foundations, rather than from wood, which was used for most contemporary bridges. It took eight hundred workers a year to complete the bridge—which still carries railroad traffic today—at a cost of $320,000 (about $9 million in 2012 values).

As the railroad reached each small community on the route, prolonged celebrations were held with feasts for the masses and speeches, often with Loder himself as the star. The partying at Dunkirk, New York, when the line was finally opened in May 1851 right through to Lake Erie was, however, on a far grander scale. Holbrook notes wryly that the myriad of opening ceremonies for railroad lines throughout the nineteenth century were "pretty much alike," but then adds, "I think the Erie doings deserve some attention." Indeed. The opening was celebrated by running two trains all the way from Piermont on the Hudson to Dunkirk on a trip that included an overnight stop in Elmira, as the overall travel time was around twenty-four hours. The guests included the US president, Millard Fillmore, and "298 assorted statesmen and political catchpoles of varying degrees of importance," who feasted first at Elmira and then, after resuming their journey apparently rather the worse for wear, at Dunkirk on the second night, where they were greeted by the USS *Michigan* firing a twenty-one-gun salute. A three-hundred-foot table positively "groaned with barbecued oxen, pork and beans in 50 gallon containers, bread baked in loaves ten feet long and two feet thick," and there was even an enormous clam chowder.[10] As railroad opening celebrations go, it was probably the grandest of them all before the joining of the Union Pacific and Central Pacific Railroads in 1869. Indeed, the building of the Erie was, in a way, the start of the process that less than two decades later would see the completion of the first transcontinental. It marked a recognition that the railroad had come of age, demonstrating that it was able to cover huge distances through difficult terrain. The local communities may well have been delighted by the arrival of the iron horse, but these folks were somewhat incidental to the line's true purpose, for the Erie was primarily intended to be a long-distance trunk line. California, or, rather more practically, the Mississippi, was the obvious next stop.

Not long after the Erie started operation, the promoters realized that the siting of both the eastern and the western terminals of the railroad had been a mistake. Piermont was too far upriver—twenty-five miles—from New York, and consequently the line was quickly extended down to Jersey City, almost opposite New York across the Hudson. At the other end, Dunkirk was soon found to be inadequate and was swiftly replaced as the western terminal by the more substantial town of Buffalo. Despite such teething troubles, once completed the Erie made an enormous difference to the transportation system of America's Northeast. As the obvious and cheapest way to carry goods inland, it greatly strengthened New York City's control of domestic commerce. The Erie also reinforced New York's stranglehold as the nation's foremost port, even though the line terminated on the wrong side of the Hudson. According to the historian of the Erie, the completion of the railroad "helped Gotham to become the continent's most populous urban center and meant secondary places for longtime rivals Baltimore, Boston and Philadelphia."[11] The promoters of the Baltimore & Ohio, therefore, had failed in their aim of making their city the dominant East Coast port, primarily because their line went to the wrong place, but also because it had taken so long to reach its original planned destination at Wheeling on the Ohio River. New York, it must be stressed, had other benefits, such as an excellent natural port and a buoyant financial district, but the Erie Railroad undoubtedly helped to consolidate its superiority.

The choice of terminals was not the only mistake made by the Erie's promoters—a number of other blunders would contribute to the financial difficulties that were to beset the line. Back in the 1830s, the directors of the company had made a fatal error of judgment when they turned down the opportunity to buy, for a mere ninety thousand dollars, the New York & Harlem Railroad, the city's first railroad. This would have given it access to New York City by virtue of the Harlem's route through Manhattan, thereby avoiding the need for travelers to take a steamer downriver from Piermont. It was not the modest outlay of a few thousand dollars that lay behind the Erie's directors' decision not to acquire the New York & Harlem, but their belief—perhaps somewhat surprising from a twenty-first-century standpoint—that its passengers would rather enjoy the boat trip along the Hudson. Even the ambitious men who built America's first trunk line would appear not quite to have understood the import of what they were doing.

They made a major technical error, too, that would ultimately cost the railroad dearly. Thinking that the land was too swampy and that positioning the railroad above the land would reduce the impact of snowfall and flooding, the Erie spent three-quarters of a million dollars driving piles into the ground on which the track would be laid. The directors had become enamored of a device called Crane's Patent Pile Driving Machine, eight of which—operated by no fewer than thirteen men apiece—were enlisted in the cause of creating a raised railroad. More than one hundred miles of piling were completed before the idea was abandoned when it was discovered that the foundations were not stable.[12] The Erie would have done well to call on the pioneering railroad engineer George Stephenson, who had successfully built part of the Liverpool & Manchester through marshy terrain in the late 1820s. Early passengers on the Erie would be bemused by the sight of mile upon mile of decaying oak piles running parallel to the line.

A further blunder was the Erie's choice of a six-foot gauge, rather than the four feet and eight and a half inches that eventually became standard. The wider gauge was chosen for a variety of reasons, including, oddly, the utterly false notion that it was used extensively in the UK. But the chief motivation behind the Erie's directors' decision, as with Isambard Kingdom Brunel when he opted for a seven-and-a-quarter-foot broad gauge on the Great Western, was the wish to differentiate the railroad from others. The directors also argued that the steep gradients on the line would require powerful locomotives, which could be more easily accommodated with the extra width. There was an obstinacy in the decision, too, the notion that it would be better if the Erie did *not* connect with any of its lesser neighbors— further evidence of the directors' failure to understand that the ultimate role of the railroads would be, precisely, to allow long-distance carriage. This isolationist stance had been encouraged by the State of New York, which, in order to protect New York's advantageous trade position, had included a provision in the railroad's charter that the line should not connect with any others across state borders. This decision not only increased costs because of the extra width required for the track, but, as with the Great Western in the UK, had to be reversed later at vast expense, a task that was not fully completed until the 1880s.

The choice of gauge may seem like a mere technical issue—and therefore beyond the scope of this book—but in fact it is of fundamental importance to railroad history. In Australia, for example, the failure to agree upon a standard gauge throughout the country fatally undermined the railroad's efficiency and prevented it from developing into the vital economic force that it became in most economically advanced nations. In America, too, there was no clarity over gauge at the dawn of the railroad age, and the Erie was far from alone among early railroads in choosing its gauge with little regard for the idea of connecting with other lines. The Baltimore & Ohio was built to what became standard gauge, four feet and eight and a half inches,[13] whereas on the Mohawk & Hudson the rails were four feet, nine inches apart, and on the Camden & Amboy a further inch separated the rails. In the South, the Charleston & Hamburg had gone for the full five feet—a common, but by no means universal, gauge for southern railroads. Louisiana, for example, went for five and a half feet. As early as 1834, the *American Railroad Journal* was advocating the adoption of a universal gauge, but this would not actually be achieved until a half century later (see Chapter 8). By the outbreak of the Civil War, there were eleven gauges in the North and almost as many in the South. A journey between Philadelphia and Charleston would, at the time, require no fewer than eight changes of gauge.

Probably the most bizarre consequence of the failure to unify gauges was the brief battle dubbed the Erie Gauge War of 1853–1854. Confusingly, this had nothing to do with the Erie Railroad, which was, in fact, named after Lake Erie and did not pass through the town of Erie, Pennsylvania, where the battle took place. The line between Buffalo, New York, and the New York–Pennsylvania border was built to a gauge of four feet, ten inches by the Buffalo & State Line Railroad. However, a passenger heading west from that border toward Cleveland, Ohio (the next state),

would have to change trains, because a twenty-mile stretch of line between the border and the town of Erie had been built, by a different company, the Erie & Northeast Railroad, to a six-foot gauge. Then, at Erie
itself, came yet another change of train—back to the gauge of four feet, ten
inches that was becoming prevalent in Ohio. Obviously, this was totally
unsatisfactory for the passengers, but for the people of Erie, as with residents of many other such junction towns, one man's burden was another's
benefit. The local carters and haulers, and, indirectly, the hoteliers, innkeepers, and restaurateurs, profited from the town's status as an enforced
stopping place.

After a year of this ridiculous situation, the owners of the Buffalo &
State Line Railroad were able to acquire two-thirds of the Erie & Northeast's stock and, in November 1853, made the decision to standardize the
whole track across this narrow northern corner of Pennsylvania using
the four-foot-ten gauge. However, the townsfolk of Erie were infuriated by
the decision, fearing that their town's very raison d'être would be
threatened by the move.

As preparations began for the gauge change, the mayor of Erie enlisted
a force of 150 townsmen under the guise of a special police force to "restore
order," which in fact involved attacking and destroying railroad property.
The legitimized mob tore down bridges and ripped up the tracks, earning
them the nickname "the Rippers." They managed to create an eight-mile
gap in the Erie & Northeast Railroad's rail line that was not restored until
the Pennsylvania legislature passed a law authorizing the state to standardize all the railroad gauges and backed it by protecting the property of the
rail companies.

The Erie Gauge War was just one of a number of conflicts triggered by
the vexed issue of gauge width. There were numerous others. When in the
1870s the evocatively named Androscoggin & Kennebec Railroad in Maine
sought to change from broad gauge to standard to enable it to connect with
Boston, local objectors managed to obtain an injunction to prevent the
conversion, but before they could serve it, the railroad, rather shockingly,
sent out teams of workers on the Sabbath to carry out the work.

The reason the apparently arcane and technical matter of track gauge
could arouse such passions was because it went right to the heart of a

much deeper issue—that of the nature of the nation these early Americans were intent on creating. The move to standardize gauge was the globalization of its day, the natural province of the free traders and the settlers who wanted to create one big America best represented by the views of the Federalist founding father Alexander Hamilton. As Mark Reutter, in the introduction to a history of the midcentury American rail network, suggests, "A standardized gauge fits a business model that places a premium on high volume and low cost, the very principles that Hamilton had advocated for his factory system."[14]

Those who favored keeping their railroads local, limiting their scope through the need to change trains and transfer goods, were more in tune with the ideas of Thomas Jefferson, whose vision had been of a land of urban factories and self-sufficient rural farms. Indeed, until the arrival of the railroad, this was the natural way of life for most Americans, who created a world where clothing was sewn by mothers and daughters, shoes were made by the village cordwainer, food was grown locally, and tools, and even crude firearms, were forged by the local blacksmith. With few roads and little reason to use them, people rarely ventured more than a few miles from where they were born. Eager to improve their lot, many of these villagers and farmers had supported the idea of the railroads, and many had even invested in them. However, they had not understood the power of what they had unleashed. The very people who had invested in the local railroad company—the farmers and the merchants keen for easier access to markets—had most to lose from railroads that could travel long distances without stopping, as the people of Erie realized in 1853. Getting produce to the local market town might be of great benefit, but facing competition from far more distant places could put them out of business or reduce the value of their produce. Therefore, "while technical journals generally advocated a uniform gauge, local politicians were more comfortable with small, fragmented railroads."[15]

This was a painful awakening for many Americans. The wonderful invention that had elicited almost universal support and whose arrival had been cheered in so many places across the nation was suddenly turning out to be hydra-headed. Until now Americans—with the exception of the odd stagecoach driver and canal owner—had regarded the benefits of the railroad to be universal, but its impact was turning out to be more complex than first thought, and moreover could be detrimental to many local interests. It was at this point that the railroads began to elicit significant levels of opposition for the first time, germinating the wider antipathy that would later be felt toward them. For a while, though, the people were mostly protected from the worst depredations of the iron road. The Jeffersonian ideals triumphed, as they accorded with the strong contemporary ethos of states' rights, but posed a barrier to the development of the railroads: "The success with which local interests managed to hobble this lusty steed [the iron horse] for over thirty years is a testament to the vigor of state and local rights in an age in which the powers of federalism were hardly realized."[16]

Ultimately, however, the Hamiltonian view was bound to triumph, as the forces of capitalism were behind it and the transportation revolution, with railroads in the vanguard, was irreversible. As time went on, the railroad companies sought to make profits by through-running—that is, by concentrating on long-distance routes on which no changes were required—because this attracted new customers and reduced costs; the obvious corollary was that as the railroads became bigger, they paid less attention to local interests. The growth of the railroads was intimately bound up with the wider development of America as a powerful economic force, and ultimately this process would ride roughshod over parochial concerns.

The Erie might have failed with its plan to run the railroad on piles, and made a huge initial mistake with its gauge, but the company was responsible for introducing a technical innovation that would become universal on railroads across America: the telegraph. It had already proved its worth during the Erie's inaugural run of May 1851 when a locomotive developed problems and the next station was alerted by telegraph to ensure that a replacement was ready. Yet despite that success, there was much skepticism about the invention until Charles Minot, the superintendent of the Erie, showed that it could be used as a way of greatly increasing a railroad's reliability and traffic, and therefore both its usefulness and its value.

Minot was one of those big characters of the early railroad industry. He was a judge's son who chose engineering rather than the law and was appointed as the first superintendent of the railroad. Portly and genial, he also had a fierce temper, which "would blow like a volcano" when someone crossed him.[17] And that is precisely what happened when he learned that the train drivers were not making proper use of the telegraphic system that he had installed along the tracks. Minot had made a stab in the dark by persuading the Erie to put up the poles to make use of Morse's recent invention, the telegraphic machine. However, the railroad's drivers and signal staff were reluctant to put their trust in the device until Minot showed them its advantages. One day in September 1851, he found himself at the small Turner's Station[18] seated in a westbound train that was delayed while waiting for a late eastbound service. As the railroad was single track throughout, apart from a few passing places at stations, and there was no signaling system, the only form of train regulation to avoid accidents was through the timing of scheduled crossing points. Minot, anxious to continue his journey, barged into the telegraph office and told the operator to wire ahead to Goshen, fourteen miles down the track, to ask if the eastbound train had yet passed. On hearing that it had not, he sent a message—the first-ever telegraphic order[19] dispatched in the United States—to hold the train there until further notice. Minot then instructed the train driver, Isaac Lewis, to proceed, but the hapless fellow, "a man of orderly mind and of little imagination," responded that he'd be damned if "he would run by that thing."[20] Minot took over the controls himself, dispatching Lewis to "ride on the cushions,"[21] where the terrified driver took up the backseat of the last wagon, fearing that a head-on crash was inevitable. When Minot reached Goshen, he discovered that the eastbound service had still not arrived. By telegraphing ahead twice more in advance, he finally met the eastbound service three stops down the line, saving more than an hour.

In fact, the telegraph and the railroad proved to be almost symbiotic inventions. In the pretelegraph era, there would be no way of knowing when a train might next arrive other than when the smoke could be seen from the nearest high point, usually a water tower, or a specially provided wooden pole fitted with cleats, which were used rather like crows' nests on ships, where the station agent, equipped with a telescope, could scan the horizon. But now telegraphs provided railroad managers with an unparalleled communication system across their networks. In return, the railroads were indispensable to the telegraph companies, giving them a ready-made route through the countryside, with the added benefit that train staff would quickly be able to spot any break in the system where a pole had fallen down or a wire had snapped. While the original system of Morse code, which uses a series of short and long signals—dots and dashes—to spell out words, had first been developed in the 1830s, it was the spread of the railroads that ensured the telegraph's rapid development and its financial success. Stations provided handy sites for telegraph offices, and although the railroad had priority use of the system, there was plenty of spare capacity available for business and personal users. There was, though, considerable cost involved in putting up the poles and laying the wires, and it had taken some persuasion by Minot to convince his company of its advantages. The incident at Turner's Station, however, marked a turning point, and within a decade the telegraph had become universally deployed across the United States. By 1866 Western Union had established total dominance by buying out most of its smaller rivals in an industry that was a natural monopoly. So, too, were the railroads, but, as we shall see, other factors prevented any one railroad corporation from acquiring monopoly power—in contrast to the experience of most other countries.

The Erie may have been the longest of the early railroads, but the construction delays meant that by the time of its completion, other big players with similarly grand ambitions had emerged. A little to the south, the Pennsylvania was also stretching far into the West. Unlike the Erie, the Pennsylvania was not originally conceived as a trunk line; rather, as was the case with most of its contemporaries, it was developed by local interests to serve their needs. Realizing that the state canal system was inadequate for their transportation requirements, fearing the dominance of the Erie as it took shape farther north, and judging that the technology was now sufficiently developed to overcome the obstacle of the mountain range that separated Pennsylvania's two biggest cities, the merchants of Philadelphia decided in 1846 to build a line to Pittsburgh. Plans for a 137-mile section between Philadelphia and Harrisburg were approved, signaling the start of what would become one of America's great railroads. The Pennsylvania Railroad would owe a great deal of its success to its fortuitous choice of John Edgar Thomson as engineer. In fact, the title of "engineer" as applied to these early railroad builders is something of a misnomer. In the pioneering days, the construction of a railroad line required a man at the helm who could cope with all aspects of the business, and, like several of his contemporaries, both in America and in Europe, Thomson was a genuine jack of all trades. Indeed, Albro Martin describes him as "a genius of planning, construction and operation," who "possessed a consuming curiosity about everything new that was being introduced into American railroading." Like many talented individuals, he could be difficult, rude, and stubborn—*pigheaded* was a word routinely associated with him—and tended to do things without consulting his directors. But, fortunately for both parties, he was generally right, and the railroad he built was so good that it was widely regarded as "the standard railroad of America": "The result was a main line and branches that were laid with a foresight which appears uncanny today."[22]

Thomson was also, perhaps oddly for a Quaker, very good at making money and at the wheeling and dealing that was another necessary part of early railroad management. Perhaps, though, it was his religious beliefs that made him stress the importance of railroads' reinvesting their profits to keep improving their assets rather than, as so many did, paying high dividends to the shareholders at the cost of establishing the long-term viability of the company. Having completed the first section in 1851, Thomson soon became president of the railroad and oversaw the crucial extension of the line through to Pittsburgh. This involved the building of an expensive and difficult tunnel and the construction of the remarkable 220-degree Horseshoe Curve near Altoona to get through the Allegheny Mountains that was partly designed by Herman Haupt, who later played a key role in the use of railroads in the Civil War (see next chapter). The challenge and complexity of these engineering projects meant that it was not until 1858 that Pennsylvania's two major cities were connected by rail. Thomson, whose vision had always extended well beyond his home state, did not stop there. He put the cash generated by the success of the line to good use and through a process of acquisition soon had a line all the way to Chicago. In the East, his purchase of a New Jersey railroad gave him terminal facilities on the west bank of the Hudson, with ferries running to New York.

The New York Central Railroad was also stirring. But, as Holbrook so elegantly puts it, the Central was "not the result of engineering and construction crews [but] rather the creature of lawyers and investors, many of whom might be said to be speculators."[23] It was, in fact, the result of a merger of ten small railroads crossing New York State. Until the creation of the Central, those traveling between Albany and Buffalo in New York State had to use a series of small railroads and make numerous changes. These lesser lines generally bore names that reflected their two termini: the Auburn & Syracuse, the Schenectady & Troy, the Buffalo & Rochester, and so on. Starting with the Mohawk & Hudson, they had been built in the previous two decades along the Mohawk Valley and the Erie Canal, and the service they offered was patchy and unsatisfactory. By the late 1840s, they had combined to offer a through service of sorts, passengers being able to stay in the same cars—owned by the Albany & Schenectady—for the entire duration of their journey, but lengthy delays were routine. In theory the 290 miles between Albany and Buffalo could be covered in fourteen hours—the average of barely twenty miles per hour was in fact not bad for the time—but in practice this was rarely achieved. A hapless traveler—sadly his or her name has not survived—who left Albany one spring day in 1850 made a note of their arduous progress, which included various unexplained stops in sidings and some twelve hours, again unexplained, in Syracuse followed by another six-hour wait in Rochester. The train finally arrived in Buffalo after a journey of more than thirty-eight hours at an average of less than eight miles per hour—about the speed of a gently trotting horse.

There was clearly money to be made by connecting these lines. The creation of the Central required the vision of a wheeler-dealer, and fortunately one was at hand: Erastus Corning, whose day job was the prosaic task of making nails but who also doubled, more important, as the longtime mayor of Albany. Corning was the president of one of the ten existing New York lines, the 78-mile Utica & Schenectady, a railroad so prosperous that in 1850 its shareholders rewarded him with a plate service worth an astonishing six thousand dollars, a sum equivalent to a present-day banker's bonus. Corning, who became president of the joint railroad on its creation in 1853, set about enhancing the new combined railroad and offering a far better service: new cars and locomotives were purchased, and the track was improved, ensuring a rapid rise in both passenger and freight traffic. To give a scale of the enterprise, which was probably around the same size as the Erie, the New York Central could lay claim to 542 miles of line and owned 150 wood-burning locomotives, 1,700 freight cars, and just under 200 passenger coaches. Indeed, it fared so well, easily surviving the panic of 1857, that it attracted the attention of a rapacious shipping magnate, one Cornelius Vanderbilt (see Chapter 8).

In the 1850s, the consolidation of smaller lines to create a larger railroad was a new idea in America, but would be adopted widely across the United States, particularly after the Civil War as the Hamiltonian ethos prevailed. Big companies like the Erie, the Pennsylvania, and the New York Central were still, in the antebellum period, the exception. Most railroads in this era remained small, rarely connecting with a neighboring company line and, if they did so, requiring passengers to change trains with all the hassle that entailed. No one thought of the railroads as a network; they were viewed, rather, as a series of disparate lines, best illustrated by the lack of any rail connection between lines in towns blessed with more than one railroad. Separate stations were the norm, and therefore railroad maps of the period can be confusing, suggesting links and connections where, in fact, there were none.

By 1850, America's railroad mileage had tripled to 9,000. As New York included both the Erie and the Central, it could lay claim to having the most mileage of any state at the midcentury point, with 1,361 miles. Pennsylvania, thanks to its eponymous trunk line, was not far behind. The railroads remained most extensive in the East, but considerable mileage had been constructed in the South. Georgia was beginning to establish the preeminence that it was to maintain for a century, and Atlanta was becoming the hub for a variety of lines. In the old Northwest, Ohio and Michigan were the leaders, but their mileage was still modest. That would change in the next decade, helped by the establishment of Chicago as the nation's railroad hub.

Chicago's dominance was by no means a foregone conclusion. Other western cities such as Sandusky, Ohio, and St. Louis, Missouri, had potential, having been reached early by the iron road, but Chicago had natural advantages that made its location as a railroad hub ideal. When the inaugural section of the Baltimore & Ohio opened in 1830, Chicago had consisted of a few wood cabins and trails scratched out of the marshy land on the southwest corner of Lake Michigan. As soon as it was incorporated in 1833, Chicago boomed. Thanks to its favorable location, it grew rapidly in the 1830s, reaching a population of four thousand by the end of the decade. Yet it came surprisingly late to the railroad, with its first line, the Galena & Chicago Union Railroad, built by William Ogden, not being completed until 1848 when, already, there were innumerable railroads farther to the west. The small, unassuming town, with problems of perpetual flooding because of its position on the banks of Lake Michigan, did not seem natural railroad territory. While the rest of America was busy building railroads in the 1830s and 1840s, Chicagoans were to be convinced that the future lay with plank roads, laid to connect the burgeoning town with surrounding communities and used increasingly by farmers to take their goods into the city. These crude highways were, literally, made of wooden boards nailed into timbers on the ground and, for a time, earned their owners huge dividends from tolls, as Chicago grew rapidly in the 1840s. But they required constant maintenance, as they were damaged by the ever-heavier wagons using them that, incidentally, were wont to bully smaller carts into the adjoining mud.

However, the focus of the region was already changing. Chicago had previously looked south to New Orleans along the Mississippi as its main economic outlet, but this was an unsatisfactory transportation corridor, as both the trip downriver and the subsequent voyage across to Europe were lengthy and expensive. With the completion of the Erie Canal in the 1820s, Chicago had begun to look eastward. The town had become the effective terminus of the waterway, because ships, after reaching the end of the canal at Buffalo, on the eastern shore of Lake Erie, could continue their journey to Chicago along the Great Lakes. Whereas previously much of the raw produce of the area, such as meat, timber, and grain, was almost worthless because of the high cost of transportation, the value of these commodities increased as eastward communications improved. Chicago's connection with the Mississippi was greatly facilitated by the completion of the Illinois & Michigan Canal in 1848, but westward extension of the waterway through the vast grain-growing area of the Midwest was impractical given the distances involved. The railroad was the obvious means of exploiting the rapidly growing economy of the region. And Chicago, at its center, with its easy connections both East and West, as well as the water-front on Lake Michigan, was its natural strategic hub. Ogden's Galena & Chicago Union rapidly became profitable, proving to be far more efficient than the plank roads. Two other, similar, railroads soon sprang up, the Chicago, Burlington & Quincy[24] and, in the same year, the Chicago & Rock Island Railroad, which in 1866 became the Chicago, Rock Island & Pacific Railroad, revealing its ultimate ambition of reaching the ocean, which, as with many similarly named railroads of the time, was never fulfilled. These were the three original "Granger" railroads, so called because their primary purpose was to bring farm produce to market. By reducing the price of transportation, these railroads increased the amount of money the farmers received for their produce and were the catalyst for the agricultural development of the huge Midwest prairies.

In 1852, Chicago was connected to the Eastern Seaboard by the Michigan Central, which later became part of the New York Central system. Like the Erie and the Pennsylvania, both of which would eventually reach Chicago, this was a very different type of railroad from those that were swiftly spreading out west of the city. The nature of this difference explains one of the great mysteries of the American railroad system: why did all railroads, from both East and West, stop in Chicago, rather than simply going around or through the Windy City, just as they traversed every other town in the vast space between the two oceans? The answer is that the two sets of railroads that terminated at Chicago—the Granger railroads to the west and the major trunk railroads to the east—were so different as to be completely incompatible in purpose and financial performance, preventing the mergers that would seem logical. The four major eastern trunk railroads—the Erie, New York Central, Pennsylvania, and Baltimore & Ohio (which had finally gotten to Wheeling, on the Ohio River, in 1852)—soon reached Chicago. The reason they stopped there and did not progress westward was because, by the time of their arrival, the Granger railroads had already established themselves. The Grangers were weak railroads, eking out a tenuous existence delivering farm produce to market, a one-way business that offered little potential for growth. The large areas they covered, and the fierce competition—at least initially—between each railroad company, meant that they earned low returns, making them an unattractive acquisi-

tion for the big trunk railroads. For their part, the Grangers could not expand eastward, as they were always too weak to take on the big railroad
companies. Once past Chicago, they would have had to build lines all the
way to the East Coast, as the existing lines would have refused them access
to their tracks, clearly an enterprise beyond them.

The decision of the big trunk lines not to go beyond Chicago was based
on caution and custom, since railroads did not like sending their trucks
onto another company's tracks through fear of losing them. This rather
unimaginative thinking would determine the somewhat fragmented nature of the US railroad network. Perhaps if one adventurous eastern railroad had decided to venture west, braving the inevitable attacks from the
Grangers, it might have been able to overcome the initial difficulties. The
prize, a genuinely national rail system that would allow untrammeled
transcontinental travel, could well have been worth it. In the event, only the
Baltimore & Ohio dared, eventually, to try to connect the two types of railroad, through its purchase of the Chicago & Alton, but that was in 1931,
when the railroads were already beginning to struggle in the face of competition from road and air transportation.

Thus, by happenstance, a combination of geography and economics,
as well as timidity and habit on the part of the big companies, Chicago
became America's preeminent railroad hub, though St. Louis became another key transfer point between eastern and western railroads. Even after
America's East and West Coasts were linked by the iron road, transcontinental services still started from Chicago rather than the Eastern Seaboard.
Throughout the history of the US railroads, in fact, there have been very
few transcontinental routes that did not require a change of trains in the
Windy City.

Chicago's position as a railroad hub became entrenched as its people
and politicians realized the advantages of not allowing traffic to go directly
through. Chicago had no genuine through stations,[25] only termini, and although a few freight lines, such as the Belt Railway, were eventually built
around the city, the whole nation's railroad industry became geared around
Chicago as a transfer station, where trains were broken up and re-formed
in massive classification yards for onward dispatch. It would sometime
take days for goods to be moved from one yard to another, and, like t'

citizens of Erie, the Chicagoans were in no hurry to suggest that the two different railroad systems serving the town should be unified. Quite the opposite. They benefited enormously from the lack of through routes, none more so than Franklin Parmalee, whose eponymous company enjoyed the highly lucrative monopoly of transferring passengers between the various stations. At least the service he provided was classy. He used old coach-style rigs pulled by the best local horses and painted a distinctive green and driven by smartly turned-out men. The latter developed a reputation for providing not only a cordial service but, more surprisingly, honest information, even if that meant they lost a fare because the destination was too close or best reached by another means, in distinct contrast to the "bunco steerers of various rackets who had been operating on American travelers since the earliest coaching days."[26] By the outbreak of the Civil War, Chicago was the undisputed rail capital of the United States, boasting no fewer than eleven rail lines.[27]

The big trunk lines in the East remained very much the exception right up to the Civil War. Most of the hundreds of railroads being promoted and built in the years before the war were small, local, and limited in intent. The pace of their growth, however, was remarkable, with thirty thousand miles having been completed by the end of the 1850s. This was roughly as many miles as had been built at the time in the rest of the world put together and represented more than a tripling of the mileage of railroad in that decade. It was still, though, not a network but rather a collection of mostly short lines with a huge disparity in standards of provision. Through journeys were, for the most part, a trial, even in the East. For example, five different lines made up the New York–Washington service, making for a long and arduous journey, and it was not until 1863 that passengers could travel between the two cities without changing trains.

Indeed, much rail travel before the Civil War was difficult, slow, and, as traffic increased, potentially dangerous (see Chapter 6). In 1840, the American railroad system was merely a "thin, broken network stretching along the Atlantic coast from Portsmouth, New Hampshire, to the Carolinas," if "network" is the right word. To go from Boston to Georgia, for example, required a trip to Stonington, Connecticut, steamers to New York and Philadelphia, followed by four different rail journeys to reach

Washington, with changes at Camden, Philadelphia, and Baltimore, where the two train stations were at different ends of the town, necessitating a cab ride.

Charles Dickens, an experienced traveler on railroads in Britain, visited the United States in 1842 and was not impressed with what he found, sparking a lifelong controversy between the writer and the new nation when his collection of musings titled *American Notes* was published in October of that year. His first journey was on the Boston & Lowell, which he found lacking in most of the amenities to which he was accustomed: "There are no first and second class carriages as with us; but there is a gentlemen's car and a ladies' car: the main distinction between which is that in the first, everybody smokes; and in the second, nobody does. As a black man never travels with a white one, there is also a negro car; which is a great blundering clumsy chest, such as Gulliver put to sea in, from the kingdom of Brobdingnag."[29]

In fact, on some railroads black people, both slaves and free, could travel in the same accommodation as white people, whereas on others, especially in the South, they were relegated to baggage or freight cars. Contrary to what Dickens says, there was first- and second-class accommodation on some railroads, with variations in fare levels much in line with European practice. When the Western Railroad opened between Boston and Albany in 1842, for example, it charged $5.50 for first class but just $3.66 in second. The Boston & Lowell, on which Dickens traveled, had second-class cars on the services that catered to factory workers, charging them just $0.75 cents compared with the $1.00 that Dickens probably paid.

Most of the early cars on American trains were based on stagecoach design, accommodating perhaps a dozen or possibly thirty people at most. Even the more modern ones were little better, and it was no wonder that Dickens found these "shabby omnibuses" not to his liking. The cars were, in fact, rather like the homes of the day: they were built of wood, poorly lit by candles, and inadequately heated by stoves, and the only ventilation came from opening their rather small windows. Worse, for Dickens, was the layout. Unlike those in the UK, which had individual compartments, the US cars were open plan, accommodating up to fifty people, with the doors at the ends. They were fitted with crosswise seats, separated by a narrow passage through the aisle, each holding two people. Dickens, a rather private man, did not enjoy the fact that Americans expected to talk to their neighbors during the journey, even raising subjects that would be taboo between strangers in England such as politics and, showing that some things do not change over time, banks. Cotton, too, was a perennial matter for discussion. Being forced to sit among the other passengers meant that Dickens met far more Americans than he probably would have done otherwise, but he used this experience merely to pour scorn on the American tendency toward patriotism and their supposed mispronunciation of the word *route* as *rout*. He was impressed with the ladies' coaches, particularly the fact that they made it possible "for any lady [to] travel alone, from one end of the United States to the other, and be certain of the most courteous and considerate treatment everywhere." However, he disliked the fact that the conductor wore no uniform and walked up and down the car "as his fancy dictates, leans against the door with his hands in his pockets and stares at you."

American informality was clearly not to his liking, either, and worse was Americans' habit, mentioned in the previous chapter, of chewing tobacco and spitting the remnants on the floor. Another, more sympathetic, English writer, Fanny Kemble, an actress who loved the nascent railroads—she was taken on a train by George Stephenson before the opening of the Liverpool & Manchester in 1830—found "a whole tribe of itinerant fruit and cake-sellers" offering their wares at every major station, as well as water boys who passed through the train with a long-spout can and glasses for the benefit of thirsty travelers, unconcerned with the lack of hygiene;[30] such a service can still be found on some trains in India today. Journeys were enlivened, too, by the news agent, often fondly referred to as the "news butcher" or even "news butch." In the early days, these were self-employed young men who had realized that passengers on long train journeys would welcome reading material, as well as drinks and snacks. They would pass through the trains offering the day's paper, magazines, sweets, soda pop, and cigarettes. Later, the individual entrepreneurs were subsumed into the gigantic Union News Company, which was given a monopoly by many train companies in an effort to deter peddlers on the trains. The "butchers"—invariably enthusiastic young men, dressed in the smart blue uniform with brass buttons of the company—would, in a falsetto voice, scramble their various wares into one word: *candycigarettescigars* or *newspapermagazines.* As time went on, they expanded their offerings. Whereas officially they were allowed to sell only respectable magazines such as *Harper's* and *Scribner's,* many privately supplied penny dreadfuls or even slightly titillating magazines that would have passed as the *Playboy* of the day. Traveling much later through America by train, Scottish writer Robert Louis Stevenson was impressed by the young men providing the service and amazed that one could buy "soap, towels, tin washing basins, tin coffee pitchers, coffee, tea, sugar, and tinned eatables, mostly hash or beans and bacon."[31] The butchers were not always benign, however. Short-changing drunks and elderly passengers and selling bogus goods were frequent rackets, as was the scam of offering cheaply bound novels for twice the normal price of twenty-five cents on the basis that one of them supposedly had a ten-dollar note inside.

In the winter, heating was a universal problem on the early trains. Dickens found that most cars were provided with a stove in the middle. This not only filled the air with what he called "the ghost of smoke" but also meant that those sitting near it became overheated, while those at the far ends of the car simultaneously froze. The stoves were a hazard, too, in the event of accidents, becoming "the cause of cremation" in later years when derailments and other disasters became ever more frequent.[32] In the heat of summer, the dilemma for passengers was that opening the windows, if they afforded such a facility, risked the perils of sparks from the chimney setting clothes on fire, while keeping them closed meant virtual asphyxiation in the hotter parts of the nation. Indeed, cinders from the soft coal used in the United States not infrequently wrecked the clothes of passengers in uncovered wagons or those unwise enough to open the windows in more modern ones. One prominent and infuriated victim was the visiting English social reformer and abolitionist Harriet Martineau, who reported that sparks had burned no fewer than thirteen holes in her gown during a short journey in the South.

In glorious overwritten prose, Dickens bemoans the lack of views, the discomforts, the noise, the smells, and the bumpy ride caused by the primitive couplings between cars:

> There is a great deal of jolting, a great deal of noise, a great deal of wall, not much window, a locomotive engine, a shriek, and a bell. . . . Except

when a branch road joins the main one, there is seldom more than one track of rails; so that the road is very narrow, and the view, where there is a deep cutting, by no means extensive. When there is not, the character of the scenery is always the same. Mile after mile of stunted trees: some hewn down by the axe, some blown down by the wind, some half fallen and resting on their neighbours. . . . Now you emerge for a few brief minutes on an open country, glittering with some bright lake or pool, broad as many an English river, but so small here that it scarcely has a name; now catch hasty glimpses of a distant town, with its clean white houses and their cool piazzas, its prim New England church and schoolhouse; when whir-r-r-r! almost before you have seen them, comes the same dark screen: the stunted trees, the stumps, the logs, the stagnant water.

He was flabbergasted by the scarcity of people at the intermediate stations, even on a journey close to a major city like Boston, and the fact that the train ran down several main streets, which was rarely the case in Britain apart from on small branch lines:

The train calls at stations in the woods, where the wild impossibility of anybody having the smallest reason to get out, is only to be equalled by the apparently desperate hopelessness of there being anybody to get in. It rushes across the turnpike road, where there is no gate, no policeman, no signal: nothing but a rough wooden arch, on which is painted "When The Bell Rings, Look Out For The Locomotive." On it whirls headlong, dives through the woods again, emerges in the light, clatters over frail arches, rumbles upon the heavy ground, shoots beneath a wooden bridge which intercepts the light for a second like a wink, suddenly awakens all the slumbering echoes in the main street of a large town, and dashes on hap-hazard, pell-mell, neck-or-nothing, down the middle of the road . . . on, on, on—tears the mad dragon of an engine with its train of cars; scattering in all directions a shower of burning sparks from its wood fire; screeching, hissing, yelling, panting; until at last the thirsty monster stops beneath a covered way to drink, the people cluster round, and you have time to breathe again.

While Dickens's description does not suggest it, the Boston & Lowell was, in fact, one of America's better-appointed railroads at the time. Other lines were far more primitive. The empty woodland stations Dickens describes were better than the halts found on many other lines that had no facilities whatsoever and where, to stop the train, the local farmer would have to wave his shirt at the approaching locomotive. In towns, trains would stop on a particular corner, or the railroad company might have rented a small shop to sell tickets and provide a few lucky waiting passengers with some shelter from the elements. Even more so than on European railroads, stations were an afterthought for the parsimonious rail companies, who found it tough enough dealing with all the engineering problems such as track, tunnels, and ties without having to consider providing for the wretched passengers. So American stations were termed *depots,* based on the French word *dépôt,* a place not so much to offer services to the passenger but, rather, to deposit goods or people with a minimum of fuss. These depots were modest, and the most common structure was a wooden barn through which the train passed as if in a tunnel. Not surprisingly, since they were made of wood, destruction by fire was an all too frequent hazard, a fate suffered by the East Boston depot of Massachusetts's Eastern Railroad on the very day the railroad opened in 1836. A few depots were fitted with doors at either end of the tracks to retain a measure of warmth in the adjoining waiting rooms, but this created an additional hazard, as locomotives occasionally crashed through them to the horror of the waiting passengers. Right from the beginning, depots began to provide food for passengers (a necessity given the increasing length of the journeys being undertaken), but it was rarely wholesome. Hapless travelers who consumed these prepared meals during a lunchtime stop at a depot often complained of indigestion, possibly caused by having to bolt down their food to ensure they could regain their seats, which generally could not be reserved. Station facilities taken for granted by rail travelers today, such as signs displaying the name of the station and warnings to advise passengers of an imminent departure, took many years to be introduced. Indeed, many railroad companies seemed reluctant to stop for passengers or provide them with even the most basic facilities. In New Hampshire, for example, the state had to legislate in 1850 to compel the railroad companies to provide depots for passengers at every stop. Other states tried to ensure that passengers were provided with information about services—timetables—so that they did not have to wait interminably at stations. As historian Sarah H. Gordon comments, "That the state had to require railroads to arrive and depart on schedule, to provide reasonable accommodation, and to build passenger depots implies a notably lackadaisical approach by railroad corporations to the social aspects of rail service."[33]

In charge of the depot was the station agent, a ubiquitous and increasingly important figure in the railroads, who, in European terms, was a combination of stationmaster, ticket clerk, and train dispatcher. He was the public face of the railroad company, and, not surprisingly, he did not always manage to juggle his many tasks to the satisfaction of passengers. His first problem was that, until the advent of the telegraph, he had no information about when a train was likely to arrive. Timetables were vague or nonexistent, and given the frequency of breakdowns, his only means of finding out if a train was approaching was to climb up to his lookout point. The agent was also in charge of selling tickets, but from the outset American railroads departed from the European practice of booking passengers in advance and only allowing people with tickets to board trains. Given the number of small, remote stations described by Dickens, that would have been utterly impractical. Instead, some passengers bought tickets from the station agents, whereas others paid the conductor, and it took some time for the railroads to work out ways of preventing fraud by both passengers and employees, which was prevalent. Early tickets came in various forms, ranging from metal discs to glazed colored pieces of cardboard. Numbered tickets were the obvious solution, but they did not become widely used until the mid-1850s and still did not prevent the conductor from simply pocketing the cash without issuing any kind of receipt, perhaps sharing the profit with the traveler, a scam known as "knocking off" that the companies attempted, often in vain, to stymie throughout the history of passenger rail in the United States.

The conductor, called the captain in early days, also had a variety of jobs to do, as nicely described by George Douglas: "The conductor took tickets, sold passage to those who boarded the train without tickets, supervised the other trainmen, settled arguments, disciplined unruly children and admonished inebriated passengers." The task of keeping passengers in check was not always straightforward. Trains were the first form of mass transportation, other than shipping, and people did not necessarily know how to behave. In the words of Sarah H. Gordon, "Passenger behavior ranged far from the traditional image of waiting quietly at the station, boarding the train when it stopped, and remaining seated throughout the journey."[34] Indeed. During the first two decades of the railroad age, when trains ran slowly—and infrequently—people would hop on freight wagons, ride in the caboose (the brake van) and the locomotive, or—tunnels being infrequent—sit on top of the cars. Passengers jumped on and off the trains at any point that took their fancy. During the numerous stops for breakdowns or to replenish the supply of wood or water, they wandered off into the countryside, either for the hell of it or to satisfy their bodily functions, since there were no toilets on board, sometimes finding themselves stranded when the train resumed its journey. Many careless souls perished, too, not understanding the unforgiving nature of tens of tons of rapidly moving metal.

Inside, they would sit with legs or arms dangling out of the windows, spit (as Dickens noted), get drunk, abuse the conductor, and try to travel without paying. It took some time for the railroad companies to obtain the legal powers to be able to deal with misbehaving passengers. The states had to pass specific laws to allow railroad companies to throw passengers off the train for not paying the fare and even to give conductors the legal right to collect tickets.

Conductors were seen by the railroads as representing the public face of the company to their customers. The cannier companies, therefore, recruited men with strong personalities, but who were also able to empathize with the passengers and help them cope with the inconveniences of rail travel. Conductors would often work the same trains week in and week out, thereby establishing relationships with the regular travelers and becoming well known throughout their route. At first, the driver took responsibility for the train and the welfare of the passengers, but it soon became obvious that the conductor was better placed to do so. According to railroad legend, it was the doyen of the early conductors, Henry—or "Poppy" as he was generally known—Ayres who changed this practice. Ayres, a "huge, genial teddy bear of a man, weighing nearly three hundred pounds . . . [who] hovered over his passengers with benevolent menace," joined the uncompleted Erie in 1841.[35] Shortly after he started working for the Erie, Ayres had a row with an engineer (driver), a German named Hamel, which is said to have established the future hierarchy on the trains. As there was no way of communicating with the driver, Ayres had rigged up a crude rope device, a kind of primitive forerunner of the emergency cord that would later become standard, to alert the driver if he wanted the train to stop. Hamel, a cussed character, refused to play ball and kept on cutting the rope. On the second occasion, Ayres threatened to beat up his hapless colleague unless he acquiesced in the arrangement, thereby ensuring that in the future, the conductor would be in charge of the train. To his passengers, however, Ayres was politeness personified. He remained with the Erie for thirty years, achieving fame and public recognition for the excellence of the service he gave to both his passengers and his employers. Ayres once persuaded an old lady who had left her umbrella, a precious family heirloom, on a connecting ferryboat that he had arranged for it to be sent via the telegraph system—an invention of mystery in the 1850s—to the next station. He knew, in fact, that lost items were generally dumped in the baggage car, but he was nonetheless rewarded for his pains with a rather undeserved kiss.

Not only were trains few and far between in these early days, with perhaps two or three services per day at best on most lines, but they also traveled very slowly by modern standards. These two apparent inconveniences had an upside, however, in terms of passenger safety, since the infrequency of the trains made collisions a rarity. And the fact that the majority of trains traveled at barely twenty miles per hour meant that the frequent derailments—often dealt with by the simple expedient of the male passengers being inveigled into helping haul the recalcitrant car back on the rails—resulted in few injuries, let alone deaths, unlike in later years, when safety would become a major problem for the railroad companies (see Chapter 7). There were, of course, exceptions, and the first recorded passenger fatality—excluding the deaths of unwary people who were hit by trains while crossing the tracks—was on the Camden & Amboy in November 1833, barely a few weeks after all the horses on the railroad had been replaced by locomotives. A train traveling from South Amboy was derailed at

Hightstown, New Jersey, when an axle broke, injuring all but one of the twenty-four passengers and killing two. The train was carrying a remarkable contingent of famous people, suggesting perhaps that early travelers were largely the better off. The infamous entrepreneur Cornelius Vanderbilt, who broke a leg in the accident, vowed never to travel by rail again, a promise he failed to keep when he gained control of numerous railroads a quarter of a century later (see Chapter 8). The former president and now congressman John Quincy Adams was the sole passenger to escape unscathed, while Irish actor Tyrone Power, who suffered only minor injuries, later wrote a detailed account of the crash, describing it as "the most dreadful catastrophe that ever my eyes beheld" and recalling how he helped a fellow passenger, a surgeon, tend to the injured.[36]

As rail lines extended, journeys lasting more than the daylight hours became necessary. Some railroad companies started running freight trains after dark, and from the early 1840s passengers, too, started being carried at night. The technical difficulties of nighttime travel, especially the issue of lighting the way for locomotives, proved hard to tackle. One company, the South Carolina Canal Railroad Company, hit upon the primitive and perilous idea of hitching a small flat wagon to the front of the locomotive with a pile of sand and blazing pine-log fire to light up the way, but this crude solution, clearly a stopgap, was soon abandoned. Instead, various types of oil lamps were tried, and eventually the rather more secure system of kerosene-burning lamps with mirrors to enhance the beam was universally adopted. Some of the early lamps were huge, more than two feet high, but soon they were reduced to a more manageable size. This was another point of divergence between railroad practice in America and Britain, where locomotives ran without any front lights until the 1880s, since it was felt that as long as there were no obstacles on the track they were unnecessary, although they were helpful to track workers. Part of the reason was that British lines were protected by fences, whereas in America railroads were never totally enclosed, which explains in part their lower construction cost. This lack of fencing increased the likelihood of collisions, both with people and—later—with cars. In the early days, however, it was animals that came most frequently into contact with trains, normally with fatal results for the latter. A fully grown cow could easily derail a train, even one fitted with a cowcatcher, and the railroad companies were by law always held liable for these incidents. Cannier farmers realized that this was a lucrative way of disposing of poor livestock. The Michigan Central, a line that traversed cattle country for much of its route, was keen to keep on the right side of the public and consequently made generous provisions to any farmer whose animals were struck by a train.

When the line was taken over by a private company, the new owners tried to reduce the bovine casualty rate by putting up fences, but still the cows kept wandering onto the tracks. As Holbrook explains, "The simple, honest agrarians along the road were quick-witted to know Opportunity when it loomed on the steel rails in the form of the Iron Horse. They began to feed their oldest and poorest stock handy to the tracks and often, it is said, plumb between the rails."[37] The company, cottoning to the farmers' ploy, reduced the compensation to half the value of the beast. The farmers, far from giving up, launched a full-scale war on the railroad, putting obstructions on the line, tampering with switches, and attacking trains with stones. It was only when the railroad infiltrated the farmers' organization and raided their homes just as an arson attack on a train was being launched that normal traffic could be restored. A dozen conspirators were convicted and jailed.

It was passengers rather than freight that kept the early railroads solvent. In fact, the rail companies were slow to see the potential of freight as a source of income, which is ironic given that today America's rail industry is dominated by freight interests. The reason for the tardiness, though, was simple. As American towns in the first decades of the nineteenth century were largely self-reliant, there was little need to transport manufactured goods around the country. As for the transportation of agricultural produce, the other potential area of freight transport, it took some time for farmers to appreciate that the railroads created new markets for their produce. As George Douglas summarizes, "The railroads didn't get into the freight business in the early days simply because there was no freight business to be had."[38] Of course, some lines were built solely to serve a mine or quarry, and mail began to be carried as early as 1834 on the Camden & Amboy and on many other railroads soon after. Indeed, by the end of the 1830s, entrepreneurs like William F. Harnden and Alvin Adams were renting space in baggage cars for their express-parcel services, but most of the early railroads earned the bulk of their income from passengers.

Whereas freight could be carried uncomplainingly at night, accommodating passengers was more difficult. Train travel in the early days was not for people of nervous disposition: "Those who travelled on the first American railroads needed every bit as much pioneer spirit as those who built them." Some trains simply stopped wherever they happened to be at dusk, with little regard for the needs of their passengers. The *New York Tribune,* in October 1846, suggested that the Housatonic Railroad in Connecticut, whose trains simply stopped at nightfall, should "either run their trains through in the course of a day or stop them where passengers can find beds." The newspaper editor was appalled that on several occasions trains had stopped overnight at the village of New Milford, where there were no hotels, and therefore, shockingly, "several ladies had to lie on the floor without beds."[39] As more trains simply continued their journeys through the night, the discomforts mounted, particularly for women. Whereas men could simply put their legs up on the seat in front, provided it was empty, for women such an indelicate move was considered unseemly, and therefore they had to keep their feet on the floor, making sleep even more difficult. A few more forward-looking railroads began introducing cars with facilities to bed down on several eastern routes, but they were still basic and uncomfortable until the man who gave his name to the sleeping car, George Pullman, transformed overnight travel in midcentury (see Chapter 7).

Sunday travel was another bone of contention. While some railroads with devout directors argued that this broke the Sabbath, others cottoned to the idea that Sundays could be a source of profitable business. The clergy themselves seemed to have an ambivalent attitude: "Pastors often extorted special Sunday excursion rates from companies, even as they argued the remainder of the week against running trains on the Sabbath."[40] The men of the cloth stressed that a Sunday excursion into the countryside for a picnic was a healthy exercise. Despite this, some railroads, particularly in the South, refused to run trains on Sundays, creating much inconvenience for passengers. In Vermont, Sunday passengers had to endure a passage from the Bible being read out above the clatter of the train by the conductor to fulfill the requirement of a state law passed in the 1850s.

Connections, in those early times, were a particular trial. As we have seen, transferring between separate stations in the same town generally required a cab ride and, because of the lack of coordination of services, could involve a lengthy wait. Right up to the Civil War and beyond, many railroads resisted investing in expensive river crossings, and therefore journeys were broken up by short rides in steamboats. Travelers on long and complicated journeys were at risk, too, of being cheated by "runners" working for agents. They would sell tickets promising connections between all the various legs of the journey, but on arrival at some distant point the naive traveler would find that the runner's voucher, often painstakingly printed with images of the latest locomotives and steamers, was just an elegant fraud.

For the rich, there is always the option of buying themselves out of inconveniences, and train travel was no exception. Railroad companies were happy to provide a flatcar on which a buggy or stagecoach could be attached with ropes and, better still, offered the affluent the opportunity of exclusive use of a well-appointed private car. The stagecoaches soon became a safety risk, as the speeds of railroads increased, but the rich continued to travel in their own railroad cars, normally hooked up to a regular service, right into the twentieth century.

The feelings of the less affluent travelers who had to slum it in the service cars were neatly summed up by one, unfortunately nameless, traveler who, after a troublesome journey on the Boston & Providence in 1835, commented: "And all this for the sake of doing very uncomfortably in two days what could be done delightfully in eight or ten."[41] Leaving aside the rather fanciful notion that eight to ten days spent in a stagecoach could be described in any way as "delightful," speed was the railroad's unique selling point, which ensured that within a generation it became the dominant form of travel. Even the average of twenty miles per hour, which the early trundlers struggled to achieve, was sufficient to give the railroads a tremendous advantage over all the alternative forms of transportation. It was speed that stimulated the boom that saw the mileage of railroads, which in 1840 was around the same as that of the canals, increase almost exponentially, whereas canal building all but stopped. In the 1840s only 375 miles of new canal were added to the network, and closures of the economically weak waterways had already begun. Railroads like the Hudson River Railroad, and indeed the Erie, were being laid parallel to existing canals or river routes, and consequently even the steamboats were beginning to feel the pinch.

The decade of the 1850s was a period of railroad mania. Whereas New England had benefited from most of the growth in the 1840s, the focus now shifted to the plains of what is now known as the Midwest but was then called the Northwest. The huge size of the territory meant that in the 1850s, Illinois and Ohio vied for the prize of building the most miles of railroad, a contest that the Land of Lincoln shaded with more than 2,600 miles of track—just 300 more than Ohio. These figures are impressive, though still modest in comparison with those achieved in the last thirty-five years of the century, after the Civil War. The premium line was the Illinois Central Railroad, which was begun in 1851 and spread rapidly southward from Galena in the Northwest of the state, running in parallel with the Mississippi down to Cairo at the confluence of that river with the Ohio at the southern tip of Illinois. The Illinois Central, when its initial phase was completed in 1856, took over the mantle as the world's longest railroad, with more than 700 miles of track, mostly a perfect straight line heading south across the Midwest plain. It was also the first to benefit from grants of land. In 1850, two senators, Stephen Douglas from Illinois and William King from Alabama, had managed to maneuver through Congress a bill that allowed land grants for two of their pet railroad projects, the Illinois Central and the Mobile & Ohio. This was to prove groundbreaking as a future way of enabling the state to support railroad projects and to make them viable. The idea was that the land would be sold profitably to new settlers, further boosting the use of the railroad and providing a perfect illustration of how the railroad became a kind of self-sustaining economic catalyst. Incidentally, Abraham Lincoln had been one of the key lobbyists for the line as a local politician and had also worked for the Illinois Central in his capacity as a lawyer. He was about to play an even bigger role in railroad history.

Ohio, which built most of its lines on an east-west axis, was messier. Its plethora of gauges made journeys across the state time-consuming and inconvenient, as did the failure to build a bridge over the Ohio River (which runs largely east-west), a task that was completed only in 1870. The states of Indiana and Missouri also built hundreds of miles in the run-up to the Civil War. By the end of the 1850s, the iron road stretched well into Iowa, which completed 655 miles of railroad from scratch during the decade. A crucial development in the railroads' westward expansion came in 1854, with the completion of the Chicago & Rock Island Railroad, which deliberately ran its tracks right up to the eastern bank of the Mississippi, facing westward, with every intention of fording the river, using an island as a support. Within two years, despite much local opposition from the Mississippi rivermen, the railroad had built a bridge into Iowa over the river at Rock Island, triggering a dispute that was to be a landmark in establishing the railroad's dominance over its predecessors. Within days of the first train passing over the bridge in April 1856, a steamboat, the *Effie Aflon,* smashed into it at full speed, and the ensuing fire from the ship's engines destroyed the whole structure. The rapidity with which a banner appeared proclaiming "Mississippi Bridge Destroyed. Let All Rejoice" suggested strongly that the collision was no accident, and it soon emerged that, rather suspiciously, it was the first time that the *Effie Aflon* had ever ventured that far upriver.

This strong whiff of suspicion did not prevent the emboldened boat owners from suing the railroad for putting the bridge in their way when it might have been expected that the railroad had a rather stronger case against them for destroying its structure! It was at this point that Lincoln made the first of his two significant—but largely forgotten—contributions to US railroad history (he will reappear later as the major political supporter of the transcontinental), as the lawyer representing the Rock Island in court. The importance of the *Effie Aflon* case went well beyond the interests of the local boat owners, as it was effectively a test of whether the right of the railroads to traverse rivers prevailed over those who sailed on them. More broadly, it was a case that pitted communities such as Chicago, already establishing itself as the hub of the rail network, against riverside towns such as St. Louis, whose interests lay with developing the waterway. The southerners, too, were on the side of the boat owners, as they were reluctant to see the West, with all the potential of its vast lands, gain access to the railroad. Lincoln, who had previously been a river pilot, spent days surveying the site and talking to those who worked on the river. In court, he tactfully acknowledged that the accident had been due to "pilot error" but argued that the need for Americans to travel between East and West to populate the vast country should be paramount. The railroad won—just. The jury in the lower court was tied, which meant that the plaintiff, the boat owners, did not win the case, and, despite a later successful appeal, the issue was eventually resolved in the Supreme Court, which declared that bridges were not a hazard to navigation.[42]

It was the last-gasp attempt of the boat owners to resist the onslaught of the iron road. Reaching the Mississippi was crucial. It enabled the railroads to offer far easier and cheaper access both to Chicago and to the river itself, the most important waterway in America, as an alternative to the tortuous route through the canals, rivers, and lakes used by shipping. Furthermore, by crossing the river, they had overcome a key barrier to reaching the Rockies and beyond. As its inhabitants had feared, the completion of the iron road through to the river was extremely damaging to the South, cutting off much of its lucrative through trade to Europe. Even worse for shipping interests, from the Midwest to the South, railroads were beginning to be built parallel with the Mississippi. The Illinois Central began to take from the Mississippi some of the trade between the Great Lakes and the Gulf of Mexico, as did another north-south railroad, the Mobile & Ohio, linking Mobile on the coast of Alabama with Cairo in southern Illinois and completed just before the outbreak of war. Other railroads, such as the more successful Louisville & Nashville, which would play a prominent role in the Civil War, soon followed.

Not only was the South losing out as the very economic orientation of the central part of the United States shifted ninety degrees to the east, but its railroads were in a sorry state, far less developed and sophisticated than their counterparts in the North. And that would cost the South dearly in the Civil War that broke out in 1861.

4

THE BATTLE LINES

In the optimistic mood that accompanied the arrival of the railroads, one of the most notable and oft-repeated claims was that they would bring about an end to warfare. The manifesto promoting a railroad between Cincinnati, Ohio, and Charleston, South Carolina, published in 1835, had suggested that once the railroad was built, "the North and South would, in fact, shake hands with each other, yield up their social and political hostility, pledge themselves to common national interests, and part as friends and brethren."[1] Henry Poor, the founder of the *American Railway Journal,* suggested that the railroads were an agent of national peace and that "the certain prevention of foreign war . . . will be one of the numerous advantages of the railroads." The *Cincinnati Daily Chronicle,* in 1843, went further, arguing that by ensuring the country would always be in a state of military preparedness, the railroads would bring about permanent peace and would be "dispelling prejudices and cementing friendships, calculated to perpetuate the institutions under which we have risen from a mere handful." Poor saw trains and Christianity going hand in hand as forces for good. As war approached and seemed inevitable, the *American Railroad Journal* somewhat rowed back on its optimism, but it still remained unreservedly positive, noting that the majority of railroads would be unaffected by the conflict. Sadly, all these assertions proved to be wrong. As Sarah H. Gordon counters, "No voice rose to predict that trains might disseminate bad behaviour as well as good, or widen the scope of war beyond imagining."[2]

In the Mexican-American War that broke out in 1846, following the US annexation of Texas the previous year, the army had made some use of the railroads to transport troops down to Texas, but their efforts were hampered by the paucity of the lines in the South and the fact that Texas itself did not join the railroad age until 1853. Nevertheless, in "the Mexican War [US] generals learned first hand just how useful the new invention could be, and they took that knowledge into the Civil War."[3]

Far from being a catalyst for peace, the iron horse turned out to be one of the most effective weapons of war invented by man, helping create a far more intense, deadly, and lengthy type of warfare.[4] Moreover, the American Civil War would prove to be a testing ground for the use of railroads to extend the scope and impact of warfare; as a result, the conflict exacted a terrible toll on the American people. The story of the American Civil War can, in fact, be told through the railroads. Only an understanding of the role that the railroads played in it can explain how the Civil War became bloodier and more intensely fought than any previous conflict.

At the outbreak of the war, the nation's thirty thousand miles of railroad could be broadly split into three. Following the railroad construction boom of the 1850s, the Midwest, all free states, now had the most mileage, with eleven thousand miles, whereas New England together with the Middle Atlantic states boasted around a thousand miles fewer. That left the slave states of the South with just nine thousand miles, half as many as the North. Moreover, while substantial railroad companies able to cover long distances were beginning to emerge in the North, and the process of consolidation of lines had already begun there, the South's—mostly poorly equipped—railroads presented a deliberately disparate picture, still entirely in keeping with the Jeffersonian model of localism. There was no southern equivalent of the big trunk railroad companies like the Erie and the Pennsylvania, which together possessed as much locomotive power as the entire Confederacy. The only route that even vaguely resembled a trunk line ran east-west in Tennessee between Memphis and Chattanooga, with branches northward to Richmond and Norfolk in Virginia and southward to Atlanta and Savannah in Georgia. Any lengthy trip undertaken was likely to require a change of train because of gauge differences.

Substantial railroad construction had taken place during the 1850s, with Virginia and Georgia the main beneficiaries, but the railroads of the South nonetheless remained largely underdeveloped. The poor condition of the southern railroads was partly due to the weakness of the local economy and the lack of capital, but there was a more fundamental reason, too, rooted in the South's history and its adherence to slavery. Broad swaths of southerners were deeply suspicious of the iron road and through their actions stymied the development of the railroad as an effective mode of transportation in their region. The dichotomy between the Jeffersonian and Hamiltonian approaches to the construction of railroads was nowhere more apparent than in the South. In railroad terms, the debate boiled down to two contrasting positions: on the one hand, for the creation of a railroad network that would make it easier for southerners to travel to the burgeoning cities of the North; on the other, for a more localized railroad, geared to funneling commerce in the direction of its own ports.

The most ambitious railroad promoter in the South, Robert Hayne, a South Carolina senator who had supported the Charleston & Hamburg Railroad, had envisaged a railroad running all the way from Charleston, South Carolina, the South's best port, to Memphis, Tennessee, but his sudden death in 1839 brought an end to the idea and, worse, seemed to sap the South's entrepreneurial spirit. It was not only the lack of promoters, however, that held back the growth of the southern railroads. The region simply did not have the right attributes for the development of an efficient transportation system: "Nothing could make up for the inferiority of the South's ports, the lack of adequate markets for imports and diversity of exports, and a slave-labor system that immobilised her capital resources."[5] Had the South managed to overcome these deficiencies and its leaders' reluctance to exploit the potential of the iron horse, it would have had the side effect of strengthening the Union and might thereby have reduced the likelihood of war, or at least delayed it.

Instead, at the outbreak of the Civil War, the South possessed a messy, ill-connected ragbag of underfunded railroads that, because of the purpose for which they had originally been built, were wholly inadequate for the needs of the military: "The Southern railroads, initially built to expand the wealth of Southern plantations and states, remained almost entirely in the control of those local interests who put states' rights ahead of the long-distance exchange of goods and people."[6] The military consequences of these failings would become all too obvious.

The hundred or so southern railroads, which averaged just ninety miles in length, were hampered, too, by a lack of gauge standardization. Although many had been built to five feet, the dominant gauge in the South before the war, there were also many standard-gauge railroads, and a variety of others. However, even when neighboring railroads were built to the same gauge, there seemed to be an almost perverse reluctance to connect the lines when a town found itself with several termini. This was, in part, due to the lack of popularity for railroads. Southern towns had simply not welcomed the iron road with the same warm embrace as their northern counterparts. On the contrary, the opposition to railroads was broader in the South than in the North. And the forces ranged against the railroad promoters included not just the usual nakedly self-interested groups of innkeepers, haulers, and hoteliers but also the powerful lobby of the large wholesale merchants. They opposed the arrival of the iron road because they realized it would destroy the profitable trading opportunities they enjoyed through the loading and unloading of produce in their locality. It was therefore in their interests to ensure the railroads remained inefficient with a lot of enforced transfers of goods and people.

There was, too, a gut feeling in the South that the railroads put at risk their very way of life. The house-proud southerners certainly did not want these foul-smelling machines, belching sparks that could so easily lead to a conflagration, anywhere near their city streets. And not only were the tracks kept away from the town centers, but local business interests prevented them from reaching the waterfronts where goods could be easily transferred from rail to water. Even when the railroads spread rapidly in the South in the decade before the Civil War, becoming a more important part of the southern economy, this antagonism from local business groups prevented a rational approach to their needs. Because the early railroads were mainly built to bring in agricultural produce from the surrounding rural areas rather than to serve local passenger needs, the railroad companies were forced to build their depots on the outskirts of towns. The Virginia legislature had actually passed a law allowing towns to prevent railroad companies from running their lines down city streets. Consequently, Richmond, Virginia, which would become the capital of the Confederacy in 1861, was the town most inconvenienced by these legislative obstacles. It had five railroad lines, all leading to different depots, yet none of them connected with one another by rail, even though three of them used standard gauge. Similarly, Savannah, Georgia, was the terminus of two railroads—the Savannah, Albany & Gulf Railroad and the Georgia Railroad—but vociferous opposition prevented a bridge being built over the Savannah River to connect the two until just before the outbreak of the Civil War. There were all too few exceptions. In a couple of inland towns, notably Atlanta, Georgia, and Columbia, South Carolina, important junctions were created to allow the through passage of freight, but for the most part any lengthy journey in the South would involve several inconvenient and expensive transfers.

A further hindrance for the South during the Civil War was the layout of its railroad network, which was blessed with few through connections beyond the region. Most of the lines ran north-south, and consequently there was only one railroad route connecting the Deep South with the southwestern states. The rivers, too, were still a barrier. Whereas the Mississippi had been traversed by the railroad at Rock Island, the Ohio River remained unbridged when the war broke out, as did the Potomac, which cuts a swath through Virginia, effectively separating much of the South from the North. As if to demonstrate just how separate the North and South were even before secession, only one railroad line—at Bowling Green, Kentucky, a junction on the Louisville & Nashville—crossed between North and South. At the outbreak of the Civil War, only one of the five railroads that went through the Appalachians, the mountain range that separates the East from the Midwest and Southwest, was in the South.

It was not only the connections that were bad on the southern railroads. The facilities on the southern trains were far worse than those in the North, with poor rolling stock and lackadaisical timetables that were often unintelligible because of the plethora of local time zones. Facilities such as waiting rooms and ticket offices were even scarcer in southern depots than in their northern counterparts. Fares tended to be high precisely because of the paucity of facilities. The fastest train in the South in 1861 ran between Nashville and Chattanooga on the Louisville & Nashville but still required nine and a half hours for the 150-mile journey, an average of barely 15 mph, whereas in South Carolina trains were expressly forbidden to exceed 25 mph.

The architect of New York's Central Park, Frederick Law Olmsted, complained about the primitive nature of the southern railroads. According to Olmsted, the southerners' attitude seemed to be that the Yankees' demands for a clean bed, digestible food, and trains that made their advertised connections at least half of the time were utterly unreasonable and demonstrated the northerners' weak-bellied nature. He was concerned, too, about safety on the southern lines and suggested that the difference in railroads demonstrated the disparity in the economic situation of the two regions: "There is nothing that is more closely connected, both as cause and effect, with the prosperity and wealth of a country than its means and modes of travelling." If, at the outset, the South was already at a disadvantage in terms of its railroad network, matters were made worse when war was declared by "a traditional dislike for mechanical pursuits in the South that had resulted in the employment of many northerners on southern roads."[7]

Many of these key railroad personnel went back to the North once war was declared. Labor shortage was a perennial problem for the South's railroads, compounded by regular call-ups of railroad men to join the military. Wisely, the Confederate government prevented many railroad workers from being called up through exemptions to the draft, which, curiously, were not so freely issued in the North. As the war wore on, however, the railroads in the South found it increasingly difficult to find labor, and many of the gaps were filled by slaves, either owned directly or "rented" from plantations, who were employed in a variety of roles.

The Civil War was the world's first railroad war, and it was inevitable that neither side exploited the new technology as fully as it might. But it would be the South's failings in this regard that would prove the most damaging. The railroads supplied all the major battles of the war, many of which took place at junctions or near key sections of line. Even the skirmish that was the prelude to the conflict, fought eighteen months before the official hostilities broke out—which gave us the famous song "John Brown's Body"—was played out on the railroad.

John Brown's raid on Harpers Ferry (then in Virginia) in October 1859 was a bizarre, almost suicidal raid backed by a group of affluent "free soilers," as the abolitionists were known. With a group of twenty fellow raiders, including five blacks, Brown rowed across the Potomac River from Maryland to occupy the federal armory at Harpers Ferry. They encountered little resistance and soon took over the arsenal. It was, however, an ill-thought-out venture, and the raiders' fanciful ambition of using the weapons to help foment a wider rebellion among the local slaves would quickly founder. Ironically, the first casualty of the raid was a free black baggage master at the railroad station, who was killed in error by one of Brown's sentries. Brown held up the midnight service at Harpers Ferry for several hours and cut the telegraph cables to prevent the alert from being given, but then, inexplicably, allowed the train to proceed, ensuring that by morning the armory was surrounded by local militia. Thereafter, the arsenal was quickly retaken by a force of US Marines commanded by Brevet Colonel Robert E. Lee, who rushed to the scene using the Baltimore & Ohio. Brown, along with several of his colleagues, was hanged a few weeks later, creating a martyr of this eccentric abolitionist and a song remembered today.

The raid was one of the more violent illustrations of the growing tension that was rapidly making war inevitable. Slavery was at the root of the conflict, but the two parts of the United States were diverging in every significant way. Whereas the North was basing its economy on industrialization and urbanization, the South wanted to remain a land of plantations based on slave labor. The South, too, was insistent that its government, led by Jefferson Davis, should remain weak, while states' rights would remain paramount. The only exception to this general doctrine of state autonomy was the fugitive slave laws passed by Congress in 1793 and 1850, which provided for the return to their owners of slaves who had escaped across state boundaries. In other words, each state was almost an independent nation in itself. These fundamental differences explain why the conflict was much more than a localized civil war—it pitted two contrasting ways of life against each other. Its scale and breadth were more in keeping with a major international war than an internal conflict, as the military operations during the Civil War were conducted over an area equal to the whole of Europe, a scale made possible by the extensive use of the railroads. The Northern railroads themselves exacerbated the antipathy between the two sides, as the South was deeply suspicious of the big companies' expansionist tendencies. In the 1850s, the idea of a transcontinental railroad had been discussed several times in Congress (see next chapter), but each time the legislation was blocked by the southern delegates, who were insisting on a southern route. There was, though, more to the dispute than simply the location of the line. The southern leaders perceived the transcontinental as the means of extending their plantation economy westward, replicating the same kind of small-town America characteristic of the antebellum South and, crucially, retaining the slave labor that was integral to their way of life: "The South saw land in a traditional light, as home and heritage, not as a natural resource to benefit capital and state."[8]

Northern business interests, led by the big railroad companies that were the largest corporations of the time, had very different ideas. To them, the railroads were the means of colonizing the interior and exploiting its resources. The railroad was the instrument through which they were able to control any amount of land under a single government. Gleefully, they considered the possibilities offered by the railroads infinite. Not for them a limited vision of small-town America: "The railroad gave them the confidence to expand and take in land far in excess of what any European nation or ancient civilization had been able successfully to control. They also saw in the railroad the ability to expand civilization beyond its historical boundaries, for the railroad seemed to promise that towns, cities, and industries could be put down anywhere as long as they were tied to the rest of the Union by rail."[9]

Steam power, and the rails along which it could run, meant that factories could be built anywhere. English novelist Anthony Trollope, who happened to be in America at the outbreak of the war and who was a fervent supporter of the antislavery policies of the North, was troubled by this expansionist policy, as he felt that Canada, a British colony, might be included in these ambitious plans and come under the Northern yoke. This nakedly commercial view, which saw the vast lands of the West as a capitalist enterprise controlled by business interests in the Northern cities, troubled the Southerners as much as the attempt to abolish slavery. Consequently, the South was opposed to the very idea of offering land grants to railroad companies to help fund their construction, as would eventually become the norm for funding railroad construction in the West. Thanks to energetic lobbying by the vested interests of southern congressmen, legislation for the building of a transcontinental railroad was repeatedly blocked in Congress during the 1850s.

The election of Abraham Lincoln, as the first Republican president, in November 1860 made war inevitable. The Confederate States of America was created by six seceded Southern states (Alabama, Florida, Georgia, Louisiana, Mississippi, and South Carolina) in February 1861, with Jefferson Davis as its provisional president. Five states—Texas, Virginia, Arkansas, Tennessee, and North Carolina—would secede from the Union by the end of May. Hostilities broke out barely a month after Lincoln's inauguration in early March 1861. The trigger was an attack by rebel forces on Fort Sumter, a fortified island four miles off the coast, guarding the entrance to Charleston Harbor in South Carolina. On April 14, after a lengthy standoff, a Confederate militia attacked the fort to prevent it from being resupplied and easily overwhelmed the defending Federal forces. This victory for the Southern forces marked the beginning of the Civil War.

Attention on both sides quickly turned to the railroads. The immediate task for the combatants was to call up large numbers of men in order to build up their respective armies. Lincoln decided to centralize his resources in Washington, which had been earmarked for early attack by the Confederates, and called for seventy-five thousand volunteers to protect the capital. His decision would lead to an incident in Baltimore, Maryland, that resulted in the first bloodshed on the mainland and demonstrated that the railroads would be a key aspect of the conflict. The failure of the railroad companies to build a connecting line between any of the termini in Baltimore—a city through which the troops arriving from the North had to pass to reach Washington—forced all passengers traversing the town to change trains or to endure the tedious process of having their coaches hauled by horses along the main streets on streetcar tracks. The first of Lincoln's volunteers, two thousand men principally from Massachusetts and Pennsylvania, who had responded quickly to their president's call, arrived at Baltimore's President Street Station on the morning of April 19. Although Maryland remained a Union state, many of its people were opposed to the Northern cause, and a crowd of protesters began to shower the coaches carrying the troops through the town with bricks and stones. When a second group of men was told to march the mile across town from the President Street Station of the Philadelphia, Wilmington & Baltimore Railroad to the Camden Station of the Baltimore & Ohio, they were provided with live ammunition, but that did not prevent them from being attacked by a local secessionist mob, and they fired back. The ultimate toll in the "Baltimore Riot of 1861" was four soldiers and twelve civilians killed, along with numerous injuries. The response of the authorities was a rather clumsy overreaction. In order to protect the area from mob violence or even from a full-scale battle between secessionist residents and Unionist troops, they decided to destroy railroad bridges on both the Northern Central Railway and on the Philadelphia, Wilmington & Baltimore, thereby cutting off Baltimore's rail connections with the North and preventing any troops from transferring through the city. This isolation could not be allowed to last. The railroads were swiftly repaired, but Lincoln was wise enough to ensure that his troops no longer traveled through volatile Baltimore. At Lincoln's instigation, a route bypassing Baltimore was created by Thomas Scott, the vice president of the Pennsylvania Railroad. The troops heading toward Washington from the North took the Philadelphia, Wilmington & Baltimore to the Susquehanna River, where they boarded a steamer to Annapolis to connect with the Annapolis & Elk Ridge Railroad and then with the Washington branch of the Baltimore & Ohio. Various sections of the line were taken over by the government, and these enforced emergency arrangements led to the genesis of the United States Military Railroads, which was to play a key part in the conflict. Scott, with the assistance of a young Andrew Carnegie, who was later to become one of the richest men in the United States through his domination of the steel industry, was given the task of supervising the railroads on behalf of the government until the government's control over them was enshrined in legislation early in 1862.

This immediate imposition of federal power over the railroads was to be in marked contrast to the situation in the South, where government control of the railroads was never properly established. Lincoln had long realized that such control was essential to the war effort. Anticipating war, two weeks before the fall of Fort Sumter Lincoln's government had already taken possession of the Philadelphia, Wilmington & Baltimore Railroad, recognizing that it would become the lifeline of the federal army protecting Washington. As the nerve center of the Unionist campaign and the seat of government, Washington was in a somewhat vulnerable location, effectively an outpost in Southern territory and uncomfortably close to enemy lines. So close, indeed, that it was not uncommon for the Unionist leaders in Washington to see, on a clear day, a rebel line in full operation over the Potomac in Virginia where Arlington National Cemetery, the military cemetery established after the Civil War, now lies. In calling up the volunteers to Washington, Lincoln told the railroad companies that trains on government business must have priority over civilian passenger and freight services. The North's railroads, despite the problem of Baltimore, were far more efficient than those of the South. As Sarah H. Gordon puts it, "The speed with which Northern mobilization took place and the numbers of men that were drawn together were both directly attributable to the availability of railroads."[10]

Lincoln was far more successful in quickly galvanizing his forces than were the Confederates, who were constrained not only by the deficiencies of their railroads but also by the reluctance of the various states to accede to the requirements of their government, even if that now represented only the eleven seceded states. The inadequacy of the Southern railroads, built principally to further local interests, greatly hindered early Confederate mobilization. The lack of connections between the various short lines meant that transporting troops and matériel across long distances was a more time-consuming and onerous business than it should have been. Logistics would be a perennial headache for the Confederates throughout the conflict.

Jefferson Davis, the president of the seceded states, who had vehemently opposed Lincoln over the bridge built across the Mississippi, now found that the parochial view he had taken on railroad development rebounded against him. Even with a major conflict looming, the Southern towns and cities were reluctant to allow the connections that they had long resisted. Davis was trapped by the contradictions of his own politics. The very essence of the secessionist ethos dictated against the imposition of unilateral demands from the center: "In the South, nothing could be strictly imposed and every compromise failed accordingly. Because the Confederates' quarrel with the North centred around their demand for freedom from interference from Washington, they were psychologically incapable of accepting that their railroads should be subject to interference from their own government." Moreover, although the Southern railroads were in theory eager to help, somehow their good intentions rarely materialized in practice. They seemed torn between patriotism and profit: "Southern railway managements regarded themselves as true patriots, but claimed that their first duty was to their shareholders."[11] Some wanted to offer their services to the government for free, but it became rapidly apparent that this was financially unworkable, and soon the railroad companies, desperately short of funds, were charging premium rates to transport troops. The very philosophy that had led the South to secede—its emphasis on states' rights and its reluctance to encourage strong central government—militated against bringing the railroads under the military yoke.

The North faced no such limitation. Lincoln had, right from the start of the war, proclaimed that the railroads must obey government orders. Now, with the war raging, he realized that it was essential to enshrine this in law. A series of congressional acts in early 1862 allowed the federal government to take possession of a range of important railroad and telegraph lines, including rolling stock, locomotive depots, and all essential equipment, and placed railroad employees under strict military control. The United States Military Railroads was formally created to operate lines under direct government control. In the event, very few Northern railroads were taken over, because the very existence of the legislation ensured that they fell into line, meeting military needs when asked to do so by the federal government.[12] But, as the conflict wore on, the US Military Railroads became a major force in the federal war effort: it assumed operational control of railroads in captured territory, built 650 miles of line, and reinstated routes damaged by sabotage—a tactic that had come into its own during the war. By the war's end, the US Military Railroads controlled more than 2,000 lines of track.

South of the Mason-Dixon line, which separated the two combatants, the Confederate government struggled to impose itself on the railroads. It established a special government section as part of its Quartermaster Bureau to deal with railroad matters and act as a liaison between the railroads, Jefferson Davis's government, and the individual states. However, the Railroad Bureau was not given the power to force the railroads to coordinate their workings or even to make them acquiesce to military demands: "Throughout the war, Confederate government policies encouraged railroads to handle civilian traffic in preference to military traffic. There was little real co-operation between railroads and senior military officers, and there was resistance to creating interchange points."[13] Over the course of the war, successive leaders of the bureau tried to push forward changes that would have improved the efficiency of the Southern rail network, but they failed. The states' distrust of a powerful center blocked any such move until the dying days of the war, when at last, in February 1865, an equivalent bill to the railroad legislation north of the border was passed by the Confederate Congress, far too late to have any impact on the outcome of the war.

Nevertheless, as soon as the conflict began, the South, like the North, was quick to realize the potential of the railroad. The railroads were to play a decisive role in the first major land battle at Bull Run,[14] in July 1861, turning an almost certain defeat into victory for the Confederates. The battle started as an attempt by the Unionists to put a quick end to the war by capturing the secessionists' capital, Richmond, which was barely a hundred miles from Washington. An army led by Brigadier General Irvin McDowell advanced across Bull Run, a small tributary of the Potomac twenty miles southwest of Washington, to engage rebel forces. The Confederates, led by General P. G. T. Beauregard, initially found themselves under pressure and retreated, until General Joseph Johnston, stationed in the Shenandoah Valley, sent reinforcements east by railroad over the Blue Ridge Mountains to support the retreating army. Although the line they used belonged to a small railroad, the Manassas Gap, that could scarcely cope with the sudden load, and the engineers at one point refused to work the trains, claiming fatigue, enough troops reached the battlefield by rail to turn the tide. With further troops arriving on the line over the next couple of days, the Confederates launched a counterattack—inspired partly by General Thomas Jackson, whose refusal to retreat during this battle earned him his famous nickname of "Stonewall"—and the Federal troops fled back toward Washington. The Confederate victory changed the course of the war over the next few months. The idea, which had been current among Unionists, that the war would be quickly over now dissipated: "The result stunned the North, emboldened the South and presaged the long and bloody conflict to come."[15]

Nowhere symbolized the importance of railroads in the war more than the small railroad town of Manassas, close to the Bull Run battlefield. It was the site of a junction linking the short Manassas Gap Railroad with the Orange & Alexandria Railroad, which would change hands numerous times during the war. Consequently, the town became a supply depot for whichever force occupied it, and both sides fought hard to seize and retain the town. After Bull Run the Confederates remained in the area and dug in for the winter in entrenchments at Centreville, six miles from Manassas. The two towns were connected by a road that was fine in the summer, but in the wet weather of the autumn turned into a muddy morass under the weight of military traffic. The six horse and mule teams that used the road to bring supplies from the railroad to the encampment of forty thousand men at Centreville proved inadequate to the task. Between December 1861 and February 1862, a six-mile line was built—mainly by slave labor—to bypass the road and ensure that supplies could be brought right up to the camp. For a couple of months, despite difficulties obtaining rolling stock, the short railroad proved a vital lifeline for the men at Centreville. On March 11 the line's brief existence came to an end as the troops were ordered to retreat, and they pulled up the tracks behind them as they withdrew. It was the first of hundreds of miles built for military purposes by both sides during the conflict.

As the Battle of Bull Run demonstrated, in the early days of the war the Confederate generals had a better understanding of how to use the railroads than their Unionist rivals. This made it all the more problematic that the Confederacy was unable to take control of its railroads because of the reluctance of the states to countenance centralized direction of the network by Davis's government in Richmond. The Confederate generals, who are generally regarded as having been far more imaginative and effective leaders than their Unionist counterparts in the initial stages of the conflict, followed a simple strategy. Knowing the Confederacy had fewer resources, they adopted a defensive strategy that relied—as weaker armies must—on fighting "smart," and the mobility afforded by the railroads was crucial to that plan. To overcome the difficulty of defending a large territory with a small army, it was essential to shift troops around its perimeter with speed and skill: "The South's leaders decided they didn't need to 'win' against a superior enemy—they simply needed not to lose. Only by effectively using its 9,500 miles of railroad could the South prevail."[16]

Unfortunately for the Confederacy, the theory could not be put into practice. A lack of coordination among the railroads, and the absence of an integrated command structure, would prove damaging to the Southern cause. Even railroads owned by individual states sometimes refused to accede to requests from the central government. Early in the war, William A. Ashe, who headed the Railroad Bureau, demanded that the Western & Atlantic, which was owned by the State of Georgia, supply six locomotives and seventy wagons to move freight out to eastern Tennessee. However, not only did Georgia's governor, Joseph E. Brown, turn down the request, but he threatened to send troops to fight any Confederate officials who tried to commandeer the rolling stock. Farther south, the head of the Florida Railroad, David L. Yulee, was no more helpful. Although his railroad was unable to operate because it had suffered damage, he refused to allow its rails to be lifted and redeployed to create a connecting line between Florida and Georgia, which was essential to keep the Confederate army supplied with beef. In yet another failure of wartime cooperation, promises made by railroads to provide transportation for free soon proved to be empty. The Richmond & Petersburg, for example, immediately raised its charges when the company realized the line was a vital part of the military buildup for the Battle of Chickamauga in September 1863.

At times it almost seemed that the Confederacy was deliberately setting out to reduce the effectiveness of its own railroads. Before the war, the South had neglected its limited industrial base by continuing to import most of its railroad equipment from the North, rather than trying to expand existing factories such as those in Savannah, Georgia, and Richmond, Virginia. Instead of being allowed to continue to produce material for the railroads, these facilities were quickly turned over to the production of ordnance, a shortsighted decision that further hampered the railroads' ability to maintain services. Moreover, even though few of the Southern railroads had the capability of repairing their own rails, many were forced to give up any spare ones to be melted down to provide armor plating for ships. The extent of the South's plight was highlighted by the fact that, in the later years of the war, the Confederacy resorted to tearing up the tracks on branch lines, the cannibalization that had so angered the Florida Railroad, in order to keep key services operating. According to railroad historian John Stover, "As early as the spring of 1862, southern railroad officials were predicting the complete breakdown of their service because of shortages of rolling stock and motive power."[17]

The canny way in which the Confederacy exploited the railroad at the start of the war was illustrated by a particularly destructive raid on the Baltimore & Ohio, whose line out to Wheeling on the Ohio River effectively formed the boundary between the warring parties. The Unionists fell victim to a clever ruse by Stonewall Jackson, who demonstrated all the ruthlessness and cunning necessary to maintain the upper hand against stronger forces in a scheme known as the Martinsburg Raid. Although the Confederates occupied the territory around a section of line seized by Jackson, Unionist freight trains were allowed to continue running along the railroad. This seemingly magnanimous gesture, though, was a trap. Recognizing that locomotive power would be crucial to the war, Jackson devised a scheme to capture as many engines as he could manage and simultaneously wreck the railroad. Jackson informed the Unionists that they could use the Confederate zone of the line only between 11:00 a.m. and 1:00 p.m., so that the passage of trains would not wake his troops. Remarkably, the Unionists accepted this flimsy argument, enabling Jackson to lay a perfect trap. On June 14, 1861, he allowed all the trains into a fifty-four-mile section of track, but then trapped them in Confederate territory by tearing up the rails. Before the Union forces grasped what was happening, Jackson's men destroyed 42 locomotives and 386 freight cars and ripped up miles of rail for use in the South. They also wrecked the machine shops and warehouses at Martinsburg, Virginia,[18] and made off with 14 locomotives, which had to be taken into Southern territory by road in the absence of a rail connection. The raid forced the closure of the western part of the Baltimore & Ohio for nine months, greatly hampering the North's logistics.

The attack was, however, a self-inflicted wound. The destruction wreaked by Jackson on the Baltimore & Ohio angered Marylanders—who saw it as *their* railroad—and turned their sympathies against the Confederacy. The company's president, John Garrett, already a strong Unionist, was therefore able to rally the local people around the railroad, keeping the rest of the line operating throughout the conflict. That was crucial, since the Baltimore & Ohio would later play a key role in the biggest troop transfer of the war, the relief of the beleaguered defenders of Chattanooga.

Despite their decision to subject the railroads to central government control, the Unionists were slower to understand how best to exploit the railroads in this new form of warfare. In the words of George H. Douglas, "Union generals took a more desultory attitude toward [the railroad's] various uses, and the leaden-footed bureaucracy of the U.S. government took a long time deciding how, whether, and for what purpose it should use the many miles of railroad in its territory."[19]

Lincoln himself, however, needed no persuading of the vital nature of the railroads. After all, he had not only, as we have seen, done so much to ensure the railroads could cross the Mississippi, but he had also pioneered the concept of politicians' whistle-stop tours during his election campaign. With the power of legislation behind him, he set about creating the appropriate organizational framework to allow him to best harness the railroads to the war effort. Lincoln was blessed by good fortune in his choice of the men to carry out the task. Once the legislation granting the federal government oversight was passed in January 1862, Daniel McCallum, the general superintendent of the Erie, was appointed military director and superintendent of the railroads. McCallum would later share his responsibilities with Herman Haupt, who can lay claim to being the world's first military railroad strategist. Both men were given honorary ranks in the army, which was important in ensuring that their decisions on railroad matters could not be challenged by the military. Haupt was notionally McCallum's deputy, but was very much a law unto himself. While McCallum coordinated activities in Washington, Haupt was out in the field overseeing the work. McCallum, a Scottish immigrant, was a brilliant organizer who combined both administrative and engineering talent—a rarity among railroad managers. His military demeanor and reputation for strict discipline would stand him in good stead. Haupt, who became known as the "war's wizard of railroading," was an equally brilliant but famously difficult character who had precisely the right qualifications for the job.[20] He had passed through West Point, the main US military academy, where he had been its youngest cadet ever, but resigned his commission to become a professor of mathematics and engineering, writing the definitive textbook on bridge building and later becoming superintendent of the Pennsylvania Railroad, where, as we saw in Chapter 3, he helped design the Horseshoe Curve. As a result of the two men's efforts, the Unionists became adept at the twin tasks needed to win the war: building railroads and destroying them. Haupt's first job for the military was to repair the Richmond, Fredericksburg & Potomac Railroad, a strategically important line that connected the two capitals, Richmond, Virginia, and Washington, DC, as well as providing the principal supply route between the main Union Army of the Potomac and the smaller Army of the Rappahannock. In response to the Peninsula Campaign launched in April 1862 by General George McClellan as an attempt to end the war quickly by capturing Richmond, the rebels' capital, the Confederates had wrecked several miles of the railroad in a fierce attack aimed at disrupting the Unionist supply lines. They had been particularly thorough and had learned from previous attempts to wreck railroads that had been all too easy to remedy. Heating up rails and twisting them was too arduous and not that effective, since the rails could be straightened. Instead, the rebels devised an iron claw that could quickly tear up both the rails and their supporting ties. Bridges were blown up and locomotives destroyed with cannonballs.

In response, Haupt had to call upon all his skills to restore the line. Despite being hampered by the lack of skilled workers, he reconstructed three miles of line in the first three days and restored the bridges at an astonishing rate. Within two weeks, up to twenty trains per day were running on the fifteen-mile stretch previously wrecked by the Confederates. Lincoln himself came to view the work, notably the perilous-looking four-hundred-foot trestle bridge over the Potomac that had been erected in just nine days using unweathered wood and a largely unskilled workforce. He was suitably impressed: "That man Haupt has built a bridge across Potomac Creek . . . and upon my word, gentlemen, there is nothing in it but beanpoles and cornstalks." The bridge gave rise to the greatest testimony to Haupt's work, this oft-used but anonymous quote: "The Yankees can build bridges quicker than the Rebs can burn them down."[21]

Despite the failure of the Peninsula Campaign, which ended in the bloody Battle of Antietam in September 1862, the importance of Haupt's efforts was recognized. The reconstruction of the line would be the first of many such projects undertaken by Haupt and the growing team of railroad engineers under him. With the backing of Lincoln, McCallum and Haupt set about making field commanders understand how best to use— and not abuse—the railroads. The generals needed to learn—and fast. Officers were wont to make outrageous demands on the railroads without realizing that unscheduled or unexpected changes could cause massive delays and inconvenience. On one occasion, when he investigated the nonarrival of four trains at the terminus in Piedmont, North Carolina, Haupt discovered that a general had held a train on the main track so that his wife could enjoy a night's rest in a nearby farmhouse. Going to the scene, he ordered the conductor to restart the train and then came face-to-face with the woman who had inadvertently caused the delay. Writing in his autobiography, Haupt recalled his reaction when the elegantly dressed lady came tripping across the field. He was nothing if not restrained, but was clearly in retrospect embarrassed by his lack of manners: "I did not display extra gallantry on the occasion, nor even offer the lady assistance. She had detained four trains in three hours in a period of urgency, and I was not in an amiable mood."[22] He told her to get back on the train and rapidly got services moving again.

This was not the only occasion that Haupt had to throw his weight around, but crucially he had the backing of the top brass. They issued instructions that were simple in expression but not always followed in practice: "No officer . . . shall have the right to detain a train, or order it to run in advance of schedule." Enforcing that rule in the field was not always easy. Railroad war historian George Edgar Turner notes that "constant bickering went on between field officers and railroad men who would order them to move a train without reference to formal plans" and that officers were wont to disobey Haupt's other rule, on the rapid emptying of wagons, too.[23]

Slowly but surely, Haupt and McCallum managed to impose railroad discipline on the military. Haupt established a series of rules and priorities for railroad traffic: the carriage of subsistence stores was given first priority, then, in order, forage for the horses, ammunition, hospital supplies, and only then the carriage of troops—on the basis that they could travel on foot, if necessary. There was a system of priorities for the men, too, with veteran infantry regiments given precedence, followed by raw recruits, whereas artillery and cavalry troops were to be kept off the railroads entirely. Haupt decreed that the train timetable had to be determined by railroad personnel rather than the military, who had no understanding of railroad operations

and constraints, and that both freight and passenger cars should be emp-
tied and returned promptly, rather than being used as warehouses, or even
offices. Indeed, Haupt once personally ejected a colonel who had set up his
office in a boxcar in a siding, dumping the hapless fellow's papers, chest,
and furniture on the side of the tracks so that the wagon could be used for
railroad operations. The rapid return of empty stock might seem like the
sort of technical issue that is of interest only to trainspotters, but it was essential in maintaining the smooth running of the railroads. Haupt took
steps to ensure that the railroads did not become clogged up with static
stock or run out of spare cars by insisting that trains had to be unloaded
quickly and the wagons returned straightaway. Simple enough, but so often
ignored in the heat of war. He reckoned that provided his principles were
adhered to, a single-track line could supply an army of two hundred thousand men, a far greater number than could ever be maintained on the inadequate roads of the day by means of horses, mules, and carts.

The importance of sticking to his rules was demonstrated by Haupt's
crucial role in the supply operations for the Battle of Gettysburg, a Unionist victory in July 1863 that is widely accepted as the turning point of the
war. The battle, in the Northern state of Pennsylvania, was the result of
General Lee's brave but ultimately foolhardy attempt—his second—to in-
vade the North. The Southern forces were in an optimistic mood after a
series of victories, and the Unionists decided to try to hold them at Gettysburg. As soon as it was realized that this was to be a key battle, Haupt went
to Baltimore to organize the operation of the Western Maryland Railroad, a
line running northwest from Baltimore to Westminster, thirty miles away,
where it eventually connected through to the Gettysburg front. The Western Maryland was an inadequate single-track line with scrap-iron rails
on poor-quality ties and no adequate sidings or even a telegraph system.
Haupt quickly drafted four hundred men to improve the line, and consequently it was used to send a series of huge convoys to the front and, crucially, bring back the wounded from what proved to be the bloodiest battle
of the war. Rather than allowing a higgledy-piggledy timetable to be run by
the military, Haupt established a service of three convoys of trains per day,
each consisting of five ten-car sets carrying fifteen hundred tons of supplies, and once the battle commenced, they were used to return to Baltimore with up to four thousand wounded soldiers each.

The other side of the coin was the destruction of lines that were of use to the enemy. This was a learning process, given the novelty of using railroads in warfare, and, as we have seen from the wrecking of the Fredericksburg Railroad, the Confederates had honed their destructive skills quickly, though later in the conflict the Unionists would eventually show themselves to be the most adept at this new but vital task: "Confederate raiders never acquired the pure destructive skill of the more mechanically minded northern soldiers."[24] Inevitably, it was Haupt who became an expert at destroying railroads as well as building them. He devised a particularly effective method of bringing down bridges that could be undertaken by just one trooper carrying all the required equipment in his pockets. The demolition man would simply drill holes into the wooden support beams and insert "torpedoes," eight-inch cylinders filled with gunpowder and detonated with a two-foot fuse, which gave the wrecker enough time to get away and watch his handiwork. In this way, three men could bring down even the largest-span bridges in just ten minutes. Once the main beams had been destroyed, the rest of the structure invariably collapsed.

Whereas most of the early destruction of the railroads was by the South, principally in preemptive moves to stop the federal armies from building up forces to launch attacks, the North had been actively wrecking railroads, too. There were a few early attacks by Northern forces such as one on the tracks around Harpers Ferry in February 1862, but the most famous of these early raids, recounted faithfully among others by the British thriller writer John Buchan, was the attempt by a young civilian scout, James Andrews, to destroy the crucial Confederate-controlled Western & Atlantic Railroad, which ran between Chattanooga and Atlanta.[25] The raid two hundred miles into enemy territory was prompted by General Ormsby Mitchel, the commander in middle Tennessee, whose target was Chattanooga, a key hub for both rail and river transport. Wrecking the Western & Atlantic would have weakened the ability of the Confederates to defend the town, and Andrews was sent in with a group of twenty-one soldiers to capture a train and sabotage the line as they headed back north.

On the morning of April 12, 1862, the group—two short, as a pair had overslept—boarded a northbound train in the small town of Marietta, Georgia, twenty miles north of Atlanta. At Big Shanty, seven miles up the line, the train conductor, William Fuller, announced a stop of twenty minutes for breakfast, giving the raiders the opportunity to take over the train. Detaching the passenger cars, Andrews commandeered the engine, The General, and headed north, cutting the telegraph wires in order to prevent the pursuers from alerting the stations ahead. Fuller, furious at the hijacking of his train, proved to be just as determined and heroic as Andrews. He chased after the train, first for the initial two miles to the next station on foot, then with a succession of platelayers' carts (known on US railroads by the wonderful term *gandy dancer carts*) operated by pushing up and down on a large lever that drives the wheels. This proved to be a versatile method of transportation, as he was able to overcome a gap in the track that Andrews's gang had torn up, dragging the trolley through the ballast and rerailing it on the other side. Then, after being derailed again, he found a locomotive, The Yonah, which was fortuitously in steam, and when, again, there was a gap in the track, he ran another two miles and stopped a train passing in the other direction to commandeer its locomotive.

And so the chase went on for a hundred miles, with the locomotives at times reaching speeds of sixty miles per hour until The General ran out of fuel and the raiders dispersed into the local countryside. Because of Fuller's effort in keeping so close, Andrews's men never managed to cause any serious damage to the track. Their attempts to burn down bridges were thwarted by damp tinder, and their efforts to tear up the track were confined to small sections, which were later easily repaired. The men were all picked up quickly by the Confederate authorities, and poor Andrews, just twenty-two years old, was soon hanged, along with seven of his gang. However, several other members of the group managed to escape back to the North, some helped by slaves, and most survived the war, with one living until 1923. All the nineteen military participants received the Congressional Medal of Honor, the first soldiers ever to receive this newly instituted award. On his side, Fuller, too, was feted for his actions and spent his later years ensuring that the story was told from his point of view, which suggests that there may have been some rewriting of history. Indeed, the raid has been mythologized, inspiring several films, most notably in 1926 *The General*, in which, interestingly, Buster Keaton portrays the conductor, Fuller, as the hero, whereas the Unionists are depicted as ruthless train wreckers, demonstrating the enduring tacit sympathy to the Confederate cause. According to George Douglas, it was the vagaries of the Southern railroads that wrecked the raid: "Andrews was undone by bad weather, by heavy rail traffic, by a single-track bottleneck, by trains not on schedule, and by other vicissitudes of the Southern railroads, as much as he was by Fuller."[26] Indeed, had he gone ahead with the original plan, which was to launch the raid on the previous day when the weather was better and there were fewer trains coming in the other direction, the story might have had a different ending and the inevitable outcome of the Civil War might have come sooner.

Most similar attacks on the enemy's railroads were carried out by cavalry rather than small groups of spies. On the Unionist side, the most remarkable was the raid commanded by Colonel Benjamin Grierson, a former music teacher, in the spring of 1863. He led a group of seventeen hundred men who rode six hundred miles through hostile territory from southern Tennessee through Mississippi to Baton Rouge, Louisiana— which was held by the Union—tearing up railroads, burning ties, and destroying storehouses, with the ultimate aim of wrecking the key rail junction at Newton's Station, Mississippi. Not only did Grierson's raid tie up large numbers of Confederate forces, but remarkably only twelve of his men—three killed and nine missing—were lost in the whole expedition. Again, this tale attracted Hollywood producers, with John Wayne starring in the 1959 film *The Horse Soldiers*.

On the Confederate side, the most effective attack on railroads behind the lines was the raid at Christmas 1862 led by General John Morgan with a force of four thousand men. Their target was the Louisville & Nashville Railroad, which, like the Baltimore & Ohio, had the misfortune of being situated on the border between the two sides. As Stewart H. Holbrook aptly describes, it was "destined to be wrecked and wrecked again by both contending armies." The Louisville & Nashville was a crucial line, as it led into the South and was initially used to smuggle supplies to the Confederates until much of it fell into the hands of the Unionists. Morgan and his men swept through Kentucky, capturing the station in the small town of Upton, where he used the telegraph system to fool the Unionists farther up the line into giving him information on the position of their forces.

The Confederates then wreaked havoc on the line, demolishing bridges and warehouses in a week of destruction, before withdrawing with two thousand prisoners. They destroyed the Louisville & Nashville so thoroughly that even Haupt could not weave his magic quickly. Hampered by floods, it took him the better part of six months to restore the line. Ultimately, however, Morgan's wrecking was to no avail. Despite the constant attacks—the bridge on the line at Bridgeport, Alabama, was blown up four times during the war—the Louisville & Nashville proved to be immensely useful to the Unionists and "could be rated as a major factor in winning the war, so far as transportation was concerned."[27]

Destroying railroads became a strategic aim precisely because they were proving so useful as a way of moving supplies and, particularly, troops. Although troops had been deployed by rail in various European wars in the previous couple of decades, the scale and extent of troop movement in the American Civil War were unprecedented. Indeed, the extent and range over which battles were fought were so large that accounts of the war refer to two theaters, eastern, broadly the Atlantic Seaboard and its immediate interior, and western, generally defined as the area east of the Mississippi River and west of the Appalachian Mountains.

That first major battle at Manassas (Bull Run) had demonstrated irrevocably the benefit of rapid troop movements by rail, and ever more ambitious transfers ensued. Chattanooga, Tennessee, some five hundred miles west of the main theaters of war, saw several major troop movements by both sides. In June 1862, anticipating a Unionist attack in eastern Tennessee, the Confederates' General Braxton Bragg, commander of the Army of the Mississippi, decided to rush his troops to try to secure Chattanooga. Although the route was circuitous, and Bragg was uncertain about the reliability of the railroads, his first batch of three thousand men arrived within six days of leaving their base at Tupelo, Mississippi. The rest of his army and equipment quickly followed, and ultimately the operation that involved twenty-five thousand men being sent nearly eight hundred miles by rail passed smoothly, despite the journey's requiring them to travel on six different lines.

A year later, in September 1863, another such mass transfer of Southern troops, involving a variety of routes and coordinated, at last, by the Railroad Bureau, enabled the Confederates to reinforce the Army of Tennessee just south of Chattanooga, which had just been captured by Union forces from northern Virginia. Despite traveling nine hundred miles on single-track railroads never intended for such heavy use, and which were not connected with one another at the termini, more than twelve thousand men led by General James Longstreet arrived in time to ensure victory over General William Rosecrans at the Battle of Chickamauga. Longstreet's aide-de-camp, Gilbert Moxley Sorrel, later summed up the move in Churchillian terms, with an emphasis on the inadequacy of the Southern railroads: "Never before were so many troops moved over such worn-out railways, none first-class from the beginning. Never before were such crazy cars— passenger, baggage, mail, coal, box, platform, all and every sort wobbling on the jumping strap-iron—used for hauling good soldiers."[28]

The defeat at Chickamauga prompted the Unionists, in turn, to trump all those moves with the biggest troop transfer of the war. Again, Chattanooga was the destination. The town was held by the Unionists under the illustrious general and later president Ulysses S. Grant, but it was under threat from the Confederates and needed reinforcements. The federal government decided to send twenty-five thousand men,[29] but there was much debate in Washington on how this could be achieved and Lincoln needed much reassurance that such an epic journey was possible by rail. Lincoln finally consented, and the logistics were quickly worked out. Railroad presidents were summoned and orders given to assemble dozens of trains. The chosen railroads were effectively taken under military control, and within a couple of days the first troops rolled out of Culpeper, Virginia, for a twelve-hundred-mile trip through Union-held territory over the Appalachians and across the unbridged Ohio River. The detail of the journey illustrates the discontinuity of the American railroad system at the time. At Culpeper, on the Rappahannock River, the troops took the Orange & Alexandria to Washington and then the Baltimore & Ohio to the Ohio River just below Wheeling. A ferry ride over the river to Bellaire in Ohio connected them with the Central Ohio Railroad to Columbus, then the Indiana Central to Indianapolis, and then the Jeffersonville, Madison & Indianapolis Railroad to Jeffersonville on the Ohio, opposite Louisville. Having recrossed the river using a pontoon, a combination of the Louisville & Nashville and the Nashville & Chattanooga took them to their destination. It was not just the trains that had to be organized. Food depots had to be established at fifty-mile intervals, and all other traffic on the lines was canceled. The whole move had been expected to take more than two weeks but in practice was completed in just eleven days. It was, according to a history of the Civil War, "the longest and fastest movement of such a large body of troops before the twentieth century."[30]

These huge troop transfers across what was most of the entire territory of the United States at the time demonstrate how the railroads extended the scope and duration of the war. The West was sparsely populated, and, with troops unable to obtain food from the surrounding countryside, such mass battles as Chickamauga would not have been possible without the supply line afforded by the railroads. It was inevitable, therefore, that the final and decisive push of the war, led by General William Sherman, should be entirely dependent on the railroads. Union tactics by then had become well established. Union armies could penetrate Southern territory only as far as supply lines allowed, and these were entirely dependent on railroads. As they headed into Confederate territory, they would destroy the railroads to eliminate their use by the enemy and then call on Haupt or his successors to reconstruct them once the territory was established. In some instances, the gauge of railroads was changed by the conquering army in order to facilitate connections with existing lines.

After Chattanooga was secured, the town became the base for the move across the South led by General William Sherman that began in the spring of 1864. Sherman's route took him along the Western & Atlantic Railroad, which, with the Nashville & Chattanooga and the Louisville & Nashville, created a five-hundred-mile supply line linking Atlanta with Louisville. As he progressed, units of the United States Military Railroads were almost constantly employed in repairing the railroads after Confederate raids, at times reconstructing tracks while further destruction of the line was taking place simultaneously just a few miles away. When the Confederates, under the notoriously reckless General John Hood, destroyed thirty-five miles of track and 450 feet of bridges, a team of two thousand men restored the line within a week and ensured the railroad was fully operational in two.

Once Atlanta was taken in September 1864, the way was open for Sherman's March to the Sea to seal the victory along with Grant's forces, who had fought their way south through Virginia. At this stage, though, Sherman was more worried about being chased by regrouping Confederate forces in the hostile territory he was crossing and therefore destroyed the railroad behind him. He became "the greatest railroad wrecker of all" and devised the "Sherman hairpin," a sophisticated way of ensuring rails could not be repaired, involving heating and then twisting the rails around trees.[31] After using the Western & Atlantic to bring in supplies, his men ripped up no fewer than eighty miles of the line and then continued the destruction as Sherman progressed through Georgia, leaving the Southern railroad network in utter disarray at the conclusion of the war. It was precisely because Sherman understood the importance of the railroad that his destruction was so thorough. In his memoirs he stressed, with military precision, the essential nature of the railroad supply line during his move south: "That single stem of railroad supplied an army of 100,000 men and 32,000 horses for the period of 196 days, from May 1 to November 19, 1864. To have delivered that amount of forage and food by ordinary wagons would have required 36,800 wagons, of six mules each . . . a simple impossibility in such roads as existed in that region."[32] Grant, who led the other part of the pincer movement taking over the South, also understood the importance of the railroads. Before Richmond could be taken, he had to build two new military lines, totaling twenty-two miles, to supply his armies as they advanced to the town.

The railroads were adapted for all kinds of purposes during the Civil War. Ambulance trains, which had previously seen only limited service in European wars, became widely used on both sides as the war progressed. As early as October 1861, the Virginia Central built two ambulance cars designed to hold forty-four casualties each, and in the North hospital cars were running between Boston, Massachusetts, and Albany, New York, as early as the spring of 1862 with basic facilities of hair mattresses, pillows, and blankets for each berth. However, neither the military nor the railroad companies anticipated the extent of the demand for proper medical facilities to which the conflict would give rise. Not only did the fierce battles result in huge numbers of wounded, but the insalubrious conditions and poor diet triggered outbreaks of disease that exacted a more lethal toll than bullets and risked overwhelming frontline medical facilities. Despite the early experiments with hospital trains, suitable medical care was rarely provided. In the Peninsula Campaign of 1862, for example, there was virtually no special provision for the wounded, with the result that injured men were simply dumped on the floors of freight cars. According to a contemporary witness, "The worst cases are put inside the covered—close, windowless boxes—sometimes with a little straw or a blanket to lie on, oftener without."[33]

On the Unionist side, the situation improved thanks to the creation of a government agency, the Sanitary Commission, which ordered a series of special "ward" cars, each holding twenty-four removable stretchers suspended from uprights with heavy rubber bands. Unfortunately, the swinging motion of the trains sometimes resulted in the injured men being tipped out of their litters, and, ironically, the rather cruder arrangement used in the South, involving the placing of large quantities of straw on the bottom of the cars, was probably a safer option for the wounded.

By the end of the war, hospital trains had become part of the paraphernalia of war. When Sherman attacked Atlanta, he had three whole trains, each capable of carrying two hundred men, operating between Louisville and Atlanta. The Confederates developed a system of mobile hospitals that transported equipment and patients by train as the battle lines moved and could be unloaded and repacked rapidly. In 1864, for example, one such unit, the Flewellen Hospital, spent five months in Barnesville, Georgia; six weeks in Opelika, Alabama; nine days in Mobile, Alabama; and two in Corinth, Mississippi.

Armored trains and railroad-mounted guns were another railroad innovation of the Civil War. The first recorded use of an armored train was by the Unionists in the early days of the war, to protect the railroad lines around Baltimore against Confederate saboteurs. On the secessionist side, it was the ever-innovative general Robert E. Lee who developed the concept. He ordered his artillery commander to build a railroad gun wagon by placing a thirty-two-pounder on a railcar protected by a wall of steel rails, and this armored battery was deployed in the Seven Days' Battle in Virginia in June 1862. A bigger gun, a thirteen-inch mortar, was fitted to a railcar by the Unionists during the siege of Vicksburg, Mississippi, in the spring of 1863, but, in truth, this was an experimental technology that was used only to a limited extent in this conflict.

Unorthodox uses of railroad equipment, however, occasionally played havoc with the trains. Haupt noted that the guards posted to protect railroad facilities were wont, especially in the summer, to take baths and wash their clothes in the water meant for locomotives. The result, comic to see but disastrous for the engine, was that hot soapy water foamed out of the boiler, disabling the locomotive. Haupt had to issue a specific instruction to ban bathing in water tanks.

The asymmetry of the two sides meant that the result of the war should never have been in doubt. The North had two-thirds of the guns, a far more developed economy, most of the industrial capacity, better railroads, and far greater financial resources. Its territory included all the cities above one hundred thousand people with the exception of New Orleans. Given the North's overall strength and all its other advantages, the fact that the conflict lasted for four years was a remarkable testimony to the South's ability to fight. The South, though, had the better generals, especially in the early stages, and was fighting for what its citizens perceived as their very survival, which was a strong motivating force. Moreover, the South's generals seemed to have an instinctive understanding of how to use the railroads in the early part of the war, but the failure of Davis's government to assume control over the railroads greatly hampered the war effort. As John F. Stover suggests, "Had the government of Jefferson Davis earlier faced up to its transportation problem and established as vigorous a policy of railroad control as it did in the field of ordnance, Southern railroads might well have provided a more adequate support for the Confederate military effort."[34]

The scale of use of the railroads by the military demonstrates the vital role they played throughout the war. Not all railroad companies kept records, but the Pennsylvania alone carried nearly a million military personnel during the conflict and the Illinois Central more than half a million. However, for the most part the railroads maintained their normal business, and, overall, military carryings represented a small proportion of their total wartime traffic. Even more remarkably, the railroads in the North continued to grow during the Civil War, and a start was even made on the first transcontinental.

It was because of the railroads that the conflict was carried out over such a large area and continued for so long. A report by McCallum after the war demonstrates the scale of the railroad operations during the Civil War. He found that the United States Military Railroads, a government agency, was bigger than any private company of the age, operating 2,105 miles of line with 419 locomotives and 6,330 cars. The railroads afforded the armies unprecedented mobility, which, as the war progressed, they learned to exploit to the fullest. The scale of destruction and carnage can be directly attributed to the railroads. The official history of the war lists ten thousand military encounters, of which more than four hundred were deemed serious enough to be called battles, about one every four days. Not surprisingly, therefore, the war was far bloodier than its predecessors. The death toll of American soldiers, some 620,000,[35] remains greater than in any conflict involving the United States and, remarkably, more than the total lost in all the nation's other wars before or since, including the two world wars and Vietnam. The railroads greatly increased the fighting power of the armies, allowed them to operate much farther from their supply depots than previously, and gave the side with the best railroad supply line a clear strategic advantage. The impact of the war was devastating to a vast swath of the country, and the railroads could be held responsible: "A war strategy that relied on railroads spread the effects of war over a vast area and left hundreds of thousands of uprooted wanderers looking for a place to settle or earn a living."[36]

Perhaps the most fascinating question concerning the relationship between the railroads and the war, however, is whether the conflict would have happened at all had it not been for the iron horse. Many historians suggest that had the Southern states seceded earlier, when there were no long-distance railroads, the Unionists would not have been able to reclaim the South. According to Franklin Garrett, a historian of the South, "If the Southern states had seceded in 1832, when South Carolina was threatening to do so, nothing could have stopped them." He also points out that Atlanta was created by the railroads, and that had it not enjoyed such efficient connections with the rest of the country, Sherman's long march through the hostile territory of the South would have been impossible. It was thanks to the railroad that "Union forces were able to strike deep into the South without suffering Napoleon's fate in Russia." Indeed, even as late as 1850, it would have been impossible to envisage that the war could have been conducted on such a wide front, as there was no quick way of traveling across the country. Secession "might have succeeded in 1850 when over 40 per cent of the nation's inhabitants formed a truly 'solid South' and the opposition 60 per cent was scattered from Skowhegan, Maine, to Mississippi with no completed means of transportation at either end."[37]

Whereas the railroads determined the conduct and course of the war, the long-term impact of the conflict on the railroads was less obvious. By 1861, the railroads were already changing, becoming more of a mass enterprise and beginning their long process of consolidation. The American public's suspicion of the big companies, which was to become an increasingly significant aspect of its relationship with the railroads as the century drew to a close, had begun to emerge even before the first fateful shots of the war were fired at Fort Sumter. For all the momentous physical impact of the conflict on the railroads, especially in the South, the trends that would define their postwar history were already visible when war broke out. The railroads were about to embark on the period of their greatest domination, and, in reality, the war was merely a blip in an inevitable process. First, however, there was a continent to cross.

5

HARNESSING
THE ELEPHANT

The war was a transforming experience for railroads on both sides of the Mason-Dixon line, but in contrasting ways. In the North, it was mainly good news. Apart from a few unlucky railroads with lines on the border that suffered war damage, the Northern railroads had not only escaped any direct consequences of the war but prospered, thanks to the increase in traffic that always results from conflict. At first, the Northern companies rued the outbreak of the war, fearing it was going to wreck their recovery from the poor economic conditions of the late 1850s. However, they soon realized that war was beneficial for railroads. Use of the railroads in the North soared, boosting income and profits: "Railroads which had suffered a decline in freight and passenger revenues in the three years immediately preceding the outbreak of war, soon found themselves swamped with business, and vied with each other in placing orders for more locomotives and more cars." According to the *American Railroad Journal*, 1863 had been "the most prosperous ever known to the American Railways," and traffic continued to grow throughout the war.[1]

The four major east-west railroads—the Pennsylvania, the Baltimore & Ohio, the Erie, and the New York Central—did especially well during the conflict. With the Mississippi closed to through traffic during the war, and poor harvests in Europe increasing the demand for American grain, all four railroads enjoyed a spectacular rise in traffic and in profits during the war. For example, whereas in 1861 the New York Central carried 2.1 million passengers, this figure had all but doubled to 3.7 million four years later. For the Michigan Central, the increase was even more phenomenal: a growth of 260 percent during the war. But it was not only passengers who used the trains. War generates a variety of demands for freight transportation, from raw materials to ammunition. Not surprisingly, since the railroads were essentially a monopoly, goods traffic rose dramatically during the conflict. As a result, there were healthy increases in dividends paid to shareholders, even on railroads that had rarely prospered. The Erie, for example, after not paying any dividends for many years, suddenly distributed 8 percent to its grateful investors in 1864. Some minor but heavily used lines such as the Cleveland, Painesville & Ashtabula, which paid a remarkable 26 percent that year, made a fortune for their owners.

As ever with the railroads, rapid growth was not entirely beneficial, because at times of such intensive use maintenance tends to be skimped and assets get overused. The war saw unprecedented increases in demand for equipment such as rails, new cars, and locomotives, which pushed up operating costs. Labor costs rose, too, as many skilled men joined the Union army, partly because Lincoln, showing a rare absence of foresight, failed to take action to stop railroad workers from enlisting. On some railroads, the situation was so bad that in the later stages of the war, they had to turn away business for want of rolling stock or personnel to run the trains.

Those Northern railroads that were safely ensconced away from the front were quick to use some of this extra revenue to expand. A total of five thousand miles was added to the US rail network in the first half of the 1860s, mostly in the North, a remarkable pace of growth given that so many resources were devoted to the war effort and an illustration of the burgeoning industrial strength of the North. Apart from a few hundred miles of the lines built by the United States Military Railroads, these tracks were intended to be permanent additions to the nation's network. Indeed, this period can be seen as the beginning of the greatest period of growth in the US railroads' history—or indeed that of any other country—as will be outlined in the next chapter.

The contrast with the railroads in the South could not have been greater. The war exacerbated the differences between the railroads in the two regions in every conceivable way. As in the North, the Southern railroads also saw increased carrying, but because of the chaotic organization of the military effort, the railroad companies rarely received any of the money this should have generated. Moreover, the lack of maintenance facilities—as most of the latter had been based in the North—together with the damage wrought first by overuse and then by military action, meant that the Southern railroad network was in a terrible state at the end of the war. Indeed, much of the system was not functioning at all, owing to a combination of war damage and the parlous financial state of many railroad companies. Several railroads had gone bankrupt during the war, as the secessionist government had run out of money to pay for the men and munitions they had carried, and there was no one to compensate them for the war damage. The bonds issued by states and railroads during the Confederacy were officially deemed void by the federal government, leaving the railroad companies holding worthless paper.

Without factories or even materials, the South had completely depleted its rolling stock by 1865, and the process of reconstruction would prove slow. The Southern railroads were further hampered in their efforts to recover from the war by a shortage of labor. As Theodore Kornweibel Jr. notes, "Slave labour was essential to antebellum southern railroading," and during the war this dependency increased, as large numbers of slaves were drafted onto the railroad to replace men who had signed up to fight.[2] Losing that free labor at the conclusion of hostilities made it even more difficult for the Southern railroads to become financially viable.

The war had a very powerful direct impact on the railroads in both North and South. However, the trends that saw the railroad expand and develop almost exponentially for the rest of the century—the consolidation of small companies into bigger railroads, the growth of financial capitalism that made it easier for the railroads to obtain funds for expansion, and the shift in agriculture away from subsistence farming toward cash crops that required transport by rail to the Eastern Seaboard—had already been in evidence before the war and simply intensified afterward. In other words, those factors that would transform the US railroads from being mostly a series of short and disconnected lines into a network were already in place. For example, whereas in 1849 no railroad company operated more than 250 miles, by 1855 at least sixteen railroads controlled more than 200 miles, and the large companies were already on their way to becoming the nation's biggest businesses. By the outbreak of the war in 1861, there were at least ten railroad companies with a capital of $10 million or more, far bigger than any other enterprise of the time.

Britain played a key role here in supplying capital. Right from the outset of American railroad development, financing had been sought in Europe and especially in the United Kingdom. Those US states that provided so much support to the railroad pioneers raised much of their capital, in the form of bonds, from the other side of the Atlantic. Indeed, when several defaulted on them in the 1840s, it was the London market that suffered most. Not surprisingly, it became reluctant to lend again, boycotting the American railroad companies. But the lure of the American railroad market was too attractive, and within a few years British investors started sending money over again, a boom-bust cycle that would repeat itself several times by the end of the nineteenth century. British investment ceased during the Civil War, but resumed by the end of the 1860s. And then it all went sour again with the panic of 1873. The author of the standard work on British investment in American railroads, Dorothy Adler, suggests that British capital helped to fuel this succession of American railroad manias: "It is not stretching the facts to draw a parallel between the late 1840s, the late 1860s and the years 1879–81. Each of these periods was characterized by a speculative movement of British capital into American railway shares."[3] She calculates that by the end of the century, British investment in US railroads totaled around £400 million (perhaps worth one hundred times that amount today, £40 billion), around 10 percent of all American railroad capitalization.

British capital played a role in most of the bigger American railroads, and the two companies that built the first transcontinental, the Union Pacific and Central Pacific, were no exception. One of the most immediate effects of the secession of the Southern states was the start of construction on the transcontinental, which, remarkably, began even as the conflict was still raging. The building of a line from the Atlantic to the Pacific had been mooted at the very dawn of the railroad age, and despite the physical obstacles and huge distances involved, the dream of uniting the two oceans had become part of the American psyche. The idea of a transcontinental railroad was integral to the very notion of creating a unified nation across

North America. The land was there, but, for the settlers to come, transportation was needed. In the early days, they traveled in wagon—rather than steam—trains, but it was obvious that the creation of substantial communities in the West was dependent on finding a better transportation solution than the horse and cart. Without the railroad, it would be impossible to open up the huge swath of land between the Mississippi and the West Coast.

Several fanciful and impractical ideas for a transcontinental railroad had been put forward as early as the 1810s and 1820s, but the first detailed proposal emerged just as the first locomotives were chugging along the Charleston & Hamburg and Baltimore & Ohio lines. In 1830, William Redfield, later the president of the American Association for the Advancement of Science, published a paper proposing a railroad from the East to the Mississippi with extensions right through to the Pacific. Redfield's paper was soon forgotten, but the people of Dunkirk, on the shore of Lake Erie in upstate New York, can lay claim to being the first to lobby for the transcontinental line to pass through their town. At a public meeting in January 1832, they passed a resolution in favor of a line connecting the Hudson with Lake Erie, suggesting it would continue on to the Mississippi River and the Pacific Ocean. Their idea was picked up by Samuel Dexter, the editor of the *Western Emigrant* of Ann Arbor, who wrote in the following month that "it is in our power to build an immense city at the mouth of the Oregon [on the West Coast] by a railroad by which the traveller leaving the city of New York shall, at the moderate rate of ten miles an hour, place himself in a port right on the shores of the Pacific."[4] Interestingly, like Redfield, Dexter opined that the expense of such a massive scheme would be insignificant in relation to the cost of war, though his estimate of $30 million would prove rather optimistic. He also suggested—quixotically perhaps, because his knowledge of weather patterns was limited—that one reason to build the line would be to facilitate the export of furs to India. But then, to be fair, the notion of a three-thousand-mile transcontinental railroad at a time when there were barely a few dozen miles of line in the whole country could be conceived only by those with a fervent imagination.

Various enthusiasts began to pick up on the idea. There was, for example, John Plumbe, a Welsh engineer who had moved to the United States in the 1820s and in 1836 began to examine possible routes for the line from his home in Wisconsin, then still a territory rather than a state. Rather presciently, Plumbe, best remembered as a pioneer of photographic techniques, argued that a transcontinental railroad "would hasten the formation of dense settlements throughout the whole extent of the road, advance the sales of the public lands, afford increased facilities to the agricultural, commercial and mining interests of the country . . . and enable the government to transport troops and munitions of war." Yet when Plumbe petitioned Congress for the idea in 1938, one congressman reckoned it was as silly as asking "to build a railroad to the moon."[5] Poor Plumbe spent much of the 1840s trying unsuccessfully to convince politicians, national and local, of his idea, but returned a broken man to the Midwest in 1857, where he soon committed suicide at the age of forty-seven.

The most serious and effective early proselytizer for the scheme was Asa Whitney, an eccentric self-made merchant whose resemblance to Napoléon Bonaparte was apparently so marked that strangers would often stare at him in amazement. He spent many years and much of his fortune trying, unsuccessfully, to convince Congress to sanction the idea of a railroad across America. More practical and thorough than Plumbe, Whitney conceived of his plan for a transcontinental on a lengthy sea voyage in 1843, as he returned to the United States from China, where he had made his fortune. It was the apparently interminable nature of his journey across the Indian and Atlantic Oceans—for this was the era before the construction of the Suez Canal—that attracted Whitney to the idea of a transcontinental. He believed the railroad would become the corridor of exchange between Europe and Asia, placing America at the center of the world's trade routes. Whitney was also an idealist who, like many early railroad promoters, saw the project as an opportunity for human improvement. As he told Congress, it would bring the dispersed population of the United States "together as one family, with but one interest—the general good of all." In 1845, after presenting the plan in Washington, he toured the country with a group of enthusiastic young acolytes, extolling the virtues of the project and exploring a rail route that went west from Milwaukee, Wisconsin—which would, indeed, be chosen by one of the later transcontinentals. Whitney became a popular speaker and a darling of the newspapers. He returned several times to Congress, where he put forward a plan to build the railroad himself in return for a grant of a corridor of land sixty miles wide from Lake Michigan to the Pacific. By selling off parcels of land as the railroad was built, Whitney optimistically believed that it would be self-financing.

Largely thanks to the idealistic enthusiasm of men such as Plumbe and Whitney, a series of railroad conventions was held in various cities across the country to explore the project and lobby for particular routes. There was, of course, one major obstacle to the building of the transcontinental about which little was said—the Native Americans, or Indians, as they were then known. As Dee Brown notes, "During the lively debates over all these various routes, no mention was ever made of the native Americans, the Indians who had lived for centuries on the lands into which the Iron Horses must intrude."[6] Uniquely among early supporters of the transcontinental, Whitney did at least give some consideration to the issue. It was not, though, that he had any more regard for Native American rights than the politicians who did not even trouble to mention them. Not at all. He was simply keen to ensure that their land titles would be extinguished and that they would be forced to settle permanently like white men or move far away from the iron road. It was not the presence of Native Americans that killed off Whitney's idea but the politics of the North-South divide. Southern legislators had no truck with talk of a route in the Far North, running along the southern shores of the Great Lakes and then west from Milwaukee, while the Northerners could not accept the idea of the line going through the South. Whitney, who even went to England in 1851 to try to raise financing for the project, gave up, and the transcontinental scheme disappeared into the government machine. It was not totally inactive, though. The Army Corps of Engineers produced surveys for five possible routes from the Missouri River to California that covered everything from geology to flora and fauna. They provide a remarkable and beautiful compendium of the virgin West before the arrival of the iron horse, but proved to be of little practical value, as the Southern interests blocked any move toward legislating for the line. The transcontinental was thus put on hold until the secessionists left Congress to the Northern interests they so despised.

Whitney, Plumbe, and various other early dreamers, however, had not wasted their time. They had established the idea of the transcontinental as a topic of popular debate and ensured the concept took hold in the public mind. When the Southern states seceded from the Union in 1861, Lincoln, himself a true railroad visionary, wasted little time in indicating that a bill to build the line was now likely to be blessed with favorable passage through Congress, given the absence of the troublesome Southerners. The strongest lobbying now came from the West in the shape of another visionary, Theodore Judah, who has the best claim to be called the father of the transcontinental. Judah, for whom the epithet *fanatic* might have been devised, had been the engineer on the first California railroad, the Sacramento Valley Railroad, a twenty-one-mile line completed in 1852. He was convinced that it was possible to build a railroad through the Sierra Nevada, even though they appeared to be an insuperable barrier when viewed from the valleys below. He had the talents of both engineer and lobbyist, and he spent several years shuttling between the West, where he surveyed the potential route, and the East, where he labored tirelessly to convince politicians of the need for the transcontinental railroad.

As the bill was being prepared in 1862, he was back in Washington as the official representative of the Pacific Railroad Convention. Remarkably, despite the fact that there was a war going on, with battles breaking out at times within earshot of Washington, both houses of Congress found time to debate the bill in great detail. It was no walkover, but the result was not in doubt, provided the various potentially hostile interests—principally states that might be bypassed and rival railroads—could be appeased. Ultimately, the Pacific Railroad Act of 1862 passed through both houses with ease and gave the concession for the construction of the line to two companies, the Central Pacific, which was to start building eastward from Sacramento, California, and the Union Pacific, which would begin at Council Bluffs, Iowa—a confusing nomenclature since it was the *Union* Pacific that started in the center of America. One simple statistic illustrates the scope of the project: the Union Pacific and the Central Pacific would become the biggest two corporations in the country. This also helps to explain the sheer, almost unbelievable, scale of corruption and graft that would accompany the construction of the first transcontinental.

The act completely ignored the interests of the Native Americans. Indeed, it was worse than that. The act clearly contradicted previous efforts to protect their territory. The 1851 Treaty of Fort Laramie between the US government and seven Plains Indian nations recognized that the Cheyenne and Arapaho held a vast territory between the Rockies and western Kansas, including what is now southeastern Wyoming, southwestern Nebraska, eastern Colorado, and the far-western part of Kansas. The deal gave the Indians the right to clearly defined territories in exchange for stopping their attacks on settlers headed west on the Oregon Trail, while the US government offered money to the signatories of the treaty and pledged to deter US citizens from entering Native American territory. Clearly, building a railroad right through Native American territory was a breach of this pledge and ended any meaningful attempt to pay heed to their rights.

In contrast, for the railroad builders, the terms of the initial act were not ungenerous, but when they were improved upon two years later, they offered an astonishing level of federal funding, given that the war effort was taxing government resources to the limit. The companies benefited from two forms of state aid: for every mile of line they completed in the plains, they would receive $16,000 in government bonds, double that in the more difficult terrain of the Nebraska prairies or the Sacramento Valley, and triple the amount, $48,000 per mile, in the mountains. In total, that represented a potential loan of $60 million to the companies, but there was also a generous land grant ultimately representing a total of more than thirty-one thousand square miles, equivalent to an area the size of South Carolina. This was to be distributed on the basis of ten square miles per mile of track in strips alternating on either side of the right of way—which itself was a substantial four hundred feet wide. The meeting point of the two railroads was not specified, giving both companies an incentive to lay track over as many miles as quickly as possible.

Certain restrictions, placing obligations on the companies, were imposed by the federal government. Most notably, no government funding was available until the companies had each raised millions of dollars and built forty miles of track. However, much of the legislation was poorly worded, and details of the precise requirements, such as the sums required and the repayment terms of the loans, were unclear. The two railroad companies, for whom the term *rapacious* is an understatement, would take every opportunity to exploit these loopholes. Each company had been given two years to build the first fifty miles, but thereafter only fifty miles per year were required, which suggested the near two-thousand-mile railroad could have taken two decades to build. In the event, it was completed far more quickly, thanks to the financial incentives and the competition between the two companies.

The act was signed into law by Lincoln on July 1, 1862, and tradition—but perhaps not historical accuracy—has it that Judah, who had continued his lobbying as a clerk to the bill committee, sent a telegram to his Central Pacific colleagues back in Sacramento saying, "We have drawn the elephant. Now let us see if we can harness him up." It was not the only crucial piece of legislation passed that year that would help bring about the transcontinental. The Homestead Act, which enabled settlers to claim land that they had farmed and developed for five years—a kind of legal guarantee to squatters—encouraged the migration westward that would be essential in making the new line viable.

Having secured the passage of the act, Judah headed back west by boat with large amounts of equipment, as none was available in California; virtually everything had to be imported via a railroad that crossed the Isthmus of Panama or by sea around Cape Horn. The war was far away, and there was nothing to prevent work from starting on the line. For Judah, it was a moment to savor, a triumphant outcome to an exhausting two years spent first surveying the Sierra Nevada in search of a route for the transcontinental and then canvassing support for the new railroad. To force through a railroad against the myriad of obstacles generally requires an element of obsession, bordering on fanaticism, a common characteristic of railroad pioneers both in America and elsewhere. Judah had worked on various engineering projects in the East when he traveled west to be the engineer of the first railroad in California, the 21-mile Sacramento–Folsom line. The railroad was a financial failure, as the gold mines it was designed to serve soon became exhausted, but that did not stop Judah from exploring the possibility of a line farther eastward through the mountains. He had tried to get a bill for a Pacific railroad through Congress but, having failed, managed to persuade the California legislature to permit the construction of a line from Sacramento to the state line with Nevada, 115 miles away. Ostensibly, it was to serve the recently discovered silver mines of Nevada, but, in fact, Judah's eyes were always on a line right through to the East.

With promises of access to that wealth, Judah was able to sell the idea of a railroad to a key group of local businessmen. Judah's breakthrough in his search for investors had come at a seminal meeting in Sacramento in November 1860, probably the most famous gathering ever to take place above a hardware store, though many of the later accounts have undoubtedly been embellished through the rose-tinted glass of hindsight. Judah had been touring the state, seeking to sell the idea of his railroad to any local notables with a few hundred dollars to spare, but he found few of the richer members of the state were forthcoming. At the meeting in the hardware store, however, a quartet in Judah's audience famously responded to his entreaties, a decision that they would never regret. Four rather unprepossessing local merchants—Leland Stanford, Charles Crocker, Mark Hopkins, and Collis P. Huntington—came forward to invest in what would become the Central Pacific, and by doing so would join the ranks of the richest men in the United States. They were to become the Big Four—or Associates, as they called themselves—of the Central Pacific, turning themselves from humble small-town businessmen into directors of one of the two biggest companies in the land. Stanford was a wholesale grocer (though, more usefully, he was soon to become governor of California), Charles Crocker dealt in dry goods, while Hopkins and Huntington were the proprietors of the hardware store in which the meeting took place. A 1930s biographer of the Big Four wrote with brutal candor of the meeting, "In later life, four of his [Judah's] listeners accepted easily the roles of men of vision, who had perceived a matchless opportunity and grasped it with courage. It was a role none of them deserved." Indeed, at the meeting Judah had sold the line not on the basis of a great project that would transform America but, rather, as a short-term opportunity to make a quick buck by tapping into the silver and other mineral wealth of the mountains. He had told the merchants what they wanted to hear: "how to sell more of their goods, how to make their property more valuable, how to expand their businesses and stifle competition."[7]

Therefore, immediately on Judah's return to California following the passage of the 1862 act, the Central Pacific was formally constituted with Stanford as president, Huntington as vice president, Hopkins as treasurer, and Crocker as the construction supervisor—and, crucially, president of the construction company that was a subsidiary of the Central and bore his name. That company was to be the mechanism through which the illicit part of their fortunes would be made and eventually led to Judah's falling out with the Big Four and, as an indirect consequence, to his premature death.

Despite the war still raging in the East, the passage of the act and the prospect of government subsidies meant there was nothing to stop work from beginning in California. Judah had brought much useful equipment with him, and the first sections of the line, on the eastern side of California's great Central Valley, were relatively easy to construct. Too easy, though, for the money-grabbing Associates, who fell out with Judah over the question of precisely where the rise into the Sierra Nevada began. This was an important and potentially lucrative matter. The cash-strapped Central Pacific was desperate to get its hands on the cheap loans it would obtain by starting construction. And, as we have seen, for each mile of track built in the mountains, the company stood to receive three times the amount it received per mile of track built in the plains. So Stanford and Crocker decided that the rise began at a place called Arcade Creek, despite the fact that the mountains, a good fifteen miles away, were barely visible from there. It would have been all too easy to pull the wool over the eyes of the bureaucracy, three thousand miles away in Washington, but Judah was having none of it. As he had personally undertaken the survey, he knew that the true beginning of the gradient was some twenty miles farther east, a difference of some $640,000 to the company.

This was the point at which the visionary, as Judah saw himself, came up against the hard-nosed "gang of corner-cutting merchants he saw the Associates to be."[8] There were other sources of friction between the Associates and Judah, notably over his survey fee and his suspicions that some of the money being spent on the first section of line was actually being diverted to a road project that was one of the Associates' other commercial ventures. These swindles had not gone entirely unnoticed in the press, thanks to the machinations of a pair of equally corrupt brothers, John and Lester Robinson, who had worked on the Sacramento Valley Railroad and leaked the story, since they were eager to obtain the contract on the Central Pacific themselves. Judah wanted nothing to do with the Associates' sharp practices.

Work on the Central Pacific had started on January 8, 1863, after the ceremony of turning the first shovelful of earth. Heavy rains had turned the streets into mud, onto which the prominent lady guests of the town refused to venture, as they sought refuge on the balcony of a local hotel. The main speakers were Crocker, styling himself as the "general super-intendent" of the railroad, and Stanford, now both president of the Central Pacific and governor of California. The straw laid out to absorb the mud made the ritual of turning the first sod rather more difficult than usual. It was somehow apt, given the fraud and deception that would attend every stage of the building of the line, that even the groundbreaking ceremony was an act of deceit, with a wagonload of earth dumped expressly for the purpose.

The inaugural part of the Central was built by Charles Crocker's eponymous company and illustrates precisely the sort of financial shenanigans that became routine on both railroads. On this first section stretching eighteen miles out of Sacramento, costs soon exceeded estimates, and Crocker's cash ran out. No matter. The extra money required, $150,000 on a contract originally estimated at $275,000, was made up from Central Pacific's coffers, a clear breach of normal accounting rules that amounted to "a polite form of embezzlement," but since the other three were all silent partners in Crocker's outfit, they benefited personally, too.[9]

It was through this type of contracting arrangement that the promoters of both the Central and the Union railroads would make most of their money. There was in fact plenty of straight money to be made, given the generous terms of the legislation, but as historian John F. Stover suggests, "none of the participants wished to be satisfied with a modest profit." Crocker's company had the contract to build the railroad only as far as the state line, at which point another contractor, the Contract & Finance Company, took over. The move away from using Crocker's company was prompted by a realization on the part of the Associates that such a patently dubious arrangement—between Crocker of the Central Pacific and Crocker & Company as the contractor—would not stand up to any scrutiny. Crocker, who incidentally had no previous contracting experience but ultimately did see the project through, later cheerfully admitted that there was no "& Company" in his organization, as he had sole charge of it. The new arrangement was no less dishonest. It was merely a subterfuge, since the Contract & Finance Company was owned by the Associates, who "managed to get their accounts into such a shape that no outsider had a chance of understanding them."[10] They were able to use the contracting company as a cash cow, given it was responsible for acquiring all the material and building the line at prices that could easily be inflated, to the detriment of the Central and its shareholders, as there was no external scrutiny of what were internal transactions.

It was this arrangement that led to Judah's disillusionment. Judah had not even been at the opening ceremony, and after a couple of difficult board meetings he understood clearly that the Associates were trying to push him out. They paid him off with $100,000, and Judah decided to try to obtain alternative financing, possibly with the intention of buying out the Associates. He headed back east in the autumn, but the journey proved fatal, as he contracted yellow fever in the tropical climate of Panama and died in New York a few days after his return, aged just thirty-seven. His death left the Associates completely free to use the railroad company to plunder the government's coffers and, through the medium of the contractor, to cheat the unwitting investors. Indeed, they were so intent on enriching themselves first that initial progress on the line was painfully slow, despite the expenditure of considerable sums of money. It was so slow, in fact, that the Union Pacific, despite starting two years later, had soon built as much mileage as the Central.

Work on the Union Pacific had been delayed not only by the proximity of the war, which sapped both men and materials, but also by its more diffuse structure. The Union Pacific did not have an obvious set of champions like Judah and the Big Four. In an attempt to ensure that ownership of the railroad was widely spread, the first Pacific Railway Act had created a group of nearly a hundred "commissioners" who were supposed to first create, and then fund, the company.

Enter Dr. Thomas Durant, the man who would become Mr. Union Pacific. A measure of the fellow can be gleaned from the fact that he had originally qualified as a doctor but had never practiced because he had become bored with medicine and turned, instead, to speculating in stocks. He had railroad experience also, as he had promoted and built the Mississippi & Missouri, the line that connected with the Rock Island Railroad through the ill-fated bridge over the Mississippi. Although many of the other characters involved in the Union Pacific, which has been aptly described as "a curious mixture of the noble and the ignoble," were every bit as corrupt as Durant, most at least demonstrated a genuine and commendable interest in pushing the project through and believed it would transform America. Not so Durant. He was the complete opposite of Judah, seeing the making of money as the only reason to involve himself in railroad construction: "Pride of accomplishment, the excitement of opening up new frontiers, and fulfilling society's need for transportation meant nothing to him."[11]

Durant, who was not named as a commissioner under the act but had quickly set out to gain control of the transcontinental project, had previous experience in manipulating stock and cheating investors in the Mississippi & Missouri. It was, therefore, with practiced ease that he managed to scheme his way into obtaining a controlling interest in the Union Pacific, despite the legislation specifically designed to prevent such control. He spent considerable time in 1863 arranging the purchase of stock through nominees whom he controlled and in October that year, thanks to his control of the votes, ensured that an old colleague, a corrupt politician by the name of John Dix, was elected as president of the company, while Durant became vice president. As Dee Brown puts it, "Durant knew that Dix would never bother him."[12]

With the Union Pacific safely under his control, Durant was keen to demonstrate progress on the scheme, but it was not easy with war waging close by and a shortage of materials, as the company was further hamstrung by a clause in the legislation that required all iron to be American rather than British. However, the need to demonstrate at least some activity was made more urgent because a rival railroad, the Atchison, Topeka & Santa Fe, had just been awarded a large land grant by Lincoln, and there were fears it might win support for a transcontinental route from a Congress easily persuaded with the right inducements. A meaningless groundbreaking ceremony was held at Omaha, Nebraska, in December 1863, but after the flag waving and earth turning, everyone had simply gone home, though Durant did use the opportunity to pick up some cheap real estate, which soon became worth millions because of its proximity to the new railroad.

Durant then turned his attention to ensuring that the already supportive legislation was made even more generous to the companies building the line and that he would be able to reap much of the benefit. As Dee Brown explains, "During 1864, Durant successfully accomplished two major maneuvers that made it possible for him and his close associates to enter upon a colossal looting of the people's treasure and plundering of national land resources." First, he established the equivalent of the Central's contracting company, an organization called Crédit Mobilier that would achieve notoriety and forever be remembered for a scandal that became the nineteenth century's equivalent of Enron. The way to set up this structure was explained to Durant by the much-traveled George Train, another of the Union Pacific's early promoters. Train was a "character": a true eccentric and impassioned orator, a supporter of women's rights and builder of tramways, and apparently the man who inspired the portrayal of Phileas Fogg, the hero of Jules Verne's *Around the World in 80 Days*. Train advised Durant of a company in France called the Société Générale de Crédit Mobilier, which was involved in several major infrastructure projects and was, in modern parlance, a way of outsourcing construction to protect the parent company from risk and, incidentally, creating a mechanism through which profits, largely obtained from government subsidies and shareholders, could be purloined without scrutiny. To establish the company, a moribund little corporation, the Pennsylvania Fiscal Agency, was acquired by Train and, as a kind of ironic tribute to the original French concept, given the pretentious name of Crédit Mobilier of America. By controlling Crédit Mobilier, Durant was effectively able to make contracts with himself at any price per mile he chose. The government subsidies were paid to Union Pacific, but since Crédit Mobilier overcharged for everything it did, the beneficiaries were its shareholders, a small coterie of Durant's friends rather than the far bigger group of Union Pacific investors. There was nothing subtle about the fraud, least of all the size of the dividends that Crédit Mobilier would soon be paying.

Having established Crédit Mobilier, Durant sped to Washington to buy politicians in order to ensure that even more money could be made through the construction of the railroad. He went there with a staggering $437,000 of Union Pacific funds in his bag, equivalent at today's prices to around $13 million, and doled out largesse to congressmen and senators to persuade them to pass another Pacific Railroad Act that offered better terms to the Union Pacific. According to Dee Brown, Durant "also spent a great deal more than that distributing Union Pacific stock to congressmen in exchange for their votes" and, it is thought, pocketed much of the original cash he took with him.[13] With the help of $18,000 (around $540,000 in today's money) spent entertaining congressmen at the sumptuous Willard's Hotel on Pennsylvania Avenue, Durant's little trip was highly successful.

The 1864 Pacific Railroad Act doubled the land grants available to twenty square miles for each mile of completed railroad, guaranteeing the railroads land equivalent to the states of Massachusetts, Rhode Island, and Vermont combined. Durant also invited Congressman Oakes Ames and his brother Oliver, who together owned a shovel-manufacturing business in Massachusetts, into his tight coterie of shareholders of Crédit Mobilier, which effectively became a license to print money.

With the new legislation safely passed, and the Civil War beginning to wind down, in late 1864 the Union Pacific needed to start laying tracks, as the company could begin claiming government subsidies only once forty miles had been completed. A few miles of track had started to be graded before Durant's trip to Washington, but setbacks for the Unionists in the war and Durant's departure resulted in the work being stopped. However, Durant had by now made the crucial appointment of a chief engineer, Peter Dey. He soon realized he had made a mistake, for Dey, like Judah, was guilty of the cardinal sin of honesty. The two men clashed over the contract for the first section of line, the hapless Dey having failed to realize that for Durant the whole enterprise was to enrich himself and his associates, irrespective of whether the railroad was built. Dey had obtained a quote from contractors for the first section of twenty-three miles out of Omaha at a cost of between $20,000 and $30,000 per mile, but was surprised to find that Durant had invited in another contractor, an Iowa politician of dubious integrity named Herbert Hoxie, who said that the work would cost $50,000 per mile, which, of course, would be paid by Union Pacific to Crédit Mobilier. Moreover, rather than using Dey's alignment of twenty-three miles, Durant opted for a new route—devised by a "consulting engineer," the dandyish Colonel Silas Seymour, who had been appointed over Dey's head—that was nine miles longer than Dey's, thanks to extra curves that had been designed solely to obtain more government subsidy. Dey, who was clearly not party to the Crédit Mobilier scam, could not accept either the route or the contract and in December 1864 tendered his resignation. Durant did not even grace his letter with a reply.

Durant, utterly unabashed, simply continued with the circuitous route (which would eventually be shortened to Dey's original alignment forty years later) at the higher estimate. Following tortuous progress in the first half of 1865, however, he realized that Seymour was not the man to drive the railroad forward and sought to replace him. Durant now made two key appointments that were to save the entire project. As chief engineer, he chose an old crony, a former Unionist general, Grenville Dodge, with whom he had made a fortune smuggling contraband cotton during the Civil War. Dodge might have obtained his position thanks to his lack of scruples and Durant's criminality, but that did not mean he was a bad engineer. On the contrary, Dodge not only was a successful soldier, but also had considerable prewar railroad experience as a surveyor and engineer on several midwestern railroads, including a spell on the Chicago & Rock Island, where, ironically, he had worked with Dey. Dodge had been Durant's first choice as chief engineer, but he had turned down the post to work on rebuilding railroads in the South, where there was more money to be made. He was well connected, having met Lincoln several times, and persuaded the president that Council Bluffs would be the right starting point for a railroad heading toward the Pacific. He was, however, "wild, nervous, and aggressive in temperament, constitutionally able to play the bully upon occasion," and therefore not an easy fellow to work with, but certainly the right man for the job.[14] Under Seymour, the line had inched forward at barely a mile a week, but with Dodge's arrival the construction of the railroad took on all the aspects of a military operation. At its peak it employed an army of ten thousand men supported by nearly as many draft animals, since there was little mechanization.

Durant's other appointment, the choice of the Casement brothers as main contractors, proved equally important. John Casement had been a colonel (and later a general) in the Union army, with a record of protecting his men in difficult situations, and had been recommended to Durant by General Sherman, who had invested money in the railroad and visited Omaha at Train's invitation to check on progress. Casement and his brother Daniel did not look like the sort of imposing characters that would be needed to control the huge army of men needed for such a project. They were just five feet four and five feet tall, respectively, but they were, in fact, an inspired choice. They adopted an almost Fordian approach of allocating tasks to specific gangs, which brought discipline to the ragbag of thousands of men on the work site.

The Casements were helped by the fact that during the Civil War, the entire country had been militarized. As the war was ending in 1865, thousands of uprooted men, both former soldiers and freed slaves, were wandering around America in search of work and headed west more in hope than expectation. By chance, therefore, the right type of workforce was available, men who were used to discipline, led by officers who understood engineering. As soldiers, they had absorbed strategy, tactics, and logistics. Given that factories were still few and far between in this preindustrialized America, the skills they had learned in war proved invaluable. The Irish, many of whom had worked on railroads back in the East, predominated, but there were large groups of Germans and Swedes also, many of whom were veterans of the separate brigades that had fought in the war.

The system devised by the Casements was ingenious and effective. To provide for the workers as they laid the track westward into lands where existing settlements became more and more sparse, the brothers devised a work train based on the model of the hospital cars used in the Civil War. The train initially had a dozen cars but grew longer as the project progressed, each with a specific purpose: one carried tools, another was a mobile blacksmith shop, a third had rough tables and a kitchen, and then there were various flatcars loaded with rails, spikes, bolts, and all the other paraphernalia needed to lay track. It was a self-sufficient small town on wheels that was, invariably, the first train to travel over each newly completed section. Behind the work train, there was a long line of boxcars with bunks in which the men took their meals and slept. The work train, of course, could not accommodate all the men on the job, and many stayed in temporary camps.

The workers themselves were organized by the Casements in a much more structured way than in any previous railroad construction. First, the surveyors would be sent ahead, leaving wooden markers to show the route, followed by the graders cutting through the hills and leveling the ground, making everything ready for the tracklayers, including building bridges and embankments (there were, incidentally, no tunnels on the Union Pacific until it reached the Rockies, thanks to the policy of avoiding expensive features by running the track along the contour lines wherever possible). The work was carried out entirely by hand with pickaxes and shovels—provided by Ames, of course—and the occasional stone obstacle was blown up with gunpowder. Then, according to Dee Brown, after the graders came "the main body of the army, placing the ties, laying the track, spiking down the rails, perfecting the alignment, ballasting, and dressing up and completing the road for immediate use." Next came the most skillful aspect of the work. The rails were brought up on a flatcar as far as the railhead and carried to the site, where they were dropped onto the ties and, according to a contemporary newspaper reporter, quickly laid: "Close behind the track-layers come the gaugers, the spikers and bolters. Three strokes to the spike, ten spikes to the rail, four hundred rails to the mile."[15] The newspaperman admired the way in which the monotonous work was carried out with such meticulousness and precision. Indeed, it had all the discipline of a factory that kept pace with the railhead.

Military discipline was not enough to spur on the work. Money was the real incentive that oiled the wheels of this massive operation. The Casements set a goal of one mile of track per day—compared with the mile per week previously achieved by the incompetent Seymour—and offered each tracklayer a pound of tobacco if the target was completed between dawn and sundown. Then, as the men's skills improved, the Casements offered three dollars, rather than the usual two, per day if the men could lay a mile and a half, and then, later, four dollars for two miles.

As a result of these cleverly calibrated incentives, and helped by the relatively easy terrain—this was, after all, sixteen-thousand-dollar-per-mile country—in October 1866 the railroad reached the crucial milestone of the 100th meridian, nearly 250 miles from Omaha. This was a critical landmark for the Union Pacific, as the original legislation had stipulated that the first railroad company to reach that point would be given the right to continue westward, and there were rivals, such as the Santa Fe, ready to pounce on any failings by either of the two railroads. Moreover, Congress had recently lifted the restriction previously imposed on the Union Pacific, which prevented the company from building beyond a point 150 miles east of the California border. With the lucrative land and subsidies available to the competing railroads, this effectively fired the starting pistol for a race across the great desert beyond the Rockies that, for the most part, was easy railroad-building territory.

The Union Pacific threw a big party to celebrate its achievement on the 100th meridian in the middle of the featureless Nebraska plain, with boiled trout à la Normande, quails on toast, and "escalloped oysters Louisiana style" on the menu. The only disappointment was that President Andrew Johnson failed to turn up. One thousand miles to the west, Charles Crocker and his Associates had rather more to worry about than absent presidents, as the Central was struggling with numerous difficulties, including the mountains, a shortage of labor, and a lack of cash. The 50-mile start that the Central Pacific had enjoyed when the first rails were laid out of Omaha by the Union Pacific was long gone, as progress through the Sierra Nevada was proving painfully slow.

First, the Central Pacific had to solve the problem of a chronic labor shortage. When work started, the war had not ended, but even when it did, few veterans wanted to travel all the way to the Pacific coast to work on a railroad, as it was much easier for them to reach the Union Pacific's work sites. Those men who did reach the West were more likely to be attracted by the mines, which paid more than the railroads. Crocker hit on the idea of importing labor from the endless supply available in China, but he had difficulty persuading his superintendent, James Harvey Strobridge, to take on Chinese workers. Strobridge was an old-fashioned contractor who wanted giant beef-eating Irish laborers, not, as he put it, "tiny rice-eaters" who looked too frail to wield a shovel. Crocker pointed out that they had built the world's biggest structure, the Great Wall of China, and that he could get away with paying them just over a dollar a day, half the rate earned by the rest of the labor force. Eventually, Strobridge was persuaded to take on a batch of fifty as a trial, and the experiment transformed the fortunes of the project. The Chinese proved to be the best workers Strobridge had ever employed, and he immediately sought to recruit more. Soon, virtually every able-bodied Chinese male in California had been hired by the railroad, and Stanford was organizing the recruitment of thousands more in Asia.

Crocker and Stanford were desperate to ensure that the Union Pacific would not be able to claim the whole of the easy territory in the deserts of Utah and Nevada; every mile of railroad completed by Dodge represented money that would be lost to the Central. The speed of construction now picked up, and by November 1866 the Central Pacific line had reached Cisco, almost a hundred miles from its starting point and nearly six thousand feet up in the mountains. Further tracklaying progress was prevented by heavy snowfalls, which had begun in October and continued for the next six months, creating drifts up to thirty feet deep that required loco- motives with a snowplow to clear the tracks. It was decided, however, that work on the twelve major tunnels required for the line to cross the Sierra Nevada would continue through the winter, the workers being protected from the elements once they were inside the tunnels. In one of the most remarkable episodes of the construction process, an army of eight thou- sand men was brought up the mountains to spend the winter in the tun- nels, working eight-hour shifts through the day and night in conditions that tested the whole enterprise to the extreme. A railhead was established at Cisco—where the weather conditions can be judged by the fact that to- day the town is a ski resort—and equipment to excavate the tunnels was hauled up the slopes of the crude wagon road on sledges. One can only guess what the atmosphere was like in the tunnels where the men worked and lived in air made fetid from their own sweat and filled with dust from the constant explosions and drilling needed to break through the rock. More snow falls in this area of mountains than in any part of the main landmass of the United States. Keeping the men supplied was a constant logistical nightmare.

Yet the plan worked. The scale of the operation can be illustrated by one telling statistic: Crocker spent more than $1 million on the black pow- der (gunpowder) that was used to blow holes into the rock, although to- ward the end of the project nitroglycerin, which was far more effective though more unstable and dangerous, was used occasionally. The constant explosions in the tunnels could prove deadly for those outside. There were numerous accidents, as the vibration and noise set off avalanches that sometimes buried whole work camps. One avalanche, near the Summit Tunnel, swept away twenty Chinese, whose bodies were found only after the spring thaw. Although no record was kept of the total death toll, sug- gesting a deplorable lack of care on the part of the company, estimates suggest that between five hundred and one thousand Chinese laborers perished on the Central Pacific.

On the Union Pacific, where conditions were easier and required less use of explosives, there were fewer deaths as a result of accidents. However, the workers faced a far greater danger from the violent conditions of the terrible temporary settlements that sprang up near their work sites. These notorious "Hell on Wheels" towns moved along with the tracks and became dens of iniquity, violent places where life was cheap, law enforcement was nonexistent, and disease caused by the unsanitary conditions claimed many more lives than accidents on the work sites. The first of these temporary towns had been North Platte, Nebraska, where the railroad stopped for the winter of 1866–1867. As Stephen E. Ambrose has described, it soon "bulged with gambling dens, houses of prostitution, taverns, music halls, hotels and an occasional restaurant." The residents were mostly workers waiting for warmer weather, with nothing to do but with a lot of spare cash burning holes in their pockets: "The chief entertainment came from getting drunk, getting laid, and losing all their money to gamblers."[16] Robbery was endemic and murder not uncommon, given that most of the men were veterans who were used to carrying firearms. According to one contemporary newspaper report, "Not a day passes but a dead body is found somewhere in the vicinity with pockets rifled of its contents." Charles Savage, a photographer, provided the most apt description when he said of Corinne, Utah, a town blessed with no fewer than eighty ladies of the night, that "it was all on the wrong side of the tracks."[17]

Although these accounts may sound exaggerated, their veracity is borne out by the fact that four times as many Union Pacific men were murdered in these towns than were killed in work-related accidents. Gun battles were commonplace, and the worst, in Laramie, Wyoming, during the final stages of construction, resulted in five deaths and fifteen injuries. The bosses of the Union Pacific did, at times, try to curb the lawlessness, but with equal brutality. When matters got out of hand in Julesburg, Colorado, where local gamblers had squatted on land belonging to the railroad, the Casements, supported by two hundred men, marched into town and ordered them to leave. Faced by their refusal to do so, John Casement simply instructed his men to start firing indiscriminately. When Dodge arrived later to see what had happened, Casement pointed to a row of graves and said, "General, they all died but bought peace. Julesburg has been quiet since."[18] In fact, Julesburg existed for only five months, and its only legacy was a cemetery with more than a hundred bodies.[19] These Hell on Wheels towns had no equivalent on the Central, as its mainly Chinese workforce was far more docile and disciplined, helped by the fact that they mostly favored the soporific drug of opium rather than alcohol.

By the spring of 1867, all the tunnels on the Central, except Summit Tunnel, had been finished. Crocker, though, decided to bypass the tunnel so that the race across the desert could begin in earnest. He set graders to work on the other side of the uncompleted Summit Tunnel, but his plan failed because, with no railroad support to transport the rails and ties, little progress was made in terms of laying tracks during the year. The Summit Tunnel was finally completed at the end of November 1867, and, to celebrate, seven hundred guests were carried up in a special train to a temporary terminus near the summit, where, after a formal ceremony, an enormous snowball fight broke out.

By the end of 1867, five years after the groundbreaking ceremony in Sacramento, only 131 miles of track had been laid by the Central, and even this section was not continuous because the climb up to Summit Tunnel remained uncompleted on both sides. Progress had been further hampered by the need to build no fewer than 40 miles of snowsheds, at considerable expense, to protect the track. These were essentially open barns with pitched roofs built over the railroad to prevent the tracks from being swept away by avalanches. Whereas snow was the main winter hazard, fire posed a serious risk to the sheds in the summer. Built, like the station structures, out of timber, they were horribly vulnerable to the wood-burning locomotives whose dramatic bulbous smokestacks did not stop the occasional emission of red-hot cinders.

Whereas the Union Pacific, laying track by the mile, was making vast amounts of money in bonds and land grants, until this point the Central had been continuously short of cash. Indeed, historians have struggled to explain how the company remained solvent given the lack of progress, the cost of labor and materials, and the corruption. But somehow the Central Pacific survived, thanks to the machinations of the four Associates and Crocker's refusal to bow to an unprecedented threat of industrial action from the Chinese workers who continued to receive barely a dollar a day.

The spring of 1868 was to be the turning point in the Central's fortunes. The tracklayers had reached the strategically placed town of Reno, Nevada, at the foot of the eastern side of the mountains that only came into being because of the railroad and was, in fact, named by Crocker at a ceremony in May 1868. As soon as the winter ice began to melt, Strobridge sent a team of men back up the Sierras to lay tracks on the 7-mile gap on the eastern slope of the mountain, completing the 154-mile continuous route between Reno and Sacramento. The first through train rumbled along the line in mid-June 1868. As if to demonstrate the scale of the achievement, its passengers had to wait near the summit while the Chinese workers cleared the tracks of snow. According to a local reporter on that epoch-making journey, the banks of snow were so close to the tracks that the cars scraped against them, bringing down lumps of ice. The completion of the route through the mountain was important in two respects. First, the Central Pacific was now entitled to claim the government subsidies, which began to flow into the company's coffers, greatly facilitated by the fact that inspectors made only the most cursory efforts to check that the work claimed for had been completed before sanctioning payment of the money. Second, the line could now be used to supply the work sites at the railhead, greatly improving the efficiency of the construction process.

Soon, the Central was averaging a mile of track a day—the kind of pace the Union Pacific had enjoyed on its easy stretches—by adopting some of its rival's methods. Now that the terrain was flat, the Central avoided any expensive engineering by keeping to the contour lines, even if that meant long detours and snakelike curves. After all, payment was by the mile, and no one had specified the route. Since now the cost per mile was far less than the subsidies paid by the government, it was almost as if such—quite literal—chicanery had been deliberately built into the legislation. In subsequent years, fortunes would have to be spent by the rail companies on realigning the track, but that was of no concern to the four Associates.

Another of the Union Pacific's ideas copied by the Central was the work train. Strobridge put together a similar contrivance, equipped with sleeping and dining accommodation, together with shops for carpenters and the men erecting the railroad's inseparable companion, the telegraph lines. Strobridge ensured that construction of the latter kept pace with the track-laying to ensure he could wire progress to Sacramento every evening. The best car was reserved for Mrs. Strobridge, who kept it so neat and homely that a newspaperman dubbed her "the heroine of the Central Pacific" and suggested that her mobile home was the equal of any back in San Francisco. Strobridge's effort, however, came nowhere near to matching later versions of the Casements' work train, which, toward the end of the project, comprised no fewer than eighty cars. A stunning reflection of the growing flexibility of the railroads, it included a bakery car, a complete feed store and saddle shop, a combined telegraph and payroll car, and even a butcher's car kept filled with fresh beef from a herd driven alongside the train as it progressed westward.

Supplied by Strobridge's trains, which echoed the modern "just-in-time" style of logistics, there was nothing to stop the Central from speeding across the Nevada landscape, memorably described by Dee Brown as "five hundred miles of white alkali beds burned by the sun, waterless, treeless, bare of vegetation except for patches of gray sagebrush and stunted junipers." The California pioneers in their wagon trains had dreaded crossing this desert, which proved fatal for many of them, but for the railroad builders, it was an opportunity for easy money at thirty-two thousand dollars per mile from the taxpayer. So eager were the Associates to cash in on this potential bonanza that they sent surveyors several hundred miles east to Wyoming, "where they encountered the red-flag markers and theodolites of the equally eager Union Pacific surveyors."[20] Both parties sent spies to assess progress, but these were easily identified and regaled with tall tales to take back to their masters.

The desperation of both sides to lay as much track as possible led in 1868 to one of the most bizarre episodes in the history of American railroads, a vivid demonstration of how the project was animated by competition rather than cooperation. Here an unlikely religious sect, the Mormons, enters the story, as their leader, Brigham Young, had the chutzpah to sign up as a contractor with both railroads. First, he agreed with Dodge to grade a route across Utah and back eastward through to Wyoming. However, given the sparse population, the Mormon settlers who had chosen Utah as their God-given land represented the only significant group of labor, and now Leland Stanford traveled to Utah to persuade Young to grade a similar route for the Central Pacific. Young took on this second role unabashedly, having been promised that his Mormon crew would be paid double the wages of the Chinese workers. Therefore, during the autumn of 1868, two separate crews of Mormons prepared separate parallel routes across Utah, one of which would never be used, with both bills ultimately being met by the unfortunate American taxpayer. The Union Pacific had its own mountain range, the Rockies, to contend with. In April 1868 its rails reached the highest point in the whole enterprise. Sherman Summit—named after General Sherman in gratitude for his efforts in protecting the railroad against Native American attacks—was, at 8,242 feet above sea level, a full 1,000 feet higher than the Central's Summit Tunnel in the Sierras, a fact that Dodge never tired of pointing out to Crocker. At this stage, too, the company was completing its most impressive engineering project, the bridge across Dale Creek, Wyoming, 650 feet long and 130 feet high, the largest trestlework on the line and a flimsy structure that swayed alarmingly in the wind and received sanction from the government inspectors only after the engineers lashed it down with cables. This jerry-built bridge was, perhaps, illustrative of how speed above all else was the determining factor in many of the engineering decisions made by both companies during construction, as it had to be replaced by an iron structure just a year after the opening of the line.

In one key respect, the Central's bosses were cannier than their Union Pacific rivals, and that was the way in which they dealt with the Native Americans. The relationship between Native Americans and the iron horse had, quite understandably, been a difficult one, made even harder by the eagerness of some settlers, and, indeed, their politicians, to use any attack as an excuse to launch a genocidal campaign. The recent "Indian wars" had seen massacres carried out by both sides—though the Native American death toll was far greater—and Durant and Dodge may have felt they had little choice but to arm their men in the expectation of attacks from Native Americans. They were, however, unnecessarily aggressive in their approach and made no effort to conciliate the local tribes. The construction of the railroads was, as the best chronicler of the transcontinental rightly suggests, "the Native Americans' story, too, for their territory was breached and their way of life was an impediment and they were brutally, calculatedly shunted aside."[21] This was frontier country where there were strong, at times even blurred, links between the military and railroad men, and both groups were keen on "disposing of the Indian menace." The relationship between the military and the railroads was embodied in the person of John Evans, who as governor of Colorado had encouraged genocide, culminating in the massacre of more than one hundred Cheyenne, mostly women and children, at

Sand Creek in 1864. Despite his clear responsibility for the bad relations between Native Americans and the settlers, he was too useful as a local politician not to be offered a lucrative directorship with the Union Pacific. Such atrocities as Sand Creek inevitably provoked a response from the Native Americans that resulted in numerous attacks and hampered progress on the railroad. Dodge ensured that arms were always available to his men, but nevertheless railroad employees, especially surveyors who operated far from the main work sites, were sometimes killed.

It was, in fact, the men working on the Kansas Pacific, which was being built simultaneously with the Union Pacific, who bore the brunt of Indian attacks, and these became the origin of the myriad tales of cowboys and Indians with which generations of children would be regaled. The Kansas Pacific, also known as the Union Pacific Eastern Division, was initially sanctioned by Congress as part of the original Pacific Railroad Act with the same generous land grants and was envisaged as a branch line off the Union Pacific, connecting Nebraska with Kansas. However, the route was changed, and, rather than heading north up to Nebraska from Fort Riley in western Kansas, the line followed the path of the Smoky Hill River and then on to Denver, Colorado, taking it through the main hunting country of several tribes of Sioux, Arapaho, and Cheyenne. The small town of Abilene, Kansas, became a crucial transfer point where herds of cattle, driven up what became known as the Chisholm Trail from Texas, were loaded onto trains heading for the growing stockyards of Chicago. Abilene and similar towns on the Kansas Pacific Railroad quickly became permanent versions of the lawless Hell on Wheels towns of the Union Pacific, and their seedy saloons were the haunts of the drovers who soon became known as "cowboys." Sporadic exchanges of gunfire broke out along the Chisholm Trail as the cowboys drove their cattle across Native American land. It was the railroad, though, that bore the brunt of Native American antagonism, and as the iron horse proceeded westward, they directed their fire against it. They hated this "snorting, whistling monster" that violated their territory and drove away the game on which their very survival depended.[22] When the tracks reached the plains west of Salina, nearly halfway between Kansas City and the Colorado state boundary, the Indians began to attack in a more concerted way. By the spring of 1867, Indian hunting parties were regularly attacking railroad workers' camps, and the graders needed military protection. General Sherman, who was in command of military forces in the West, had devised a plan to drive Native Americans away from the route of the railroad to create a large swath of "no-man's-land." With the military burning tepee villages and killing indiscriminately, a protracted and bloody war broke out in the Great Plains on both sides of the Kansas Pacific.

The tracks became a forbidden area for Native Americans, and the more bloodthirsty military commanders simply ordered the killing of any found near the railroad. The skirmishes had little of the romance of the westerns that immortalized them but rather were short, bloody battles that left many dead and maimed on both sides. Dee Brown suggests it was the railroad workers, often unarmed, who bore the brunt of the attacks, but their story has largely been left untold: "A few hundred railroad workers in Kansas and Nebraska probably took more punishment from Indians than did all the thousands of cowboys from Texas to Montana."[23] The reality of the situation is hard to extract from the myths and tales that have formed the huge canon of western films and books.

The Indians at times managed to derail trains, but they could never inflict permanent damage on the iron road. Nevertheless, they aroused such fear that the Kansas Pacific took to distributing guns to its passengers. As the military resistance on the Kansas Pacific intensified, groups of Indian raiders shifted their operations to the Union Pacific, but they achieved only one notable success, the ambush at Plum Creek in August 1867. A team of repair workers, including a Briton, William Thompson, was sent to Plum Creek in Nebraska on a handcar to investigate a break in the line. There had not been any Indian activity in the area, so they were taken by surprise when they were ambushed by a group of Cheyenne who had cut the telegraph wires as well as ripped up a section of track. Thompson's four colleagues were killed instantly, and he was shot, knocked to the ground, and scalped. He survived by playing dead and watched helplessly as the following train was derailed and plunged down the embankment, killing the two-man crew. Although the pain from his skull was excruciating, Thompson took advantage of the Cheyennes' interest in the loot from the freight wagons to escape. Picking up his scalp, which they had dropped, he hid for a while and then, remarkably, jogged back the fifteen miles along the track to Willow Island, the nearest station. He had kept his scalp in a bucket of water, hoping that a doctor would be able to stitch it back, but his effort was to no avail, and it resides today as a gruesome relic in the Union Pacific Museum in Council Bluffs, Nebraska. The Plum Creek attack hardened the attitude of the Union Pacific toward the Native Americans, and General Sherman redoubled his attacks to clear the swath of land needed for the railroad. Inevitably, the military and the railroads prevailed, although it would take a couple of decades before the Native Americans were finally suppressed.

In contrast to the Union Pacific, the Central adopted a much more conciliatory approach to the Native Americans. There were, admittedly, fewer of them on their territory, but they could have been equally troublesome had the same aggressive attitude prevailed. Instead, the Central made deals with them, offering the chiefs passes to ride on the trains and allowing the rest to ride free on the freight cars whenever they wanted. The Central even employed both male and female Native Americans alongside the Chinese and noted that "the women usually outdid the men in handling crowbars and sledgehammers."[24]

By the end of 1868, it was clear that the transcontinental would be completed the following year, far earlier than originally envisaged. The only doubt remained about precisely where the two railroads would meet. By the beginning of 1869, the Central Pacific had reached Carlin, Nevada, nearly 450 miles from Sacramento, whereas the Union Pacific's rails stretched nearly 1,000 miles west of Omaha to Evanston, Wyoming.

This remarkably rapid progress had not gone unnoticed. The story of the transcontinental was already becoming the stuff of legends, which it remains today. All America was watching, excited and eager for a conclusion. In the autumn of 1868, swarms of newspaper reporters began arriving from the East, dispatching daily bulletins from the front, as if it were a war zone, with details of every mile of track laid and tales of the derring-do of the army of laborers. Never before had the construction of a railroad line become an issue of such moment. The corruption that underlay its building would be exposed later, but for the time being, nothing was allowed to get in the way of this epic achievement.

The great race, which had been launched a year previously, was now being fought in earnest. At the start of the year, the gap between the two railroads was just 400 miles, and, thanks to the crazy contest across the desert between the two railroads, much of the intervening section had been graded in parallel lines by the Mormon contractors, who now departed the scene as the main railheads reached Utah. Although the location of the obvious meeting point was pretty clear to the engineers of both railroads, their acquisitive employers continued to work on their separate routes in an attempt to maximize their mileage. The ultimate absurdity was in the Promontory Range, where the Central Pacific line crossed a deep valley on a large embankment, only for the Union Pacific to ford it with a trestle bridge just fifty yards away. The proximity of the two parties inevitably led to hostility. At one point the Irish of the Union blasted away rocks without warning their Chinese rivals above, several of whom were hurt by flying debris. The Chinese promptly retaliated by deliberately cascading rocks down the slope, burying several Irish workers. Fortunately, the defiance of the Chinese, whom the Irish, like Strobridge before them, had underestimated, prompted a truce before these antics cost any lives.

The precise location of the meeting point was sorted out not in the desert of Utah but half a continent away, in Congress. There, another type of war was being fought by representatives of the railroads lobbying their respective friends. Whereas Huntington of the Central had the ear of the incumbent president, Andrew Johnson, Dodge and Durant were close to president-elect Ulysses S. Grant, the former Civil War general, who as the Republican candidate had visited the Union's work site shortly before his victory in the 1868 election. The decision he made soon after he took office in March 1869 was a fair compromise: he decreed that the railroads should be joined six miles west of Ogden, at Promontory Point in Utah. For all its lofty place in American folklore, Promontory was just a temporary town, a street of tents and false-fronted wooden shacks stretching a few yards from the railroad line, set in a bleak, waterless basin surrounded on three sides by mountains. It was just over 1,000 miles from Omaha and just under 750 miles from Sacramento, which showed that the Union Pacific had won the race, building a third more track than the Central.

If the ceremony was all about PR, so was a stunt organized a few days before the ceremony by Crocker, who had taunted Durant by suggesting that 10 miles of track could be laid in a day. Durant responded by wagering $10,000 that it could not be done, and Crocker and Strobridge made elaborate preparations to ensure all the equipment was in place. A crew of eight men, whose names—which betrayed their Irish origins—have been immortalized in the history books, was handpicked to carry and spike the rails. In twelve hours, a full working day, they had passed the 10-mile point by 50 feet, and Crocker could claim the money, though Dodge, who viewed the proceedings, complained it was a con because so much preparation had been undertaken beforehand.

The eventual meeting of the two railroads took place on May 10, 1869, a couple of days later than originally planned. The reason for the delay, according to Durant, was that a section of the Union Pacific's track had been washed out in a rainstorm, but Dee Brown, the chronicler of the railroads of the West, says this was a cover story for a rather better tale that almost prevented the ceremony from taking place: "On May 6, when the Union Pacific special [carrying VIPs from the East for the ceremony] pulled into Piedmont, Wyoming, an armed mob of several hundred railroad workmen surrounded Durant's private car, switched it onto a side-track and chained the wheels to the rails."[25] The workers were protesting about their overdue wages, and their action is thought to have been supported by Brigham Young, who was also owed considerable sums for his grading contract. The involvement of Young, a powerful local man, would explain why the military failed to respond to Durant's pleas to be released, and eventually he had to wire to New York for the money to be paid. The amount Durant's kidnappers managed to extract from him remains unknown, though some estimates suggest as much as $235,000. Meanwhile, the Casements were forced to entertain Stanford and the other Central dignitaries with a trip along the line to Ogden, Utah, on a train stocked with "a beautiful collation and oceans of champagne," an expense that would not have pleased the hapless Durant, either.

On the big day, Stanford and Durant shared the duties of the traditional ceremony of knocking in the last two spikes. Even this historic demonstration of the Central and the Union finally cooperating with one another was marred by the collective incompetence of the two company heads, who together missed the spikes with their first attempt at wielding the sledgehammer. The ceremony, in truth, was a pretty confused affair. Few witnesses were able to hear the speeches, and, with no cordon around the main players, it was impossible for onlookers to see what was happening. Nevertheless, "oratory and whisky flowed in almost equal measure," and not just in Utah.[26] Across America, a large proportion of the 40 million population, alerted by telegraph, celebrated. In Chicago, a seven-mile-long parade jammed the city streets, while in New York a hundred-gun salute was fired in City Hall Park and Wall Street business was suspended for the day. Across the newly connected continent in San Francisco, the party carried on well into the night. In Sacramento, birthplace of the Central, thirty locomotives that had been specially brought together were steamed up to whistle out a celebratory but tuneless concert.

After the golden spikes had been hammered in and the champagne drunk, there remained a rather thorny question: What, precisely, had all this effort been for? Certainly not to allow people to travel from one coast to another, the province of the affluent, of immigrants seeking a better life and occasional adventurous travelers like Robert Louis Stevenson (see Chapter 7), a traffic that was by no means able to justify the expense or even pay for the operating costs.

There are two ways of viewing such grand schemes of transportation infrastructure. Some are built to meet an existing need, filling an acknowledged gap, such as the world's first major railroad line, which connected the already busy towns of Liverpool and Manchester. Or they are constructed to connect undeveloped regions as a way of attracting settlers and stimulating economic development. Almost all major railroad lines designed for passengers fall into one of these categories, and there is no doubt that it was the latter description that befitted the transcontinental. This type of project, however, invariably requires government support and usually a lot of it. There was no potential for immediate profit from the transcontinental, given the enormous distances it covered and the lack of local traffic. Without government subsidies, it would never have been possible to build the line, but, of course, that is no excuse for so much taxpayers' money ending up in the promoters' pockets.

In fact, the various supporters of the project had been divided over what the railroad was actually for. There was no shortage of proffered reasons. Asa Whitney had harbored the fanciful dream of exploiting the vast markets of Asia;[27] the Wisconsin settlers wanted military protection from the "Indian

menace," despite the fact that it was the railroad that provoked the worst attacks from Native Americans; then there was the vague notion that the line
would open up the West for European settlers, but there was no certainty
that they would come. The truth is that there was no clear purpose: "For all
the fanfare that accompanied the building of the first Transcontinental, and
for all the romantic nonsense that has been written about it since, the importance of this accomplishment for many years was mainly psychological."[28]

There was no cunning plan. The building of the transcontinental was
like such feats of exploration and endurance as the conquest of Everest or
the journey to the poles, often undertaken simply because "it's there." The
most coherent of the various motives, but still a vague one, was the notion
of conquering the West, and that was what was celebrated at Promontory
Point on the day the last spike was hammered in. The West was a movable
feast drummed up by the early railroad promoters for whom it meant west
of wherever they happened to be or even just anywhere sparsely populated,
such as, oddly, in one example of rail promotion, northern Vermont. The
West was seen as a land of plenty, a biblical vision that was America's mani-
fest destiny. The first editor of the *American Railroad Journal*, D. Kimball
Minor, had repeatedly used precisely that description in his journal, calling
the land between the Great Lakes and the Rockies "the garden of the world."
The West was to be America's empire, "a metaphor that emphasized fertil-
ity, the potential richness that lay locked in the untapped western regions."[29]
By midcentury "the West" had come to mean the lands west of the Mississippi, but that was still a pretty imprecise concept. Before the railroads,
there had been some sparse settlement in the West, mostly by newly arrived
Spanish-speaking immigrants, but the lack of transportation meant that
they could only eke out a life of subsistence. The prairies were not blessed
with great forests out of which homes and fences could be built, game was
sparse once the vast herds of buffalo had been wiped out by settlers with
guns, the climate was harsh, and much of the land was not particularly fertile. The stagecoaches, wagon trains, and mail companies like the Pony Express had all struggled to provide any kind of regular connection with the
East for these sparsely populated areas.

The railroad, therefore, made all the difference, enabling a journey that
would have taken six months to be completed in just a few days. But settle-

ment remained a slow process and did not really intensify until a couple of decades after Stanford and Durant's brief moment of collaboration. It was not until other railroads followed the first transcontinental, blessed with land grants that helped them attract investors who now felt a little more confident about the potential for making money out of western railroads, that the population of the West began to expand rapidly. As a result, it would be many years before the first transcontinental and its various successors were intensively used. And, oddly, they would hardly ever be used to carry passengers from ocean to ocean. Technically, the coast-to-coast journey by railroad was not possible until the bridge over the Missouri was completed in 1872, finally relieving passengers of the need to transfer to a rickety old ferry. But even then Chicago would remain a break for most travelers, for which they were grateful, given the primitive conditions on the trains. The very name *transcontinental*, therefore, is a misnomer—despite its widespread use and the celebration its construction engendered—as there has never been a single railroad company stretching from East Coast to West.[30] Richard White brilliantly encapsulates the contradictions within the transcontinental project: "The very term 'transcontinental' communicated the hubris and power of a new technology that wrapped the continent in iron and steel bands . . . for the transcontinentals did not really span the continent."[31]

None of this is to deny the amazing achievement of the construction of the first transcontinental. Sure, there was corruption, cheating, purloining of government funds, reckless building practices, and astonishing greed—in short, a total lack of principles and scruples shown by the majority of the key players. The result, however, was to enable America to be governable as a single nation and to realize the dream of a single country stretching from coast to coast, unlike in South America, where history and geography were so different and resulted in a patchwork of nation-states that were weaker both politically and economically than their northern counterpart. The United States would not have become a united nation without the railroad in general and the transcontinental in particular. That is why the story of the building of the transcontinental and the ceremony at Promontory Point have assumed such a prominent place in American history, spawning countless books and articles and, in a way, skewing the history of American railroads by placing too much emphasis on the building of this one line.

The initial legacy of the first transcontinental, however, was a rather less happy one. Long before the last spike had been hammered in, the allegations of corrupt practices began to emerge, but their extent only really came to the fore after the euphoria of the celebrations had abated. Mostly, attention focused on the Union Pacific, probably because its greater proximity to the East gave journalists easier access as well as making it more newsworthy. Not that the business practices of the owners of the Central Pacific were any less scandalous. According to a government commission, the four Associates on the Central were reckoned to have pocketed $63 million and obtained 9 million acres of land between them, hardly trivial sums. Maybe it was the sheer nakedness of the Crédit Mobilier scam that led to its arrangements with the Union Pacific being the prime focus of public scrutiny. Perhaps, too, it was the fact that a none too mysterious fire destroyed the Central's financial records soon after the completion of the railroad, making it difficult to work out precisely how the money had been purloined. More likely, it was because the shares in the Central's construction company were held by a very small group consisting of the four Associates and a few colleagues, whereas Crédit Mobilier shares had been distributed widely to politicians and to prominent businessmen as bribes. The anger felt by many Americans at the extent of the corruption of the railroad magnates was mitigated by a feeling that however scurrilous these rascals were, they had completed a Herculean enterprise that was to have a tremendously beneficial impact on the nation. Stanford, Durant, and their cronies may have been in it for the money, but they did get the railroad built when it would, at numerous points, have been all too easy to have abandoned the enterprise. Giving up, though, would not have been an attractive option. Not only would there no longer have been the prospect of fortunes to be made, but it would, too, have attracted the wrath of politicians and most likely the attentions of the justice system, with the distinct possibility of jail sentences for the miscreants. Their motives, therefore, were hardly altruistic. Indeed, most historians concur with George H. Douglas, who wrote in his account of the American railroads that after the Civil War, "Men of the better sort were crowded from the stage, while crude, unprincipled robber barons came into the ascendancy. If such men had also been men of vision or men of superlative technical skill, there might have been sufficient justification for them, but with few exceptions, although bold and audacious, they were inept and unsuited to the task that lay before them."[32]

If the four Associates of the Central really did cream off $63 million from their enterprise, on the face of it they seemed to have done better than the good Doctor Durant. However, Crédit Mobilier was not his only scam. Reputedly, Durant took 10 percent of every contract and received kickbacks from subcontractors who undertook excess work on his instructions in order to earn extra and then paid him a percentage. As far as Crédit Mobilier was concerned, it would have taken no great investigative skill to spot that something was amiss when, in December 1867, the company paid out the equivalent of 100 percent dividends to its small coterie of investors, as the Union Pacific was stumbling from crisis to crisis. Yet despite the occasional story in the newspapers, the plundering continued unabated. During 1868, Crédit Mobilier paid out no fewer than five sets of dividends, by which time it had disbursed a total of three times the amount investors had contributed, whereas the Union Pacific struggled to pay its bills and was $6 million in debt. Indeed, the Union Pacific was in such a bad state during the final year before completion of the railroad that a notorious financial speculator, Jim Fisk, tried repeatedly but unsuccessfully to wrest control of the company from Durant, probably in the hope that he would be able to get his hands on some of the ill-gotten gains. Had Fisk enjoyed a more honest reputation, his efforts might have led to more attention being paid to the financial irregularities at the heart of the relationship between Crédit Mobilier and the Union Pacific, but the affair evaporated in the heady atmosphere of the run-up to the Promontory Point ceremony. It was not until 1872, an election year, that the Crédit Mobilier scandal hit the headlines, starting with a story in the *New York Sun* under the bold headline "The King of Frauds: How the Crédit Mobilier Bought Its Way Through Congress." The six months of congressional hearings that ensued focused more on the involvement of politicians than on the likes of Durant and Dodge. Their principal target was the shovel manufacturer Congressman Oakes Ames, who had distributed shares to some of his fellow members of Congress. Even Vice President Schuyler Colfax and future president James A. Garfield were caught up in the scandal. Colfax was replaced on the Republican ticket for the 1872 election by another, cleaner, candidate, but Garfield denied the charges and went on to be elected president in 1880. The Crédit Mobilier scandal would rumble on for many years and was one of the main catalysts for the antipathy toward the railroads that grew in the postwar period and would do them so much damage. In the words of Keith L. Bryant Jr., "The financing of the Central Pacific and Union Pacific railroads produced scandals that rocked the industry for 50 years."[33]

6

RAILROADS TO
EVERYWHERE

The first transcontinental stimulated a rapid growth of railroads in the West that was part of a wider nationwide expansion in the network far beyond the scale of anything that had gone before. After the war, there was no brake on the growth of the railroads in the newly reunited nation, which, during the 1870s and 1880s, a period dubbed the Gilded Age by Mark Twain, grew faster than at any other time in its history. The route mileage of the railroads doubled between 1865 and 1873 and, after a brief lull caused by the financial panic that year, would double again by 1887, reaching nearly 164,000 miles by the end of the decade. These impressive figures do not take into account the large amount of reconstruction work on the wrecked railroads of the South or the improvements carried out on older parts of the network.

To put this achievement into perspective, the British railroad network in its heyday before the First World War had just under 20,000 route miles. Even the whole of western Europe had fewer miles of railroad than America. Or to express it another way, on average the Americans built an additional 15 miles of railroad every day in the two decades up to 1890. The labor force required for such a massive scale of construction can only be guessed at, as there is no reliable source of figures, but clearly would have numbered tens of thousands. Sure, fewer men were required than before because of technical developments. The invention of dynamite and the gradual adoption of steam-powered pile drivers and shovels improved the efficiency with which railroads were built, but there was still a considerable need for sheer muscle power, and the workforce employed by the railroads represented a substantial proportion of manpower in a country whose population reached only 50 million in the middle of this period. Railroad labor mostly consisted of recent immigrants, especially Irish, and later Italians, though on several of the western projects large numbers of Chinese were hired. As with the Union Pacific, there were, too, many veterans of the Civil War who, inculcated with military discipline and sometimes even engineering skills, made ideal rail construction workers, as they had also proved on the Union Pacific.

There was a symbiotic relationship between the exceptionally rapid expansion of the railroads and the wider changes occurring in American society. The nation was industrializing rapidly, with the railroads as the catalyst. However, the pattern of growth contrasted markedly between the regions, as they were in different stages of economic development. The East already boasted a well-developed network. In the West with its vast expanses served only, in the early years of this period, by the transcontinental line, the promotion of railroads was principally designed to encourage settlement. In the South, for the first decade or so after the Civil War, most effort was focused on the postwar Reconstruction, and it was not until the withdrawal of the last Union troops in 1877 that business really picked up and the South began the process of connecting its local lines with the major systems of the North and West. Various new lines began to be added to the network in the 1880s, the peak decade for railroad construction in the South, as in the rest of the United States.

The Southern railroad network had been devastated by the war: "With ruined cities, and a much poorer and smaller population than the North, the South found it difficult to rebuild railroads."[1] In the early postwar years, numerous short lines were rebuilt, financed by the bonds being issued freely by the new administrations of the states, which were now run by a combination of Northern whites and some freed blacks who briefly dominated local government in the South. But, as before the war, the rail network still consisted mainly of short lines with few connections. Although by the end of the 1860s every state in the South had some railroad track in working condition, and on the map the South appeared to have something resembling a coherent network, in practice it was still a patchy, disconnected system offering a primitive level of service likened by experienced travelers to a journey in the North on the early railroads of the 1840s. Longer journeys in the South required numerous changes of train, and on most lines there was only one scheduled passenger train a day, with perhaps an additional one carrying mail.

Indeed, the postal and rail services throughout the United States had long been intertwined. The first trains to carry letters had been on the Camden & Amboy in New Jersey as early as 1832, and six years later Congress designated all railroads as "post roads," which qualified them for the carriage of mail. After the war, railroad post offices—specially designed coaches in which postal workers sorted mail—became commonplace. These coaches were equipped with ingenious openings and chutes that allowed mail to be collected from hooks by the side of the track without the train having to stop. To drop off mail, there was the rather less sophisticated method of throwing the bag out of the train. Letters and parcels developed into an important part of the economics of many railroad companies, nowhere more so than in the South, where few people could afford to travel by train. The southern railroads remained much more expensive than those in the North due to the paucity of passengers, with travelers in the South paying around six cents per mile, twice the rate of average fares in the North. Mail carriage was thus particularly important in maintaining the solvency of many southern railroads and was often carried in wagons attached to passenger trains, which made for infuriatingly slow journeys because the mail trains, unlike the railroad post offices, stopped at every station. As there was no food service on these trains, a passenger could go all day without a meal, and, worse, trains would not infrequently break down for lengthy periods, far from any hotel.

Travel on the southern trains in the immediate postwar period was not very different from travel in the supposedly wilder West and probably even more perilous. Badly laid track led to frequent derailments, and the rickety-looking trestle bridges were not for the fainthearted. On the lower ones, built over minor creeks, the weight of the train could make the foundations sink, causing water to lap over the track. It was not unknown for the foundations to give way completely, sending the coaches into the creek. There were dangers inside the trains, too. Nimrod Bell, a conductor for various southern railroads of the time who wrote about his experiences, says

he frequently carried a gun and had to resort to hitting argumentative passengers and even crew with a stick.[2] At one point, a fellow crew member, a
mail agent, was shot by a sniper from nearby woods, and in another incident Bell had to hold a number of black men at bay with his gun as they
were insisting on traveling to Chattanooga without paying the fare. The
tense relationship between the races and immigrant groups—Irish and
Chinese as well as black and white—frequently led to fights and brawls that
the conductor had to sort out.

The South still lacked any equivalent of the big east-west railroad systems in the North, which had consolidated their position in the postwar
period. There were few through services, since the state line invariably
marked the border between different companies, which remained state-
sponsored enterprises and were therefore confined to one state. And any
change of train might entail a long wait, as connections were not synchro-
nized. The Virginia & Tennessee, for example, had 204 miles of track but
operated just one scheduled passenger train a day, making a lengthy wait
almost inevitable for connecting travelers. Even if through routes were advertised, as when a group of southern short lines cooperated to provide the
"Great Southern Mail Route," journeys were painfully slow. This service
was, in fact, anything but "great": it took four or five days to cover the 1,200
miles between Mobile, Alabama, and New York City because of the need to
change trains.

The only two lines in the South that could lay any claim to trunk status
were the Louisville & Nashville and the Mobile & Ohio, both of which followed a north-south route from the Ohio River to the Gulf of Mexico. The
hub of the southern rail system remained Tennessee and Kentucky, and
lines radiated from these states to all the Atlantic ports. The South, in
other words, was still linked with the outside world rather than the rest of
the country, and it was not until the 1880s that the railroad system began
to improve connections with the North: "This long delay in uniting the
two rail systems persisted despite efforts by Northern bankers and investors to rebuild the Southern railroads in such a way that they complemented the interests of the major Northern roads."[3]

The focus on the South by northern interests was by no means benign,
nor motivated by philanthropy. The weak financial condition of the south-

ern railroads left them vulnerable to precisely the type of northern profiteers whose ambitions had helped provoke the South into war. The expression *carpetbagger* was born, to describe these northern adventurers looking to make a lucrative career in the southern states.[4] There was certainly no shortage of sharp-eyed Yankees trying to profit from the Reconstruction by promising to undertake repairs or rebuilding work on the southern railroads, much of which was carried out to a low standard or, worse, never even completed, though it had been paid for.

Northerners also traveled south to swallow up ailing railroads on the cheap. Bankers and investors from New York and Boston who had funded many developments in the North and the Far West now reckoned that the best profits could be made from the Reconstruction of the South and bought up southern railroad company shares and state bonds cheaply to sell, at a profit of course, in the Northeast and even Europe. The carpetbaggers, though, often lost their shirts or at least those of their backers. The railroads in the South were unable to earn the profits they needed to repay the loans they had raised from both the private banks and the states to build or reconstruct them. This was partly a result of the low number of passengers, but it was also due to the sheer scale of the railroad boom: "[The collapse of many railroads] was caused in part by building more railroads than any town or state would ever need—in order to make money on financial speculation, without regard for the future usefulness of each line." This was often the case during periods of railroad boom—called railroad manias—both in the United States and, indeed, in other parts of the world. A kind of self-perpetuating madness would engulf potential investors, who would pour money into ever more dubious schemes. In fact, in the words of Sarah H. Gordon, "looked at from both business and personal perspectives, the efforts of Northern investors appear not only self-interested but unsuccessful."[5] In particular, they subsequently lost much of the money they had invested in the panic of 1873 and the ensuing downturn.

These failures took place despite the fact that there was no shortage of low-paid, or even free, labor available for railroad companies in the South, enabling lines to be built on the cheap. Slavery may have notionally been ended by the Civil War, but the railroads took advantage of a corrupt judicial and prison system to obtain large amounts of poorly remunerated labor for their construction work. The southern railroad boom in the quarter century after the Civil War would not have been possible without what effectively amounted to a massive state subsidy through the provision of near-free labor, which was overwhelmingly black. Theodore Kornweibel Jr. has no doubt that it was a deliberate policy of the judicial and political systems to create a cheap labor force that worked under such harshly punitive conditions that were often worse than those endured in the prewar days of slavery: "From Reconstruction into the early 1900s, southern courts purposefully convicted large numbers of blacks—many for minor property crime—and sentenced them to lengthy prison (not jail) terms to ensure that railroads and railroad construction companies . . . could obtain cheap labor from the state." Under the convict-lease system whereby these prisoners were "rented out" to railroad companies and others to carry out demanding physical work, the states were relieved of the need to pay for the upkeep of their prisoners, while the companies who "employed" them obtained cheap labor. As Kornweibel suggests, the convict system "replicated slavery but with an earlier death sentence."[6]

The contractors who took on the convicts were often well connected politically, sometimes being the very politicians who created the system. Young blacks were literally railroaded straight from local courtrooms to work camps on the railroads and, indeed, mines and plantations. Kornweibel cites an example: "Of the 30 unfortunates sent to help build the state-owned Western North Carolina Railroad in January 1879, 24 were convicted of larceny." That effectively meant theft, defined as taking from a person, often of a small amount—*mugging* in modern parlance—rather than robbery, and would earn the defendant a sentence of up to fifteen years. Not that they were likely to live that long. Convicts were, in fact, cheaper than slaves, who had been hired from owners before emancipation for much greater sums than the three dollars per month that, for example, the Greenwood & Augusta paid in the 1870s. Moreover, the railroads were even less concerned about the welfare of the convicts than the plantation owners had been about their slaves: "Its workers, who labored in chains, were underfed, poorly housed, and medically neglected." On the Greenwood & Augusta, almost half of the 265 prisoners working on the line died, but there were always more to replace them. On some other railroads, nothing was paid for convict labor. Although the contractors were required to feed and house the prisoners, the meager rations were usually insufficient for the hard labor they were required to perform, and they were often housed in thin tents. Death came easily, frequently, and in many forms: accidents were common, disease endemic, and violence routine. In Alabama, which, according to Kornweibel, "set the record for barbarity," in the mid-1880s, convicts survived on average just three years, and one in ten perished within the first four months. Florida was hardly better: a commander of various Florida convict camps, J. C. Powell, who later wrote about the system, described how one group was sent into the tropical marshes with no provision for shelter or even food and forced to scavenge to keep alive.[7]

The railroads were crucial to the South's recovery and central to the Reconstruction efforts because of the investment they attracted. As Sarah H. Gordon suggests, "In connecting the population centers of the South, and in bringing supplies, money and mail from the North, the railroad, for all its inadequacies, was one of the only links holding this ruined society together and tying it to the rest of the Union."[8] Within a decade of the end of the war, too, a more rational railroad system was beginning to emerge in the South, triggered, ironically, by the panic of 1873, which forced many penurious railroad companies to consolidate. After the financial collapse, the surviving railroad companies took over many of their weaker peers. The largest and strongest of the southern railroad companies began the process that their counterparts in the North had embarked on a quarter of a century previously, becoming, at last, systems and networks rather than simple routes. Railroad empires were finally starting to emerge in the South.

Meanwhile, the trend toward bigger unified networks was becoming even more marked in the Northeast, where the substantial network built before the war limited the scope for further growth. This was particularly the case in New England, whose railroads had initially been the fastest to develop. Expansion mostly took the form of branch lines or links between existing railroads, although there was one spectacular project, the belated completion of the Hoosac Tunnel through the western Massachusetts mountain range. At four and a half miles, it was, at the time of its completion in 1875, the longest in America and the second longest in the world after the Mont Cenis Tunnel under the French Alps. The tunnel, which was originally conceived as a canal connection back in the 1810s, was intended to provide a direct link between Boston and the Great Lakes to the west. It was the brainchild of one Alvah Crocker (no relation to Charles of the Union Pacific), a self-made paper-mill proprietor and owner of the Fitchburg Railroad, which ran from Boston to Greenfield, Massachusetts, eighty miles to the west. The tunnel was needed to get through the Hoosac Range and connect northern Massachusetts directly with routes to the west without travelers having to first head south toward New York. It proved, however, to be a much more difficult enterprise than anticipated, and very costly in terms of both lives and money.

Work had started in 1852, nine years before the Civil War, and had been expected to be completed in just five years at a cost of $2 million. That ubiquitous genius Herman Haupt was again involved, designing the tunnel and the lines leading to and from it, and for a while progress was steady. As well as the obvious problem of blasting through a mountain, the project was dogged by a host of geological, financial, and political difficulties. A thousand-foot vertical shaft was dug in the mountain to provide access to the middle of the tunnel to speed up progress, but this central shaft was an unsatisfactory and dangerous arrangement, resulting in an explosion that killed thirteen men in an accident in October 1867. Inevitably, too, as costs mounted, the project was caught up in political controversy because such an expensive piece of infrastructure needed considerable state funding. Worse, Haupt was forced out by opponents of the tunnel who argued, wrongly, that his methods were at the root of the engineering problem. With his departure, work on the tunnel ground to a halt, as the money from the private investors had run out. After a delay, the Commonwealth of Massachusetts stepped in to ensure completion, demonstrating yet again that the state was often the investor of last resort in railroad enterprises, especially those that it hoped would produce extensive benefits for local people.

In the event, further technical difficulties, and opposition by rival railroads to increased state funding, meant that the tunnel was not completed until 1875 at an eventual cost of $20 million, ten times the original estimate. Moreover, nearly two hundred men died during construction, a huge number in comparison with the death toll on much larger projects. As on the first transcontinental, it was explosive material that was the main danger, with the old black powder and the newer nitroglycerin, introduced in the latter stages of the project, proving to be equally deadly. Because of state involvement, once the tunnel was open, there was a rather unusual operating arrangement. Rather than granting a monopoly, the Commonwealth of Massachusetts had encouraged various railroads to build their lines up to the tunnel and actually charged a toll for every train passing through to help pay for the investment. Despite the difficulties of construction, the tunnel was to demonstrate its worth over many years after its completion, becoming a vital part of New England's transportation system.

Such extravagant construction as the Hoosac Tunnel was very much the exception on American railroads, especially in the East, where *consolidation* became the watchword. For example, in New England, the dozens of railroads started to amalgamate, and by 1900 just six major concerns controlled all but 20 percent of the local network. In 1872, the 131-mile-long New York, New Haven & Hartford was created by merging the New York & New Haven and the Hartford & New Haven. By the turn of the century, it had become a system boasting more than 2,000 miles of track, mostly through acquisition rather than construction. Ironically, this type of consolidation arguably did more to improve the experience of passengers traveling on the railroads than the construction of so many new, disconnected, and—by now—often superfluous lines. Whereas before the Civil War there had been some measure of unification across the rail network in the East, for most passengers long journeys remained an ordeal, involving several changes between lines and overnight stays at hotels that, according to contemporary reports, were rather better than the restaurants providing lunch at the enforced stops. After the war, however, the major trunk lines of the East started to establish through services by building connecting links and taking over neighboring railroads.

There had been no direct rail service between New York and Washington, as passengers had to change trains at Philadelphia, until the war, when at last through services to the capital started to operate. The *New York Times*, which had been a persistent critic of the poor service between these two major cities, complained that Philadelphia "has not entirely out-grown the village peevishness manifested at Erie."[9] It was only when the railroad companies found a route bypassing Philadelphia that through trains to Washington were made possible.

There were improvements, too, for passengers heading west to Chicago via Pittsburgh. From 1869 they no longer had to change there because the Pennsylvania took over the Pittsburgh, Fort Wayne & Chicago Railroad, which had previously insisted that passengers travel in its rolling stock through to the Windy City. However, it would take several years before the timetable was sorted out to guarantee a through service for all Pennsylvania passengers. The routes between major cities immediately became so lucra-tive that they attracted keen competition for patronage that did not always work to the benefit of passengers. The rival New York Central soon estab-lished its own through route, acquiring the Lake Shore & Michigan South-ern to take its trains between Buffalo and Chicago. Within a few years, there were four main lines between the two cities, as the Erie took over the At-lantic & Great Western, which fortunately used the same six-foot gauge, whereas the Baltimore & Ohio, unable to find a suitable acquisition, built its own line across northern Ohio and Indiana to reach Chicago in 1874.

These developments were part of a remarkable pattern of expansion of the railroads of the Midwest, where the rapid pace of growth before the war actually accelerated in its aftermath. The Granger railroads were pro-gressing ever farther westward into the upper Midwest area but needed to offer inducements to attract settlers, without which they served little pur-pose. The railroads were rapidly connecting the Midwest with the West through building across the plains, where railroad construction was at its most feverish.

The idea of encouraging settlers through the construction of a railroad was not new. The Illinois Central, which had difficulty attracting labor, let alone passengers, pioneered the idea in the 1850s with newspaper adver-tisements and what were called "fairyland pamphlets" depicting idealized versions of rural farmhouses. The ploy worked, with Illinois quickly be-coming a destination for immigrants. After the Civil War, with several western railroads vying for settlers, far more sophisticated methods were used to induce people to "go west." In 1870, the Chicago, Burlington &

Quincy[10] (known as "the Burlington") employed a land agent, one Edward Edginton, in the port town of Liverpool in northwestern England, from which many emigrants set off on their journeys to the New World. Edginton's job was to hand out leaflets and talk to the emigrants on their ships before departure and the boardinghouses where they lodged, extolling the virtues of settling in parts of Iowa and Nebraska served by the railroad.

Soon, Europe was flooded with railroad company agents. By the early 1880s, the Northern Pacific alone employed nearly a thousand of them. Most railroad agents operated in the UK, but they were also scattered through Scandinavia, Germany, and Switzerland. The railroads flooded European newspapers with advertisements offering cheap land for sale and even created their own newspapers in order to promote these deals. Immigrants arriving at New York were targeted by railroad company agents who would approach newly arrived fortune seekers as soon as they disembarked. Then there was old-fashioned PR. Journalists were plied with fine wines and Havana cigars to produce articles extolling the virtues of settling in the West. The companies produced false rainfall statistics for the areas they were promoting and issued pseudoscientific advice suggesting, for example, that "rain followed the plow," because the moisture released from the soil when it was churned over would later fall as rain. Possibly the most outlandish effort was made by one Burlington agent who organized a trip to America for a buffalo hunt led by "Buffalo Bill" Cody. The sixty lucky Englishmen chosen for the excursion were then expected to return to their homeland to convince their compatriots to settle. Even the fine arts were co-opted to lure settlers west. The Burlington commissioned an artist to produce eighty-five huge canvases of views of the areas to be settled, which were exhibited in a lecture tour around Britain under the bizarre title of *Sylphorama of America by Sea, River, and Railroad.*

The world portrayed in much of this publicity material was far divorced from the harsh reality. The promoters tended to exaggerate the attributes of these remote parts of the United States, many of which were actually difficult to farm because of their dry climates and cold winters. No mention was made of the fierce blizzards that were a regular feature of the midwestern winter or the less regular but even more disastrous plagues of grasshoppers. The railroad companies, and indeed the settlers, were fortunate that, with a couple of exceptions, the 1870s and 1880s were a wet period when farms could be cultivated without the need for irrigation. However, many settlers were to suffer appalling privation in the last decade of the nineteenth century, when the Great Plains suffered one of its periodic bouts of drought, destroying their crops and forcing them to slaughter their cattle prematurely. By then, they had realized the railroad companies had conned them.

On the other hand, not all the publicity produced by the railroads presented the West as a land of milk and honey. The railroad companies did not always hide the fact that conditions were likely to be harsh and that they wanted people prepared to work on farms, not clerks or even doctors and architects. In this respect, at least, the publicity material was, at times, brusquely honest: "Clerks ought not to think of coming unless they have thoroughly made up their minds to lay down pen and paper and take up spade or plough."[11] This honesty was partly motivated out of self-interest, as the railroads were keen to deter the destitute and the feckless, who would not be able to afford to purchase the land and were likely to fail as farmers. Ideally, from the railroads' point of view, they needed people who could afford the $26.80 fare from New York to Omaha, Nebraska, even if it used up their life savings. Few were able to afford the return fare, which was deliberately set far higher by the railroad. In any case, not many would have been willing to repeat the experience of a transcontinental train ride. Conditions on these trains were appalling, with the immigrants, who were treated as freight, stuffed ninety to a coach fitted only with hard wooden seats. The settlers also needed sufficient funds to put down deposits on the land that the railroad companies had been granted for the construction of the lines. The Burlington, for example, offered land at $12 per acre in Iowa and at just $8 per acre in Nebraska. The company made loans available for the purchase of further acreage at a rate of 6 percent interest, which was cheaper than other railroads, which normally charged 10 percent.

Of course, it was not just the sophisticated recruitment methods of the railroads that attracted the immigrants. Conditions back home were often a spur to emigration. Many were eager to leave the Old World and had good reason for doing so, particularly the Irish, who started arriving in the mid-1840s, fleeing the Great Famine. Scandinavia also experienced a series of disastrous harvests in the mid-nineteenth century. In particular,

Sweden, with terrible weather and then an impoverished backwater rather than the affluent country it is today, endured a particularly severe famine in the mid-1860s that drove many people to leave. Then there were the wars. The political upheavals caused by the 1870–1871 Franco-Prussian War and the subsequent rise of the militaristic Bismarck induced large numbers of Germans to head for the New World. The Burlington was quick to send agents to Alsace-Lorraine—annexed to Germany following the Franco-Prussian War—to lure its defeated and disgruntled inhabitants away from the newly imposed German yoke. The railroad company agents' skill at targeting persecuted minorities reaped the richest dividend with the Mennonites, the most successful group of settlers to be recruited. They were a religious sect in czarist Russia who had enjoyed special exemption from military service, as it was against their nonviolent principles. When this immunity was abolished by the czar in 1870, they needed little persuasion to emigrate to the United States when Carl Schmidt, a German-speaking agent of the Santa Fe, discovered their plight. Schmidt entered Russia disguised as a farm-machinery salesman and visited thirty villages with the aim of convincing the Mennonites that the Kansas plains offered wheat-growing land just as good as that of the Russian steppes. He made no mention of locusts and blizzards and dismissed the threat from Native Americans. Despite discovering these difficulties, the Mennonites were delighted with what they found when they arrived in the Midwest.

Inspired by Schmidt's salesmanship, thirty-four families from the Crimea turned up in Kansas in the summer of 1874. To the locals, they were a strange bunch, tall and thin, clad in Russian blouses and billowing trousers, who seemed particularly ill-suited to the rigors of farming the dry land. How wrong the skeptics were. The Mennonites, who incidentally had a long tradition of emigration, did everything right, unlike many of the other groups of settlers. They had cashed in their belongings and smuggled out gold with which they immediately purchased some of the railroad's land. They had also brought with them jars of wheat seed, a variety called "Turkey Red," which was particularly well suited to the local climate. As a result, they proved to be the best-adapted settlers, so sought after that railroad land agents began competing with one another to attract them. Indeed, in one instance, an unprincipled Burlington railroad agent in Atchison, Kansas, persuaded a group to board his train rather than the Santa Fe service that had been specially provided to pick them up. "I stole the whole bunch except less than a dozen unmarried young men, and carried them all by special train, free, to Lincoln, Nebraska," he later boasted. Eventually, as many as fifteen thousand Mennonites emigrated to Kansas. Those left behind suffered under the czar, with many being sent to Siberia, where wheat cannot be grown. Dee Brown notes the irony that a century later, "the descendants of those who came from Russia to the Great Plains in the 1870s were growing wheat in the 1970s for export to Russia, shipping millions of bushels to ports on the railroads that had brought them to America."[12]

Attracting men was the easy bit. But without women, the settlements would soon die out, and so the phenomenon of the mail-order bride, made possible by the railroads, emerged. There were very limited numbers of respectable women available for marriage in the West. The daughters who arrived with their parents or were born there were mostly far too young for the men who had come in search of work. Among them were a few schoolteachers, but nowhere near enough to satisfy demand. There was no shortage of prostitutes, but for marriage the men began to seek "mail-order brides." So, in a precursor to online dating, men would advertise in eastern newspapers for a wife, and, similarly, eastern women who might be seeking a different way of life would send pictures and descriptions to the western newspapers. Often, a group of women would travel together to a western town, where "socials" would be arranged at which the men and women could mingle and become acquainted, rather like an early version of speed dating. Invariably, these women would travel west on the railroads. They would be met at the station either by the specific man they had come to marry (the true mail-order bride) or by a local organizer, who would house them and arrange for the socials.

The railroads in the West made concentrated efforts to attract settlers because it was their only hope of salvation. Building railroads in the West was "a cutthroat business at the very best," which came at a heavy price. Many projects never saw the light of day, and those that did were invariably constrained by a lack of cash. In truth, the railroads were not built to satisfy any existing need or demand. Far too many railroads in the West, especially the proliferation of transcontinentals, were built too quickly.

One after the other, the resulting businesses, fed by generous subsidies, were for the most part not viable but dependent on a diet of state funding and the deployment of much sharp practice: "These Western railroads very often should not have been built when and how they were. Their costs over the long term, and the short term, exceeded their benefits."[13]

The railroads in the West faced other difficulties, ranging from disease and drought to attacks by Indians whose territory was gradually, with the permission of a pliant Congress, being further invaded. The workers building the lines often needed the protection of a militia, which could be either the US regular army or, more likely, a bunch of well-armed mercenaries. It was not only the Indians who attacked the railroads. There were internecine fights, too, most notably over the right to build through the Raton Pass, the only feasible route from Colorado down to New Mexico, and subsequently over another key route, the Royal Gorge of the Arkansas River. Both the Atchison, Topeka & Santa Fe (usually known as the Santa Fe) and the Denver & Rio Grande Railroads wanted to use the Raton Pass, and in theory there should have been plenty of room for the two lines, but, rather than negotiate, both railroad companies hired militias consisting of an unprepossessing bunch of hustlers and gunslingers. Legendary cowboy figures like Marshal William Barclay "Bat" Masterson of Dodge City and the notorious gambling gunfighter-dentist John Henry "Doc" Holliday were enlisted by the Santa Fe, which recruited a team of seventy gunmen, whereas the Rio Grande's force at one point numbered two hundred men. The Santa Fe got there first in February 1878 and held the pass, and in the event managed to gain control without a shot being fired in the first stage of this "railroad war." The dispute then shifted to the Royal Gorge, through which both railroads sought to lay tracks in order to access a key mining region. Even though the matter was going through the courts, a series of minor battles ensued, in one of which two Santa Fe men were killed, and at one point several Santa Fe train crews, working on Rio Grande tracks, were set upon and beaten: "For several months both sides maintained small armies in the field, spying on each other, committing acts of sabotage, kidnapping public officials, cutting telegraph wires, and diverting Colorado very much."[14] Eventually, a peace agreement was thrashed out two thousand miles away in Boston in February 1880, giving the Rio Grande, which had won the court case, rights over the Royal Gorge. Legend has it that the gun skills developed by the Santa Fe men during the two-year war later prevented a train wreck. Charles Watlington, the freight conductor of a train stalled by a washout,[15] was running up the tracks to prevent the following passenger service from smashing into it. The driver failed to see him, but Watlington, remembering his shooting skills, pulled out his gun and fired into the brake air hose between two passenger cars, which automatically brought the passenger train screeching to a halt.

Apart from trying to shoot its rivals, the Rio Grande was a pioneering railroad in another, less violent, respect. It was the first major narrow-gauge railroad in the United States and would be the harbinger of a short-lived fashion for building these cheaper railroads. Its tracks were constructed to the three-foot gauge rather than the standard four feet and eight and a half inches because its promoters realized that would reduce the costs dramatically in the hilly but sparsely populated terrain of Colorado. The narrower gauge not only saves on construction, as the right-of-way is smaller, but also allows cheaper and lighter rails, cars, and locomotives to be used. One calculation suggested that the first 25-mile section of the line was built at a cost of just twenty thousand dollars per mile, compared with estimates of ninety thousand for a standard-gauge railroad. According to the *Encyclopedia of North American Railroads*, "The Denver & Rio Grande 'baby railroad' captured everyone's imagination and seemed to ignite the narrow-gauge explosion."[16] The Rio Grande eventually extended to 2,000 miles, and within fifteen years 11,700 miles of narrow-gauge railroad had been built across America, in all but a handful of states. The advantage was that narrow gauge, an idea that had been copied from the UK, where the Ffestiniog Railway in North Wales had been completed in the 1860s, allowed many towns and villages to have a railroad at a cost that made it economically feasible. These narrow-gauge lines served a variety of freight purposes, too: there were farm-to-market lines, which were mostly killed off by the trucks; forestry railroads, which were abandoned when the trees were all chopped down; and mining railroads, which disappeared once the mines were exhausted. The lack of connection with other railroads, and the limitation on the weight of freight that could be carried on them, resulted in the rapid waning of the narrow-gauge lines, and by 1920 all but 4,000 miles had either been abandoned or been converted to standard gauge. The Rio

Grande, however, lived on until after the Second World War and 45 miles of the line survive as a scenic heritage railroad.

Neither battles, financial difficulties, Indian attacks, nor the tough terrain prevented the railroads in the West from expanding exponentially, thanks largely to the land-grant system. The pattern of development of these western railroads was generally to complete the main line and then add a network of branches, turning them into extensive systems reliant on the settlers they could attract to the farms that had to be, of necessity, within easy reach of the rail lines. The scale of growth was staggering. At the end of the Civil War, there had been just under 1,000 miles of railroad west of the line stretching between the eastern borders of the Dakotas and Texas; by the outbreak of the First World War, there would be more than 90,000 miles. These first railroads were lengthy affairs that aimed to reach the Pacific coast, since otherwise they would have ended up, quite literally, in the middle of nowhere. The line built by the Union & Central Pacific quickly spawned imitators. The next two transcontinentals opened in 1883, and inevitably both included the word *Pacific* in their names, which seemed to be de rigueur to convince investors to part with their money. The Southern Pacific, whose terminus was in Los Angeles, then a modest Mexican-style town, ran along the border with Mexico through New Mexico and Texas and eventually to New Orleans, the mouth of the Mississippi. It was the brainchild of the Big Four of the Central Pacific, who were reliant on expanding their rail network in order to allow them to pay off the debts incurred in building the original transcontinental. To them, railroad construction was like a giant Ponzi scheme:[17] they had to keep building in order to disguise the fact that their company was in financial trouble—although, personally, they had all enriched themselves. The Southern Pacific was not a single line but rather a collection of existing railroads that the Big Four had built or purchased in California, and in 1907 it joined with the Atchison, Topeka & Santa Fe Railway to form the Northwestern Pacific.

The Santa Fe, however, having reached Chicago in the East, had been keen to push its own rails all the way to the Pacific and funded itself through the sale of land it had been granted by the government. Sales offices were set up, and potential buyers were lured with cheap rail tickets—whose cost would be discounted from any future purchase, a clever strategy that brought in immediate cash and potential passengers. Despite its name, the railroad actually bypassed Santa Fe—which would later become the state capital of New Mexico—because the terrain was too difficult and instead continued west toward the Pacific. Eventually, a branch line did connect the railroad with its eponymous town. The main line of the Santa Fe extended as far as Deming, New Mexico, from where, under an agreement with the Southern Pacific, its trains were able to reach Los Angeles and the Pacific. This provided a connection between the interior of the United States and Australia, one of its key markets, that was 1,400 miles shorter than the route via San Francisco. Extension to the Pacific made the Santa Fe briefly the longest railroad in the world (until the Trans-Siberian was completed around the turn of the century). Later it acquired or built several other lines in California to ensure access to several ports. Consequently, despite its late start and a bankruptcy in 1893, when many other railroads went under because of an economic downturn, the Santa Fe would become the most successful of the transcontinental lines. A key factor was that it eventually had control of its own metals all the way between Chicago and the West Coast, whereas other companies had to use tracks belonging to other railroads, which would invariably prioritize their own services.

Meanwhile, two other transcontinental railroads had been built to the north. These were epic affairs, on a scale with the original transcontinental. The Northern Pacific was a completely separate enterprise from its southern namesake and one that suffered, like its predecessor, from constant cash shortages that delayed progress. On the same day in July 1864 that Durant's bribery had obtained from Congress those generous arrangements for the financing of the Union Pacific, the lawmakers also granted a charter and land to a second transcontinental railroad, with a route from the shores of Lake Superior in Minnesota to the northern Pacific coast. Whereas the first transcontinental had been completed within five years, it would take nearly two decades to build the Northern Pacific, not least because its construction was even more demanding than that of its predecessor. History has a habit of being unfair to runners-up, and the story of the Northern Pacific is rarely told. It was a massive enterprise, passing through territory that General Sherman said was "as bad as God ever made or any one could scare up this side of Africa," which may explain why the land grant was even more generous than for the Union Pacific, totaling a staggering 46 million acres (71,852 square miles, larger than the state of Missouri).[18] Built by a single company, unlike the original line, which required two, the Northern Pacific was the biggest railroad enterprise undertaken up to that date. The line progressed well initially, stretching nearly 500 miles from its starting point at a junction in Minnesota to Bismarck, North Dakota, on the Missouri River, but there it stalled for several years following the 1873 financial panic. The line, which had a checkered history, having been at one time controlled by the railroad baron Jay Cooke, and then fallen into bankruptcy, was taken over by Henry Villard, a German immigrant and reporter who had covered the Civil War. He managed to raise $8 million from investors and restart construction initially from the West, where he had gained control of the Oregon Central Railroad, but later work proceeded from both ends. With a workforce of twenty-five thousand men, more than on the original transcontinental, half of whom were Chinese, the line was completed in September 1883 when the two teams eventually met at the appropriately named Gold Creek, Montana, and celebrated with the usual gold spike ceremony.

The achievement of building the Northern Pacific was matched by that of the Great Northern, which ran parallel to it, hugging the Canadian border. Remarkably, the Great Northern was built without the benefit of the generous land grants allocated to the other transcontinentals. Unlike many of the other pioneers of western railroads, its creator, an eccentric, one-eyed Canadian, James J. Hill, was a true railroad man, having "twenty years of frontier freighting, merchandising and transportation experience" when he decided, along with some Canadian associates, to stretch his railroad to the ocean.[19] Hill, who was given the nickname of "Empire Builder," was one of those hard taskmasters who nevertheless respected his men and knew most of his superintendents by name.[20] He once arrived in his special coach at a place where a train had been blocked by a heavy snowfall and not only started shoveling snow himself but also told the men to get coffee from his coach.

Hill started by taking over the bankrupt St. Paul & Pacific (again!) and built his railroad in fits and starts, recycling the profits from completed sections to pay for the next stretch. As Hill progressed westward, he would throw out branches where he could see easy potential profits. Unlike those of his rivals, therefore, the financing of his railroad was generated by its transportation activity rather than through land deals.

By the time the line reached Seattle in 1893, it was already profitable, and its financial strength soon allowed Hill to take over the rival Northern Pacific. Hill had also ensured the line was built to a high standard, with lower gradients and gentler curves that, while increasing the cost of construction, reduced operating expenses. He had the satisfaction of being able to watch all the other transcontinentals collapse into bankruptcy during the financial panic of 1893, while his railroad continued to flourish. Moreover, Hill's railroad continued to expand, with branches and new routes. According to John Stover, "Between 1891 and 1907, the year Hill retired from its presidency, the Great Northern built an average of one new mile of road for every working day."[21] Some of these lines proved to be largely useless branches that were soon abandoned, but others survive today.

Remarkably, therefore, before the century was out, five transcontinentals (not counting those in Canada) and innumerable branches and connecting routes stretched across the West. Although all sorts of crooked deals had helped bring them about, the sheer extent of the engineering achievement should be celebrated. However, as we will see in the next chapter, the unscrupulous nature of the railroads' western expansion would be one of the reasons they became so reviled.

These railroads had a common purpose: to allow the colonization of the western half of the United States. As Keith Bryant Jr. writes in the *Encyclopedia of North American Railroads*, "The old concept of the 'Great American Desert' disappeared as freight trains laden with wheat, corn and cattle flowed eastward and returned with finished goods from metropolitan manufacturers." However, the West was not won as swiftly or as easily as Bryant's description implies. Unlike in Europe or even in the eastern states of America, where the railroads served existing communities or gained business from other modes of transport, in the West they created communities and the transportation links between them from scratch. Their claim to have brought civilization to the West was, certainly at first, something of an exaggeration. The towns that sprang up along the line

1. The Atlantic, built by Phineas Davis at York, Pennsylvania, was introduced on the Baltimore & Ohio Railroad in 1832, pulling cars based on stagecoach designs. (The photograph is undated but is clearly from a much later period, suggesting it depicts a celebratory run marking an anniversary.) © UNDERWOOD & UNDERWOOD/CORBIS.

The "Best Friend," the First Locomotive built in the United States for actual service on a Railroad.

The "Best Friend" was built at the West Point Foundry Shops, in New York City, for the South Carolina Rail-Road, and after several experimental trials, in November and December, 1830, made the first excursion trip, as above, on Saturday, 15th January, 1831, being the anniversary of the commencement of the road. See extract from *Charleston Courier*, page 152.

2. In December 1830, the Best Friend of Charleston, the first locomotive built in America to haul a passenger train, began operating on the Charleston & Hamburg railroad, which was briefly the world's longest line. Not long after, the locomotive met with an unfortunate end when a fireman closed a safety valve and was killed in the subsequent explosion. GETTY IMAGES.

3. The most famous picture in American railroad history: the rather chaotic ceremony to mark the completion of the first transcontinental by the Central Pacific and Union Pacific rail in May 1869 at Promontory Summit, Utah. © Bettmann/Corbis.

4. The arrival of the iron road changed the landscape of America in various unpredicted ways, such as helping to speed up the virtual extinction of buffalo. Getty Images.

5. Until the First World War, agents were widely used to sell train tickets, often offering a discount on the normal price. © BETTMANN/CORBIS.

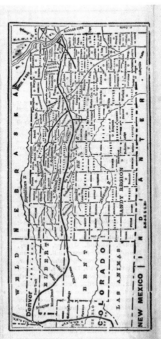

6. The railroads used advertising and even speaking tours in order to attract settlers onto their land. © BETTMANN/CORBIS.

THE FARMER AND THE RAILROAD MONSTER.
WHICH WILL WIN?

7. Of the many opponents of the railroads in the later stages of the nineteenth century, the farmers proved to be the most effective and vociferous, helping to bring about regulation of the industry. © CORBIS.

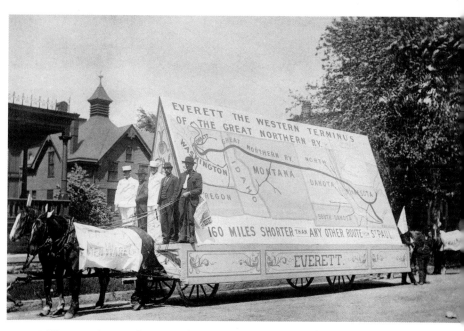

8. The completion of major railroads was a cause for celebration and, sometimes, innovative publicity campaigns. © MINNESOTA HISTORICAL SOCIETY/CORBIS.

HISTORICAL CARICATURE OF THE CHEROKEE NATION.

9. The railroads did much to hasten the demise of the Native American culture both directly, through land grabs, and indirectly, by encouraging settlement. © CORBIS.

10. As this 1904 picture of Houston, Texas, shows, freight was key to the profitability of many railroads. © CORBIS.

11. 1885: At times the railroad companies struggled to keep up with demand for their services. CLASSICSTOCK/ALAMY.

12. The railroads were used extensively to take vacationers to resorts such as the one served by this typical small station in the Catskills in upstate New York, shown here in 1905. © BETTMANN/CORBIS.

13. The elevated railroad in New York was well used but proved unpopular with residents and workers in offices near its tracks. It was eventually replaced by the subway, although a similar system of elevated railroads survives in Chicago today. GETTY IMAGES.

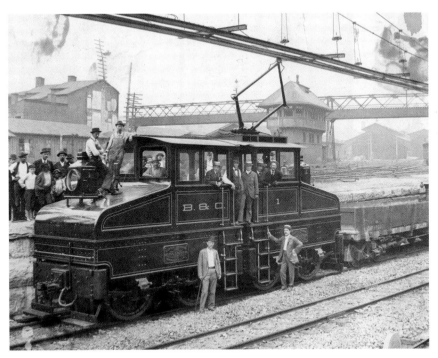

14. Although some electric locomotives, like this one on the Baltimore & Ohio Railroad, were introduced in the early twentieth century, electrification, with the odd exception, never spread much beyond the Eastern Seaboard states.
© SCHENECTADY MUSEUM; HALL OF ELECTRICAL HISTORY FOUNDATION/CORBIS.

15. Starting from humble beginnings, Edward H. Harriman became the biggest owner in railroad history who, at the time of his death in 1909, controlled the Union Pacific, Southern Pacific, Illinois Central, Central of Georgia, and Wells Fargo Express Company, among others. © CORBIS.

16. As this picture of nicely turned-out Dutch immigrants shows, the railroads were crucial in encouraging settlement in the Midwest and West. © MINNESOTA HISTORICAL SOCIETY/CORBIS.

17. At their peak, there were more than 250,000 miles of railroad line across the United States, far more than in any other country of the world. © PEMCO-WEBSTER & STEVENS COLLECTION; MUSEUM OF HISTORY AND INDUSTRY, SEATTLE/CORBIS.

18. The railroads' influence on politicians was seen by the general public as contributing to scandals such as the Crédit Mobilier affair involving the builders of the Union Pacific. GETTY IMAGES.

19. The railroads played a crucial role in the First World War, bringing troops and matériel to the ports. © Minnesota Historical Society/Corbis.

20. Though they looked perilous, trestle bridges proved a cheap and effective way of fording rivers. © Corbis.

21. Railroad workers began to organize in the 1870s, and their unions eventually became very strong, resulting in numerous strikes, such as this one in Illinois in 1904. © Bettmann/Corbis.

22. New York's Penn Station, completed in 1910 and seen here in 1934, was demolished in 1963, although trains still operate from the lower level. © Bettmann/Corbis.

23. Redcap porters were employed at many stations to carry luggage for passengers, who often took vast amounts on train journeys. © H. ARMSTRONG ROBERTS/ CLASSICSTOCK/CORBIS.

24. These sleek, streamlined locomotives, seen in a New York Central yard in 1939, were another attempt to attract customers to the railroads. © BETTMANN/CORBIS.

25. The Twin Cities Zephyr passenger train running between Chicago and Minneapolis–St. Paul was so successful after its introduction in April 1935 that extra trains had to be quickly ordered. © UNDERWOOD & UNDERWOOD/CORBIS.

26 and 27. In the interwar and immediate postwar years, the railroad companies, facing competition from the car, launched publicity campaigns using top artists of the day to produce a range of stunning posters. © Swim Ink 2, LLC/Corbis.

28. All sorts of facilities, such as secretarial services, gyms, lavish bars, and even a cinema, depicted here in 1947, were introduced on the prestige train services. © Bettmann/Corbis.

29. The railroads were so heavily used in the Second World War that the government tried to deter ordinary passengers from using them—to no avail since, with fuel shortages, they once again became the main way to travel. © Swim Ink 2, LLC/Corbis.

30. The presidential campaign train, such as this one being used by Harry Truman in 1948, became a routine part of the election process. © Bettmann/Corbis.

31. Rail accidents, such as this one on the prestigious Santa Fe Chief that killed four people near Lomax, Illinois, in August 1954, were relatively infrequent but nevertheless attracted considerable publicity. After a slow start in relation to safety in the early days of railroading, for the most part, railroad companies reacted after accidents by improving safety features on trains and introducing new technology. © BETTMANN/CORBIS.

32. Amtrak's Acela Express, pictured here in 2005 at Union Station in Washington, DC, is the most prestigious train service in the United States today. © KEN CEDENO/CORBIS.

were little better than the Hell on Wheels temporary settlements described in Chapter 5. As the railroads spread west, so did the cowboys, and they seemed to get more disreputable the farther west the railroads went. In the words of George H. Douglas, "As the lines inched forward they invariably planted a series of towns that were savage and undisciplined— blights on the unspoiled landscape." The Santa Fe left a particularly vile and violent set of shanty towns in its wake, including the most legendary, Dodge City, not only named after a crook but full of them. As Douglas puts it, "Dodge City collected so many bad characters so quickly that it needed a lockup even before the railroad was able to bring in the lumber to build one."[22] When the town did at last acquire a jail, it was little more than a huge hole in the ground that flooded in the rains, creating a pool into which the town drunks were thrown, notionally to "dry out." The West was truly wild at this stage, and it would be some years before the railroads, by continuing to bring a stream of more respectable settlers and make it easier to establish the rule of law, could be said to have brought civilization. It is no exaggeration, however, to say that the railroads created the West. Before the iron road arrived, there were no settlements, vile or otherwise, other than the mostly peaceful villages of the Native Americans. It was the railroads that not only enabled people to go west, but also induced them to settle through their extensive publicity campaigns.

Eventually, the railroads tamed the Wild West that they had created. As they began to crisscross the vast lands of the West, they created enclosures, and soon the cowboys lost the open spaces that had made possible their long cattle trains north from Texas. Settlers began to fence in with barbed wire the lands that the railroads had sold them and, inevitably, ended the practice of cowboys driving the cattle over the prairies. The railroads could transport the beasts all the way to the stockyards of Chicago with much less loss of weight, and soon they would be traveling as carcasses in refrigerated wagons. The wilder elements of the population soon found their freedom curtailed: "Outlaws, gamblers, hoboes and other wanderers saw a gradual reduction in public wilderness land outside the bounds of any law, as most Western lands came into private hands before 1890."[23] The freedom of movement of the Native Americans, too, was curtailed. Not only was their land purloined by the government to give to the railroads, but the fences restricted their hunting grounds and effectively destroyed their way of life. Within a couple of decades of the arrival of the first transcontinental, the railroads had enabled the East to colonize the West and to impose its legal, economic, and social forms over it. It was not so much the union of two distinct parts of the United States, but rather the triumph of the East over the West and of the white men over the "red savages."

7

GETTING BETTER ALL THE TIME

With the rapid expansion of the railroads all across the United States, travelers benefited from a great improvement in the passenger service. Not only were there more trains, operating regularly to published time-tables, but they were also becoming more comfortable for passengers. During the 1870s, many railroads began to offer more amenities and luxuries to the traveling public, although provision of these facilities remained patchy. Probably the most important improvement, at least to those who could afford it, was the Pullman sleeping car, which was essential for comfortable travel in such a vast country where journeys of three or four days were commonplace.

In the early days of the railroad, as we have seen, trains stopped for the night and, indeed, for meals, but this was impractical and unsatisfactory. A different arrangement was clearly needed, and it was not long in coming. Although indelibly associated with the name of George Pullman, the sleeping car was not his invention. Indeed, a primitive version of the sleeping car had been introduced on the Cumberland Valley Railroad, in Pennsylvania, as far back as 1839,[1] consisting of a pair of carriages each with four sets of three-tiered berths—no more than hard boards with no bedding or mattresses—that allowed passengers to lie down parallel to the tracks and were folded away during the day. A few years later, the New York & Erie Railroad provided two cars equipped with iron rods that could be used to link facing seats to create a crude and uncomfortable bed. However, as the cushions were made of horsehair cloth that penetrated all but the thickest clothing and were often liberally infested with a variety of ravenous insects, getting to sleep in conditions described as "cramped, crude and uncomfortable" must have been solely the province of the inebriated. Furthermore, the poor condition of the track made it seem "like sleeping on a runaway horse," according to one early traveler.[2] The railroad did not provide pillows or bedding, and passengers went to bed wearing their boots and breeches. By the 1850s, several American railroads were advertising sleeping-car accommodation that represented a slight improvement on what had gone before. The first real innovator was Webster Wagner, who is credited with the invention of the sleeping car, though he was merely building on the work of others. Wagner was a stationmaster on the New York Central, which had just come under the control of Cornelius Vanderbilt (about whom we will hear much more in the next chapter). Wagner had previously been a wagon maker and developed the idea of a car with a single tier of berths and bedding closets at each end, a definite improvement on all predecessors. Vanderbilt embraced the idea and provided the money to build four such cars. They immediately proved popular, demonstrating the viability of the concept, and soon different versions of sleeping cars appeared on several of the longer-distance railroads. It was, however, George Pullman—whose name would become synonymous with his product—who developed the concept and revolutionized overnight travel on the American railroads.

Like many of the early railroad entrepreneurs, Pullman had previously been successful in another field. Born in upstate New York, he had entered the contracting business with his father, who made a fortune from moving houses—the whole house, that is, not its contents—which happened to be in the way of the expansion of the Erie Canal. The apogee of Pullman's house-moving career came in 1861 with the raising of the four-story Tremont House Hotel, Chicago's tallest building at the time. The hotel owners had thought the building would have to be demolished when the local authorities decided that Chicago's streets needed to be raised to clear the local swamps. Pullman, however, had other ideas. He placed the whole building on five thousand jacks and, with the help of twelve hundred workers, who repeatedly turned the screws 180 degrees on Pullman's signal, slowly raised the hotel by a total of six feet, while not interrupting the lunch service or the chambermaids making the beds in the rooms above.

Many more such moving jobs ensued, and creating a mobile hotel on rails, therefore, could be seen as a logical next step for Pullman. He first converted two carriages on the Chicago & Alton Railroad in 1858 to provide upper and lower sleeping berths. The innovative idea was that the upper berth was suspended from the ceiling by ropes and pulleys and when not in use could be pulled up snug with the roof. Curtains were used in front and between the berths, but the crudeness of the accommodation could be judged by the fact that lighting was still by candles and heating provided by a woodstove, which—given the presence of the flapping curtains—posed an awful fire risk. At least blankets and pillows were provided, but not sheets, and it still proved difficult, according to the conductor on the first service, to persuade passengers to remove their boots, possibly because they may have been the most valuable thing they owned. This was not a trivial issue. For many years, every Pullman car had notices stating, "Please take off your boots before retiring," which was also printed on all Pullman tickets. Although the scheme was moderately successful, and a third car soon introduced, Pullman went to seek his fortune elsewhere, running a store in Colorado during a mining boom for four years until returning to Chicago in 1863. He had, however, kept on teasing away at the sleeping-car idea by sketching designs. On his return, he improved the concept by fitting a hinged upper berth that, when folded away, could also be used as a headrest for the seating accommodation during the day.

Now, with the enhanced design, there was nothing to stop Pullman. Legend has it that the catalyst for his success was to provide the funeral train for Abraham Lincoln after the president was assassinated in 1865. By then Pullman had been working on his superior sleeping car for almost a year. The idea was to bring luxury to the train traveler, and Pullman, together with a boyhood friend, Ben Field, designed a new type of coach, developed from scratch rather than by adapting existing stock. Appropriately named The Pioneer, with eight sections and a washroom and two compartments at each end, it was first put into service on the Chicago & Alton in 1865. However, Pullman had a problem. To accommodate all the facilities, Pullman's coach exceeded what is called the "loading gauge" of the railroad—that is, the size of the envelope created by tunnels, bridges, and platforms that can accommodate the locomotive and coaches. Pullman's coach was longer—which meant it could not handle sharp curves—and wider than conventional stock. Mrs. Lincoln is said to have seen the coach on a visit to Illinois shortly before her husband's death and been enchanted by its style and elegance. Consequently, when his funeral cortege was being organized, she insisted that The Pioneer be used, and the Chicago & Alton had to go to the enormous expense of rapidly adjusting its tracks to accommodate the width of Pullman's coaches. The Chicago & Alton soon ordered more coaches, and other railroads followed suit, despite the cost of the requisite track work.

It was here that Pullman's business acumen came to the fore. Rather than merely produce coaches for these railroads, Pullman retained control over them. Pullman cars were hooked to existing train services, sometimes in tandem with the railroad companies' existing sleeper cars. Although Pullman charged a premium of 50 cents per night, his coaches proved so popular that they soon displaced their rivals. Pullman's key selling point was the luxurious nature of his cars. The Pioneer had cost twenty thousand dollars to produce, but subsequent models were even more expensive, stretching to twenty-four thousand dollars, sums that can be put in perspective by the fact that no previous coach had cost more than five thousand.

Pullman's version of the sleeping car, which became the American standard and survived well into the second half of the twentieth century, as demonstrated by the train scenes in Billy Wilder's 1959 comedy film *Some Like It Hot,* remained very different from the European style, where single compartments, with up to six beds, were the norm. Instead, Pullman's design was open plan, with makeshift folding seats, pull-down berths, and only curtains for privacy, but with nothing to stop a bullhorn snorer from keeping the whole car awake. Women, indeed, got rather a bad deal from the arrangements. The editor of the British *Baedeker's* guidebook strongly approved of the open-plan design of normal passenger cars, but was appalled at the design of Pullman's sleeper cars. In particular, he complained about the fact that men were allocated twice the space of women in these open-plan cars, despite the fairer sex's having more elaborate dressing requirements. The company argued that there were far more men to accommodate in these unsegregated cars and that separate restrooms were provided. But the *Baedeker's* scribe was not appeased: "It is not considered tolerable that they [women] should lie with the legs of a strange, disrobing man dangling within a foot of their noses," he snorted. However, another British visitor, an anonymous "London parson," could hardly contain his excitement about the prospect of sharing sleeping accommodation with thirty-odd people of both sexes, especially as he was allocated the lower bunk below "a young married couple sleeping in the berth above mine. The lady turned in first, and presently her gown was hung out over the rail to which her bed curtains were fastened. But further processes of unrobing were indicated by the agitation of the drapery which concealed her nest . . . "[3] One can almost feel the clergyman's palpitations . . .

In fact, Pullman cars continued to provide twice as much room for men to smoke, dress, and perform their toilette than they did for women, but thanks to another innovation by the company, the intercar vestibule, the ladies could enjoy wandering about the train from coach to coach. Previously, getting between cars had been a hazardous process, exposing passengers to the open air between the platforms at the ends of each coach, and women were loath to take the risk. Now, however, the connections between cars were protected with pleated leather coverings. According to Pullman's publicity for the introduction of this facility on the Pennsylvania Limited in 1887, "Ladies may now make social calls or wander at will, may even take long walks for exercise or to relieve monotony, so perfect are the arrangements and appliances."[4]

It was not just the coaches that were luxurious. Pullman set a standard for service that increased his renown and did so by retaining control over every aspect of his business, which was entirely integrated. He did everything from manufacturing the cars—which eventually took place in a company town covering a massive thirty-six hundred acres at Lake Calumet on the outskirts of Chicago—to ensuring that all the right linen was available. Pullman was, in modern parlance, a control freak, as indeed were most of the early railroad pioneers who were, in essence, establishing capitalist disciplines for the first time over an industry spanning huge distances. His eponymous town, America's first planned industrial estate, which was built in the 1880s, was run as his personal fiefdom, with strict rules governing the behavior of the residents. In return for the high-quality accommodation, literally a stone's throw from the factories, the workers were banned from reading newspapers other than the company's ever-cheery *Pullman News* and were expected to keep their houses in good order or face eviction.

Goods had to be bought from the company store, simply because there was no alternative, and the rent was not cheap. (This would eventually provoke the bitter and cruel Pullman strike, described in the next chapter.) Much of the town survives as pleasant housing today, even though the factories are now mere burned-out shells. The imposing fifty-room Florence Hotel, built to accommodate the various suppliers' representatives—of iron, steel, upholstery, and other commodities—who visited the town in its heyday, became a rooming house in the 1930s, but is now being renovated as a museum.

Whereas the factory workers were white, the train service staff were black, with the exception of the Pullman conductor,[5] an arrangement that replicated the overseer-and-slave relationship of the prewar plantations. Pullman's motives in employing solely black train staff were anything but altruistic. The growth of Pullman's empire, which built up quickly to nearly fifty cars by 1867, coincided with a vast pool of former slave labor coming on the market. At first he offered African American attendants no wages, forcing them to live off tips. Conditions were tough, with the attendants not being allowed to sleep on duty, as they were required to be on call twenty-four hours a day. Inevitably, they sometimes dozed off, risking being disciplined by inspectors, or "spotters," as they were called. Pullman liked the idea of having black people serve his white clientele, who were either used to being looked after by African Americans or flattered by the attention if they were not. Pullman said blacks were "by nature adapted faithfully to perform their duties under circumstances which necessitate unfailing good nature, solicitude, and faithfulness." The attendant's job was arduous and was "a cross between a concierge, bellhop, valet, housekeeper, mechanic, babysitter [passengers were encouraged to leave their children in his care] and security guard . . . prepared at any moment day or night to be a good listener, answer questions, find lost articles [and not steal them, since leaving valuables around was another ploy used by the "spotters"] and handle emergencies."[6]

The attendants were invariably known as George, a kind of demeaning joke and probably shorthand for "George Pullman's boy." The name was, according to Kornweibel, "particularly galling to porters."[7] Although transgressions resulted in firings, the porters became experts at passive resistance in response to the worst experiences of rudeness from their white clients. When a passenger called out "George!" some porters would simply respond, "George not on t' train today." The rudeness toward the attendants outlived Pullman. Traveling in a Pullman coach shortly after the Second World War, the Duke of Windsor had been measly in his tips, giving just a few cents to a porter who carried out numerous special chores and then, remarkably, asked for his eighty cents back. This proved, in fact, to be the duke's idea of a joke, and he promptly rewarded the attendant with fifty dollars, but it was the initial humiliation that stuck longest in the man's memory. A more common trick was to tear a ten-dollar bill in two and give half to the attendant, with the implied promise to give the other in return for good service. Despite these indignities, in many respects being a Pullman attendant was an excellent job at the time, as it offered rare stability and a steady income—Pullman did soon start paying a basic wage—that could be supplemented by occasionally generous tips. Indeed, the jobs were much sought after and invariably were either passed on from father to son or obtained through the recommendation of a friend or relative.

For all their sometimes shabby treatment by the company and some of the passengers, the attendants and the waiters provided a service that was second to none. They followed rules set out in a primer by Pullman himself that detailed, for example, twelve steps on how to serve a beer, beginning with "1) Ascertain from passenger what kind of beer is required" through to "12) Remove bar tray with equipment not needed by passenger and return to buffet." Each car was equipped with one hundred sheets and pillowcases, forty blankets—employees were only allowed to use specially provided blue ones and could be fired for using the emblematic brown linen reserved for passengers—and towels of various kinds. All bedding was removed and cleaned nightly. For his part, Pullman made a fortune, eventually breaking or taking over all his competitors to create a virtual monopoly. One of the last rivals to go was poor Wagner, with whom Pullman had a series of legal spats and who eventually perished in a rear-end accident in one of his own cars in 1882. Pullman expanded rapidly in the 1870s and 1880s, both by creating new business and by taking over competitors. Soon he was producing special cars for the megarich of the day, coaches that cost upwards of a half-million dollars, some twenty times more than his already expensive standard models, and which, for a modest fee, would be attached to the back of normal service trains without, of course, a connecting vestibule. These were the "mansions on wheels" that are celebrated in coffee-table art books and represented the apogee of train travel. One was laid out at such expense that, according to a guest, "the only thing that's economical about our car is the solid gold plumbing. It saves polishing, you know."[8]

Geoffrey Freeman Allen, a chronicler of luxury trains, reports that "the most splendid of them ran to marble baths, hidden safes, Venetian mirrors, an open fireplace burning balsam logs [this was John Pierpont Morgan's] and even an English butler to supervise the car's private cellar and the Lucullan output of its kitchen."[9] J. P. Morgan's efforts, though, were bested by the train built for railroad baron Jay Gould (of whom we will hear much more in the next chapter), which consisted of four coaches, one of which housed a special cow to produce fresh milk with just the right proportion of butterfat to meet the needs of the ailing magnate's digestive system. A doctor, too, was permanently on board. But neither the proximity of the cow nor Gould's precarious health prevented every evening from being an occasion, with guests expected to don full evening dress and the whole train teeming with footmen, butlers, and ladies' maids, all in appropriate uniform.

Although the service in Pullman cars may have been solicitous in the extreme, that was not the case for those unfortunate enough to breathe their last in one of his cars. The company rule was simple and immutable. The corpse had to be taken off at the next station stop, even if there were no undertaking facilities there. The conductors, more humane than their employers, were on occasion known to break the rule surreptitiously, allowing the deceased and their companions to continue to the next town that had an undertaker rather than leaving them with the body of their loved one at some godforsaken, lonely halt.

The logical extension of the sleeping coach was the dining car, and here too Pullman was an innovator, though not the inventor. The provision of food had long been a neglected issue for passengers and one that the railroads almost cussedly failed to address. Travelers were encouraged to bring their own food or to buy from the hawkers who congregated at stations and sold their wares through passenger windows. On some routes, the railroads allowed brief meal stops during which passengers rushed off the train, gulped down a usually rather unsatisfactory meal in specially appointed restaurants on the platforms, and were herded back by hustling and whistling train staff eager to keep the service on schedule. On the Minneapolis & St. Louis Railroad, for example, stations were marked on the timetable with an *e*, for "eats." Before stopping at Grinnell, Iowa, the conductor would make his way through the cars asking how many people needed supper and then wire ahead to the local Hotel Monroe to ensure the right number of meals would be made available. For his pains, of course, he would get a free meal.[10]

It was not until 1862 that the first dedicated food-service car was introduced by the Philadelphia, Wilmington & Baltimore, a predecessor of the Pennsylvania Railroad. This was not a proper dining car but a stand-up counter at which precooked meals could be purchased and eaten. The meals were reheated in an oven powered by steam from the locomotive, a not entirely enticing prospect.

As he had done with the sleeping car, Pullman revolutionized the concept and was the first to provide what were called "hotel cars," with their own kitchen facilities and table service. Initially, the idea was to install a small galley on a sleeping car, serving steak meals for sixty cents at temporary tables, but in 1868 Pullman's Delmonico—he always gave his cars names, often with classical references, or, in this case, to a chic New York restaurant—ushered in a new era of on-board refreshment, as it was the first vehicle dedicated purely to the preparation and serving of meals. This development broke the railroads' long resistance to providing dining cars, born, quite possibly, of the realization that they were likely to be a loss maker, as, in fact, has proved to be the case, since the cost of staffing and providing quality food at an acceptable price generally outweighs what can be reasonably charged for a meal. Nevertheless, Pullman's initiative was soon followed by other companies, and by the 1880s dining cars had become standard on long-distance routes. Interestingly, although the range of food varied considerably in both quality and variety, with many companies specializing in regional dishes, the layout of dining cars has remained largely standard right through to the present day.

For Pullman, the dining car was a chance to further indulge the luxury market. And how. The hotel cars on the Chicago–Omaha leg of the transcontinental route listed no fewer than fifteen seafood dishes—kept fresh with vast quantities of ice carried in a separate car—and no fewer than thirty-seven meat entrées, including a prodigious selection of game. On the highly competitive route between New York and Chicago in the 1880s, according to Geoffrey Freeman Allen, Pullman's mouthwatering menus included, besides staples such as chicken, ham, chops, and porterhouse steaks, "exotica such as English snipe, quail, golden plover and blue winged teal; or oysters and clams, raw, stewed, boiled, fried or 'fancy roast' as you might wish, all at around 50 cents per person."[11] If you still had the appetite, a rum omelet would set you back only a further forty cents, and a good brandy could be had for just thirty cents. Life on the crack trains for affluent passengers was rather like a permanent party. The sexes, in good Victorian fashion, were separated, with lounges for ladies and club cars complete with card tables for the men, who could drink, smoke, and gamble without being bothered. Nothing was spared in the decor, with its rich upholstery, heavy drapes, massive freestanding armchairs (discreetly bolted down to cope with the vagaries of the track), perhaps even a piano, and always a well-stocked library.

Of course, things were not like that for everyone. Hoi polloi traveled in more modest style, but the introduction of sleeping and dining cars was part of a wider improvement to rail services that began as soon as the Civil War ended and continued through to the end of the century.

Technical improvements to trains made a difference not just to passengers' comfort, but also, crucially, to their safety. The poor safety record of the railroads had become a national scandal after the Civil War. As we saw in Chapter 3, there were few accidents in the early days, but as trains speeded up and services became more frequent, both the frequency and the seriousness of rail disasters increased.

Most early deaths came about not through accidents but as a result of passengers, unused to even the modest speeds of the trains, jumping on and off cars while they were in motion. The American design of coaches, with a platform at both ends, was far too tempting for passengers who saw a train departing, and not a few ended up under the wheels. Leaning out of the window was another bad idea, as there was very little clearance. One early victim on the Erie soon after its opening was a Mrs. Walters, who made the mistake of trying to ensure her luggage had been taken on board and was killed instantly when her head hit a station support.

The most common victims, however, were trespassers, or simply "track strollers," whose deaths attracted little attention because they were seen as largely their own fault. Track walking was a deceptively hazardous activity that, in a way, was almost encouraged by the lack of fencing. As mentioned in Chapter 2, this was partly the result of American railroads being built on the cheap, but also of the fact that they stretched far into virgin territory where fencing was simply unnecessary. It was, perhaps, understandable that it took time for people to comprehend the danger posed by the speed at which trains traveled. As today in parts of Asia and Latin America, the railroad track often represented the best route for walking between neighboring villages, but those who used these shortcuts were unaware that a train traveling at just thirty miles per hour covers forty-four feet per second and, on the single tracks that were the norm in those days, could come from either direction. Walking in the same direction as the wind was particularly hazardous, as the sound of a train behind the hapless stroller might not be heard until it was too late. Drunkenness, too, was a contributing factor in many track fatalities.

Right from the beginning, "trespassers"—who included suicides, since standing in front of a train ensured that no second attempt was required—were the biggest category of casualties. As Henry Poor, the editor of the *American Railroad Journal*, wrote in 1855, "Of the hundreds who are annually maimed or slaughtered on our railroads, more have certainly fallen victim from careless walking or lying [!] on the track than from any other half-dozen causes put together." Mark Aldrich, a chronicler of disasters on the American railroads, reckons that "railroads killed children by the hundreds who were playing on the track or gathering coal."[12] The State of New York responded to these accidents in 1850 by requiring fencing, but this was a rare exception, and the American railroads remain largely unfenced to this day. By 1890, deaths by "trespassing" had reached an annual rate of more than three thousand and would attain a peak of more than fifty-five hundred during the First World War.

These statistics did not include deaths at grade crossings, which were a major source of accidents and remain one of the greatest risk areas of train travel in the United States.[13] As mentioned in Chapter 2, the American railroads differed from their European counterparts by the proliferation of grade crossings, or "level crossings" as they are called in Europe. On main lines European railroads in general separated roads from railroads with bridges or tunnels. In America the railroads, built quickly and cheaply, crossed roads without a bridge or underpass being provided. There were no crossing keepers, and accidents were inevitable. In the days when only horses and carts trundled along the road, damage and injury were largely confined to the road users, although there was the odd exception when the accident caused a train to derail. However, as roads became busier—ironically as a result of the very development stimulated by the railroads—the risks increased.

It was not just passengers, trespassers, or road users who lost their lives on the railroads. It was, in fact, railroad employees who faced by far the greatest risk, and within a couple of decades of the start of the railroad age, the annual death toll had already reached three figures. Indeed, railroad employees have always suffered far more fatalities than passengers, and in the early days there was little regard for their safety, despite the great variety of risks they encountered, which attracted little attention in the press. Working on the open track was ever hazardous, but the biggest danger was in shunting yards, where drivers, firemen, and track workers were often hit by engines. Even though the locomotives moved only very slowly, the result of such collisions was frequently fatal. Boiler explosions were a far greater hazard than they were in Europe, as locomotives were pushed harder over longer distances and at higher pressures to get up the steeper gradients, and there was no inspection regime. Indeed, unlike in most European countries, the US government did not initially inspect new railroads before they opened. The first such inspections were introduced at the state level in New York only in 1855, but there was no universal system until much later. Nor was there a systematic way of investigating accidents. Again, New York was the pioneer, setting up a commission to investigate accidents based on the British Board of Trade, but only a few states followed suit before the Civil War.

Indeed, there was a lack of regulation of all aspects of the railroads until the later years of the nineteenth century. Although there were a few regulations in some states, generally introduced as a response to a particular disaster, there was what could be described as a deliberate "want of government regulation." America was a country of pioneers, different from staid Europe, and it was in keeping with its spirit that perhaps less regard was paid to safety than on the other side of the Atlantic. The contrast between European and American attitudes was summed up by an Englishman, Charles Weld, whose train was derailed because of the crew's efforts to make up time. He found that most of the passengers commended the train crew's attempts to get back on schedule and commented, "Accidents on railways are thought so little of in America it is useless to remonstrate." Not entirely. Gradually, the situation changed as accidents, and the publicity surrounding them, proliferated. The tone of the most extreme newspaper coverage can be gauged from a comment in the *Ogdensburg (NY) Republican,* which in 1852 claimed there had been "a proposal in the state legislature to abolish hanging and substitute for punishment a ride upon some of our railroads."[14]

In terms of bald statistics, rail travel was generally very safe, especially when one considers that it was a novel technology that was still bedding down. The death toll of passengers was small in relation to the millions using the railroads, but by the mid-1850s the perception of danger was understandably heightened as these accidents came to the notice of the public through a press that was never restrained in its reporting of disasters and tended to illustrate its coverage with lurid line drawings. The clamor for legislation increased as the trains grew in number and traveled ever faster.

The year 1853 was a seminal one in terms of rail accidents and the public attitude toward them. It had started particularly badly with the death in January of Bennie, the eight-year-old son of the president-elect, Franklin Pierce. The family was traveling from Boston to their home in Concord, New Hampshire, on the Boston & Lowell Railroad, when a coupling broke, sending the Pierces' car down an embankment. Although the coach was rather more luxuriously appointed than most contemporary cars, it was still a flimsy wooden affair that broke up easily on impact, and poor Bennie was killed instantly, crushed under a seat. It was a tragedy from which his father, who along with his wife was unhurt in the crash, never really recovered during his undistinguished four-year term in the White House.

That relatively minor accident was a portent of far worse to come later in the year. Two major disasters took place within a fortnight of each other in the spring of 1853, and their proximity exacerbated the sense that railroads were dangerous. The first was at a railroad intersection near Chicago accurately known as Grand Crossing. Chicago was experiencing its initial surge of railroad construction, and railroad lines were being laid with little thought for safety or operating convenience. At Grand Crossing the tracks of the Michigan Central had been built right across those of the Lake Shore & Michigan Southern, two hostile rivals. The procedure for such intersections was crude and required all trains to stop, but the rules were not always followed by engineers who believed that trains of other companies were simply unwanted intruders.[15] On April 25, an eastbound Michigan Central express bound for Toledo, Ohio, ran into the side of a heavily loaded Michigan Southern immigrant train that failed to observe a stop signal, causing the death of twenty-one German passengers and injuring many more. Less than two weeks later, on May 6, the first major railroad bridge accident in the United States occurred on the New Haven Railroad, and again it was a driver who was responsible. The drawbridge over the Norwalk River in Connecticut was operated by a signaler who had correctly imposed a stop signal, which the driver ignored. The train plunged into the river with the loss of forty-six lives, and the driver narrowly escaped being lynched by the angry survivors, a fate that, according to George H. Douglas, "would befall numerous engineers—some culpable, some totally innocent—in the years ahead."[16]

The proximity of two accidents of such magnitude led to much anguished speculation in the newspapers about the safety of the railroads. There were several more high-profile accidents that year, but with lower death tolls. At the time, the most spectacular accidents were the growing numbers of head-on crashes, known with tombstone humor as "cornfield meets." Since almost all railroads were single track, with no signaling, early train schedules were simply set by intervals between trains. But without telegraphic communication, which only began to be introduced widely in the 1850s, it was impossible to communicate between train and dispatchers (known as controllers in Britain), placing broken-down trains in great peril. The conductor was supposed to run down the track to put down warning flares, but on occasion this procedure broke down, resulting in disaster. Operating rules were crude and at times vague. Remark-ably, the rules of several railroads, including some major ones such as the Camden & Amboy, the Western & Atlantic, and the Georgia Central, decreed that if two trains met, the one closest to a loop (or "turnout," sections where there were two tracks to allow trains to pass each other) should reverse. According to Aldrich, "This encouraged train crews to speed, both to go beyond a turnout and if that failed, to back into it."[17] The result, on the Camden & Amboy, was predictable. In August 1855, a train from Philadelphia had arrived at Burlington, the normal crossing point, early and, according to company rules, was allowed to leave after waiting ten minutes when the train from New York failed to show up. However, once under way, the driver spotted the train coming from New York, and it was up to him to go back. He reversed at great speed, hitting a horse and buggy driven by an elderly doctor. The rear coach was derailed by the col-lision with the buggy, pulling four other coaches with it and causing the deaths of twenty-three passengers.

The deadliness of "cornfield meets" was all too baldly demonstrated at Camp Hill on the North Pennsylvania Railroad on July 17, 1856. The world's worst railroad accident to date, with fifty-six fatalities, it became known as the Picnic Train disaster because it involved a Sunday excursion train. (In the history of rail accidents, both in the United States and else-where, excursion trains have featured regularly. The reasons for this in-clude the fact that they did not appear in the regular timetables, often used old stock, and were frequently overloaded.) Packed with at least one thou-sand passengers, mainly Irish teenagers from the local Catholic church heading for a hot day in the park, the train smashed head-on into a local service because the driver, though knowing that the other train would be coming in the opposite direction, was speeding along the line in the hope of reaching the next turnout in order to catch up on lost time. The two trains met at a bend with such force that the explosion was heard five miles away, and the resulting fire caused most of the deaths. The driver of the local train blamed himself and immediately committed suicide by tak-ing arsenic, although in fact he was exonerated by the subsequent inquiry.

The disaster speeded up the introduction and use of the telegraph, bringing about a major improvement in safety. A system of issuing train orders, which authorized a train crew to proceed to a particular point such as a station or a loop, was developed. However, cornfield meets continued to occur when there was confusion over the orders, or procedures were not followed properly. Silent films would later portray robbers trying to arrange train wrecks by deliberately forcing the dispatcher to issue false orders so that they could steal from the wreckage, but no evidence exists of such a crime ever actually being committed. Head-on collisions were the most spectacular of the litany of possible accidents, but derailments caused by broken rails or proceeding too fast around bends, bridge failures, livestock on the line, and broken axles all contributed to fatal accidents in the early days of the railroads. At root the problem was that the rapid spread of the railroads had not been matched by the technological changes required to keep them safe. For a time, anger about rail safety subsided as the number of spectacular accidents declined significantly. The Civil War diverted attention to the far-bloodier tragedy taking place before the eyes of the public. In the aftermath of the war, however, as both the numbers traveling and the mileage of railroad increased rapidly, safety again became an issue, fueled by a series of yet more eminently preventable accidents.

In many respects, the technology was improving. More powerful locomotives were able to travel faster and to haul a larger number of cars that, since weight became less of a concern, could be fitted with all sorts of extras to make travel more comfortable for passengers. Longer stretches could be covered without stopping, as a locomotive could typically travel around a hundred miles without needing to be resupplied or changed. Furthermore, longer rails, manufactured from steel rather than iron, made for a smoother ride and reduced the number of broken rails, a frequent cause of accidents. However, overall safety was lagging behind. There was no excuse. In the postwar period, the technology was being developed, but there was a lack of will to introduce it. Faced with the obvious need for better safety devices, the railroad companies were not so much resistant as downright obstructive, seeing accidents as an unfortunate but unavoidable side effect of an industry in which large machines moved at high speed. They failed to see that investing in safety would improve both the reliability and the image of their product.

Two related safety devices, the automatic coupler and the air brake, were crucial and would make the biggest difference in terms of safety, but it took a lengthy campaign of lobbying to bring about their universal adoption. Coupling and braking had been a technical and safety problem for the railroads since their very invention. The coupling between cars involved a crude link-and-pin device that required a brakeman to stand between the cars, guide the link into a socket, drop the pin in place, and, if necessary, hammer it down. Not easy, not safe. In the dark, with a slippery oil lantern in one hand, it was even more perilous. It was said that if a man was looking for work as a brakeman and claimed to be experienced, he was asked to show his hands—missing digits were the key confirmation that he had previously worked in the job. The device had the disadvantage, too, of breaking as a result of metal fatigue and causing accidents with runaway cars or wagons. Soon after the Civil War, several better couplers were devised, notably one designed by Ezra Miller that involved a platform with buffers and was adopted by several railroads. Critically, Miller's platform prevented the oscillation that was a risk with link-and-pin devices because they allowed slack. But his invention was not perfect. Although the platform reduced the risk of "telescoping" of cars in an accident, a very dangerous phenomenon, it did not prevent the possibility entirely, especially at higher speeds. An improved device patented by Eli Janney in 1873 had the added advantage of being automatic, which meant that men no longer had to stand between cars to couple and uncouple trains (though they still had to go each time on the tracks to open "the jaws," the mechanism that enables cars to be connected with one another).

Braking, too, was primitive in the extreme. Locomotives had no mechanism to slow them down apart from putting them in reverse, which good drivers did only in an emergency. Instead, once the driver gave the signal to slow down, a brakeman had to clamber along the roof of the train from the rear and apply the brakes fitted on each car. Normally, there would also be a brakeman at the front who would work his way toward the back of the train. There was no end of potential for accidents with this arrangement, not least the risk to the brakemen themselves. As a former brakeman described the process, it "took nerve, coordination, timing and a perfect sense of balance, to go over the top of a freight train—winter or summer . . . rain, snow, sleet, ice all over the roofs and on brake wheels and handholds."[18] And it was a very unsatisfactory way of slowing down trains that were becoming increasingly fast. Uneven braking could lead to a snapped coupling, with the risk of runaway cars.

George Westinghouse, a remarkable young engineer, already had a couple of inventions under his belt before devising a solution to this problem: continuous braking. Legend has it that Westinghouse witnessed a railroad accident in which two engineers saw one another, but were unable to stop their trains in time using the existing brakes. Westinghouse's idea was to place a compressed-air tank in the locomotive and run a hose connected to a cylinder on each car that operated the brake shoes. Switching on the air would push the shoes down onto the wheels. It took him a while to overcome various difficulties, such as how to stop the front cars from braking before those at the back, but after three years of development, the method was patented in 1872. A rival invention was the vacuum brake, which operates when air is allowed into the vacuum. There was much debate about which system was superior—both devices were certainly a great improvement on what had gone before—but ultimately it was the air brake that would win out in America, as it would in most European countries.

Janney's coupling and the Westinghouse brake combined well to improve rail safety. However, although some rail companies introduced one or both systems relatively quickly, many resisted or used them only on passenger trains, which meant that freight trains remained a major hazard. It took the fanaticism of one man, with the appropriate name of Lorenzo Coffin, a tall, bewhiskered farmer from Iowa, to badger the lawmakers into making the Westinghouse air brake and the Janney coupler mandatory.

Coffin is an unlikely hero of the history of the railroads. Initially, he had no official role in the rail industry but was one of those local busybodies whose letters appear in the local newspaper when there are no others. He was a self-styled lobbyist on railroad matters and developed considerable knowledge by touring the country, mainly on freight trains, and talking to railroad workers. He had first become interested in the issue when he observed an accident in which a brakeman on a freight train lost the two remaining fingers of his right hand while coupling two cars, having lost the others in similar incidents. Coffin, who had been a chaplain in the Civil War and was blessed with both religious fervor and technical expertise, began to lobby for the railroad companies to install automatic couplers along with air brakes that could be operated from the locomotive.

This system not only provided better braking but also made the brakeman's job safer.

Coffin traveled around Iowa promoting railroad safety and was appointed the state's first railroad commissioner in 1883 at the age of sixty, a mostly honorary position but one that at least gave him a locus from which he could lobby the rail companies. He drafted Iowa's first Railroad Safety Appliance Act, but even after it became state law, railroads ignored its requirements. Coffin realized that federal legislation would be required, and he became something of a one-man-band campaigner, writing countless articles in obscure journals. According to Stewart H. Holbrook, he "invited himself to conventions of railroad officials and equipment builders, and here he was as welcome as leprosy." Eventually, the Master Car Builders Association was persuaded to hold a series of tests on an eight-mile stretch of the Chicago, Burlington & Quincy Railroad. The Burlington Trials, as they became known, were intended to test the ability of various braking systems to stop fifty-car freight trains. Initially, none of the systems, even Westinghouse's, performed well, which seemed to vindicate the skepticism of the railroad companies, which doubted that these new types of brakes would ever be adequate for anything but short and light trains. However, Westinghouse adjusted his system, and at the third trial, in the summer of 1887, the test train was stopped from forty miles per hour within five hundred feet, a huge improvement on anything previously recorded. The following year the Interstate Commerce Commission (ICC), the federal regulatory board for the industry (about which much more in Chapter 9), had begun examining safety in the industry and was influenced by Coffin's arguments. The commission started recording statistics on the industry's safety record that revealed, shockingly, that two thousand workers were killed and ten times that number injured on the railroads in 1888. No fewer than three hundred men died in coupling accidents alone. Coffin, no longer a commissioner, gatecrashed a meeting of state railroad commissioners that year and made a speech that proved highly influential in creating the right political climate for the legislation to be passed. He had been hired by the unions representing brakemen and conductors to lobby for the equipment to be made mandatory and used his powers as an orator to recount, in great detail, numerous tales of needless deaths and personal tragedy on the railroads: "He piled horror upon horror, and interspersed the bloody statistics with pitiful tales of the aftermath of accidents." Although Coffin's efforts helped influence public opinion, it took another five years before Congress passed the bill that he had drafted. In March 1893 President Benjamin Harrison finally signed the Railroad Safety Appliance Act, by which all American railroads were required to adopt air brakes and automatic couplers. Coffin, whose efforts had done so much to bring about the legislation, was given the pen used to sign the bill into law: "Coffin [was] a fanatic to the last, one of the most useful fanatics this country has produced, the man Westinghouse and Janney needed to give their inventions real and widespread use."[19]

The railroads, as ever, objected. Not, of course, because they were oblivious to the mounting death toll, but because they argued it would be a mistake to tie them to a particular technology, rather like Apple being forced into using Microsoft software today. It was a familiar argument of industries wishing to resist regulation. Faced with mounting public pressure as a result of the large number of deaths, the railroads inevitably lost the argument. After the usual delays to give time for the railroads to make the necessary changes, the Railroad Safety Appliance Act became fully operative by August 1900. A further safety feature, and one that did not become widespread until the early years of the twentieth century, was the all-steel coach, which was much more fire and crash resistant than its wooden predecessors, but again it took a long time for the railroad companies to make the required investment. The act, indeed, entrenched a rather different approach to safety from that in Europe. Rather than trying to avoid crashes entirely, which was the European philosophy, America has tended to focus on crashworthiness. This has resulted, for example, in uniquely heavy coaches being mandated and, as we will see in the final chapter, has proved costly to the railroads and detrimental to their interests.

These developments were all part of a wider process of standardization and equipment and operating procedures, which further reduced costs and made it easier for railroads to operate their trains on the lines of other companies, creating the beginnings of a truly national rail network. This was a period of rapid expansion and consolidation, during which the very nature of the rail system changed visibly. For example, many towns with two or more stations built one central "union" station, linking lines that had hitherto been separate. The first such joint station was opened in Columbus, Ohio, in 1862, and the concept was picked up in subsequent decades in many major cities, though also in some relatively small towns such as Worcester, Massachusetts, where the station served no fewer than five railroads.

A key development was the near-universal adoption of the standard gauge of four feet and eight and a half inches for the tracks, which became inevitable after Congress had decreed that the transcontinental line would use it. The decision had been hotly debated. Lincoln favored the five-foot gauge that was in use throughout much of the South, but he eventually bowed to northern interests who lobbied for standard gauge. There were some who thought it was a mistake: "That additional 3½ins of track width would have meant even more inches of car width, hence roomier seats, wider aisles—making it possible for two fat people to pass each other in the aisle without danger of throwing the train off the track."[20] Even more useful today in the age of obesity! Following the transcontinental decision, the vast majority of railroads built in the aftermath of the Civil War used standard gauge, and many other lines were converted in this period.

As railroad companies expanded to serve national rather than local interests, the idea that it was better for a railroad to have a separate gauge from its local rivals had become redundant. *Cooperation* rather than *confrontation* was now the watchword. Railroads work best as an integrated system: the longer that passengers and freight can travel without changing trains, the better the service. Even the Erie, with its magnificent broad gauge of six feet, had to swallow its pride in order to allow through trains on its tracks. In the South, the five-foot gauge was changed to standard over two days in the early summer of 1886, large gangs of track workers moving one of the rails on thirteen thousand miles of track. The operation—staggering in its organizational scope—also required converting eighteen hundred locomotives and forty thousand coaches, although some of these already had adjustable axles. Until this time, trains heading in and out of the South had been subject to a delay of up to a half hour as their cars were lifted by hoists and attached to wheel sets of the right gauge. The efforts of tens of thousands of workers over a momentous thirty-six-hour period on May 31–June 1, 1886, created—at last—a unified railroad for almost the whole United States.

Apart from accidents, railroad passengers faced a rather more mundane risk, but one that was all too common: robbery. Although exaggerated in films and popular culture, this was a genuine danger in the last decades of the nineteenth century. According to the *Encyclopedia of North American Railroads*, train robberies "grew into a uniquely American phenomenon" that plagued the railroads for a half century.[21] Numerous figures emerged, many of whom have been mythologized in westerns: Sam Bass and the Reno brothers from Indiana, the Younger and James brothers from Missouri who formed a joint gang, and the Daltons from Kansas.[22] Initially, most robberies were in the Midwest, but as the railroads expanded in the West, so did the number and location of attacks. Contrary to legend, Native Americans did not attack the passenger trains that now crossed their land. Although, as we have seen, they had occasionally tried to disrupt construction of the railroads, by the time the lines were completed, the indigenous peoples of the plains and farther west had been defeated, massacred, or pacified. Indeed, passengers heading out west were often excited by the prospect of coming across Indians, with romantic notions of seeing half-naked "noble savages" with feathered headdresses skillfully riding their horses, suggesting there were sexual undertones in these Victorian ladies' descriptions of their encounters with Native Americans. The reality was sadly different. In some cases, as with the Central Pacific, the Indians had been given free passes to travel on the lines, and, as trains full of tourists and immigrants started arriving, they would congregate at stations, begging or selling a few knickknacks. Although through the car window the Native Americans might present an exciting image, travelers began to fear encountering them for rather more prosaic reasons than being attacked: "On the train or at close range in the station they did not appear to be as clean as some tourists would have liked."[23]

The white robber gangs, however, were another matter and remained a problem for the railroad companies right until the end of the century and even, occasionally, beyond. The many armed and rootless men left by the Civil War were for the most part the perpetrators of these audacious crimes. The earliest recorded attack, near Cincinnati on the Ohio & Mississippi during the last few days of the war in May 1865, was probably the result of military action. A gang of thieves derailed the train and promptly

robbed the passengers, though sparing the women, and escaped over a
river toward Kentucky. The first peacetime armed train robbery was in
October the following year at Seymour, Indiana, on the same railroad. The
target was an express mail wagon that the messengers were forced to open
after being threatened with a gun. The two masked robbers snatched thirteen thousand dollars from the safe, pulled the bell cord to stop the train,
and escaped into the night. This was a typical pattern. For the most part, it
was the high-value mail and the safe in the mail car rather than, as in the
cowboy films, the passengers who were targeted.

Several similar successful attacks were carried out that year on midwestern railroads, and most were the handiwork of the Reno brothers'
gang. Their biggest heist, on the Jeffersonville, Madison & Indianapolis
Railroad in May 1868, netted a staggering ninety-six thousand dollars and
resulted in the death of a messenger, beaten and thrown from the train,
but a few months later vigilantes and sheriffs caught up with the three
Reno brothers along with a fourth gang member, and they were later
lynched. After a two-year lull, in the early 1870s there was a spate of robberies in several states, from Kentucky to Nevada, and even one in the
East, on a train run by the Boston & Albany. Most of the attacks followed
the same modus operandi. At a remote stop, the robbers would climb on
the baggage car, where they could not be seen by either the locomotive
men or the train crew, and would clamber over the roofs of the coaches to
the tender, where they forced the driver to stop the train. There were, in
truth, probably not as many attacks as suggested by the sensationalist
publicity they attracted, but the robberies certainly had an impact on the
railroad companies. Anxious to maintain the image of being a safe form
of transportation, they strengthened their mail cars and improved their
security. Most controversially, they employed security guards from the
Pinkerton Agency to act as a kind of private army not only to protect
the trains but also to pursue actively the perpetrators. The Pinkertons,
whose uncompromising methods came to the fore in strikebreaking toward the end of the century (see next chapter), almost matched the robbers in their ruthlessness. The most famous of the train robbers was the
James-Younger gang led by Jesse James and his brother Frank, former
Confederate guerrillas in the Civil War who turned to a life of banditry.

Having robbed various banks and become outlaws, in July 1873 the gang turned to train robbery on the Chicago, Rock Island & Pacific Railroad near Adair, Iowa. Their method—simply removing a rail—lacked subtlety and caused the death of the driver, who was crushed under the locomotive when it keeled over, but that did not stop them from raiding the safe and grabbing valuables from the passengers. Several more robberies ensued, and the Pinkerton men were soon on the case. After a shoot-out in March 1874, in which one gang member and two Pinkerton agents were killed, it was, strangely, the Pinkertons who attracted the wrath of the public by committing a crass public-relations blunder through an unlawful attack on the James home in Missouri early the following year. Unbelievably, the Pinkerton men used the rather unsubtle method of simply shoving a hefty bomb through a window, killing a half brother and injuring the mother of the James boys, who, contrary to their information, were not in the house at the time. The resulting press onslaught against the Pinkertons' methods did much to make the James brothers, ruthless murderers though they were, almost respectable. Their image was helped by the fact that when robbing trains, they usually left the passengers alone while they robbed the safe and took the mail. Most of the gang were eventually captured or killed in a bank raid in Northfield, Minnesota, in September 1876, though Jesse survived until April 1882, when he was shot in the back by a bounty hunter who had infiltrated the gang.

Although passengers were rarely targeted in these robberies, one attack did have catastrophic results. In December 1896, a gang dislodged a rail on a bridge on a branch of the Louisville & Nashville, sending a local train plunging into the Cahaba River near Birmingham, Alabama. The death toll was twenty-seven, and the robbers compounded their calumny by going through the cars to steal from the dead and injured before help could arrive.

An attack such as this was, however, very much the exception, which explains, perhaps, why the public attitude toward these attacks was surprisingly sympathetic. The James gang, in particular, attracted favorable publicity, thanks to the support of the founder of the anti-Republican *Kansas City Times,* John Newman Edwards, who saw Jesse James as a potential leader of a revived Confederate insurgency and published a series of letters from him proclaiming his innocence. The action of the gangs, too, reflected, albeit in extreme form, the growing public dislike of the railroads as corrupt and domineering organizations that had become too powerful. Indeed, Stewart H. Holbrook suggests the James gang was able to continue operating for so long because "the public attitude towards the railroads in the 1870s . . . was one of fear and hatred combined." The robbers were perceived as Robin Hood figures, with the wealthy railroad companies and the more affluent travelers as their target—even though in truth for the most part the robbers were intent only on getting their hands on large amounts of cash. A few attacks, however, notably by the outlaw Chris Evans and various associates against the Southern Pacific in California, were motivated by anger at the railroads' exploitation of their monopoly position against the interests of local settlers: "Many people had no sympathy for the railroad and saw train robbers as democratic heroes rather than villains."[24] Countless songs and poems were composed in honor of the thieves, often recounting highly sanitized versions of their actions in which they stopped a train, restricting themselves to robbing the rich and raiding the safe, and then rode off on horseback into the desert. It was part of a folklore that was both born of the growing antipathy toward the railroads and also further stimulated it, a phenomenon that will be analyzed in the next chapter.

It was the same suspicion and dislike of the railroad companies that led to the romanticization of the hoboes who jumped freight trains and traveled free. Like train robbers, they enjoyed a measure of public support because they were perceived as getting one over on rapacious corporations who saw fit to hand out huge numbers of free passes to VIPs, especially politicians, who might be useful to them and were contemptuously known as "deadheads" or "fare beaters." The phenomenon of hoboes jumping trains had its roots in the chaotic aftermath of the Civil War, when large numbers of rootless men traveled the country with little clear purpose. Some were tramps, living life permanently on the road and never seeking work, but most men jumped trains in order to seek work or a new life, most commonly out west. It was a precarious way to travel. If possible, they boarded the trains at stations or freight sidings, but sometimes they hopped on trains trundling slowly through towns, running the obvious risk of being dragged underneath. There was a constant game of cat and mouse between the train conductors and the hoboes, who rode anywhere on the train where they could keep out of view of the crew. The most perilous hiding place was on top of the cars, where falling asleep could prove fatal, but it could be equally dangerous to ride between or underneath the cars. The lucky ones found an empty wagon or broke into one, which they raided for any food or portable valuables. They risked the wrath of the conductors, who, however, sometimes turned a blind eye to these freeloaders, not least because many of them were former railroad workers or, indeed, were seeking a job on the railroads. Many of the hoboes, of course, had a drinking problem, as did many railroad workers, especially the drivers. According to Dee Brown, "Pioneer engineers on the Western railroads had a reputation for heavy drinking" as an antidote to the stresses of operating trains in such dangerous conditions, with the risk of attacks by robbers, derailments caused by the poor track, or collisions with other locomotives or livestock.[25] Passengers occasionally attributed particularly bumpy rides to the lack of sobriety of the train crew, and, although drinking was a fireable offense, the railroad companies often took a lenient attitude, recognizing the pressures of the job. Use of alcohol was so prevalent that after his successful campaign, Coffin, the great safety campaigner, turned his attention to the issue and established a Railroad Temperance Society in an effort to try to reduce drinking among railroad workers.

Drunk engineers were only one cause of discomfort for ordinary passengers. By the last quarter of the nineteenth century, with the railroad well established as the only means of traveling long distances, rail travel was still rarely a happy experience. Indeed, the conditions that passengers were obliged to tolerate would be one of the reasons the railroad companies gradually became pariahs. The Pullman cars were one end of the spectrum of services offered by the railroads. At the other end, even during the Gilded Age of the 1870s and 1880s, when the railroads were expanding at a ferocious rate, train travel for the masses remained pretty grim.

The conditions that immigrants had to face were undoubtedly the worst. Despite improvements in services and connections, there were no coast-to-coast services, and it was only toward the end of the century that there were regular through trains between New York and Chicago. The completion of the bridge over the Missouri in 1872 theoretically allowed for an easier transfer, but the eastern railroads refused to cooperate with the Union Pacific, forcing passengers laden with their baggage to use the wagons of a special transfer company to reach the other side. Given the need for all these changes, and the slowness of the trains, an immigrant might take seven days to reach the West Coast, whereas passengers enjoying the faster and better-appointed trains might complete the journey in four or five. Even after the Missouri bridge was built, the journey necessitated several changes. People arriving at Chicago heading west would already have been "forced to change trains once or several times, probably at Buffalo, Pittsburgh or Detroit." And Chicago itself inevitably brought a change of train: "During the heyday of American railroad passenger travel, one of the common sayings was that a hog could travel across country through Chicago without changing cars at Chicago, but a human being could not."[26]

Immigrants were designated special cars—and sometimes entire trains—consisting of the oldest and least-comfortable equipment. Thus, they traveled in wooden coaches with flat roofs, fitted out with hard wooden benches, and still heated with the potbellied stove in the middle that fried those near it and was of no use to those farther away. There was a "convenience" at each end of the coach, a mere hole giving out onto the rails. There was no running water of any kind. The news butcher (see Chapter 3) provided bottled water and other basics, but the trains still stopped for meals that had to be bolted down with great haste, as the railroad staff were intent on avoiding delays. According to George H. Douglas, "Crews on immigrant trains were apparently especially sadistic, and would sometimes start up after only five or ten minutes, without the slightest warning to passengers, perhaps delighting in being able to leave part of their troubling horde for the next day's immigrant train."[27] Pullman service it was not.

In 1879, before he achieved fame as the author of *Treasure Island* and *The Strange Case of Dr. Jekyll and Mr. Hyde*, Robert Louis Stevenson traveled on an immigrant train nearly ten years after the completion of the first transcontinental. On these trains, conditions were not much better than those described by Dickens nearly forty years earlier, as cited in Chapter 3. The discomfort began the moment he boarded the train at Castle Garden

Station in New York: "There was no waiting room, no refreshment room, the cars were locked; and for at least another hour or so it seemed, we had to camp upon the draughty, gaslit platform."[28]

After several changes of trains, Stevenson was put on an immigrant train at Council Bluffs, Iowa, consisting of just three passenger coaches—known for some unaccountable reason as "Zulu trains" in the West—to which were added a baggage car, various freight wagons, and a caboose and which, at times, carried entire families along with their chickens and even a goat or cow for milk. One of the passenger cars was reserved for Chinese, at least fifty of whom were crammed into the car with their baggage. Indeed, in this period in America, the Chinese suffered much racism and were generally provided with separate cars, just like the separate "Jim Crow" cars that were becoming standard for black people on the segregated trains of the South. Stevenson was shocked to find his fellow travelers discussing the Chinese in terms of such stereotypes as uncleanliness—in fact, the Chinese were likely to have been cleaner than most of the Caucasians on the train—deviousness, and clannishness, the last being an all too understandable and sensible response to their pariah status. Stevenson also found the train staff almost brutally rude. He asked a conductor three times when a dinner stop would be made, and the man merely "looked me coolly in the face for several seconds and turned ostentatiously away."[29]

Stevenson installed himself in the men's car, where for $2.50 he managed to buy three straw cushions and a board on which he could sleep when placed across the backs of seats. Except he found sleep almost an impossibility, as Dee Brown reports, "with his fellow travelers sprawled on boards, seats, and flooring, all being continually shaken by the rough motion of the train groaning and muttering in their half slumber."[30] Stevenson thought it strange that women, with their children, had no compunction about wandering into the men's car, despite the spitting, swearing, and card playing. The car was spartan in the extreme, with no upholstery, no springs to soften the journey, and poor ventilation. And the journey was slow, all too slow. Stevenson moaned that the train was constantly driven onto sidetracks to wait for other services, all of which were given priority over the immigrant trains, with the result that their final arrival time could not be predicted even within a day or so. On the tracks, the trains managed as little as nine miles per hour in sections where the track had been hastily laid and perhaps thirty-five at best. In the early 1870s, the average speed was around twenty miles per hour, but this improved quickly and would double in the following decade.

Stevenson also complained that at the dinner stops, "the train stole from the station without note of warning," whereas on all other trains a warning cry of "all aboard" was issued.[31] He just missed out on the big improvement in meal services brought about by the innovative Fred Harvey, who realized that there was good money to be made from providing better-quality eating houses for the great majority of train passengers who could not afford Pullman. Harvey, who had worked for the railroads as a caterer for several years, decided in 1878 to set out on his own and opened the first of a series of restaurants at the stations of the Atchison, Topeka & Santa Fe Railway, which became renowned for service and quality and in particular for the "Harvey Girls," the waitresses chosen for their attractiveness and attentiveness. These young women were subject to a strict regime, being made to wear prim uniforms and required to live in hostels where they were barred from consorting with passengers—or any other men, for that matter. They acted as a civilizing influence on the customers, who previously had a reputation for being so unruly that the girls' predecessors, mostly black men, had to carry firearms. The Harvey Girls achieved such widespread popularity that they featured in a raucous eponymous 1946 musical. These restaurants were to become a feature of rail travel in the West, providing a vital service, until dining cars became universal,[32] and even then Harvey, credited with creating the first American restaurant chain, responded by opening several eateries in the big union stations springing up in places such as Chicago, St. Louis, and Los Angeles that survived until the decline of the railroads after the Second World War.

Whereas immigrants were at the bottom of the scale in terms of the service they received, many poorer travelers on branch and local lines fared little better than before. There was a fantastic proliferation of such railroads, most still serving local interests and businesses, and the service on these lines usually consisted of just a few mixed-traffic trains, combining a few freight wagons with a couple of passenger cars per day. The trains would stop at all stations, often taking a long time to unload freight, but they would still represent a lifeline for local people. Traveling conditions remained primitive. Whereas the large railroad companies were, by the 1880s, introducing improvements such as electric lighting and steam heating on the trains, most passengers on these smaller lines did not see such progress until well into the twentieth century—if ever, given these lines were among the first to close.

These short lines, as they are known, tended to live off hand-me-downs from the larger companies, both locomotives and rolling stock. Sometimes these were ill-suited for purpose, such as on the West River Railroad in Vermont, where longer trains had to be split in two to be hauled up the sharper inclines. On the Walla Walla & Columbia River Railroad in Washington State, the engineers reportedly had to fill up the water tank with bucketfuls hauled up by rope from the local creek. It was not unknown, either, for the passengers to have to help out when the train was held up: "Obstacles such as rainstorms, which revealed leaky roofs in the cars, or blizzards . . . stopped trains for days while the passengers and crew dug [them] out."[33] Nevertheless, most of these lines survived because they were a lifeline for the local economy, and many, too, benefited from mail contracts that were an effective hidden subsidy.

Since roads and road transportation were still primitive, branch lines were built to the remotest places, often at the whim of the local landowner. Their very names evoke a world that seems rather more than just over a century away. Take the eight-mile Narragansett Pier Railroad, which opened in 1876 to serve the fashionable Rhode Island resort of that name on a branch from the New Haven Railroad. It was family owned and "employed only the ricketiest of engines and rolling stock once the summer people were gone." At one point, for obscure reasons, the Pennsylvania sought to buy it and sent a telegram to its president asking for the price. The response is part of railroad legend: "Mine not for sale, how much for yours?" Journeys on such lines might be delayed by the conductor's deciding it was a good time to shoot a rabbit or, more seriously, because beavers had decided to make a meal of a bridge, a common hazard on the two-foot-gauge lines in western Maine. These lines were run informally, and rarely for profit: "The engineer might well be the president of the company, the brakeman his brother."[34]

One kind of local line did prosper, however. This was the period when the number of commuting services began to spread, notably in Boston, New York, Philadelphia, and Chicago, stimulating the growth of the urban sprawl that would later be served so much better by the automobile. In fact, as early as the 1840s, a few railroads had begun offering "commuted" tickets—reduced fares for regular use—to stimulate travel, but demand was limited, as there were few businesses needing such workers or, indeed, suburbs from which they could commute. Boston was an exception, as it boasted eighty-five commuter stations within fifteen miles of the city center by 1848 when a fifth of its managerial class lived in surrounding suburbs and came to work by train.

However, for the most part, it was not until after the Civil War, when industrialization began to attract vast numbers of workers to the cities, that the need for commuter services became pressing. The relationship between the railroad companies and developers was instrumental in stimulating the demand. Typically, suburbs were built around a main square housing a railroad station, to which the commuters were expected to walk, which meant that stations were spaced about a mile apart. The lines would often extend out farther to "exurban" areas, past the suburban fringe to where the really wealthy lived on "larger estates, horse farms and country retreats whose occupants would be driven to the nearest station by carriage, or, later, 'station wagon.'"[35] By the 1880s, commuting was becoming commonplace in numerous eastern towns and even as far west as San Francisco, where the first commuting line opened in 1864. Soon, on the busiest lines, there was a differentiation between the types of worker, with manual and blue-collar employees taking earlier trains, as they worked longer hours, whereas white-collar and managerial staff traveled later. The more affluent groups organized their own club cars, supplied by the railroad and paid for by subscription. These coaches were for the exclusive use of members, who joined by invitation, and were furnished with comfortable chairs, card tables, and, principally for the return journey home, a bar. The suburban sprawl was, of course, to be the urban railroad's undoing, as it spread beyond easy reach of the railroads and therefore was better served by the automobile, which would supplant these suburban rail services within a couple of generations. The effect on the towns was to relieve pressure on housing. People crammed into tenements could, at last, breathe more easily as they moved into suburban houses cheap enough for even modestly paid workers to afford the rent.

Black people, many of whom were becoming more prosperous, as demonstrated by the emergence of a small black middle class, were flocking to the railroads, too, but had a varied experience on the trains. In the aftermath of the Civil War, the trains were integrated, even if individual whites were wont to show their displeasure at sharing accommodation with blacks. However, it was not long before the southern railroad companies soon began to create what became known as "Jim Crow" cars. However, segregation was not universal, depending often on the whim of the conductor and the courage of the black passengers to face up to discrimination. Whereas poor blacks obviously used coach class—the American trains were largely unclassed, but on some services there was "coach" and "parlor" accommodation—some of the more affluent ones were carried for a time without problem in the parlor cars: "Segregation policies were not hard and fast during the 1880s and 1890s, and no individual, black or white, could know with certainty what the policy on services for black people would be in any given part of the country." The railroad companies themselves disliked the policy of segregation for practical reasons, as it imposed an unnecessary cost on them. However, white travelers, especially those in second class, pressed for it, since to many segregation was seen as necessary for the protection of female virtue. They were concerned, too, about the less servile generation of blacks who had no memory of slavery and thus "did not know their place," in the way their fathers had. In the early years of the twentieth century, therefore, attitudes hardened: "By the turn of the century, segregation had fastened its grip on practically every arena in the South where the races might come into public contact."[36] Conditions were supposed to be "separate but equal," but that was a sham that the Interstate Commerce Commission failed to enforce. In fact, lives were even put at risk by the habit of putting black people in old wooden cars in trains where the white folk traveled in steel cars that, in the event of an accident, would plow into their wooden neighbors.

The train companies operating on the border between South and North at times had to go to extraordinary lengths to impose segregation, since they could not disobey state laws, whatever the cost burden. The Pennsylvania Railroad was forced into making cumbersome arrangements for its trains on the Cumberland Valley Railroad that crossed Maryland, which had passed a Jim Crow law, and West Virginia, which had not, on their way to Virginia from Harrisburg, Pennsylvania. Black passengers were not willing to be segregated in states that did not require it, and therefore the railroad took to carrying partitions that were hastily installed when entering a segregated state and then removed when it left. Remarkably, this practice continued until passenger services on the line ceased in the late 1940s. In the North, where there had been a few instances of racial segregation on trains, attempts to reimpose it were rare and unsuccessful. Just before the First World War, the Central Railroad of New Jersey started separating its white and black passengers at its restaurant at Jersey City Station but soon abandoned the idea when the blacks simply went over to using the rival Pennsylvania Railroad.

Inevitably, with the rapid takeoff of the American economy, the demand for freight transport boomed, too. Until the immediate post–Civil War period, freight transportation had been a pretty haphazard process. The discontinuous nature of the railroad network meant that transshipments, which increased cost, were the norm on even relatively short journeys. The shippers needed a continuous point-to-point service, and that started to be provided in earnest after the war, when a number of railroads cooperated to provide fast—in other words direct—freight lines. These were either separate companies that coordinated the shipment of freight through several separate railroads or groups of railroads that cooperated to provide the service. By the mid-1870s, virtually every major railroad company belonged to one or more of these freight-line arrangements, which greatly improved the efficiency of rail transportation. Along with the vast number of new lines that were being built, rail was now able to dominate the freight market as never before, with water transportation becoming far less competitive. The railroads took over most of the grain trade from the Midwest, which was principally shipped through Boston rather than downriver to New Orleans. This changed the nature of some of the major trunk companies, which now started earning the bulk of their revenues from freight. The Pennsylvania, for example, earned $3.6 million from carrying passengers in 1876, but more than four times that amount, $15.9 million, from freight. This highlights an important fact that can be forgotten in the history of the US railroads and one that made them different from European networks: they have been, for the most part, focused on the carriage of freight. Of course, this was not universally true, and there were many lines that, for some periods, were dominated by passenger travel, and passengers played a key role in revenue terms on many others. Overall, however, freight has been the most important component of railroad economics for long periods of US railroad history and certainly since the post–Second World War demise of the passenger network. Indeed, that very collapse of the passenger traffic can be partly explained, as we shall see, by the existence of a lucrative freight trade.

The capture of the freight market by the railroads led to an odd paradox. Freight rates became very competitive. Boston, for example, had no fewer than thirty-one fast freight services feeding into it, while in 1880 there were as many as twenty competing routes between St. Louis and Atlanta, ranging in distance from 526 to 1,855 miles, which suggests the longer ones would take the business at a loss. Not surprisingly, this fierce competition led to reductions in freight rates during the boom times of the 1870s and 1880s. Yet the farmers complained about being ripped off by sky-high prices and regarded the railroads as monopolistic villains. This perception helped turn the public against the railroads, as the farmers began a campaign that would lead to regulation and severe restrictions on the rail industry. Just as the railroads were fulfilling their promise, delivering untold economic benefits to America, they began to lose their popularity.

8

THE END
OF THE AFFAIR

By the end of the century, the railroads were by far the biggest business enterprise in the United States. Their mileage had increased to two hundred thousand, as the tentacles of the ever-expanding iron road crept relentlessly across the country, connecting every sizable community and many small ones. By then, almost every American lived within easy access of a railroad station, and the railroads carried everything from livestock to lobsters, ice to rice. The tracks went everywhere, to the mountaintops or down into the valleys, to the hotel door or the dock beside the oceangoing liner. They were quite simply ubiquitous, and their impact on both the development of the economy and the American way of life was universal. Given the sheer breadth and scale of their achievements, the railroads should have enjoyed a golden age, feted by a grateful populace, rather like the car is loved by so many today. It should, indeed, have been the height of the love affair between the people and their railroads. For a time, but only a very short one, it was. Richard White, the author of a book on the transcontinentals, suggests rightly that Americans appreciated their railroads despite their failings: "Nineteenth-century North Americans became quite aware of what transcontinental railroads failed to do, but initially they embraced them, as they embraced all railroads, as the epitome of modernity. They were in love with the railroads because railroads defined the age." As White points out, the claims made for the railroads were akin to those lavished on the Internet before the collapse of the dot-com boom. This age of unbridled optimism could not last, and it took barely a generation for the climate to change.

During the final quarter of the nineteenth century, the railroads became, first, disliked and, then, widely resented. It was partly a natural cycle. At first the railroads had been the plucky innovator, the new kid on the block bringing prosperity and opening new horizons, then they became an established but respected business, and eventually they turned into the rapacious monopolist, reviled by almost everyone: "As the rail industry grew in size and became more distant from the public's everyday concerns, it lost that sense of being the underdog that had long endeared it to the American public. Americans could readily identify with the idea of a courageous David fighting vast odds, and such an image enabled them to champion the tiny locomotives struggling against nature's worst elements."[1]

As the railroads became bigger, they lost the public support they had enjoyed in the early days. Sure, the man at the depot was still old Fred whose kids went to the local school, but he now worked for an organization that was remote and disconnected from the local community. But it was not just the growth that changed people's perceptions. The railroads had indeed misbehaved and were guilty of all sorts of calumnies, but the level of antagonism they engendered was undoubtedly way beyond what they deserved, given the positive changes they had inspired and the economic wealth they had created. They were the bankers of their day, widely distrusted and too big to fail.

Their achievements are, though, worth spelling out in some detail. It is, indeed, difficult to discern much in the lives of late-nineteenth-century Americans that had not been affected by the iron horse, and mostly for the good. America's industrial takeoff was stimulated by the spread of the railroads in a synergic relationship where cause and effect are difficult to disentangle. Let's start with a few statistics. The United States in the late nineteenth century was a very different place than in 1830. It now stretched across the North American landmass from coast to coast and included all but a couple of today's states, nearly double the number that existed when the Best Friend chugged down the track of the Charleston & Hamburg. The nation's population had increased in that period from fewer than 13 million to more than 76 million. Of course, this was not entirely due to the railroads, but it would have been difficult for the Union to hold together without them. By facilitating immigration and the flow of goods, the railroads cemented the ties between states and ensured there were no further attempts at secession. Without transportation infrastructure, the United States could not have been held together, and the railroads, rather than turnpikes or canals, were the only viable mode of transportation in terms of speed, scale, and accessibility. And the telegraph lines laid alongside them added another form of vital communication.

At the macro level, the changes were all too obvious but relatively gradual as the rail system expanded. From the opening of the first railroad, it took fifty years to go through the stages of development to make it possible to travel from town to town, from state to state, from region to region, and eventually from ocean to ocean. At the micro level, the changes arising were more complex but no less significant and would happen quickly once the iron horse arrived. Picture that isolated village mentioned previously, where the blacksmith shod not only the horses but quite possibly the people, too, and where otherwise most of the inhabitants were self-sufficient, making their own clothes, hoarding food for the winter, and barely registering on the money economy. That way of life could not survive the railroad, any more than could the traditional culture of the Native Americans. The railroad was both creator and enabler, but also destroyer. In a country as vast as the United States, its impact varied greatly from place to place, but in the East the pattern was clear: the railroads stimulated the growth of towns and cities at the expense of their rural hinterlands.

Most of the changes brought about by the iron horse were beneficial: economic growth, creation of jobs, more efficient markets, opportunities to travel, easier distribution of goods, and so on. But by no means were all the effects positive. It could, for example, be argued that the railroads exacerbated the differences between rich and poor. The railroads were promoted by their developers as a great democratic institution, open to all and enabling everyone to travel around the country. The reality was rather different. The rich and the middle class could flock to the cities for work or pleasure, and consequently urbanization accelerated at a ferocious rate. According to Sarah H. Gordon, "The cities quickly grew to unprecedented, and unmanageable proportions."[2] They prospered thanks to the crowds who boosted their economies as they shopped, ate in restaurants, and stayed in hotels. Railroads, as with all transportation improvements, benefit the areas where people want to go, and although there may have been the occasional rural excursion, for the most part it was the cities that profited from people's ability to travel more easily. They developed central business districts located near railroad stations, and in order to maintain as much density as possible, the office block, and later the skyscraper, was born. These buildings, full of white-collar workers, were the new factories of the age, housing hundreds, if not thousands, of office workers in the way that the manufacturing industry had done earlier.

The effect of the arrival of a railroad connection on a community was immediate: the very nature of the village or town would be transformed overnight. The town that acquired a station would prosper to a greater degree than its local rivals that were not so blessed. There were disadvantages, too. A small town that had been self-sufficient could quickly change into one dependent on the regional, or even the national, economy as people switched to using the larger town's amenities, in much the same way that today downtowns have been killed because local residents have access by road to big-box stores and strip malls.

The station, or depot, however modest, would become a hub, the start or the end point of most people's visits or of journeys by local inhabitants to distant places. The relationship between the town and the station would be symbiotic, and again it is difficult to disentangle interwoven threads of cause and effect. Gradually, as more people used it, the station would improve, with the erection of bigger shelters, the introduction of signs showing arrivals and departures, the employment of more staff, the installation of ticket and information offices, and, of course, food counters. More often than not, the local Western Union office would be part of the station area, allowing people to send telegrams to the rest of the country. The larger stations would provide facilities like shoeshine boys, newsstands, and even hotel accommodation, and the area around the station would prosper—at least initially.

There were numerous other ways in which trains and stations stimulated local economic activity. The trains brought in mail-order goods from department stores in the city, fresh produce for the local shops, mail, packages, and newspapers. Even the station clock was a useful public amenity, providing what was probably the best local estimate of the time. Indeed, the standardization of time was yet another side effect of the spread of the railroad, but given the angst that the time difference caused both railroads and their passengers for journeys on the east-west axis, it was remarkable that it took a half century after the opening of the first railroad for the problem to be sorted out. Because of the size of the American landmass, dawn is typically more than three hours earlier on the East Coast than in California. Therefore, a train heading 750 miles west would gain around an hour by the sun, but in practice every town had its own local time, creating confusion. Buffalo in upstate New York, for example, had three clocks set outside its elegant station: one gave New York City time for the New York Central services; the second was set to Columbus, Ohio, time, used by the Michigan Southern and other midwestern railroads; and the third showed local time. According to Stewart H. Holbrook, "In Pittsburgh, the situation was even worse, for the railroads touching there used a total of six time standards."[3] There were twenty-seven local times in Michigan and thirty-eight in Wisconsin, and coast-to-coast travelers between Maine and San Francisco would have to change their watch twenty times on the journey.

In Britain the standardization that mainly affected the Great Western, the principal east-west railroad, had largely been completed by 1852, but in the United States it took a long time to overcome the opposition of what Holbrook calls "traditionalists" and "obscurantists." The humble principal of a ladies' college in Saratoga Springs, New York, Professor C. F. Dowd, first urged the adoption of time zones in 1869 and prompted the creation of a group of railroads to lobby for the change. The plan was refined by William Frederick Allen, the former engineer of the Camden & Amboy who is immortalized for his efforts in a small tablet in Washington's Union Station, with the suggestion of four time zones, based on the longitudes of Philadelphia (Pennsylvania), Memphis (Tennessee), Denver (Colorado), and Fresno (California). The plan was adopted at a convention in October 1883 and, with remarkable haste given how long the chaotic situation on the railroads over the issue of time had been allowed to continue, was scheduled to be introduced on the eighteenth of the following month at noon. There were still dissenters who balked at the notion that the railroad rather than the sun was now the determinant of time. In Bangor, Maine, Mayor Dogberry vetoed a city ordinance to adopt eastern standard time, suggesting, "It is unconstitutional, being an attempt to change the immutable laws of God Almighty and hard on the working man by changing day into night."[4] The local sextons were even banned from ringing the church bells at the new times.

Despite the fear of God's wrath, the day passed off smoothly. It was not an easy task, but sensibly, rather than risk changing over in the middle of the night, the appointed time was noon. Trains were ordered to stop while the clocks were adjusted, and there were no accidents, though there were inevitable delays and many people missed their trains, even the attorney general, who had opposed the adoption of railroad time by government departments but found himself late for a train as a result.[5] There were no riots, despite the fury of the fundamentalists, but there were convoluted details to sort out, such as whether an insurance policy, which expired at noon, would pay out during the extra time gained when the clocks were put back. Few Americans today know that it is because of the needs of the railroads that they have four time zones. As Holbrook explains, little mention of it is made in the history books, and "most Americans seem to be of the general but rather fuzzy idea that the time zones were invented by either Benjamin Franklin or George Washington."[6]

If there was a minority sentimental about the loss of local time, there were many more who mourned the loss of a whole way of life, interrupted both literally and metaphorically by the arrival of the fierce and steaming iron horse. Radical change on this scale inevitably engendered downsides. The railroads were creating a different America, and, inevitably, there was a sense of lost community, as "towns where all the members of the community knew one another" were transformed into places with "any number of strangers and crowds, whose numbers became one important measure of the economic vitality of the town."[7] In other words, the railroad created the very notion of a bustling town thronging with people going about their business. Scenes of crowds that perhaps, at most, had been seen on one market day a week or month now became a daily occurrence. The railroads contributed to the creation of ever-bigger towns, which attracted ever-larger crowds and ultimately, the mass society that can be seen as the product of the railroad's ability to allow ever more efficient and rapid travel.

If having a station was a bit of a gamble, since it might stimulate an outflow rather than an influx of facilities, not having one was generally far worse. Towns left out of the rail network were in danger of contracting or even withering and dying. To counter this effect, some states passed laws requiring railroad companies to provide stations for all communities through which they passed. In 1872, Massachusetts enacted a law requiring the railroad to provide a service of cheap trains, morning and evening, if more than two hundred people signed a petition. Rather like American airports today, vying with each other to facilitate flights from discount carriers such as JetBlue or Allegiant Air, town councils would negotiate with railroads to obtain a station, offering inducements such as tax relief or cheap bonds. As trains speeded up, however, services made fewer stops, and more and more communities faced an uphill struggle to establish or merely maintain their train stations. On occasion, people power was used to improve facilities. In Tennessee, the railroads were required to provide every town of three hundred or more inhabitants with a waiting room for the use of passengers. For their part, the railroads were not always amenable to serving small communities. They wanted to serve the profitable mass market as much as possible, siting their stations in the biggest towns or where there was the greatest movement of freight. Small towns with few inhabitants, mostly poor, were not their priority, because the maintenance of such stations would be a financial burden, as would the need to stop trains there. Most radically, sometimes whole towns simply picked up and moved to be on the railroad. Cleora in Colorado, for example, was bypassed by the Denver & Rio Grande, which laid out a nearby town, called South Arkansas (later Salida). The inhabitants of Cleora realized that this newcomer would wreck their town and consequently simply resettled to be nearer the railroad.

Sometimes, though, there was an obvious synergy between railroads and the local communities. Big events such as state agricultural fairs, or even the "World's Fairs" held in the second half of the nineteenth century in New Orleans, St. Louis, and Chicago, inevitably attracted large numbers of railroad travelers. Indeed, for most people it was almost impossible to attend these events without taking the train. Town authorities soon realized that creating fairground sites near a railroad station would make them much more likely to attract large numbers of visitors: in Ohio, for example, just before the war, "the state board of agriculture arranged to have the railroad tracks into Cincinnati stop quite close to the Ohio state fairgrounds." Soon the railroad companies were providing special rates, or even additional trains, for people attending these events. This newfound potential for association created by the railroad was felt first at the state or regional, rather than at the national, level. The limitations of the railroads before the Civil War meant that it was relatively easy to travel across a state, but rather difficult to go beyond its boundaries. This helped cement the unity of individual states, a notion that reached its apogee at the outbreak of the Civil War. After that, the railroads were able to claim, with some justification, that they were a unifying force on a national level: "The middle class traveled to the early political conventions held before the Civil War; to schools that drew students from all parts of the country; to professional gatherings in law, medicine, teaching and library work."[8] The emergent middle class, created in part by the railroad's ability to generate wealth, were inveterate travelers, able to pursue both business and leisure interests ever farther from home.

The railroads encouraged collective travel. Any group, whether it was a local Sunday school or an association of retailers, would negotiate a cheap rate with the railroad company, perhaps even chartering a whole train. Thanks to the railroads, national organizations, representing all kinds of interests such as particular trades, professions, campaigns, or even hobbies, could emerge. The range of groups seeking discounted tickets was remarkable and provides an insight into the new America in which organizations could now function at a regional or national level as a result of the availability of relatively cheap rail travel. The records of the American Association of Passenger Traffic Officers reveal applications for cheap fares from those attending an array of diverse organizations that give the flavor of life in nineteenth-century America, such as the Millers' International Convention held in Cincinnati, a national meeting of the Phi Delta Theta fraternity, the Colored People's World Exposition, and the Women's Christian Temperance Union.[9] Civil War veterans had numerous reunions for which they requested reductions on the normal ticket price, and although all these requests were accepted, for some unaccountable reason—perhaps racism against the predominantly Chinese owners—the application from the National Laundry Association was turned down. The effect on American society of this ability to travel the country cannot be overestimated: "Organizing nationally was the work of the age, and ticketing records show that railroads made possible the growth of organizations with a national membership of people with middling means."[10] Even groups of shoppers, coming up to town for the day, had access to group discounts.

One major section of society was largely excluded from the sense of national cohesion created by the railroads: the poor could not join in the fun, as they could not afford the fares. However, although long-distance travel was beyond their means and the unemployed could never afford train fares, low-paid workers could occasionally indulge in the odd day trip when the railroads started to stimulate what eventually became the world's biggest industry: tourism. Even the poorly remunerated factory worker could afford to spend a day at the beach, a practice that started to become commonplace in the final two decades of the nineteenth century. Every major city established a nearby center for these day trips. For New Yorkers it was Coney Island for the beach and the fairground, reached by the Prospect & Coney Island Railroad, or in the other direction Brighton Beach, which was served by the Brighton Beach & Brooklyn Railroad. Either way, the fare was just thirty-five cents round-trip. For Philadelphians, there was a ride to Atlantic City in New Jersey for a dollar, while Bostonians, via a trip on the Boston & Maine and then a tramcar ride, could reach Revere Beach, described rather snootily in the 1893 *Baedeker's* guide as "a popular holiday resort for Boston's lower classes." A little farther away from Boston was Nantasket Beach, which on a sunny weekend day could attract fifty thousand visitors or more. In the Midwest, Chicagoans were spoiled with choices. They could either just saunter to the beaches of Lake Michigan, literally a few hundred meters from downtown, or hop on the local train service, which in a few minutes would take them to the larger beaches on the lakeshores of Indiana to the east. The richer residents might go farther north along the Illinois and Wisconsin shores of the lake or "inland to resorts such as Fox Lake, where private homes and hotels afforded accommodation for vacationers."[11] This was typical. Whereas those who toiled by hand usually had to be content with day trips, the middle classes could enjoy longer breaks, allowing them to travel farther. The more affluent professionals or businesspeople might even have a summer house, but it had to be easily accessible by the railroad. Towns that were pretty or pleasant enough to attract tourists began to compete for this custom, turning themselves into resorts that would advertise their amenities at stations.

For the seriously rich, as ever, it was a different ball game, although even they were dependent on having a nearby railroad connection. The real mark of distinction, however, was to have one's own station, or, better still, one's own railroad. After the Civil War, escaping the summer heat of the bustling cities of the East became imperative, and the Adirondacks, in the northeastern corner of New York State, developed into the favored destination of the rich. This was an unspoiled area of mountains, lakes, and forests that was first reached by railroad tracks soon after the end of the Civil War. The line was gradually extended, and soon the hunting parties, who had had to "rough it" in tents and shacks, had large country houses at their disposal. These "cabins," as their owners modestly called them, were actually enormous log houses, usually sited next to a lake, with a boathouse and outhouses for guests. Thomas Durant, of the Union Pacific, was instrumental in pushing railroads farther into the mountains, as was, later, William Seward Webb, who married Cornelius Vanderbilt's granddaughter Eliza. To ensure that his elite customers were not disturbed by hoi polloi on the various railroads like the Fulton Chain and the Raquette Lake, which he controlled, Webb provided a "private service to the owners of homes along the route and barred the public from riding the trains."[12] A list of passengers on the railroad reads like a roll call of the new American aristocracy of the time, including J. P. Morgan, Vanderbilt, and various banking families, such as the Guggenheims. Amazingly, Oliver Jensen, in a book published as recently as 1975, recalled traveling on just such a branch line in the Adirondacks, the romantic-sounding Grasse River Railroad. It was a haphazard experience. According to Jensen, "It posted no signs and listed no telephone number." Instead, he simply turned up, "hoping to ride behind their steam engine in an ancient coach with black leather seats and beautiful, if cracked, woodwork." The "astonishingly large crew" of three men in lumber jackets took him the fifteen miles from Childwold to Cranberry Lake, where it left off a mail pouch and a few express packages, which, as Jensen points out, provided what was effectively a government subsidy to the tiny line. Then, after a short pause, the train "heaved and bumped home, passengers being permitted to throw a few switches, look at the beaver dam, and inspect a long and decaying Wagner palace parlor car" in a siding.[13]

Similar areas of countryside were opened up by the railroads in this period. In Florida, a line that was designed principally to serve the tourist market must rank as the most ambitious American railroad ever built. This was the Florida East Coast Railroad built by Henry Flagler, not so much a railroad entrepreneur as an obsessive who was ready to throw his fortune at his dream of making the farthest point on Florida's coast into an opulent and exclusive resort. Flagler, who had seen how the French Riviera had quickly been transformed from a series of sleepy fishing villages into a tourist honeypot thanks to a railroad running along the coast, decided to do the same for Florida. The state had been something of a railroad desert, having seen only a few short, unconnected lines built since the Civil War. Worse, various gauges had been used, and the tracks, therefore, could not be connected. Flagler, who had made his fortune as John D. Rockefeller's partner in creating Standard Oil, first came to the state in the late 1880s and saw its potential as a tourist haven because of its climate. He ignored the fact that this very climate was, in fact, a source of disease and poverty and was one reason the state was so sparsely populated. Flagler bought up one of the largest railroads, the Jacksonville, St. Augustine & Halifax, and began to create a continuous line along the eastern side of the state to serve a series of resorts that he developed on the coast. First he built the massive 540-room Ponce de León Hotel in St. Augustine, followed by the Royal Poinciana at Palm Beach, which was twice as big. The railroad was gradually extended down to Miami to serve two more vast hotels,[14] with the help of convict labor leased from the state at a monthly rate of $2.50 per man, plus food and lodging, a fraction of the cost of the $2.00 a day that was the going rate for free labor. Flagler's line reached Miami in April 1896, and he then began to scope out the crazy ambition of reaching Key West, a dot 128 miles out in the Atlantic Ocean connected to the mainland by a string of rocky islands broken by stretches of sea. Virtually none of the route was on land where tracklaying was easy. The line, which became known as "the railroad that goes to sea," involved crossing no less than forty-two miles of ocean, including one seven-mile section, and the construction of seventeen miles of viaducts and bridges and twenty miles of embankments on filled causeway. Flagler's pockets, though, were almost bottomless, thanks to his oil money. He needed a great deal of it. On three occasions, severe hurricanes, each worse than the previous one, wrecked completed sections of track. In the third, a particularly violent storm, 134 men, many of them in a boat, were killed. In the aftermath of the disaster, many others, fearing for their lives, walked off the job, but still Flagler plowed on, offering better wages and providing the workers with storm-proof dormitories. Even so, the conditions for the railroad workers were appalling. Mosquitoes were a constant menace, accompanied, for part of the year, by even harder-biting sand flies. And there were still numerous fatal accidents, given the dangerous working conditions.

The completion of the line in January 1912 was marked by a special train, with the eighty-two-year-old Henry Flagler aboard, from New York to Key West, where it was met by a crowd of more than 10,000 people, many of whom had never seen a train before. Key West, later Ernest Hemingway's hangout, was actually nearer to Havana than Miami, and the main service, which was supposed to take four hours from Miami but often took six or seven because of the difficult conditions, was called, fittingly, the Havana Special. Flagler, who enjoyed nothing more than a ride in the cab between Miami and Key West playing folk tunes like "Long Caleb McGee" or "Old Dan Tucker" on the locomotive's whistle, died the following year, too soon to realize that the enterprise was a failure. Few tourists ventured all the way down the line, and the hopes that Key West would become a major freight port since it was the nearest in the United States to Central and South America never materialized, with the result that few freight trains used the railroad. The rail service lasted less than a quarter of a century, as yet another hurricane, on Labor Day 1935, destroyed the railroad. Flagler's work was not wasted, however. The railroad company gave up trying to run any trains on the line, which in any case had been reduced to just one service a day. Cars had begun to use the tracks, and now the arrangement was formalized. The rails were ripped out, and the line of the route remains today as the base for US Highway 1, running to a series of exotic resorts as well as the port and naval base of Key West.

If tourism was largely stimulated by the advent of railroads, so was the creation of professional sports. The railroads not only enabled matches between teams in major cities to take place by providing transportation, often overnight, for the big-league teams, but also allowed supporters of the away team to travel, greatly enhancing the atmosphere in the stadiums. Baseball was the pioneer. The game itself had started becoming popular during the Civil War, when troops on both sides played during lulls in the fighting, and it expanded rapidly after the war. Boston and Chicago were the big hitters in the first professional league established in the early 1870s, and clearly such rivalry would not have been possible without the two teams being able to travel to each other's city by rail. In fact, "city size and railroad travel feasibility defined the major baseball leagues," and generations of baseball players spent much of their time on the railroads.[15] A whole culture of life on the rails developed, enlivened by practical jokes, such as the one played on Babe Ruth, the greatest ever baseball player, who was told to rest his arm on the little netting shelf that was next to the bed for personal effects. Ruth, a pitcher at the time, did so and found that in the morning he could barely move his arm.

It was, in fact, the limitations of travel by rail that prevented teams from the West from joining the Major Leagues before teams took to the air in the 1950s. Until then, St. Louis, the most westerly town reachable by overnight train from the East Coast, was as far west as the so-called national leagues could stretch. Other professional sports developed later than baseball, but also made heavy use of the railroads, for both players and spectators. Indeed, match and tournament schedules were arranged around railroad timetables. Circuses, too, traveled by rail in whole trains specially provided for them. In one much-recounted episode, an elephant managed to remove the pin between carriages, splitting the train without the driver realizing what had happened. Tragically, one of the country's worst rail disasters occurred on a circus train when 86 people died, along with numerous circus animals, and another 127 people were injured, after a locomotive engineer fell asleep and ran his empty troop train into the rear of the Hagenbeck-Wallace circus train in June 1918 near Hammond, Indiana. Many of the victims were burned beyond recognition and are buried anonymously in a special circus cemetery nearby. Another similar disaster, also in the Midwest, involving two trains of the Wallace Bros. circus, a predecessor of the Hagenbeck-Wallace, had occurred in 1903, with a death toll of 23 and numerous animals.[16] Despite these tragedies, circuses have proved one of the most durable users of the railroad. Even today the Ringling Bros. circus travels around the United States in a pair of special mile-long trains of sixty cars each—carrying everything from acrobats and trainers to elephants and pythons. It has been using the tracks since 1872, except for a short break during a failed experiment with road travel in the 1950s.

The most significant and profound impact of the railroads was on the economy, where there was both a direct and an indirect effect. Quite simply, the railroads were by far the biggest business, and their need for basic materials was a stimulant for several other industries. Whole forests were cut down to provide millions of ties for the tracks, massive amounts of ballast on which they rested were quarried, unprecedented amounts of coal were mined to fuel the locomotives, and huge quantities of ore were needed to produce the iron for rails. Indeed, the whole method of production was transformed as a result of the huge demand for iron. Integrated mills were created where all the processes were carried out on one site, and the principal output of these early factories was rail. Other materials in great demand included copper, glass, and india rubber. The machine-tool industry also expanded rapidly to provide increasingly sophisticated tools required by the railroads.

The indirect effect was even broader. By bringing down the cost of transportation, the railroads stimulated demand for both manufactured goods and raw materials. Mass-production techniques had been constrained by the lack of constant supply and the cost of transportation. By ensuring that the supply of materials and parts was both cheaper and more reliable—since railroads, unlike the canals that froze up, operated year-round—manufacturers could now rely on a regular supply of parts and materials, revolutionizing the production process that, therefore, moved from small workshops providing for the local neighborhood to larger factories serving a state or even the whole nation: "These techniques [of factory production] were adopted to mass produce shoes, clothing, clocks, watches, locks, sewing machines, harvesters and other agricultural implements, and also guns and revolvers." The railroads changed the nature of agriculture, encouraging the production of cash crops by reducing the cost of transportation and allowing produce to be carried over much greater distances to both domestic and export markets. Although economists have long argued about the precise impact of these changes, it is undeniable that "the railroad was a significant force in the growth of the American economy during the second half of the nineteenth century."[17]

The railroads were also responsible for the development of modern business methods. The post–Civil War boom in the railroads brought with it a change in their nature that was to have a lasting effect on the way that America conducted business. Indeed, the early large railroad companies were the nation's first modern corporations, and they were as expensive and complicated to run as they were to build, especially when they consolidated into far larger businesses. The many tasks of running a railroad necessitated a vast array of skills, a requirement that increased as train services became more frequent, faster, and more complex. To mention but a few of these: railroads needed technical expertise to maintain the infrastructure and provide the locomotive power, operating skills to establish and keep detailed timetables, sophisticated management techniques to deal with the scattered workforce, and, of course, a wide variety of financial skills, whether it was assessing capital needs or determining freight rates and ticket prices.

The very notion of management grew symbiotically with the expansion of the railroads. No other businesses of the mid- to late nineteenth century were so complex nor spread over such a vast geographical area. None, either, employed so many people. At the time, manufacturing concerns were located on a particular site, with none of the difficulties entailed in running an organization extending hundreds or sometimes thousands of miles across the country. The assets the railroads had to manage were also extremely varied, ranging from bridges and tunnels to workshops and stations. The numbers of people required to carry out these tasks was also on a scale never previously encountered anywhere in the world, except, perhaps, for vast one-off construction exercises such as the building of the pyramids or the other "wonders of the world." While factories of the time employed at most a few thousand people, the labor requirements of the railroads were far greater and more diverse. There were customer-facing people such as porters, conductors, and ticket clerks—the railroads were effectively the first mass service industry—and swaths of behind-the-scenes men (they were almost entirely male until the First World War) such as track workers, mechanics, engineers, signalers, and armies of clerks. To give an example, as early as the mid-1850s the Erie employed more than four thousand people, probably the largest workforce of the day in any industry, whereas a mere thirty years later the ever-growing Pennsylvania, which controlled around seven thousand route miles, had nearly fifty thousand workers on its books.

Again, no other company could match that figure. This gave rise to a host of new management techniques, especially given the fact that telephone communication did not become routine until the last fifteen years or so of the century: "Every day railroad managers had to make decisions controlling the activities of many men to whom they rarely talked or even saw."[18]

Uniquely, running a railroad involved a myriad of vital and often safety-critical decisions to be made daily, often by quite junior staff. Working out the requirements of each station and freight depot and allocating the right resources and monitoring performance were new tasks that required both detailed management decisions and an overall strategic perspective. Even before the Civil War, the big trunk railroads of the East such as the Pennsylvania and the Baltimore & Ohio had begun to create sophisticated management structures involving, for example, the separation of sums of money allocated to investment, the capital account, from those relating to train operation, the revenue account. This may all sound banal, but was, in fact, the genesis of the corporate arrangements that are the basis of all modern-day business.

As the railroad industry became more competitive in the 1870s, there was a far greater emphasis on cost analysis, which suggests that the dominance of "bean counters" in modern business practice has far deeper origins than is generally realized. All this depended on much more sophisticated flows of information to enable managers to make informed decisions, rather than relying on instinct or experience. Statistics on all aspects of the business, whether the amount of tallow being used as a lubricant or the cost per mile for an engineer and fireman, were collected for the first time as the railroad companies strove for efficiency. In this respect, American practice was far ahead of contemporary European methods. As an illustration of the modern corporate thinking of the railroads, in 1856 Daniel McCallum, the general superintendent of the Erie who, as we have seen, would later play a key role in the North's railroad management during the Civil War, wrote to the president of the company, emphasizing the need for the collection of statistics on at least twenty different measures. He stressed that the real value of such information was "in its practical application in pointing out the neglect and mismanagement which prevail, thus enabling us to remedy the defect."[19] One can almost hear today's management studies lecturers echoing such thoughts. These tasks, of course, became even more complicated and demanding when the great series of amalgamations and consolidations took place toward the end of the nineteenth century, creating even bigger organizations. The big railroads, therefore, were the first companies to develop modern business accounting methods.

Another aspect of the railroads that made them uniquely difficult to manage was that they could never stand still. During the whole of the nineteenth century, they were constantly expanding, adopting new technology (albeit reluctantly at times), investing in improvements, adapting to new demands that they had often helped to bring about, and dealing with a constantly changing political situation that inevitably affected them as the nation's most significant business. Change had to be built into the system, and that, too, was unique. The very nature of the business was mobile.

The vast number of people taken on by the railroads made them unwitting catalysts for the development of new patterns of industrial relations, stimulating the creation of mass labor organizations. The railroads were the first businesses to employ people in such numbers that the rigidity of the division between workers and management became entrenched. It was precisely because the railroads had far more sophisticated management techniques than other industries that it became possible for the two groups, management and labor, to bargain with one another. That transformed these mid-nineteenth-century railroads into the first modern corporations. The labor force was different, too. The men had a key advantage over their counterparts in other industries in that they had sellable skills that could not easily be replaced. The withdrawal of labor was a powerful weapon, and threats to strike were seen almost as a declaration of war. Strikes represented a real threat for companies with enormous fixed assets on which they needed to obtain a return in order to satisfy shareholders. Increasingly aware of their industrial muscle, railroad workers were among the first to form local unions and then, crucially, to expand these into national federations that "quickly became the most powerful and effective unions developed in the United States before the twentieth century."[20]

The first stirrings of labor organization occurred before the Civil War, but they were very local in scope and generally involved only a small number of skilled workers. In 1863, a Brotherhood of the Footboard, later becoming the Brotherhood of Locomotive Engineers, was formed in Michigan, and this was soon followed by similar brotherhoods representing railroad conductors and "locomotive firemen and enginemen." These were still, however, not modern-style unions organized to put pressure on management to improve wages and conditions, but rather fraternal organizations providing mutual support and holding social events. Throughout the 1870s and 1880s, larger brotherhoods and craft unions began to emerge. Not surprisingly, the railroad companies were reluctant to recognize organized labor.

However, the size of the railroad companies meant that it was not the owners who would make decisions about union recognition, but rather the new breed of professional managers who were employed to run these big corporations. Gradually, they realized that negotiating with the men was unavoidable. Attempts to hire unskilled "scabs" inevitably led to failure, since most railroad jobs required skills and experience. The managers were faced with uniquely powerful opponents who were further strengthened by their sheer numbers. It is hardly surprising that the railroads were fertile territory for union organization and, indeed, would become "the seedbed of the American labour movement."[21] The brotherhoods' industrial and political strength meant that they could pioneer methods of collective bargaining, union organization, and grievance procedures that later would become universal across the labor movement. Railroad workers were able to exploit their skills by moving to rival railroads, often in the expectation of bettering themselves, even if by only a few cents an hour. This practice became so prevalent that those who drifted from job to job in this way became known as "boomers."

Railroad workers were involved in three major strikes in the last quarter of the nineteenth century, and although all of them were effectively defeats, these actions were an inspiration for the railroad workers to form strong unions. Labor relations were to be an Achilles' heel for the industry. Having initially made too few concessions regarding working practices, the railroads' vulnerability to industrial action led them at times to concede too readily to union demands. This would later result in significant levels of overstaffing, endless damaging disputes over job demarcations, and a lack of flexibility that would cost the railroad companies dearly.

The railroad companies reacted to the first major strike, in 1877, which was in response to the imposition of wage reductions, with typical heavy-handedness. After a period of economic decline caused by the panic of 1873, several railroad companies had unilaterally cut wage levels, arguing that the reduction was necessary in order to maintain or reestablish profitability. Many found their action particularly galling, since it was the railroads' overinvestment and borrowing that had been largely responsible for the 1873 crisis in the first place. The panic had been triggered by the collapse of Jay Cooke & Company, a bank that had loaned heavily to the Northern Pacific Railway but then found itself unable to sell the resulting bonds. It was, in fact, the culmination of years of overbuilding on the railroads, fueled by speculators. Collapse was inevitable. With the Crédit Mobilier scandal breaking at around the same time, all confidence in the banks was lost. Rather cheekily, Cornelius Vanderbilt suggested that the underlying problem was that government money had been wasted on "building railroads from nowhere to nowhere," which, he said, was not a legitimate undertaking, although he insisted he remained a friend of the iron horse.[22] The panic spread quickly, other banks went under, and a lengthy depression, the longest in American history to that date, set in. The railroads, hit by falling demand and with large fixed costs—railroads are asset-hungry behemoths that cannot easily cut spending when there is a downturn in the economy, which is why so many around the world have ended up in state hands—tried to reduce wages, one of the few areas of expenditure under their control. The workers, however, for the first time began to resist in a united show of force. The men on the Baltimore & Ohio, whose wages were already lower than those of their counterparts on other railroads at $3.00 per twelve-hour day for engineers and a mere $1.75 for brakemen, were the first to crack. In response to the second pay cut in a year, on July 14, 1877—coincidentally the anniversary of the French Revolution—workers began to prevent wagons from leaving the depot at Martinsburg, West Virginia, until the cut was revoked. The militia was sent in but refused to fire on the workers, and the strike soon spread to Cumberland, Maryland, where a serious battle between strikers, supported by many local people, and the militia resulted in ten rioters being killed. Soon workers on the Pennsylvania Railroad, which had also cut wages, and other railroad companies began to join in, often with considerable support from factory workers in other major industries such as steel and mining. Thomas Scott, the president of the Pennsylvania Railroad, inflamed matters by suggesting that strikers should be given "a rifle diet for a few days and see how they like that kind of bread."[23] Indeed, as the strike extended well beyond the rail industry, there were concerns among industrialists that it was the start of a revolutionary movement. With good reason. In Pittsburgh, the militia called in from Philadelphia killed twenty people as they sought to regain control of the streets, but this merely served to infuriate the mobs. When at least twenty thousand people took to the streets and destroyed large amounts of railroad property, including burning down the roundhouse and destroying a hundred locomotives, the guards could only stand and watch. In Harrisburg, Pennsylvania, the mobs were so strong that the military retreated and handed in their weapons to the strikers. There were major strikes and confrontations in Chicago and East St. Louis also, but the action petered out after a few weeks when President Rutherford Hayes sent federal troops from state to state to quell the protests. Although a few local brotherhoods were involved in the strike, for the most part it was a spontaneous uprising by workers, with railroad men leading the way.

A precursor of the powerful rail unions that eventually emerged was the Knights of Labor, which flourished briefly in the 1870s and 1880s. The Knights led the second of these major struggles, the Great Southwest Railroad strike of 1886, which at its height saw two hundred thousand men withdraw their labor. The Knights were less concerned with the immediate terms and conditions of the workers, but rather sought to replace the wage system with cooperative enterprises—in the words of their leader, Terence Powderly, "to make each man his own employer."[24]

However, in March 1886, when one of their members in Texas was fired for attending a union meeting by the Texas & Pacific Railroad, owned by the railroad baron Jay Gould, the men walked out, and Powderly used the opportunity to demand a minimum wage of $1.50 and recognition of the union. Gould refused to make any concessions, and thousands of men on his other railroads, which included the Union Pacific and the Missouri Pacific, also walked out. Crucially, the Brotherhood of Engineers did not support the strike and kept working. Gould brought in strikebreakers and the well-organized Pinkerton thugs, boasting, "I can hire one half of the work-ing class to kill the other half." Violence escalated. The workers destroyed many railroad facilities and indulged in acts of sabotage—for example, let-ting locomotives run out of steam, thereby putting them out of operation for at least six hours. However, the workers were under fierce pressure, and the intimidation from the militia in several states, supported by gangs of thuggish Pinkerton men recruited by Gould, forced them back to work in the summer of 1886.

The failure of these two strikes highlighted the difficulties of organiz-ing railroad workers on a national scale. The unions were still in embry-onic form and based locally, but this was changing rapidly. In the 1880s, union leaders sought to move away from the restrictive craft-based model of organizing and, instead, sought to create a single union that would rep-resent all railroad workers. It was not an easy enterprise. The sheer variety of jobs carried out by railroad employees and their tendency to guard de-marcation lines with as much determination as Davy Crockett defending the Alamo were almost insuperable barriers.

Nevertheless, Eugene V. Debs, a founder of the brakemen's national union and later an iconic figure in the annals of the American Left, formed the American Railway Union in June 1893. He emphasized that the union was open to all railroad workers and even those employed by suppliers such as repair shops and factories making parts. The union had an early success when it staged a walkout against the Great Northern Railway, persuading the normally obdurate James J. Hill to make substantial concessions. Within a year of the creation of the union, however, its members found themselves up against an even tougher opponent when it became enmeshed in the rail-roads' most notorious industrial-relations battle of the century, the Pullman strike of 1894. Again, the trigger was an economic depression following the panic of 1893, which like the previous slump was the result of a combination of bank failures and overbuilding of railroad lines. Early in the year, the Philadelphia & Reading Railroad went bankrupt. Then, following a series of bank failures, three major railroad companies—the Northern Pacific Rail-way, the Union Pacific Railroad, and the Atchison, Topeka & Santa Fe Railroad—also went under in the last two months of 1893, starting a reces-sion. The Pullman Company, which was dependent on the economic health

of the railroad companies that hauled its cars, announced redundancies at
its factory along with cuts to the remaining workers' wages, claiming that
these moves were necessary to maintain profitability. That was bad enough,
but the workers were particularly angered by Pullman's refusal to reduce
rents on the houses in the company town where most of them lived. In May
1894, Pullman workers, who had formed an active American Railway Union
local branch, started walking off the job, and soon 3,000 were on strike,
bringing the works to a halt. They asked Debs, who was a cautious and
conservative trade unionist, to support them, and, though reluctant, he had
no choice but to throw the weight of the union behind them. The strike
quickly became a national one, as railroad workers across the country refused to handle Pullman cars. Within four days an estimated 125,000 men
on twenty-nine railroads had walked out in sympathy and refused to cross
picket lines. They were emboldened by the growing Populist movement,
with its demands for the national ownership of the utilities and railroads,
which had reached its height at this point. Few of the Pullman Company's
large number of black on-board staff dared to strike, fearing they would
lose their jobs because of discrimination, which gave a nasty racial edge to
the dispute.

Despite all the support and solidarity, defeat for the workers was inevitable. It was not a propitious time for a national strike, given the recession
and the importance with which the railroads, still the country's largest business apart from agriculture, were regarded by politicians and industrialists.
Both managers and politicians quickly set their faces against the union. The
General Managers' Association, representing the railroad company, pushed
the federal government into action, and the president, Grover Cleveland,
appointed Richard Olney as a special federal attorney to deal with the strike.
Olney had experience in this respect. He had been the chief lawyer for the
Chicago, Milwaukee & St. Paul Railroad, and as attorney general he had previously tried to prevent strikes through the use of the law. Now he instructed
state district attorneys to issue injunctions against strikers on the basis that
they were preventing the delivery of mail, which was a federal offense. It
was a legal precedent, as such injunctions had not been used before, but it
was not enough to break the strike. That required calling up 12,000 troops,
who, together with the local states' national guards, proved ruthless in com-

bating the massed strikers and ensuring the trains kept running. It was not an easy process, nor a foregone conclusion. The strikers had considerable support and in several towns received favorable coverage from the local newspapers, particularly in California, where even the *San Francisco Examiner*, owned by William Randolph Hearst, was sympathetic to their cause. Moreover, marshals sent in by the authorities were often reluctant to act against the strikers: "All over the West, the failure of marshals either to act or to act effectively and the peacefulness of the strikers frustrated railroad attorneys who wanted much more vigorous federal intervention."[25]

Ultimately, Olney won, thanks to his readiness to exploit legislation: "Olney intervened not so much to enforce federal laws, or move the mail, or protect federal property, as to demonstrate the power of the government, its right to intervene and to break the strike."[26] Altogether, thirteen railroad workers were killed in fights with the men sent in by the federal government, and many more injured during a series of confrontations. Olney, however, was not satisfied, pursuing Debs and several other strikers through the courts for breaking the injunction and interfering with the mails. Along with several other strike leaders, Debs was sent to prison for six months, despite an impassioned defense from the renowned civil liberties lawyer Clarence Darrow. Imprisonment radicalized Debs, who became a Socialist, standing five times for president on that ticket, and receiving, incidentally, an impressive 6 percent of the vote in 1912 and 1920.

Many thousands of workers who took part in the 1894 strike were blacklisted and effectively barred from future employment on the railroads, as their service letters were written on stationery secretly carrying a watermark showing a swan with a broken neck. George Pullman himself paid a heavy price for the conflict. From being a much-feted entrepreneur, he spent the remainder of his life being hounded by supporters of the strikes. When he died just three years later, he was buried at night in a lead-lined coffin, and several tons of concrete were poured around it to prevent his body from being exhumed and desecrated by militants.

Although these strikes all resulted in defeat for the workers, they helped change the public's attitude toward the railroad companies. As John Stover, writing about the 1877 events, explains, "The strike was broken, but the railroad workers and much of the general public could not help recalling the huge estate of the late Commodore [Vanderbilt] and the dividends still being paid by the Baltimore & Ohio, the New York Central and the Pennsylvania."[27] Indeed, the railroads and, crucially, the major owners were becoming increasingly unpopular. Although the more conservative elements of the public generally supported the railroads against the workers, they were very much the minority. Most people's instinct was to support the little man against the corporation. As the railroads were experiencing their unprecedented boom, they were also accumulating enemies among various groups across the nation, and this mistrust of the railroad companies would ultimately prove very damaging to their interests. Although this change in attitude toward the railroads had various causes and was gradual in its development over the second half of the nineteenth century, the impetus behind it came from the change in the structure of the railroad companies themselves, as they grew larger and more powerful. Crucially, there was also a negative shift in the public's perception of the men who owned and controlled them, who became known as the "robber barons." Indeed, these characters, such as Vanderbilt, Daniel Drew, and Jay Gould, have been lurking in the shadows of the past couple of chapters in much the same way as they did in the boardrooms of the rail companies, but their role in changing public attitudes toward the railroads cannot be overestimated.

In the 1880s, the railroads were at the height of their pomp: tracks now spanned the full width of the United States and were generating more wealth and prosperity than ever before. As the railroads proliferated, their gradual consolidation eventually led to the creation of local monopolies. This process was already under way by the 1850s and gathered pace after the Civil War. For a generation or so from the late 1860s, railroad companies were the biggest corporations in the United States and indeed the world. However, the growing unpopularity of the railroads did not just spring from their monopoly position or their vast size, though they would have struggled to retain public support even if they had been entirely straight and honest in their dealings—and clearly they were not. Their underhanded methods were personified by the more famous of their leaders, the barons whose activity attracted widespread coverage in the press and stimulated the interest of the rather unfairly termed "muckrakers," the journalists who investigated them. The barons attracted opprobrium for various

aspects of their behavior, often but not always justified: speculation, purloining state funds, corrupt management, stock manipulation, exploiting
monopolies, and, above all, taking advantage of the little man. Thus, during
what was in many ways the "golden age" of the American railroads—a time
of expanding and improving services—the attention of the American public was focused on what one commentator called the "rail rogues."

The first of the barons to attract public attention was Daniel Drew, who
was the leading power on the board of directors of the Erie, a railroad that
always seemed to be one step away from financial collapse. It was built, as
we have seen, to a high standard but with great difficulty, and the resulting
huge legacy of debt led to the collapse of the original company in 1859, two
years after Drew had joined, when it became unable to service the loans. It
was then reorganized with Drew as company treasurer, becoming profitable, and he realized that there was a fortune to be made through manipulation of its share price. Drew had once been a cattle drover, taking stock
to the New York market, and he learned an old trick to boost the price
of the animals—making them drink a lot of water just before they were
weighed. This was the origin of the term *stock watering*, and in company
parlance it means artificially inflating the "price" of shares beyond the value
of the assets they represent. It was the way that Drew now used his privi-
leged position inside the company to good effect, a scam that would be
taken up by numerous other railroad directors. As ever, the company was
short of money, and in 1866, as he had done several times before, Drew, as
treasurer, agreed to make a loan. As security against the huge sum of $3.5
million that he provided, Drew accepted new stock—which obviously diluted the holdings of existing shareholders—and bonds that could also be
converted into stock. Then came the clever bit. The stock market was buoyant, and the price of Erie shares was rising. Drew started selling tranches of
stock and then, suddenly, just as the price started to fall from its peak, he
converted his bonds and flooded the market with the new shares before the
market makers could react. From that one coup, he made around $3 mil-
lion, which the lax rules of the day on share trading allowed him to get
away with. It was entirely legal, but hardly principled.

Oddly, Drew, who came from a humble background and had difficulty
reading, was a deeply religious man and came across to those who met him

as rather downbeat and pessimistic: "Shrewd and unscrupulous, he cultivated an appearance of sombre piety, looking, despite his stove-pipe hat,
like a Puritan elder oppressed by the thought of Original Sin."[28] He en-
dowed a theological college, but had no compunction making a fortune in
the underhanded way that today would be called "insider trading."

It was Drew's rivalry with Vanderbilt that attracted the most attention,
in particular their battle over the Erie. Drew was a natural "bear" in his
stock dealings, always assuming that prices would fall, whereas Vanderbilt
was the opposite, a "bull" who would seek to buy to make a profit. Oddly,
both Vanderbilt and Drew had originally made money out of owning
steamboats, but, for both, railroads would eventually prove far more lucrative. Cornelius Vanderbilt, known as the Commodore because of his shipping interests, came from a background as humble as Drew's but had a
rather grander vision, seeking to make huge sums out of the railroads by
ensuring they gained a dominant position. Vanderbilt had made a fortune
from his steamboat interests, notably owning the Staten Island ferry in New
York, and later oceangoing ships, taking emigrants heading for California
down to Panama.[29]

He had a long-standing dislike of railroads, which might have had its
roots in the injury he received in the wreck on the Camden & Amboy in
1833 (mentioned in Chapter 3), but as the rail network expanded, it was
clear that there was far more money to be made on the tracks than on the
water. In the 1850s, he started moving his money from shipping to the
railroads and joined the board of several railroad companies in which
he had invested. It was not, though, in his makeup to be simply a dormant
minority shareholder, and he soon sought to gain control of numerous
railroads. His first targets were two minor railroads operating from New
York, the New York & Harlem Railroad and the Hudson River Railroad.
He bought substantial holdings in these railroads and soon gained total
control of them, thanks to stock manipulation that enabled him to buy out
the other shareholders on the cheap. He had his eye on bigger fish, however, as owning these minor railroads gave him the opportunity to gain
control of the far bigger Central. Running from Buffalo in upstate New
York, the Central did not have a terminus in New York, and its passengers
had to endure the inconvenience of transferring onto ferries to get across

the Hudson to Manhattan. However, in the winter, when the river was frozen, they used the New York & Harlem Railroad instead. The seasonal nature of this traffic did not please the Commodore, and in January 1867 he suddenly refused the Central access to his lines, essentially blocking off its route to New York. As a consequence, the share price of the Central plummeted, and Vanderbilt began buying its stock on the cheap. He quickly accumulated a large holding, and by the end of that year he was being asked by the leading shareholders of the Central to become president of the line, despite his role in the company's troubles. There was an almost comic scene when, later, Vanderbilt was asked to justify his refusal to allow the Central onto his tracks to a New York City legislative committee hearing, and he claimed that he was playing whist at the time the trains were canceled. "I never allow anything to interfere with me when I am playing that game," remarked the unflappable Vanderbilt.[30]

The Central was a cash cow, as New York was booming and it was the line of preference for both freight and people heading upstate. However, the Commodore liked monopolies and hated competition, and to establish total dominance over New York's railroad system, he needed to take over the Erie. That ambition was to trigger the Erie War,[31] the most infamous company battle in nineteenth-century US corporate history. Drew had been relatively inactive during the Civil War, but still indulged in a bizarre form of manipulation, buying stock just before the annual election of directors, and then selling it when his power was confirmed at the meeting with the help of his voting rights. However, his position came under threat when Vanderbilt, flush with money, accumulated enough Erie stock in 1867 to obtain a seat on the board. Vanderbilt and Drew had history. They had clashed numerous times over their respective steamship interests, and Vanderbilt had invariably gotten the better of the less talented, and, indeed, less combative, Drew. Not this time, however. Drew managed to ally himself with two men, Jay Gould and Jim Fisk, who were even better versed in the dark arts of stock manipulation and corrupt business practices than Drew himself and who had also started buying up shares in the company.

At the beginning of 1868, Vanderbilt increased the rate of his stock purchases but found that there seemed—mysteriously—to be ever more shares available. The reason for this was simple. The trio of Gould, Fisk,

and Drew were printing large numbers of share certificates without au-
thorization from the board. They did this through a complicated legal
loophole that allowed them to issue stock on the basis of any other railroad they leased. They had gained control of an obscure and useless railroad company called the Buffalo, Bradford & Pittsburgh—which never
reached either Buffalo or Pittsburgh, as it was just thirty miles long—in
order to issue $2 million worth of stock. Vanderbilt eventually realized
that he was being "hornswoggled," as he put it, and resorted to the law,
seeking arrest warrants for the three for cheating him out of his money.

Nothing is straightforward in this story, and that includes the judges
who presided over the case. Since they were elected to their posts, these
judges could easily be bought. Therefore, it was not difficult for Vanderbilt
to find a judge to do his bidding, one George C. Barnard, who was prepared
to fire injunctions "like bolts of lightning."[32] After further maneuvering by
Drew, Fisk, and Gould, he issued arrest warrants for them, forcing them to
flee outside his jurisdiction across the Hudson River to New Jersey, where
they holed up in the Taylor Hotel in Jersey City with a large swath of the
company's files and a few million dollars of its cash and were protected by
hired hands wielding everything from shotguns to knuckles. To counter
Vanderbilt's legal maneuvers, the trio began to obtain their own injunctions from friendly judges, and even reincorporated the company in New
Jersey. With writs flying, and the action moving for a time to Albany, the
seat of the New York State legislature, the three managed to hold off Vanderbilt with the help of politicians bought off with company cash. Even
though at one point Gould was arrested for contempt of court, the three
triumphed, fleecing Vanderbilt of $7 million, much of which was returned
to him when peace eventually broke out between the warring parties. Vanderbilt had suddenly caved in, failing to oppose a bill in the state assembly
that had effectively handed victory to the Drew-Gould faction. This suggests that a deal had been struck, as Drew, who oddly rather disliked confrontation, did not relish continuing the fight. Drew had been something of
a reluctant coconspirator anyway. He resented being stuck in New Jersey
and restricted to visiting his family in New York across the Hudson on Sundays, when arrest warrants did not apply.

Indeed, it was Drew who would be the ultimate loser. He was quickly
discarded by the far more ruthless pair of Gould and Fisk, who, with yet

more manipulation of the stock price, managed to cost him $1.5 million and consequently his seat on the board. The importance of this battle over the Erie was not so much the convoluted facts themselves, which were covered in great detail by the press of the day, but rather the impression that it created in the public mind. Together with the Crédit Mobilier scandal, which unfolded a few years later, the Erie War tarnished the image of the railroads.

Gould and Fisk, who quickly became president and vice president of the Erie, respectively, were not obvious bedfellows, given their contrasting personalities. Gould was, like Drew, a churchgoing man and cut a rather lonely and enigmatic figure. Of the railroad barons, Gould was probably the cleverest, but also the least principled, despite his strong Christianity, and was accused of causing several suicides as the result of his harsh behavior in business dealings. He was a retiring character who liked money but was also rather dissatisfied by its mere acquisition, and therefore his ultimate motives are very difficult to discern. Fisk, on the other hand, was a *bon viveur,* as witnessed by his growing corpulence, testimony to an overfondness for good food, and scandalized New York with his all too public sexual adventures. His notoriety in New York society surprisingly made him quite popular with the Erie's staff: "Many railroad employees regarded him as a heroic figure, probably little realizing that his only contribution was in draining the railroad's coffers and picking the workers' pockets."[33]

With Drew out of the way, Fisk and Gould kept issuing more stock to keep Vanderbilt away, but of course that meant existing shareholders found the value of their stock being constantly diluted. In the first four months of Gould's presidency of the company, the nominal value of shares in the company rose from $34 million to $58 million, entirely as a result of more shares being issued, leading Vanderbilt to complain ruefully that he could afford to buy the Erie, but not the printing press. For political leverage, they appointed to the board William "Boss" Tweed, a New York Democratic politician notorious for his corruption in "Tammany Hall" politics, and in return they obtained favorable legislation from the city administration.

The pair enjoyed themselves, too, at the Erie shareholders' expense. With railroad company money, they bought the redundant Pike's Opera House, a huge white marble building in the classical style on Manhattan's Eighth Avenue, which they promptly leased back to the Erie at $75,000 per year. The

Erie's offices in the building, which they renamed the Grand Opera House—remember, this was a company that was for the most part bankrupt and barely ever paid a dividend in its history—were "reached by a grand carved staircase leading to a pair of huge doors with a tessellated marble hall beyond—all stained glass, Pompeian frescoes and glass chandeliers." The offices themselves were decorated in a similar ostentatious style, and a company safe, extending from the basement to the roof, was installed. In the theater below, Fisk put on operatic productions, partly to please his mistress, Josie Mansfield, "a good-looking though heavily-jowelled gold-digger with theatrical aspirations but without the requisite talents."[34] Fisk was so enamored of Mansfield that he arranged for a special underground passageway to be built between her apartment and the Erie headquarters, but she was to prove his undoing, as, in 1872, he was murdered by another of her lovers.

Gould remained in control of the Erie Railroad until 1874, when he was ousted by British stockholders and reformers who wanted to put a stop to his constant raids on the company coffers. Gould, though, simply moved west, gaining control of various lines and building up a network amounting to more than ten thousand miles of railroad. His skill lay in knowing precisely when to move in on a railroad to buy stock cheaply and using his considerable managerial prowess to turn around the fortunes of ailing businesses. Indeed, unlike Drew or Durant of the Union Pacific, who were interested only in making money, Gould actually strove to improve the railroads he took over, making them more efficient and viable. At his height, in the 1880s, he controlled about one-seventh of the entire rail network of the United States, including all of the elevated system in New York. For the most part, he left his railroads in a better state than when he acquired them, despite purloining vast amounts of money from them in the process. The Erie was an exception to this generally positive picture: much of the money allocated for improvements such as new rails and cars ended up in Gould's pockets, and after 1872, when he left it, the line did not pay a dividend until 1941, when the Second World War improved its fortunes.

Vanderbilt, though chastened by his defeat over the Erie, and already aged seventy-three by the time he had gained control of the New York Central, nevertheless continued to acquire railroad companies and expand his empire for the remaining decade of his life. He bought up the Lake Shore &

Michigan, which ran from Buffalo in upstate New York through to Chicago, and later the Michigan Central and several other lines. He was also responsible for the construction of the Grand Central Depot in New York, to provide a terminal for his three New York railroads together in one large station. It was conceived as the grandest railroad station in the world—though it had several European competitors in that respect—and had a rather eccentric arrangement to prevent smoke from damaging the great room beyond the buffers with its huge chandeliers lit by gas jets. Rather than allowing locomotives to haul the trains into the platforms, the Central adopted the "flying switch" method of bringing its cars into the station. A short way from the end of the journey, the locomotive would be uncoupled from the coaches behind it, and routed onto a sidetrack that did not lead into the station. With a quick change of the switch rails, the rest of the train would be allowed to roll into the platform, brakemen controlling it to prevent the cars from smashing into the buffers. Amazingly, this remarkable and perilous system was used for many years without accident, leaving the chandeliers unsullied by smoke.

Vanderbilt was succeeded by one of his surviving children, William Henry Vanderbilt, who, unlike many sons of millionaires, had most of the skills of his father. PR was not one of them, however. Questioned about the scrapping of a popular train service, he notoriously responded, "The public be damned! . . . I don't take any stock in this silly nonsense about working for anybody but our own." The attribution of this quote is unclear,[35] but even if the younger Vanderbilt never uttered these infamous words, they did untold damage to the image of the railroad millionaires. William Henry, despite not being held in high regard by his father, who frequently called him a "blockhead" or "blatherspike," was actually extremely successful in continuing to build up the railroad empire. Already valued at a staggering $100 million at the Commodore's death in January 1877, it had doubled in value by the time William Henry died a mere nine years later, aged sixty-four.

As the railroads consolidated in the postwar period, a new breed of barons emerged, even more powerful than their predecessors, as they ran vast networks of lines in what were now massive businesses. They were, though, different from the earlier barons, who had been focused purely on enriching themselves. Just as Gould seems to have changed from a man who sought only to make money to, in his later railroad dealings, one who realized the value of running a good railroad company, the later moguls, although not shy about enriching themselves, were also concerned with the viability of the businesses they controlled. However, although they were not such out-and-out rogues as their predecessors, that did not stop them from being equally disliked.

A case in point is James J. Hill, who constructed the Great Northern between St. Paul and Seattle without benefit of any government subsidy and is often perceived, with some justification, as America's "greatest railroad builder." Hill did indeed become immensely rich thanks to the railroad and lived in great opulence. Although without a doubt as ruthless and aggressive as the likes of Gould, he was a railroad builder rather than a stock manipulator. However, he was not averse to making the profits of his operation seem lower than they were in reality, with the aim of using the money to continue constructing the railroad. This practice lay behind the one incident in Hill's career that sullied his copybook and made him appear in the same bad light as the barons. In 1893, Hill's company issued $50 million worth of bonds that were then sold cheaply, at 10 cents per dollar, to the main stockholders in what appeared to be a classic case of stock watering. Hill claimed that this was a way of ensuring continued investment, as it meant that money that would have been paid otherwise in dividends was used to increase the capitalization of the company. However, as David Mountfield, the author of a history of the railroad barons, puts it, "his argument did not cut much ice with the increasingly vociferous opponents of big business." Mountfield goes on, however, to support Hill, saying that the railroad mogul and his partners "made their railroad a blue-chip concern. Dividends were regularly maintained, and the value of the stock remained constantly above par [that is, higher than the original offer price]." Hill also attracted criticism because one of the ways he kept his company solvent was by cutting his employees' wages several times following the panic of 1893, but in fact he restored them after negotiations with Eugene V. Debs and the American Railway Union. Hill later gained control of the Chicago, Burlington & Quincy Railroad in partnership with J. P. Morgan, who, though mostly famous for his banking interests, cut his teeth on building up a railroad empire. He was quite the opposite of Hill, not at all a railroad man, but rather the money man, controlling investment money that went into "his" railroads: "He came to choose their managers, dictate their policies, and shape them to his principles. . . . His methods included reducing wasteful competition, consolidating competing companies, and reorganizing shaky operations."[36] In effect, he "Morganized" his railroads, turning companies that had overstretched themselves or faced too much competition into profitable entities.

Morgan's first foray into railroads was a successful battle with Gould over the Albany & Susquehanna, a line of just 143 miles but potentially lucrative because it provided a useful connection between four larger railroads and several Pennsylvania coal mines. The struggle for control of this small railroad was one of those epic fights that brought disrepute on the industry. In 1868, our old friends Gould and Fisk began buying up shares, intent on using the connection with the Erie, but were opposed by the company's president, Joseph Ramsey, who not only started issuing thousands of shares to his supporters but actually took away the company's books and buried them in a cemetery. Both sides adopted a twin approach of resorting to the courts whenever possible but not shrinking from hiring thugs to do battle with their rival. Indeed, at one point, the two ends of the line, at Albany and Binghamton, were under the control of the opposing factions. In a situation that would not have been out of place in a Broadway farce, sheriffs from the two towns, armed with conflicting injunctions from local judges, boarded trains at either end to impose control on one group or the other. A train was derailed, and the two parties attacked each other until the state militia was called in as peacemaker.

At this point, Morgan, who had loaned a half-million dollars to the Albany & Susquehanna, bought a chunk of shares and became a director of the company in support of Ramsey. He managed to see off Gould and Fisk, and when the matter came to the New York Supreme Court in 1869, Ramsey and Morgan triumphed and were able to retain control of the line. Morgan would later be often called upon to sort out similar disputes, always managing to protect his own interests as he did so.

Reorganizing and refinancing railroads was Morgan's forte. A decade after the Albany & Susquehanna coup, he was involved in a much bigger operation when William Henry Vanderbilt enlisted him to help sell half of his vast stock of New York Central shares without the market realizing what was happening, as this would have sent their value plummeting. Morgan achieved this quietly and slowly, ensuring the market did not panic at the availability of a huge number of shares, and as a reward was made the railroad's principal banker. In the mid-1880s, his troubleshooting skills were employed on, among others, the New York, West Shore & Buffalo Railroad, the Philadelphia & Reading (twice), and the Chesapeake & Ohio. In the 1890s he brought order to the railroads of the Southeast, creating for the first time in the region a reasonably coherent network with his Southern Railroad, which operated forty-four hundred miles as its centerpiece. Morgan was forever trying to consolidate and integrate railroad systems, knowing that this was likely to make them more profitable. Twice, in 1889 and 1890, he organized conferences of railroad presidents in order to help the companies respond to the creation of the Interstate Commerce Commission and to negotiate agreements that would help stabilize freight rates. These conferences were a catalyst for the process of consolidation that by the middle of the first decade of the new century would see the emergence of seven dominant systems, accounting for the greater part of the nation's railroad network (see next chapter).

The largest of these systems would be controlled by the other big railroad magnate of the late nineteenth century, Edward Harriman, who is "generally recognized as the greatest rail baron in American history, not only for the extent of his empire but for the revolutionary and enduring nature of his accomplishments in operations, business practices and safety." His background, in common with most of the barons, was modest, as he started as a messenger boy on Wall Street at the age of fourteen, but within a few years he had made enough money to purchase a seat on the New York Stock Exchange. His interest in railroads was initiated by his marriage to Mary Averell, whose father was president of a branch line, the rather romantic-sounding Ogdensburg & Lake Champlain in upstate New York. His first direct venture into the industry, however, came in 1881 with his purchase, helped by the Averell family, of the Sodus Bay & Southern Railroad, which ran inland from the best harbor on the shore of Lake Ontario. Harriman judged, correctly, that he would be able to sell it to one of the larger local railroad companies, stimulating a bidding war between the Northern Central and the Erie. The former won out, but Harriman pocketed a tidy profit from his three-year tenure of the railroad, and as a result caught the railroad bug. Harriman, like many of his contemporaries—and unlike the earlier barons—made his money through an attention to detail and a clear idea of how to run railroads at a profit rather than by financial manipulation. In fact, he used the little railroad as a testing ground for his ideas, renovating the track, investing in new rolling stock, and simplifying the management structure. Harriman's philosophy could not have been more different from the likes of Drew, encompassed in his assertion that "the only way to make a good property valuable is to put it in the best possible condition to do business."[37] He realized that the age of speculation was over and that the key to making money was having a sound railroad business, rather than manipulating stock or, as he had done himself in his early days, constructing clever deals. Indeed, Harriman left every railroad that he controlled in a better state than when he bought it.

His first venture into major railroads was with the Illinois Central, joining the board in 1883 with the help of a director of the railroad, Stuyvesant Fish, and becoming a vice president four years later when Fish assumed the presidency. It was Harriman, though, who transformed the railroad, and brought about its expansion. The Illinois Central had long harbored ambitions of becoming a major north-south artery, but had failed to do so until Harriman oversaw the completion of the line all the way through to New Orleans. Harriman created such an efficient railroad that it survived the panic of 1893 without a blip in profitability.

However, other railroads suffered even worse than during the previous depression twenty years before. Of America's 364 railroads, 89 went bankrupt, representing forty thousand route miles, around a quarter of the total. As with America's major airlines, which have frequently sought protection under Chapter 11 of the US Bankruptcy Code that allows them to keep flying despite being technically bankrupt, most of these railroads continued running, as they could be operated profitably provided their debt burden was ignored. The multiple bankruptcies resulting from the panic of 1893 enabled Harriman to move to even bigger pastures, the massive Union Pacific. Like all the transcontinentals except the Great Northern (fittingly, the only one not to have received government aid), it had gone under following the panic, and by 1898 Harriman managed to assume control. And he transformed it. He saw that the potential to make it a money spinner was by hauling freight long distances at lower rates than the other guys. The Union Pacific still suffered from the economies made during its construction, and so Harriman straightened curves, reduced gradients, and installed signaling that allowed greater frequencies. As a result, it could carry more trains, which were both heavier and faster, making the railroad highly profitable. Harriman then used this money to expand. He did battle briefly with old Collis Huntington, the sole survivor of the four Central Pacific pioneers, who controlled the Southern Pacific and resisted its takeover. However, the timing of Huntington's death, in 1900, proved opportune for Harriman, who then assumed control of the railroad and improved it in the same way. By the early 1900s, Harriman controlled the greatest-ever mileage of railroads of any individual in the history of the American railroads. The dream of many railroad entrepreneurs was to control a coast-to-coast network of lines, and none really achieved it. Harriman came closest, as for a while he owned the Baltimore & Ohio and the Chicago & Alton as well as the Union Pacific, but he never managed to consolidate these holdings into a unified railroad. He nearly became the only person to own two transcontinentals when he fought with James Hill over the Northern Pacific, but at the last minute the two men reached a compromise, resulting in joint ownership through a holding company mostly controlled by Hill. Like the other barons, Harriman attracted widespread opprobrium, mostly because he was not only very rich, but also pugnacious and ruthless. As an example, he got rid of Fish, who had previously been his mentor from the Illinois Central board, because the latter cooperated with the investigation of an insurance company in which Harriman was involved. Yet now, as his biographer in the *Encyclopedia of North American Railroads* suggests, "with a century's perspective, his reputation has rebounded, and he is now considered on balance to have been a positive force."[38]

The image of the robber barons was nevertheless long lasting, as it was in railroads, more than any other industry, that these men made their fortunes. It was highly damaging to the railroads, whose image suffered from the barons' infamy. The later barons, who included the reformed Gould, may have been somewhat different in their aims and methods from their predecessors, who were out-and-out rogues, but the damage had been done. As rail historian Keith Bryant Jr. comments, "Journalists created the image of the 'robber baron' who displayed no interest in operating a railroad for profit or in improving the property, but simply used the carrier's stock and bonds as vehicles for personal gain. . . . [This image] never dissipated and was used again and again by the detractors of the industry as representative of all railroad executives."[39]

But there was more to the growing antipathy to the railroads than merely a dislike of the corrupt moguls. As we have seen, labor had started organizing, and although the series of workers' strikes beginning in the 1870s ended in defeat, they attracted considerable support from the wider population. Moreover, the railroads in general and the barons in particular seemed to show a particular disregard for the safety of their workforces, always blaming the workers themselves for any accidents.

It was not, though, the workers who were to attract the most sympathy in their battles with the railroads, but the farmers, who were by far the best-organized group of railroad opponents; even though their case was at times tenuous, they ran a highly effective lobbying campaign that would force the railroads on the defensive. The railroads changed the nature of farming. In the prerailroad days, markets were still local enough for the farmer to transport his produce there with his horse and cart, and the use of any possible transportation system, such as a river or a railroad, was entirely optional. If it were cheap and convenient enough, then he might use it, but otherwise not. The railroads were sensitive to this, as they were mostly local concerns, and therefore ensured their rates were tailored to the farmers' needs. However, as the West became settled, and large farms created out of the land given to the railroads began to emerge in the 1870s, the situation became very different. In states such as Nebraska or Iowa, farmers were no longer self-reliant producers, but, as John Stover puts it, "had no choice but to use rail facilities offered at the rates ordained by a largely absentee ownership." There simply was no local market. The farmers were growing cash crops that had to be transported long distances to the east or for export, and "it was the rare western farmer who had the choice of two rail routes to market."[40] The farmers were consequently at the mercy of the railroads, and they perceived the cost of transportation as an unavoidable tax.

Not only were the farmers tied inexorably to the railroads, but in some cases they had even helped finance them by raising mortgages on their farms. Now, though, they were in a powerless position, as the railroads imposed what the farmers felt were punitive rates. According to Stover, "The farmer's transition from railroad proponent to railroad antagonist came earlier along the eastern prairie than it did farther west."[41] The standard complaint was simple: why did the railroads charge more per mile for shorter journeys than for longer ones, which seemed to put local farmers at a disadvantage? There were, in fact, understandable reasons, since much of the cost of a journey occurs in the loading and unloading at each end, but this argument was dismissed by the farmers. They blamed the low margins they could earn on their produce on high freight charges. Even when rates began to fall in the 1880s, there was continued resentment because of the railroads' dominant position as the sole viable means of transportation. Probably apocryphal stories spread through the Midwest about the Illinois farmer who returned from selling his load of grain with the amount it had cost him to buy a pair of shoes for his son, or the similar tale from Iowa of a smallholder who burned his corn for fuel as, at fifteen cents a bushel—compared with the dollar he would have received in the East—it was cheaper than coal. In fact, there were bigger forces at work that affected the farmers. Much of the land in the West was in areas with poor rainfall, and yields were not as good as promised; also, partly thanks to the opening up of vast swaths of land in the United States and Canada as a result of the spread of the railroads, worldwide prices for grain were falling.

No matter. The railroads were an easy target. The weather and global prices could not be influenced by pressure from the farmers. The railroads and the state legislatures could, and consequently the railroads became the great symbol of grasping capitalists who were responsible for all the farmers' ills. Helped by the antipathy to the barons, the farmers captured the zeitgeist and became the first organized force against the power of the railroads. The railroads were perceived as having destroyed the traditional American way of life, a feeling encapsulated by Henry George in an 1868 essay: "[The railroad] kills little towns and builds up great cities, and in the same way kills little businesses and builds up great ones."[42] The hostility started in Illinois at the back end of the 1860s, whereas in Nebraska, farther west, it did not emerge until the deprivations in the depression following the panic of 1873. Although the farmers' complaints were hardly new or even noteworthy, they were given added strength because they were backed by a curious but effective organization, the Patrons of Husbandry, better known as the Grange. It was created by a brilliant orator and organizer, Oliver Kelley, a Minnesota farmer who had decided that farmers needed an association to press for their interests. He used the model of the Masonic order, creating a series of local Granges and a structure based on "degrees," as members rose through the ranks. Unlike the Masons, women were admitted on the basis that they would be crucial in winning over their menfolk. After a slow start, as Kelley toured first his own state and later neighboring ones giving rousing speeches with the aim of setting up local groups, the movement blossomed and by 1875 had eight hundred thousand members in twenty thousand local Granges.

The feelings of the farmers toward the railroads were evoked powerfully in a series of books and pamphlets on the Mussel Slough tragedy of May 1880 in California's San Joaquin Valley, in which seven men died in a shootout between local settlers fearing eviction by the Southern Pacific Railroad and a marshal and his three associates who, it was thought, had been sent in to clear the land. The most famous was Frank Norris's 1901 novel *The Octopus*, which describes the railroad as that "great monster, iron-hearted, relentless, infinitely powerful." On this occasion, the issue was not freight rates, but, rather, the railroad was accused of misleading the settlers about the rent levels they had to pay on their land and was portrayed as callous in trying to evict them. The Southern Pacific was victorious in various court decisions, helped by sympathetic judges, but the widespread publicity given to the incident ensured public support for the settlers, which in turn helped stimulate wider feelings of antagonism toward the railroad companies. The understandable failure of the public to comprehend the historic role of the railroads in light of their oppressive behavior is brilliantly encapsulated by railroad historian Richard Saunders Jr.: "[The Southern Pacific] made enemies in California even though, probably more than any other institution, it also made modern California possible."[43]

The farmers pressed for the states to bring in legislation controlling railroad rates. It was no coincidence that it was the states where the Grange was most active that became the first to control freight charges. Minnesota, the birthplace of Kelley's movement, passed a law fixing railroad rates and providing for a railroad commissioner in 1871. Two years later, similar legislation was introduced in Illinois, where many Granges had also been formed. Iowa and Wisconsin followed suit the next year, and by the end of the decade another four states, including California, had passed laws restricting the freedom of the railroad companies to set rates. The railroads, however, did not stand meekly by, accepting their fate. Quite the opposite. Their lawyers challenged the legislation in the courts, arguing that the states did not have the power to set rates. Here, another railroad practice that had attracted widespread criticism came into play, the issuing of passes to prominent people, such as judges, sheriffs, both local and national politicians, and, of course, journalists, allowing them free travel on request on the railroad. Favoring the great and the good with free travel might seem like a rather trivial matter given the other ways in which the railroads had made themselves unpopular, but it had widespread resonance. It was seen as yet another abuse of railroad power, and paying passengers hated sitting near the "deadheads," as they were termed, who did not have to contribute to the railroad company's coffers. The benefits of having politicians on their side were all too obvious to the railroads. Giving a pass to a town assessor, for instance, might well result in a lower tax bill; alternatively, the railroads were not averse to withdrawing passes from politicians or officials who did not do their bidding. The scale of this crude PR can be gauged by the fact that by 1897, the railroads of North Carolina alone were giving out passes for no fewer than one hundred thousand journeys per year, costing them more than three hundred thousand dollars in revenue foregone. The public's interest in these concessionary arrangements was so strong that legislation banning the practice became law in 1906.

Legislators and even judges could also be influenced by the issuing of these passes, and even when battles in the courts were lost, the railroads at times simply ignored the legislation. It was not easy. The question of what was a fair rate for freight, and how it could be enforced, was far from straightforward. Some legislatures tried to control passenger fares, too, and the railroads played a nasty game of trying to make the journey of passengers on these regulated services as unpleasant as possible, using old stock and introducing timetables with longer journey times. The balance of interest in the court cases was neatly poised, as Stover aptly suggests: "The Grangers had votes; the railroads possessed money."[44] It was not only high rates that angered the farmers and, indeed, other shippers. The railroads tended to favor big shippers and granted them substantial rebates. The pricing arrangements with these larger clients were secret, and this lack of transparency was seen as masking the railroads' preference for dealing with fellow big corporations to the detriment of the little guy. Worse, on many routes, the railroads simply pooled their income and operated jointly in order to prevent uneconomic competition, which was seen as operating an unfair cartel.

Yet favoring large clients was standard business practice in other industries. Moreover, in reality, the last quarter of the nineteenth century was a period of intense competition during which freight rates fell dramatically, from 1.88 cents per ton mile in 1870 to 0.73 cents in 1900. At various times, fierce rate wars broke out between competing railroads, and the large number of bankruptcies following the panic of 1893 suggested that this was *not* an industry where monopolists were constantly exploiting their customers. And the railroads could not be accused of a lack of innovation. One key development in the 1880s was the widespread introduction of the refrigerated boxcar. Although there had been earlier attempts to use refrigeration to keep cars cool, it was only in the 1880s that satisfactory methods were developed. The new refrigerated cars revolutionized the transportation of beef, since the animals could now be slaughtered locally before being transported to the Chicago stockyards; as a result, these yards grew to enormous proportions, eventually employing forty thousand people in the 1920s and processing nearly all of America's meat. The expansion of the Chicago yards, which also continued to deal with live meat, was another indirect consequence of the network of railroads that had concentrated in and around Chicago.

Nevertheless, with so many factors running against them, the railroads were ripe for a good kicking. The farmers might have been the best-organized force opposing them, but there was no shortage of popular criticism of the huge railroad companies, thanks to the activities of the barons.

Safety concerns, too, had not gone away. As we have seen, it took consider-able efforts for the railroads to take safety matters seriously, and, despite the gradual improvements, there were still several major crashes in the last twenty years of the nineteenth century. The years 1887 and 1888 were par-ticularly bad ones for rail safety, with a series of high-profile accidents, several of which were caused by bridge failures. The worst was the Great Chatsworth train wreck in Illinois, which took place on the night of August 10, 1887, when a trainload of Pullman sleepers and coaches, bound for Ni-agara Falls, was derailed by the failure of a wooden trestle underneath it, resulting in 84 deaths and around 280 injuries. The following year, in Octo-ber, another accident with a high death toll attracted particular attention because it involved a train chartered by the Catholic Total Abstinence Soci-ety, returning from a meeting of the organization at Hazleton in the Ap-palachian Mountains on the Lehigh Valley Railroad. Two of the eight special trains collided with one another at Mud Run Station, Pennsylvania, resulting in 66 deaths in the flimsy wooden coaches used for the excursion services, yet another example of a disaster occurring on a special train.

The opposition to the Granger laws had resulted in a series of court cases, and though the states largely won these, it was becoming obvious that federal, rather than state, legislation was needed. In the 1880s, there-fore, interest in railroad regulation passed from the states to the federal government in Washington. As early as 1871, there had been moves in Congress to create some kind of regulatory body, and the consolidation of the railroads into bigger companies increased the pressure. This was helped by the almost universal adoption of the standard gauge of four feet and eight and a half inches, as described in the last chapter. In the 1880s, 425 railroad companies, nearly a quarter of the total, came under the con-trol of other lines through mergers or leasing arrangements, and the net-work was expanding rapidly through new construction, with nearly seventy thousand miles being built during the decade. It became clear to Washington politicians that these huge organizations, which crossed nu-merous state boundaries and had become the most powerful companies in the land, could not be controlled by state legislatures.

Two events in 1886 forced the issue. A committee set up by the Senate to investigate the railroad industry headed by Shelby Cullom, a former governor of Illinois, uncovered the whole gamut of bad practices outlined above, from stock watering and discriminatory pricing to secret rebates and illegal kickbacks. Not surprisingly, it recommended the establishment of a commission to regulate the nation's railroads. That became inevitable after a Supreme Court decision in the same year involving the Wabash, St. Louis & Pacific (the use of *& Pacific* lingered on!) found that the state could not regulate rates on shipments that traveled beyond its borders.[45] That made federal regulation inevitable.

By the mid-1880s, the Granger movement was on the wane, but it had been supplanted by the even more vociferous Farmers' Alliance, which later joined together with a number of other groups to form the Populist movement and was equally hostile to the railroads' power. There was, too, growing support beyond agriculture for regulating the railroads. The increasingly important oil companies, who were entirely dependent on the railroads for transportation, together with the powerful merchant interests in New York, had joined the Grangers in seeking legislation. Many railroad owners, too, had recognized that legislation was unavoidable, and they preferred, for the most part, the simpler option of having one federal system rather than a series of different rules in each state. Indeed, the increasingly fierce rate wars in the mid-1880s led several railroad magnates to welcome the notion of regulation in order to stop their rivals from carrying goods at rates below cost and to deter them from building tracks parallel to profitable lines in order to poach the business. As a Chicago newspaper reported just before the legislation was passed, "Perhaps the strongest argument that can be presented in favour of the passage of this bill is found in the fact that many of the leading railroad managers admit the justice of its terms and join in the demand for its passage."[46] Many of their successors, however, would have cause to regret the support given to the bill by the industry. Nevertheless, in early 1887, the bill was passed, creating the rather confusingly named Interstate Commerce Commission, which, faced with a difficult and complex task, would ultimately have a disastrous effect on the railroad industry.

9

ALL KINDS OF TRAIN

The creation of the Interstate Commerce Commission was a response to the growing power of the railroads and fears that they would exploit their monopoly position. The commission, though, proved rather toothless in its early years, losing a series of challenges from the railroad companies, and could only watch as the consolidation of the railroads into bigger corporations intensified. This process was hastened by the panic of 1893, which pushed many rail companies into bankruptcy, facilitating their takeover by solvent rivals. This consolidation had, as Stover suggests, "been accompanied by financial manipulations so unscrupulous that they would have excited the envy of [Jay] Gould, Drew or Commodore Vanderbilt."[1] The result was that by the middle of the first decade of the twentieth century, two-thirds of the total mileage of the railroads, which had reached more than 225,000 miles, was in the control of just seven large corporations. The biggest was the Harriman group centered on the Union Pacific, with 25,000 route miles, but all of these conglomerates had more than 15,000 miles, and names like Gould (Jay's son George), Morgan, and Vanderbilt remained prominent.

The consolidation had been a way of clearing out dead wood and writing off unpayable debts. As Albro Martin suggests, before the depression that followed the 1893 panic, the railroads were "overbuilt, financially undernourished, divided into hundreds of poorly integrated corporate entities, and riddled with rate wars which reduced the profits of the best-situated roads drastically and drove the weaker ones to the wall of bankruptcy."[2] In truth, the railroad network was still very uneven. A map of the railroads in 1900 shows the eastern half of the country covered in a tangle of spaghetti, whereas the West remains almost bare, with just a few strands stretching across the huge plains and deserts. But that was as much a reflection of the pattern of settlement as the development of the railroads. The western lines were, for the most part, a separate system, with actually few people and not many goods making the full transcontinental coast-to-coast journey. The South, too, had fewer railroads, but now, thanks to J. P. Morgan, who melded its network together, they were better connected with the North, and indeed, apart from the seasonal vacationers, their main purpose was in carrying the raw materials such as coal, wood, and cotton required by the industrialized North.

The shakeout caused by the 1893 panic and the subsequent consolidation resulted in the growing power of these seven groups and entailed a reduction in competition, as the existence of the commission failed to prevent considerable, but mostly tacit, cooperation between rival railroads on many routes. The industry was changing from one ruled solely by raw competition to one where the value of cooperation was recognized. One sign of this was the growing number of "union" depots or stations that housed trains of several companies, although only very few, such as Los Angeles and Washington, DC, ever put all their trains in one station. The period running up to the First World War was the heyday for the building of union stations in imitation of European railroads, which had been constructing such palaces since the middle of the nineteenth century. Union Station in the capital, opened in 1907, is probably the most famous of these celebrations of the power and affluence of the railroads, with its triumphal arch entrance, grand high-ceilinged lobby, and eclectic classical style leavened with a hint of modernism. The equally classic and enormous Pennsylvania Station in New York City, opened in September 1910 and covering twenty-eight acres, was another product of the prewar period, but has subsequently been demolished, with the trains and concourse now hidden beneath the city streets. It was not only on the East Coast that these massive structures sprang up. The largest outside New York was in Kansas City, Missouri, which, tucked away in the deepest Midwest and built in the beaux arts style favored by the French, would not have been out of place on a Parisian boulevard. Completed in 1914, it was a genuine "union" station, housing no fewer than a dozen railroad companies and with thousands of passengers daily crossing the vastness of its cathedral-like concourse. It survives today, after a period of decline and disuse, having been restored as a "Science City," and offers a mere trio of Amtrak services daily, serving just 400 passengers. At St. Louis, on the other side of Missouri, one of the earliest union stations was built in a style variously described as "Romanesque, Norman Revival, and Chateau"—perhaps "eclectic" would have done the job. The busiest station of the period was the art nouveau–style South Station in Boston, a terminus for many suburban services that was used by 1 million people per week when it opened in 1900.

Another benefit for passengers of the consolidation of the railroads into bigger networks was that they were able to run longer continuous services, making it possible, for example, to travel between Maine in the far-northeastern corner of the country down to Florida in the South without changing trains. With such grand schemes and even bigger ambitions, it was, on the face of it, a good time to be in the railroad business. The automobile was not yet threatening rail's hegemony, and the airplane was just a funny idea dreamed up by a couple of innovative brothers from the Midwest working in a barn in North Carolina. Moreover, America's economy, after the postpanic depression, was growing again, and the population, boosted by the arrival of immigrants, was expanding rapidly too, reaching 100 million just before the outbreak of the First World War.

Consequently, between 1896 and 1916, it was boom time on the tracks. The core network was complete, though the construction of secondary lines[3] continued until mileage reached its peak of 254,000 miles at the point the United States entered the war in 1917. This reduction in construction activity by the railroads allowed them to devote more capital investment to making improvements, such as reducing curves and gradients, and four-tracking busy sections, rather than the far more expensive process of having to carve out new lines. The healthy state of the industry can be gauged by the generosity of the Pennsylvania Railroad, which only a few years earlier had tried to cut wages but now, in 1902, raised the pay for its 100,000 workers by 10 percent. This was because, according to the company president, Alexander Cassatt—a particularly forward-looking railroad manager—the cost of living had risen by about a quarter since the depression of the mid-1890s, and "we have more business than we can handle and can't see our way out of that difficulty unless we keep our men loyal to the company and help them when they help us." This enlightened attitude was by no means universal, but the other trunk railroads mostly followed suit. In fact, while pressure from the unions and shortages of skilled workers resulted in a sharp increase in labor costs during the prewar period, the high rate of inflation meant that real wages barely increased at all. The growing strength of the unions, now far better organized, meant the railroad companies were inclined to settle disputes through arbitration often under the auspices of the Interstate Commerce Commission, in contrast to their previous obduracy. There were consequently only a few local strikes, with no national action on the scale of the Pullman conflict. The unions even managed to make some progress on the length of the working day, which was still routinely twelve hours, managing to reduce it to a maximum of ten. The proliferation of unions, representing different skills and groups of workers, led to a series of demarcation disputes that would dog the industry for decades. By 1910 labor issues were never far from the surface: "Demands from one railroad union or another were almost continuously before the railroads. As technological changes revolutionized railroading, they added to labor problems."[4] Indeed, for much of the twentieth century, industrial relations topped the list of problems for railroad managements.

Labor issues were only one of the numerous problems faced by the railroad companies. Although Martin suggests that "the two decades before World War I were the golden age of the railroad passenger train in America," as ever with claims of so-called golden ages, the gilt is easily scratched off. Despite rising revenues and sensible consolidation, the years between the bankruptcies of 1893 and the First World War were not an unequivocally happy time for the railroads. Certainly, the railroads enjoyed remarkable growth during this period, with the number of passenger journeys tripling in the twenty years to 1916. And it was not just impoverished immigrants hopping on overcrowded special trains. Pullman journeys increased fivefold, from a mere 5 million in 1900 to 26 million in 1914. Interestingly, this was a rare period in American railroad history when passenger growth far outpaced the rise in the carriage of freight. In a way, this was not surprising. When it came to passenger travel, the railroads had it all, cornering every market since, for most journeys, there remained no viable alternative. Apart from a few trips that could be made by boat, either along the coast or on lakes, the railroads catered to everyone, "from the travelling salesman who was making his way through his territory in ten and twenty mile hops to the well-to-do family setting out in Pullman drawing room comfort for a tour of the great American West."[5] Although freight carriage did grow in this period, the marketing efforts of the railroad, together with the increase in population and greater prosperity generally, resulted in a far faster rate of growth for passenger traffic. A measure of the extent of rail travel can be ascertained from one particularly busy day marking the end of the vacation season, September 4, 1910, when the two main New York stations coped with 200,000 arriving passengers. On that day, the Adirondack Express from upstate New York, which usually had around ten cars, consisted of no fewer than sixteen trains of similar capacity that arrived at five-minute intervals at New York Central. Over at Pennsylvania Station, the Seashore service from Atlantic City in New Jersey had to be run as nine separate sections, with a couple of extra trains solely for baggage.

The growing affluence of the American people ensured that demand for travel rose rapidly. It would be false, however, to suggest that Americans were constantly hopping on trains. Although the number of journeys annually in this period was constantly above 1 billion, that still meant only ten or so rail trips per year for every American, a rather modest amount in comparison with, say, the number of journeys made nowadays by car. The vast majority of people stayed at home, as they always had, and contemporary surveys suggest that around 5 percent of the population accounted for most of this travel. Apart from immigrants, tourists and business travelers were the mainstay of the railroad companies' passenger market. Business travel was greatly stimulated by the fact that, thanks to the railroads, corporations now saw the whole country as a unified market, encouraging businesses to expand beyond the borders of a particular state or region. America was now a national economy, rather than a series of regional ones, and the railroad as a whole was a monopoly provider for many journeys, albeit often with competition between railroads.

The railroad companies set out specifically to cater to this high end of the market, although, interestingly, before the First World War there was only one railroad fare, with no first class other than the Pullman supplement and occasional provision of "parlor" cars. There was fierce competition on the most profitable routes in the East, notably between New York and

Chicago, where, by the start of the 1900s, there was a choice of no fewer than eighteen different routes. The railroad companies introduced high-profile luxury trains, partly to tap this lucrative section of the business market, but also because such trains created widespread interest and attracted favorable publicity. These prestige services were conceived by the passenger traffic managers of the major companies who began to take on a public relations and proactive selling role, again something of a first for the railroad, since the very idea of marketing was a new notion that was little known in other industries. The publicity emphasized the time savings on these new trains that, cunningly, were branded with names designed to set them apart from the standard services. The Pennsylvania Railroad had led the way in 1887 by introducing the Pennsylvania Limited between New York and Chicago, which was promoted as an all-Pullman service, boasting a barbershop, a bath and valet service for gentlemen, and a maid for their female companions. There was an impressive and varied wine list, and the publicity blurb explained at length how the latest fashionable cocktails would be mixed in the observation car (another innovation, though domed ones would be introduced only after the First World War) at the rear.

The New York Central responded with an emphasis on speed by introducing a fast day train between New York and Buffalo called the Empire State Express in 1889. Two years later, in a highly publicized exercise, it ran the train with a specially designed engine numbered 999 that covered the 436 miles in just over seven hours, an average of 61 mph. It reached a speed of 82 mph, but there were claims, which attracted widespread attention despite much evidence to the contrary, that the train reached 112 mph, which would have made it the first wheeled vehicle to exceed 100 mph on the planet. Of course, the routine journeys never reached anything like those speeds, with 60 mph being the highest that passengers experienced, but journeys were now generally much faster. Whereas in the aftermath of the Civil War averages of 25 mph or at best 30 mph might be the norm, now many fast trains averaged nearer 40 or 45 mph. A pair of contemporary timetable analysts, E. Foxwell and T. C. Farrer, who looked at express trains across the world in 1889, found that the fastest US train was the Baltimore & Ohio's Royal Blue, which operated the 40 miles between Washington and Baltimore in forty-five minutes, an average of 53 mph, the fastest regular service in the world. Two years later that service ran all the way to Jersey

City, on the other side of the Hudson River from Manhattan, and Washington at the same fast average speed, taking just five hours for the whole trip. However, it was the Pennsylvania Railroad that boasted the largest number of fast services. Foxwell and Farrer also found numerous trundlers, notably in the West, where no train passed their test of being an "express" (which required an average speed of 40 mph), but also in the East, where they noted disapprovingly that even many services designated "Flyer" or "Limited" were slow. They were most scathing about a service that ran between Jersey City and Buffalo, New York, that averaged just 31 mph.

The success of the Pennsylvania Limited led to other companies' naming their prestigious trains, but rather unimaginative names predominated, with much use of the words *flyer, express,* and *limited.* There were a few more evocative names, such as the Fast Flying Virginian, but many of the best ones, such as the White Train between Boston and New York, so called because it was painted in white trimmed with gold, were not adopted officially by the railroad company. One name and train, however, stood out, and that was the Twentieth Century Limited, devised by a dynamic railroad manager, George Daniels, who ran the New York Central's passenger business for nearly two decades. It was not only the name that was ingenious but the whole marketing exercise. Daniels had already been responsible for one major innovation, the redcap service of free porters (though since everyone tipped them, a charge was soon introduced) who carried passengers' baggage at stations and became a universal feature of US railroad travel. Daniels, though, had a consuming passion, and that was to establish a fast and luxurious daily service between New York and Chicago. The usual timing for the nearly 1,000-mile route was twenty-four hours, but with the introduction of the daily luxury service between the Big Apple and the Windy City in June 1902, with its clever name, Daniels cut the journey's duration to twenty hours. This was achieved through improvements to the line and by keeping stops to a minimum, partly via the technical innovation of providing lengthy troughs between the rails at key points to allow the ever-thirsty locomotives to replenish their water supply without stopping, an innovation imported from the UK.

The Twentieth Century Limited was, at first, more of a PR exercise than a commercial venture, as was Daniels's claim that the Central was "the world's greatest railroad." The inaugural train, consisting of five cars, was designed to accommodate just forty-two passengers, and although they paid a premium, it was insufficient to cover even the running costs of such an enterprise. The image of the train was perceived as so important to the company that operating staff were told to prioritize the Limited at all costs, even if that meant causing delay to many other passengers. The most impressive feature of the Twentieth Century Limited was its on-board service, which was better than anything that preceded it, apart from the railroad barons' personal trains described in Chapter 7. Barbers and stenographers were on hand, and there was a smoking room and a library. The decor in the diner was notable enough—"Heavily molded mahogany, leaded upper lights to the windows, pot plants on the walls between them, flowers on every table and specially-commissioned high quality linen, crockery and silverware"—but the dinner itself was even more so.[6] A typical offering in 1904 consisted of a half-dozen courses or more, depending on the passenger's appetite or, more accurately, gluttony, starting with a consommé julienne, followed by chicken, beef ribs, goose, and both dessert and cheese, along with extras and adornments such as olives, capon patties (*financière* was the inappropriate name they were given), salads, and, of course, coffee. Perhaps the most remarkable aspect was the price of the meal: just one dollar, definitely a "loss leader," long before the term had been invented. So keen was the Central to impress its prestigious passengers—whose names were printed in newspapers, in the same way as luxury-liner passenger lists—that they were refunded a dollar for every hour that the train was late. It was the Twentieth Century Limited that gave us the expression "red-carpet treatment," since at both New York and Chicago crimson carpets embossed with the company's insignia were laid out so that passengers did not risk soiling their shoes on the surface of the platform. And it was the Twentieth Century Limited that later featured in one of the most famous railroad film scenes when Cary Grant, in the 1959 Hitchcock movie *North by Northwest*, is saved from capture by the beautiful but prim Eva Marie Saint.

In response to the Central's introduction of the Twentieth Century Limited, on the same day in 1902 the Pennsylvania relaunched its Pennsylvania Limited as the Pennsylvania Special. It later became the Broadway Limited, a reference not to New York's theater land but to the fact that its railroad, mostly four-tracked rather than two, was broader than its rivals. Although the Pennsylvania's route between New York and Chicago was about eighty miles shorter than the Central's, it was hampered by the steeper gradients on its line and by freight congestion around Pittsburgh, and consequently was less reliable. However, both the Pennsylvania and the Twentieth Century services were successful and became profitable, so much so that at peak times both companies required two full-length trains to operate the service. The rival companies each tried to reduce timings by a couple of hours in the first decade of the twentieth century in much-publicized initiatives, but the practicalities and the not inconsiderable cost of speeding up services stymied their efforts, leaving twenty hours as the norm until 1932, when diesels were introduced.

As with the earlier luxury coaches provided by Pullman, these prestige trains cannot be seen as typical of contemporary train services, but their introduction suggests that many companies were now making concerted efforts to improve what modern marketeers would call "the passenger experience." These enhancements reflected the fact that the railroads now realized that passengers had to be attracted to the railroad, as they could not be relied upon as a captive market, especially in the highly competitive East, where there usually was an alternative route available for most journeys. Making it easier to purchase tickets was an obvious innovation. Most of the major companies established ticket offices in locations that were more convenient than the local station, such as downtown or in affluent shopping districts, allowing people to avoid that irritating trek to the railroad station on the edge of town, where, invariably, there was a lengthy line for the understaffed ticket office. Independent brokers sprang up, selling tickets on behalf of all the local railroads, and wielded considerable power, since they could recommend particular routes to their clients. In addition, numerous rival agencies could be found along the streets near stations that made money by obtaining a discount from the railroads, rather than charging an extra fee to the passengers. This proliferation of ticket agencies opened the door to corrupt practices, as different railroads vied to gain their favor. Most notable was the practice of selling tickets below the normal fare, known as "scalping." Agents would obtain discounted tickets, such as unsold special-rate deals intended for group travel or the second portions of unused returns, and sell them cheaply. It was not unusual, though, for these scalped tickets to be invalid, leaving the passenger having to pay twice over. Another colorful character involved in ticketing was the broker employed by the railroads to persuade the various agents of the superiority of their particular company's service. These men and, interestingly, women were chosen, according to Martin, on the basis of "personality and ability to hold your liquor [that] were believed to be of the greatest importance in the serious business of persuading a local ticket agent to punch the box opposite the name of one's own railroad on the yard-long tickets with which long-distance travelers often had to contend."[7] Hotel porters, too, carried on a lucrative trade in obtaining cheap rail tickets for guests and pocketing a commission. By and large, this little subindustry of independent ticket sellers disappeared during the First World War, as the railroads became, once again, the sole vendors of their tickets.

The most famous marketing campaign featured Phoebe Snow, a virginal lady who was devised for the Delaware, Lackawanna & Western Railroad, by Earnest Elmo Calkins, one of the great advertising men of the twentieth century, who later went on to create his own agency, Calkins & Holden. The Lackawanna had a unique selling point that might seem obscure now, but was actually quite important in the days of steam engines. Its locomotives burned anthracite from its own mines, a far-cleaner fuel than the bituminous coal used by other companies, which regularly ruined the clothes of their passengers. So, in 1900, Calkins dreamed up Miss Snow, who was prone to speak in nursery-rhyme ditties, to publicize the cleanliness of the Lackawanna's trains:

> *Says Phoebe Snow*
> *about to go*
> *upon a trip to Buffalo*
> *"My gown stays white*
> *from morn till night*
> *Upon the Road of Anthracite"*

This proved so popular that the coy Miss Snow, who always seemed to be going to Buffalo, presumably because it rhymed with her name, was made the central figure in the company's advertising right up to the

First World War. Nothing was too minor or insignificant for Miss Snow's enthusiasm:

> *No trip is far where comforts are.*
> *An observation Lounging Car*
> *Adds new delight to Phoebe's flight*
> *Along the Road of Anthracite*

In other rhymes, Phoebe praised the cooking and the electric lights, but cleanliness was her recurring theme: "No other lips have touched the cup that Phoebe sips." If the whiter-than-white Phoebe was not telling fibs about the Lackawanna's crockery, the railroad was either throwing away china cups after each use or using disposable drinking vessels. She became the best-known advertising mascot of the early years of the twentieth century, a Ronald McDonald of her day, and even made a graceful exit: at the outbreak of war, the government forced the railroad to use coal rather than the anthracite that was needed for the war effort, prompting Phoebe, in her final jingle, to say: "Good bye, old Road of Anthracite!"[8]

It was not only on the Lackawanna that passenger travel on trains improved around the turn of the century. Electric lights, first used in 1887, became standard, as did steam heating, initially introduced a couple of years later on the Pennsylvania Limited. Special magazines were published by the bigger companies, rather like airlines today, containing both PR material about the railroad and articles of general interest to readers. George Daniels of the New York Central was again a pioneer, producing a magazine called *Four-Track News* (a reference to the fact that the railroad boasted both slow and fast lines on much of its route) along with various guidebooks to places that could be reached by the railroad.

Tourism was seen as the key to profitability by many companies. As we have seen, whole resorts were created by railroad interests, but now the companies started promoting the virtues of sites of interest and attractions in their area. The Northern Pacific, which had lobbied for the creation of Yellowstone Park with its famous Old Faithful geyser in the 1870s, began to exploit the connection, producing elegant advertisements and devising promotional deals to attract its passengers. Many other railroads realized the potential of the tourist dollar: "The Great Northern promoted Glacier National Park; the Santa Fe, the Grand Canyon; the Lackawanna and the New York Central, Niagara Falls." When war broke out, even the government got in on the act, by publishing detailed guides to railroad travel to the West in order to encourage people to remain in the United States rather than risk the perils of traveling to conflict-torn Europe. Native Americans, who had so recently been displaced by the railroads, were now promoted as anthropological curiosities, dressed up in their feathers and war paint for the benefit of the visitors, who were encouraged to buy Native wares. Some of the blankets and cloth sold by the Indians had, rather incongruously, images of trains and even railroad company logos woven into their fabric. One government publication, listing sights on the Santa Fe Railroad, advised tourists that "Hopi villages are the objective of many tourists, especially on the occasion of the far-famed [sic] snake dance, which occurs in August."[9]

The railroads were also investing in better accommodation for passengers. The wooden-framed car, so dangerous in the still all too frequent train crashes because of its fragility and combustibility, was at last beginning to be phased out. By 1907, all-steel cars began to be introduced, and no more wooden-framed ones were produced after 1913, though some stayed in service until the 1950s. The introduction of steel cars was a neat illustration of the way the railroad companies could never stand still, always having to fund improvements or renewals. Steel was much heavier than wood, and therefore the new cars had to be introduced in tandem with more powerful locomotives, an added burden on the railroads' finances. Indeed, the bigger locomotives were just part of a wide range of improvements necessitated by the desire to speed up services. To improve timings, other technical changes, including more sophisticated signaling systems and better wheels, were introduced alongside more mundane measures, such as reducing the number of stops. Since trains had to slow down when crossing built-up areas, because of the large number of perilous road crossings, more protection was given to railroad tracks in towns, with fences being put up at particularly dangerous places, although by and large the railroad remained unfenced even in towns and cities. This actually remains a problem on many parts of the network today and explains why trains are so noisy compared with their European counterparts—at every road, however small, crossing the tracks, the engineer is required by law to sound the horn.[10]

The lower end of the business market was the conference delegate. As we have seen, the railroads created the potential for organizations to hold national conventions, and now, in the first decade of the twentieth century, much of America seemed to be attending conferences with the help of special rates. The railroads had to provide them, but running extra trains for such events proved on occasion more trouble than it was worth for the companies, as they disrupted existing traffic, both passenger and freight.

Another source of business was special excursions, usually on a Sunday, but these also were not always profitable for the railroads, as Martin explains: "The traffic man [who was in charge of the operation of trains on the railroad] complained that the railroad usually had to supply the attraction, and often ended up with no profit after deducting the cost of free transportation of brass bands, baseball teams, and watermelons."[11] Presumably the fruit was for refreshing the hot passengers in the days before air-conditioning! Even the Pullmans could be a burden. With the increase in traffic that Pullman enjoyed, the company churned out huge numbers of the luxury cars, trebling the number in service between the turn of the century and America's joining the war in 1917. However, the railroad company received only its usual fare for the journey from the Pullman passengers but in return had to haul the heavy Pullman coaches, which normally carried at most twenty-seven passengers each. And all the risk and costs of hauling empty spaces was with the railroads. That was fine on busy routes, but on poorly traveled lines, the railroad company could end up in the red.

These difficulties encapsulated the railroad companies' financial dilemma and exposed the fundamental reason that, across the world, they have struggled to make a profit even in the good times. Although the railroads enjoyed a virtual monopoly on many types of journey, making money out of their position was not as easy as their opponents—who were numerous and vociferous—felt. Moreover, the railroad companies were hampered by the actions of the Interstate Commerce Commission and constrained by the continuing hostility toward them. Although the establishment of the commission in 1887 had marked a turning point in railroad history, it took time for the regulator to have an effect. Until 1906, for the most part, the ICC was powerless, unable to impose its rules on the industry and given the runaround by clever railroad-company lawyers who found loopholes in the legislation and exploited them. The ICC had come into being as a result of the growing antipathy toward the railroads and concerns about their monopolistic power. The commission was charged with setting rates and fares that were "reasonable and just," but what did these words mean? In trying to find out, the pompous commission members, mostly lawyers, held lengthy hearings, with decisions taking an average four years to emerge. Naturally, both shippers and the railroad companies were dissatisfied with such delays, but gradually, as the nineteenth century gave way to the twentieth, a policy emerged that favored the former at the expense of the latter. Tighter regulation was introduced by President Theodore Roosevelt's administration in 1906, preventing the railroad companies from granting favorable rates or, as we have seen, even issuing free passes. Moreover, despite inflation returning—prices had been stable or falling for much of the last quarter of the nineteenth century—the commission almost invariably turned down requests for rate increases by the railroad companies. They saw their role as protecting the public's interest, and that was to keep rates low, even though the railroads had a strong case for being allowed to make extra profits in order to invest. Borrowing money, too, was made difficult by the commission's policy, since investors were deterred from putting money in an industry whose profits were limited by regulation and that faced ever-increasing costs. In 1910 Roosevelt's successor, William Howard Taft, passed further legislation that made it even more difficult for railroads to prove the need for increases and gave the commission additional powers over the way it assessed the railroad companies' finances.

These continued moves against the railroads were rooted in the spirit of the Granger movement and the muckrakers who exposed the corruption of the industry when the railroads were like high-spirited teenagers, misbehaving and transgressing the law. The industry, however, unnoticed by the public and the legislators, had grown up, and the tightening of regulation, together with the routine refusal to allow the railroad companies extra revenue through rate increases, constrained their ability to respond to the new demands of the twentieth century. The railroads had few spokesmen prepared to defend them, but one of the exceptions, James J. Hill, who had built the Great Northern, reckoned the industry needed $5 billion to modernize, a quite staggering sum at the time. They were not asking for public money, of course, but merely seeking to be allowed to make sufficient profits through the regulatory system to pay for these improvements. There was never any chance of their getting it. The zeitgeist of the early twentieth century was captured by the Progressives, who were hostile to the giant corporations, which they saw as corrupt and responsible for social evils such as child labor and workplace accidents. The Progressives held ambivalent attitudes toward government, being confident, on the one hand, about the ability of the state to improve social well-being—hence supporting measures to better regulate the railroads—but, on the other, remaining deeply suspicious of big-city politics that at the time were riven with corruption. A Populist movement motivated by a desire to eliminate both waste and corruption, Progressivism was a response to the rapid industrialization of the late nineteenth century. The railroads, as one of the most visible manifestations of that process, were an obvious target for the Progressives, who were suspicious of the power of the railroads and their ability to make profits out of their monopoly position as the core of the nation's infrastructure.

These prewar years should have been the heyday of the railroads. The companies wanted to invest, to improve their product offering—as it might be expressed in modern business parlance—but instead they had to struggle just to keep up. They were squeezed between rising costs and fixed rates, and the growth in traffic was not enough to provide them with the income for vital investment. Railroads, as we have seen, are a capital-intensive business and cannot stand still in the face of changing demands. The economy was, apart from the occasional blip such as the panic of 1903 and the short recession of 1907–1908, growing at an unprecedented rate, but the railroads were constrained in their response by the rules that their own past misbehavior had brought about. By denying the railroads the profits they could have earned through higher rates, the government dealt them a fatal blow. At the time when they most needed to modernize and prepare themselves for the coming onslaught from motor vehicles, they were stymied. Martin is unequivocal about the damage this "repressive policy of rate regulation" caused, arguing that it was not only the immediate loss of the huge amount of investment but the very ability of the railroads to respond in an entrepreneurial way: "The great tragedy of this failure of human beings intelligently to order their economic environment lies in the long-term effects on the railroad system as an enterprise. American railroads, quite literally, never got over the shock which archaic Progressivism's cruel repudiation of their leadership produced. . . . [W]hat was lost was the spirit of enterprise which had produced such remarkable results from 1897 to 1907 and which had seemed then to stand on the threshold of even greater accomplishments."[12] This is a bit harsh on the Progressives, whose suspicions of the railroads' motives were well founded, given the rail companies' dubious recent history, which was precisely the reason the commission refused to acquiesce to their demands. Could the railroads really be trusted not to pass on the additional revenue to their shareholders or waste it by failing to control their ever-growing costs? The railroads pointed out that two pieces of government legislation had contributed to their rising costs: first, labor legislation aimed at improving the condition of workers, and second, antitrust legislation that prevented the companies from working together and therefore encouraged them to build parallel lines. The railroads were undoubtedly treated badly by the commission, but even though they were now for the most part a mature industry and not the gung ho capitalists of yore, they had not earned the trust of the people.

All this was taking place in the context of a changing transportation world. Although the automobile had not yet started to impinge on the railroads' profits, remarkably, a new type of railroad had done so. This was the streetcar or, after electrification, trolley, because of the "trolley pole" connecting with the overhead wire. The streetcar had recently been transformed by the change of traction from horse to electricity, and, later its mutation, the interurban, which was a hybrid between streetcars and conventional railroads. The first streetcars, horse-drawn of course, appeared in 1832—on the New York & Harlem—a natural development of the omnibus that had appeared a few years previously when it was realized that putting the coaches on rails ensured a far smoother and more reliable journey than on the muddy urban streets and reduced the amount of effort required from the horses. Streetcars flourished and soon spread to towns and cities around the country, but they were always inefficient: the horses or mules they used were expensive to feed and soon required replacing as they died or became exhausted from pulling the heavy vehicles, which strangely were mostly based on train-coach design.

In the 1880s, a few pioneering towns such as Boston, Massachusetts, and Richmond, Virginia, began experimenting with electric traction. These tests proved so successful that it took less than two decades for almost every system in the country to adopt electricity, and by 1902 only a handful of systems relied on animal power. The remarkably rapid adoption of this new technology inevitably led to the use of electric traction being considered for longer journeys. As we will see below, there was some electrification of conventional railroads, particularly around New York City, but it was the interurban network that grew exponentially in the first decade of the 1900s.

Electric streetcars enjoyed a remarkable boom in the following years. Before electrification, in 1880 there had been around three thousand miles of track in cities and towns across America used by around twenty thousand horsecars. Major cities like New York, Philadelphia, and Chicago each boasted several hundred miles of line, but electrification, together with the rapid increase of urban populations as people were attracted to work in the factories springing up as a result of industrialization, stimulated a remarkable expansion of streetcar systems. The transformation was swift and virtually universal. By 1902, more than 90 percent of streetcar lines had been electrified, and the new technology inspired a remarkable boom in construction, which resulted in the track mileage across the United States reaching twenty-two thousand, operated by more than sixty thousand streetcars. Apart from, oddly, Manhattan and a few small towns, the horses had disappeared, as had the cable systems that had once been seen as the natural successor to animal power—with the exception of San Francisco, where cables had long been used because horses were unable to cope with the steep hills.

The electrified streetcar lines accelerated the growth of suburbs started by the railroads and resulted in the low-density cities of today's America. The suburbanization of America was a joint enterprise of the railroads and the streetcars. Without efficient transportation systems, it would have been impossible for developers to make profits out of building homes far from the town centers where most of their potential customers worked. With the car and roads not yet ready to challenge the railroads, the decades around the turn of the century saw a massive expansion in suburban services: "Between 1880 and World War I, the pattern of railroad commuting to bedroom suburbs became a fixture of American social life."[13]

The iron road had initially stimulated the rapid development of towns and cities, and now, as much by accident as design, it allowed urban areas to sprawl: "Suburban railroad traffic changed the American landscape in the 1880s and 1890s [forging] a new kind of link between the city's core and pastoral environs that had once been thought of as far away."[14] The railroads' role in creating suburbia was key. A common pattern was for developers to identify a greenfield site in the environs of a town or city and buy up land cheaply on which to build houses without revealing their intent. The developer had to ensure that there was either an existing railroad connection or one that could be easily extended to the site and then persuade the railroad company to provide a station. Failing that, the developers themselves would have to spend their own money on building the station, because without it, the housing would have little value.

The railroads not only created the early suburbs but also established the rhythm of life that went with them. Daily travel by train meant a regimen determined by the clock, as people generally traveled on the same service every day: "Office routines in the city were in fact adjusted to fit the times when railroads actually ran the largest number of trains on the most rapid schedules." Office hours were determined by the arrival of trains, and the nine-to-five routine was born. Railroad commuting bred a lifestyle of habits and fashion and created countless Groundhog Days. People would use the same car, the same seat even, every day, often sitting with the same fellow commuters, and read the same paper or play the same card game. They might even be on first-name terms with the train conductor. They wore the same clothes, bought their coffees at the same kiosks, and even followed the same trends: "Briefcases, attaché cases or other accoutrements went in and out of fashion over the years; they were highly stylized but uniformly accepted."[15] The most affluent commuters would often club together to pay for a special coach to be attached to their regular service, solely for their use—hence the expression *club car*. Schedules tended to remain pretty much the same, too, over the years, often serving generations of users. The Lackawanna could boast the longest-running US commuter train service, which left the railroad's Hoboken terminal in New Jersey at 4:15 p.m. every afternoon to travel nonstop to the leafy towns of Madison and Morristown. It was introduced in 1883 and retained the same spot in the Lackawanna's timetable until the demise of the company in the 1970s. The popularity of the train among the wealthy elite earned it the unofficial moniker the "Millionaire's Express," which suggests that the elite of the white-collar workforce did not have to endure long hours in the office. The Lackawanna could also lay claim to having carried America's longest-serving commuter, W. Parsons Todd, onetime mayor of Morristown and founder of the town's museum, who reportedly regularly traveled between his New York office and his home between 1899 and 1970.

The early commuting lines, described in Chapter 7, had by the first few years of the twentieth century proliferated in many eastern and midwestern states. Towns with suburban rail services included not just New York, Boston, Philadelphia, and Chicago, where the rail-commuting habit survives and which had developed very extensive suburban networks in the three decades before the First World War, but also Milwaukee, Cincinnati, St. Louis, and New Orleans, where the local rail networks have all but disappeared.

For the railroad companies, this burgeoning commuter market was a mixed blessing. If there were sufficient concentrations of commuters and available train paths—that is, sufficient space in the timetable without disrupting longer-distance services—suburban rail could be profitable. However, the trains themselves were expensive to provide and might be used just twice daily, sitting idle in sidings the rest of the time, unlike stock used for longer journeys that could earn revenue all day long. The commuters themselves could be a demanding bunch, dissatisfied with the service provided in return for their expensive season ticket—though they received a considerable discount as regular travelers—and therefore ever pressuring the railroad to improve its facilities. The tribulations of the longest commuter line in the United States, the Long Island Rail Road, demonstrate the difficulties of achieving consistent profits over a long period out of commuter traffic. Despite also being America's busiest commuter service by some measure, the Long Island has had a turbulent existence with periods of prosperity interwoven with leaner times. The company went broke in the 1870s, then prospered under the inspired leadership of Austin Corbin, until the 1903 panic again plunged it into difficulties. In 1900, the Long Island was taken over by the Pennsylvania Railroad, which saw the benefits of combining long-distance services with suburban traffic in a single new, massive New York terminal. With passenger numbers growing rapidly, the

Long Island prospered, thanks to New York's population explosion, electrifying large sections of its routes, and taking over several connecting lines and streetcar services, only to start closing lines in the 1930s. Then, after the Second World War, the Long Island Rail Road fell into difficulties again (see Chapter 11), not least because it was prevented by the authorities from raising fares between 1918 and 1947, despite a doubling in operating costs.

Commuters also needed to get around towns, and one solution was the elevated railroad. Subway systems were initially rejected as being too difficult technically, despite the example of the London Underground; instead, the idea of putting railroads on raised platforms down the middle of the invariably straight city streets (US cities were required by planning statutes to be built on a grid pattern) was taken up in several places. New York's extensive network of elevated railroads started with the opening in 1870 of the West Side and Yonkers Patent Railway, a four-mile line operated by cable. The company collapsed almost immediately, but its assets were picked up by the Manhattan Railway, which built a series of lines. Soon, four of New York's avenues—which are essentially on a north-south axis—were overshadowed by heavily engineered metal structures stretching up to sixty feet in the air and carrying steam locomotive–hauled trains. By the end of the decade, there were more than fifty miles of track in New York, but, not surprisingly, given their ugly infrastructure and the smoke and cinders they rained down on the public below, the New York elevated railroads, or Els, were never particularly loved. The fact that they were owned by the reviled Jay Gould, who eventually gained control of the whole network, did not make them any more popular. They were also slow, never averaging more than around 12 mph, and difficult to reach. Nevertheless, with no alternative yet available—the subway system would not open until the early years of the twentieth century—they were heavily used. In their heyday, the mid-1880s, they carried well over 100 million passengers annually and were so profitable that they were able to reduce their fares to the five cents universally charged by streetcars of the age. Inevitably, though, their days were numbered. The Els were an intermediate technology that was never quite satisfactory, even when, soon after the turn of the century, the network was electrified. After Manhattan's first underground railroad was completed in 1904, the Els started to be gradually replaced by the subway. Most of the Manhattan Els survived into the 1950s, whereas in the other

New York boroughs many of the overhead structures were incorporated into the subway system. The other city that favored elevated railroads was, of course, Chicago, where much of the system survives and where the "L" (oddly, the system was known as the "El" in New York but the "L" in Chicago) has become a proud part of its transportation heritage. Its first line, which was steam operated, opened in 1892, and the system, which was soon converted to electricity, expanded rapidly in the years before the First World War. Elevated railroads, though, were expensive and cumbersome, and conventional railroads could not be built profitably to serve the local needs of smaller towns. The railroads had gotten in there first, taking advantage of the easier sites, but the streetcars' greater flexibility and lower costs enabled them to reach places that the railroads could not have served profitably. Once the streetcars were electrified, their flexibility and cheaper infrastructure allowed them to become the key driver of the expansion of the suburbs. There was almost no place too small to sustain a viable trolley network. While large towns soon had tracks on every major thoroughfare, almost every town with a main street was getting in on the act: "Streetcar lines were designed with the express purpose of opening new residential tracts whose appeal would be to people of some means who were repelled by conditions in the central city. They were called streetcar suburbs." Until the First World War, streetcars were highly profitable: "The expectation—actually, the faith—was that ridership and profits, even with the 5 cent fares seemingly inviolate, would continue to grow far into the future." Most lines started out as local concerns but were soon consolidated, first into urban networks, and later into major streetcar corporations that owned systems in several cities and were regarded by the public with increasing suspicion since they were effectively monopolists. That perception was not entirely fair because the streetcar companies did invest heavily in new equipment and cars after they consolidated into bigger concerns. Apart from a few affluent suburbs whose residents were worried that streetcars would attract the local riffraff, "the expansion of street railroads was regarded as a municipal boon even as the men who controlled them grew richer and lost favor in the eyes of the public."[16]

Every small-town mayor and councilor saw street railroads as the harbinger of growth and prosperity. Initially, their main purpose was to carry commuters to work and back, but soon streetcars were built to connect the city with a host of other destinations: "There were lines running out be-yond the suburbs to the countryside, to cemeteries (there were special fu-neral cars), or to scenic sites for picnics and outings." The weekend was indeed big business, and the streetcar companies expanded into providing leisure activities. A census in 1907 found that there were no fewer than "467 'parks and pleasure resorts' owned or operated by street railway com-panies," all, of course, connected to the streetcar network.[17] The ride in the trolley was part of the day's fun, especially when the windows were taken out in the summer, affording the passengers a welcome cool breeze.

The streetcar companies also began to venture into rural pastures, stimulated by demand from people living a few miles out of the cities who had no adequate means of getting there since horse-drawn transportation was expensive and slow. However, it was the interurban railroad, run by separate companies, that most effectively catered to the needs of people living out of town. Largely ignored by railroad historians because of its short life span and rather crude construction, the interurban was none-theless remarkable for the speed of its expansion and the rapidity of its demise. Mostly separate from both the streetcar and railroad networks, in-terurbans were electric trains that connected outlying areas of cities with the center or connected neighboring towns. They were essentially long-distance streetcar lines, ranging in length from a few miles to fifty or sixty, built rapidly—six months to a year was typical—and on the cheap, usually by the side of existing highways or on agricultural land offered at little cost by farmers eager to have a rail line adjoining their property. The in-terurbans filled a gap in the market: catering to relatively sparsely popu-lated areas, which it was widely expected would make its owners a profit.

It was an expectation that would be rarely met. A few interurban schemes were built in the 1890s, and a small number in the decade after the First World War, but the vast majority were built in two short bursts during the first decade of the 1900s in the expectation they would be huge money-makers. The owners' hopes were, sadly, far too optimistic. Some of the early lines were indeed profitable, but that served only to stimulate the construc-tion of a large number of schemes that could never hope to earn a decent rate of return. This rush to create interurban lines constitutes one of those periodic bouts of commercial madness that litter the history of economics, from the Dutch tulip boom of the 1630s to the rush to invest in dot-com companies in the 1990s: "Even though the interurbans built to connect major cities or to tap rural areas of considerable population density were not, in light of the expectations of the time, irrationally conceived, their construction was accompanied by an outpouring of optimism and a rash of ill-considered projects that, in retrospect, can only be called one of the classic manias." They were part of a wider movement toward electric traction during the early 1900s, when "electric railway track of all types was being built at about ten times the rate of [conventional] railroad track."[18]

Interurbans have no precise definition, since the cruder systems were like streetcars and the more sophisticated versions morphed into suburban electric railroads, but they appeared in one form or another in thirty states. The industry enjoyed a meteoric growth, which in a way mirrored the expansion of the railroads in their early years and, similarly, was stimulated by local entrepreneurs, although larger concerns began to consolidate systems in the years running up to the First World War. By 1900, there were already twenty-one hundred miles of interurban railroads, and this figure leaped to nine thousand by the end of 1906 and fifteen thousand by 1913. It was in the midwestern states where they were most prominent. Ohio had far more mileage than any other state, with just under twenty-eight hundred miles of interurban track, and only three towns of more than five thousand inhabitants in the whole state did not have a system. With its well-populated farming areas, largely flat terrain, and numerous medium-size towns spaced twenty or thirty miles apart, Ohio was perfect territory for interurbans. So was neighboring Michigan, which had the next biggest system with nearly two thousand miles. Pennsylvania, Illinois, California, and New York also all developed extensive networks remarkably quickly. By 1910, many areas of the United States were covered with these slightly ramshackle railroads, the only regional exceptions being the Deep South, the northern plains, and much of the West. Even so, Los Angeles was the hub of the extensive Pacific Electric, "a 1,100 mile interurban system whose 'big red cars' skirted mile after mile of sandy shoreline, swept past endless acres of orange groves and climbed into the foothills of the San Gabriel Mountains." Interestingly, it was this network of streetcar systems, rather than the car, that created the sprawling nature of Los Angeles and its suburbs. All its main highways had a streetcar line running down them, and therefore it was the distance to the streetcar stop that was the limiting factor in local development. The Pacific Electric interurban system was the brainchild of a developer, Henry E. Huntington, who built it as a loss leader financed by profits from his housing projects. He saw that good transportation was as essential as ensuring the houses had water and electricity and therefore was not concerned that he lost money on providing it: "The result was the characteristic low-rise form of the region, with mile upon mile of 'California bungalows' spreading along the tentacles of the Pacific Electric Network. This extensive urban spread gave Los Angeles a reputation, which has lasted to this day, as the very model of urban sprawl."[19] Lots that were a half-dozen blocks away from the streetcar were simply left undeveloped, but once the car became commonplace, they were built upon and their residents' automobiles soon displaced the streetcars on the highway.

Development of these interurban streetcars was so intensive in parts of the Midwest that it was possible in 1910 to travel continuously by interurban from Elkhart Lake, Wisconsin, to Oneonta, New York, a distance of nearly eleven hundred miles. Since their average speed was under twenty miles per hour, because of the frequency of stops, the low power of the electric motors, and the tight curves, it is doubtful that anyone in those pre-trainspotter days would have undertaken such a trip. However, in that year a group of businessmen did travel a similar distance entirely on interurbans, from upstate New York to Louisville, Kentucky, using an electric car borrowed from the New York Central, in order to promote the interurban network.

Profitability, though, proved a mirage. Passenger railroads, with their expensive infrastructure and high costs, need dense populations and intensive use, and the interurbans had neither. One or two companies even carried freight in a bid to be viable, but few remained in the black for very long. Consequently, "the interurbans were a rare example of an industry that never enjoyed a period of prolonged prosperity."[20] The United States was littered with redundant interurban projects whose promoters had failed to raise the capital. Other lines collapsed as soon as they were built: in the case of the Indianapolis, Crawfordsville & Western (even the interurbans had western ambitions!), for instance, the railroad's opening ceremony and its filing for bankruptcy were simultaneous events.

The maddest of these schemes—and there are a lot to choose from—was the plan set out in 1906 by the Chicago–New York Electric Air Line

Railroad for a double-track electric railroad in a straight line between the two cities. It was to be the equivalent of a rail superhighway: no crossings with roads or other rail tracks and only the gentlest of curves to ensure they could be negotiated at ninety miles an hour. Whereas previous crazy schemes for express railroads in the Northeast had never gotten off the drawing board, remarkably some construction on the Air Line Railroad was actually carried out, thanks to its promoter, Alexander Miller, selling enough stock for work to begin in Gary, Indiana. Some fifteen miles of track were built to a very high standard, the cost of which was one of the reasons for the scheme's failure. Inevitably, though, despite the support of its shareholders and the optimism expressed in its own promotional magazine, *Air Line News*, the company stopped building and went bust in 1915.

There was a lot stacked against the interurbans: the hostility of the railroad companies, the limited market they served, the cheapness of the construction (which increased operating costs), and ultimately, after the war, the advent of the Ford Model T and other cheap cars. Yet for a while, the big railroads felt threatened by this crude competitor, not least because many interurbans were backed by powerful electricity companies. Despite the fact that interurbans seemed to cater to a rather limited market and ran, at best, hourly trains with single cars, some railroads were so fearful that they ran concerted campaigns against them and were quick to challenge them in the courts at every available opportunity. The railroads most hostile to the interurbans were the largest, the Pennsylvania and the New York Central, both of which regularly sought injunctions against the interurbans. The trigger for disputes was often the need for the interurban to cross the line of a railroad. On several occasions, injunctions were obtained to prevent the crossing. In one case, in California, the Petaluma & Santa Rosa was banned from crossing the line of the California Northwestern and had to provide a horse-drawn shuttle service to carry its passengers into the town of Santa Rosa. When the Petaluma again attempted to install a crossing over the Northwestern's line in January 1905, its men were confronted with two locomotives on the tracks that were used to douse them with boiling water, an incident known as the Battle of Sebastopol Avenue. In fact, at the local level, "outright violence between interurban employees and railroad men was not uncommon." When the Ohio Central Traction Company completed its tracks to the village of Crestline, Ohio, a fistfight broke out between its construction gang and men employed by the Pennsylvania and New York Central. A more common—and civilized—response from the railroad companies was to try to improve their competing service by cutting rates and running more trains. However, their costs were always higher, partly because they were unionized, and they were unable to compete effectively. That did not stop the railroads from continuing their hostility even once the local interurbans were built: "The typical railroad executive was convinced that the interurbans had no ethical right to exist, and was eager to do what he could to eradicate them."[21]

The interurbans might have survived the hostility of the railroads, but it was the basic lack of a market—and the impossibility of making money from a schedule that ran just one single car per hour over the tracks—that would prove their undoing. The demise of the interurbans came almost as fast as their construction. Most interurbans had a life span of around twenty to thirty years, and they were killed off by a combination of competition from the car and the deterioration of their equipment. Many of the promoters were given twenty-five-year franchises that ran out around the time of the Great Depression, and since that coincided with the need to buy new equipment, the municipal authorities simply shut the systems down rather than issue new franchises. A few interurbans stuttered on until after the Second World War, but soon succumbed to the automobile, which not only destroyed their remaining customer base but eyed jealously all that extra space next to the highways.

Interestingly, the authors of the key history of the interurbans suggest that they could have been as damaging to the conventional railroads as the Ford Model T, whose very invention stymied their development and killed them off: "Both [interurbans and the Model T] threatened the position of the railroad train as the principal means of passenger transportation; by 1960 [when the book was published] the automobile was providing 90 per cent of intercity passenger miles." By then, "no trace of the [interurban] industry remained in its original form," although a handful of routes had been converted to suburban rail use or to freight service.[22] It was particularly unlucky for the interurbans that cars became a viable alternative to rail just a decade or so after their introduction, which made them, like the fax machine, the punch card, or even the Els, a short-term technology that was rapidly superseded.

The main railroad companies were now adopting modern technology that allowed them to explore new solutions to old problems. America may have been slow to develop subway systems, but it can nevertheless lay claim to the greatest railroad engineering achievement of the early twentieth century. This was the construction by the Pennsylvania Railroad of the tunnels under the East and Hudson Rivers that separate Manhattan from the mainland, a feat that was all the greater since it required the electrification of a large section of the tracks. The Pennsylvania had long been frustrated by its lack of access to Manhattan, as its New York passengers had to traverse the Hudson on ferries. It was Alexander Cassatt, the company's president, who pushed the idea through, though unfortunately he was to die in 1906, before the completion of the project. Of the options available at the time to the Pennsylvania, a bridge was deemed technically too difficult and would have required the cooperation of the New Jersey port authorities, which was not forthcoming. However, the building of a tunnel raised a number of concerns, most notably fears that the use of steam locomotives underground on such a busy commuter route was too much of a safety risk (although by the 1900s, the London Underground had been operating with steam engines in almost continuous tunnels for more than thirty-five years), and therefore the state authorities mandated the use of electric propulsion. The twin-bore tunnels under the Hudson took seven years to build—no mean achievement given the challenges of working under the river, which included using compressed air to keep the water from seeping in. With access from the tunnels, the Pennsylvania Railroad could, at last, have a station on Manhattan, and the decision to cross both rivers meant it had to be a through station rather than a terminus. And, of course, it had to be bigger and grander than the Vanderbilts' nearby Grand Central, which was being rebuilt simultaneously with many beaux arts features. Pennsylvania Station was, indeed, majestic and massive, extending over seven acres, the largest covered indoor space in New York, and was shared with its subsidiary, the local Long Island Rail Road. It, too, was built in the beaux arts style that was the fashion of the day, although the exterior was dominated by a seemingly endless colonnade of pink granite Doric columns. The interior was eclectic in style, with carriageways inspired by the Brandenburg Gate in Berlin and a vast waiting room in the style of the Roman Baths of Caracalla. It was, regrettably, to survive barely a half century. In a

piece of architectural vandalism akin to the destruction of the Great Hall
and the arch of Euston Station, Penn Station was, to outrage both in America and abroad, demolished in the early 1960s. That was the result of a desperate bid by the Pennsylvania Railroad, which was already in its death
throes before its fateful merger with the New York Central, to save itself
through the construction of Madison Square Garden above today's entirely
subterranean and dismal but bustling station.

Following an accident in a tunnel in 1902 that cost fifteen lives, the New
York State legislature prohibited the use of steam on Manhattan, and consequently the Pennsylvania spent the years of construction of the tunnel con-
sidering how to implement electrification. Apart from the now universal use
of electricity for streetcar operation, several railroads had begun to experiment with this new and highly efficient form of motive power. Indeed, even
before the need to electrify the New York services, America was in the forefront of railroad electrification, rivaled only by Switzerland, prompted by
the eagerness of two rival companies, General Electric and Westinghouse,
who saw the railroads as an almost unlimited market for their different systems of electric power. General Electric favored the third-rail system used
extensively on underground systems, while Westinghouse developed the
overhead-wire system.

As early as 1887, there was an electric-powered coal train operating on
the short Lykens Valley Colliery line in Pennsylvania, and a few other mining lines followed suit. The Baltimore & Ohio, pioneering as ever, was the
first railroad company to use electric power for passenger trains when it introduced a General Electric system in a 3-mile tunnel section of a new line
around Baltimore in 1895. The experiment proved successful, but the technology was still too unreliable for large-scale mainline operation. A small
railroad in California, the narrow-gauge North Shore Railroad, was the first
to electrify a suburban service, but it was New York, with the densest rail
traffic in America, that was most in need of the new technology. For the
New York Central and the New York, New Haven & Hartford that shared its
tracks, the change was essential. The number of suburban services operated
by the two companies was beginning to outgrow the capacity of the Grand
Central terminal. Given the high cost of land on Manhattan, the obvious
solution was to create new tracks under the existing station. The effects of
steam locomotives were increasingly giving rise to complaints from the af-

fluent Manhattan residents and to concerns about their safety: "The smoke, steam and cinders of some 700 daily trains were a nuisance to the neighborhoods along the line, and low visibility in the 2-mile Park Avenue Tunnel created a severe safety problem."[23] The ordinance by the New York State legislature banning steam, which was due to come into effect in 1908, gave the railroads no choice, but the Central embarked on a far more ambitious scheme than required, electrifying the nearly 60 miles of track on the Hudson River and Harlem routes with a third-rail system similar to that used on the El. For its part, the New Haven used the overhead system for 33 miles of track up to Stamford, Connecticut, whereas the Pennsylvania, after much deliberation, decided on the third-rail system—even though it was recognized as posing a hazard to track workers and trespassers—for both its Long Island Rail Road and the services using the Hudson Tunnel.

The success of the Baltimore & Ohio experiment, and the electrification of so many railroads in New York, encouraged other companies to follow suit, especially in long tunnels, which were a particular hazard because of the risk of asphyxiation when steam locomotives stalled. In 1908, Canada's Grand Trunk Railroad became the first, electrifying a mile-long tunnel linking Ontario with Michigan that had seen some dangerous incidents. Others soon followed, notably the Boston & Maine, which had particularly serious ventilation problems in its nearly 5-mile—and very busy—Hoosac Tunnel (see Chapter 6), where waiting for smoke to clear had become a limiting factor on its capacity, and the Great Northern, whose Cascade Tunnel through the mountain range of that name in Washington State was especially hazardous, as it had a steep gradient that locomotives struggled to climb. Electric locomotives not only had the advantage of being smokeless, but were also more powerful—when used in twos or threes—and therefore were introduced in several other such locations, even though that necessitated changing locomotives from steam to electric and back again. The longest and most ambitious scheme, initiated in 1915 by the Chicago, Milwaukee, St. Paul & Pacific Railroad (the Milwaukee Road), electrified 440 miles of its route through Idaho and Montana, and later through to Tacoma in Washington State, a total of more than 650 miles. This was to be the only long-distance electrification west of Chicago, and it was not, ultimately, a success, as it went bust in 1925. Despite many suburban networks' turning to electricity before the First World War and New York's becoming the first city anywhere in the world to have an all-electric train service, which meant that America was at the forefront of railroad electrification technology, the failure to introduce electric power more widely was to be another lost opportunity for the US railroads.

As well as electrification, there were several other significant improvements in this period. The building of the Lucin Cutoff over the Great Salt Lake in Utah completed in 1904 cut 43 miles from the transcontinental journey, bypassing the line's original route through Promontory Summit. In the state of Michigan, a tunnel under the Detroit River connected the city of Detroit directly with the East for the first time. There were, too, numerous small enhancements to the network that in parts included relaying the entire track with heavier rail. Martin suggests that the scale of investment in the early years of the twentieth century was such that, in effect, "America's railroads were, indeed built *twice*; once in the nineteenth century, and again in the exhilarating era we call, with so much justification, Progressive."[24] Nevertheless, thanks to the failure of the Interstate Commerce Commission to recognize the investment needs of the railroads, it was not enough, and they would enter the First World War unprepared for its demands.

The railroads had continued to expand in the first decade of the 1900s. Inevitably, the growth rate had slowed down, as networks were virtually complete; at least in the East and much of the Midwest, every little town was now served by a railroad or an interurban, but there were still a few additions made to the system. Most of the new lines were built in the still sparsely populated West and were principally branches tacked on to the transcontinentals. (In Canada, two of the three transcontinentals were not completed until after the start of the war in Europe.) The Great Northern, the Union Pacific, the Western Pacific, and the Milwaukee Road all built substantial sections of track in the first decade of the 1900s, and old Henry Flagler's madcap line to Key West was not completed until 1912. By and large, however, this was the end of nearly a century of railroad building. In the 1910s, Flagler's scheme aside, very few new lines were being built. Overall, route mileage increased from 193,000 at the turn of the century to its peak of 254,000[25] miles in 1916, about a quarter of the route miles ever built in the world. Already sections were being abandoned, as they proved unprofitable or an unnecessary duplication. In New England, for example, closures began in 1907 after consolidation by the New Haven resulted in several branch lines becoming redundant. For the most part, though, it would not be until after the Depression of the 1930s that track mileage began to be reduced more quickly.

The First World War put an end to further expansion, but the railroads would experience an unprecedented period of traffic growth during the conflict. Although from the start of the war in 1914 there had been a debate about America's involvement, the railroads were unprepared for the demands that the conflict placed on them. Many railroads were already in deep trouble. The continued obduracy of the Interstate Commerce Commission to allow rate increases had pushed numerous major companies, such as the Rock Island, the New Haven, and the Wabash into receivership, and although they kept running, they were not in a position to invest. Just as America was about to enter the war, the railroads found themselves embroiled in a bitter labor dispute that turned into a battle with the government. The labor unions had been arguing for an eight-hour day, rather than the ten they worked normally, but the railroad companies were adamantly opposed, despite being pressed on the matter by President Woodrow Wilson. Instead, he managed to persuade Congress to pass legislation to that effect, but the new law, when introduced in January 1917, was ignored by the rail companies, who argued it was unconstitutional. The matter came to a head just as America was about to enter the war. The unions threatened to go on strike on March 19, 1917, but that morning the companies finally yielded to the eight-hour day and that very afternoon the Supreme Court ruled that it was not unconstitutional.

Even without these industrial-relations problems, the railroads were already in a state of chaos as a result of increased demand, the lack of investment, and terrible winter weather. The difficulties had been mounting since the beginning of the previous winter, which had come early, with considerable snowfall in the autumn of 1915. The bad weather, which had broken previous temperature records, could not have come at a worse time. Overall demand went up by 10 percent, but traffic to the eastern ports—Baltimore, Boston, Philadelphia, and New York—soared by a third, boosted by demand from war-torn Europe. The railroads could not cope. By February 1917, the ports were clogged, and, to make matters worse, many merchant navy captains were refusing to allow their ships to leave the protection of the port, as Germany had announced that any boat carrying supplies for the Allies was a legitimate war target for its submarines. Moreover, the railroad companies failed to understand the imperatives of wartime, even if America was not directly involved until April 1917. Albro Martin suggests it was the legacy of the previous decades that caused the crisis: "Americans paid dearly in 1916 and 1917 for the neglect of their railroads. Not only were the lines short of virtually every kind of physical facility, notably locomotives, but the timid structure of the railroad business itself, based as it was on the old-fashioned philosophy of competition, turned out to be an intolerable incubus." Indeed, as another historian, Richard Saunders Jr., points out, there were some absurd practices on the railroads: "Trains of war materials rolled into congested eastern ports, while southern ports remained idle. . . . Pennsylvania coal might go to customers in the West while Illinois or Kentucky coal moved east." The railroad companies tried to muddle through, and there were occasional acts of cooperation, but they were prevented from working closely together by antitrust legislation passed in 1890 at the height of public antagonism toward the railroad barons. Even when the presidents of nearly seven hundred railroad companies signed an agreement to coordinate their services, they found they could not do so legally. The efficiency of the rail network, measured in terms of daily mileage of freight cars, reduced by 20 percent, and the effect was compounded by the extra demands being placed on the system. In short, the railroads were simply not in a state to deal with the task facing them. Samuel Rea, the president of the Pennsylvania Railroad, told the Interstate Commerce Commission, "The condition of the railroads today presents a menace to the country."[26]

By the autumn of 1917, matters came to a head. There was a national shortage of freight cars estimated at 158,000, and more than that number were piled up around the eastern ports waiting to be unloaded. The basic lesson of railroad operation that had been learned in the American Civil War by Herman Haupt, the great railroad strategist, had been forgotten: cars must be unloaded and returned before new trains can be accepted, as otherwise bottlenecks form and the cars are not available for further trips. The railroads responded by creating a series of committees to try to sort matters out, but each collapsed in the face of the antitrust legislation that specifically prevented railroads from pooling resources and the mutual antipathy between the different companies. Another early and severe winter was taking its toll. Coal and food prices were soaring, and the people, many of whom had been opposed to America's entry into the war, were becoming restless and taking to the streets.

Behind the scenes, the government tried to spur the railroads into action. A bizarre scheme to prioritize military cargoes went spectacularly wrong when government agents dispatched around the country to put preference tags on cars needed for the war effort handed them out so indiscriminately that the Pennsylvania reported that as many as 85 percent of its cars were tagged. The average daily distance moved by a freight car declined further during the year from twenty-six miles to just twenty-one, which suggested that an already inefficient system had gotten worse.

There was therefore no choice but for the government to take the unprecedented step of nationalizing the railroads in late December 1917 under the control of the United States Railroad Administration, headed by the well-respected William McAdoo, the secretary of the Treasury in Wilson's government. McAdoo took a very active role, replacing several railroad bosses with federal appointees and, crucially, ensuring the nation's stock of locomotives and cars was pooled, so that their use could be maximized. For the railroad companies, it was a humiliating experience that they would work hard to ensure would not recur when America entered another world war a quarter of a century later.

In the land of free enterprise and raw capitalism, it was a source of great shame for the railroad companies that it took government control to sort out their problems, and they complained they were given a raw deal under the nationalization arrangements. The government leased the railroads as a profitable business, guaranteeing that they would receive the same income as the average of the past three years. However, since that included the year to July 1, 1915, a remarkably bad period for the industry, the average was reduced well below the receipts of the two most recent profitable years. Worse, in order to buy off any strikes or industrial-relations problems, the government immediately granted a raise of twenty dollars per month to all those earning less than forty-six dollars per month. This was a necessity, since wages were rising because of a shortage of labor caused by loss of men to the armed forces and also to the well-paid armaments industry. Ironically, the government also gave the railroads the increase in rates that had been turned down on numerous occasions in the past couple of decades by the Interstate Commerce Commission, which was put into abeyance during this period. Martin sums it up succinctly: "This episode reveals that sometimes the much put-upon businessman's best haven from a government agency is another government agency."[27]

The railroads were essential to the war effort and were intensively used, both to carry troops and for war matériel. There was, effectively, no other form of long-distance inland transport, and the railroads catered to all needs, from taking the troops and freight to ports to organizing ambulance trains to care for the wounded. Under nationalization, the companies were obliged to send freight by the shortest route and to accept tickets from rival railroads and were no longer subject to antitrust legislation.

Although the nationalization was successful in improving productivity, with fewer empty cars having to be carried around and circuitous routes to avoid traveling over a rival's tracks curtailed, there were structural barriers to efficiency. The ingrained habits of cutthroat competition could not be cast aside instantly. For some companies, it was a long-awaited opportunity to do over their rivals. A casual remark by a New York Central executive said it all: "I've always wanted to issue *orders* to the Pennsylvania Railroad and now I have my chance."[28]

Moreover, many locomotives could not travel too far from their home bases because they were of a specific type that had to be maintained by their parent company, which had both the expertise and the spare parts to repair them. In fact, standardization of equipment was a prerequisite of a truly integrated national operation, and consequently the government ordered two thousand new locomotives of a standardized design and fifty thousand freight cars to make up for the chronic shortage of equipment. The relative success of the federal government's takeover of the railroads inevitably led to questions about their future after the end of the conflict. It was a shame that this debate on the future of the American railroads was finally being held just as they began to face their greatest threat, the spread of motorized transportation supported by the improvement of America's highways. As ever, the policies that resulted from this debate harked back to past issues rather than attempting to tackle future ones.

10

THE ROOTS
OF DECLINE

The First World War left the railroads in a parlous state.[1] They had been overused and starved of investment funds, a situation that had close parallels with other countries involved in the conflict, notably the United Kingdom. Financially, too, they were struggling. The wage raises imposed by the government and the sharp increases in operating costs from the rapid rate of inflation and shortages of material were not fully compensated by the rises in freight rates and fares that they had been allowed. To make matters worse, the boom created by the war ended abruptly when peace returned in 1918, causing revenues from freight—though not immediately from passengers—to plummet. The profit margins of the railroad companies were therefore being squeezed, and many were losing money, a state of affairs that was viable only as long as they remained under federal control. And things would get worse. In the interwar period, a combination of public demand, technological developments in the automobile industry, incoherent regulation, government policies, and subsidies favoring rival modes of transportation conspired to begin the shift from a national rail-based transportation system to one dependent on the roads, a process that would take place within little more than a generation.

The rot started in the 1920s when the federal government dithered over what to do with the railroads that they controlled. As in the UK, there was a debate on the future ownership of the railroads in which some support was expressed for leaving them in government hands, but not from the Republican-controlled Congress. Another suggestion was to consolidate the railroads into a series of major companies, rather than the seven hundred in existence before the war. Again, this sort of thinking was paralleled in the UK, where in 1923 the nearly two hundred private companies were molded into just four. The thinking behind consolidation was that combining profitable and loss-making railroads would ensure that most lines would be able to survive. As the debate raged, the railroad companies were left in a state of limbo, run by a federal government that seemed to be at a loss as to what to do with them. At the heart of the debate was the age-old question: What were the railroads for? Were they simply private enterprises, like any other, whose fate should be dictated by market forces, with the weak being allowed to go to the wall with no government intervention on their behalf? Or did they have a wider social function that meant that regulation was needed both to ensure they provided a decent service and also to protect the public against monopoly exploitation? The free-market logic that suggests loss-making railroads should simply be allowed to founder ignores the fact that railroads are a capital-intensive business with huge fixed assets that are valueless when the trains stop running. A weak railroad can, with temporary government help or a change in local or national economic circumstances, become strong again. Railroads are a long-term business that play a crucial role in the areas they serve and therefore cannot be allowed to flourish or founder solely on the basis of unfettered market forces. Convincing American politicians of the strength of this argument would always be an uphill task.

It might, for a time, have seemed that the political climate was ripe for such a profound departure from the usual American way. This was a radical period when soldiers returning from the conflict were not in the mood to settle for low wages and poor services, and all sorts of grievances were bubbling under the surface. Hostility to big business, already prevalent before the war, had intensified. Events abroad showed that change was afoot: in Russia, the Bolshevik Revolution was in full flow, and there was unrest in many European countries following the end of the war. Even in America, with its long tradition of hostility to the power of the federal government, the notion that the railroads should be owned by the state was not so far-fetched. After all, as historian Richard Saunders Jr. asks rhetorically, given that the government was about to fund and build a huge highway system across the country—the first of two such networks that would be built over the next fifty years—"why should it be so natural that the government build and operate highways, but not railroads?" Elsewhere in the world, this was a time when governments were nationalizing or rationalizing their railroads, but America was reluctant to follow suit. The radical elements in the population were still a minority, and support for nationalization was undermined by a series of "Red Scares" promulgated widely in the media. It was not long before the proposal for rail nationalization, which had been promoted by a labor lawyer, Glenn Plumb, was being portrayed as a left-wing plot smacking of bolshevism and consequently far too dangerous to be considered. As Saunders says, "The railroad plans of other democracies underscored, even at this early date, how isolated the United States was in its rigid defense of the right of capital alone to make decisions that affected everyone."[2] The failure to recognize the right of the public to have a say in the control of the railroads would fundamentally undermine US passenger rail services after the Second World War.

Despite American suspicions of government interference, there was no appetite for a return to the preregulated days of the nineteenth century: hostility toward the big railroad companies was almost as strong as the fear of communism. The result was a compromise, created largely by Albert Cummins, a senator and former governor of Iowa, where back in the 1890s he had pushed through a series of laws that imposed strong controls on the local railroads. As a member of the Interstate Commerce Commission, he had been one of the strongest voices against allowing the railroads to increase their rates and had become something of a hated figure in the industry. Nevertheless, after the war he was widely recognized as the most rail-savvy politician, and he put forward a plan to control the railroads—which remained at the time the second-largest industry in the United States—while still giving them the space to flourish. A more powerful and proactive Interstate Commerce Commission was to be created that would set the rates and fares at a level that would produce a return of 6 percent on the capital value of the railroads. However, this was to apply not to each individual railroad company but rather to the totality. Any excess earnings from the most profitable railroads would go into a pool that would be shared between those lines that were not managing to reach the 6 percent threshold. The idea was classic railroad economics: the weak would be supported by the strong, this cross-subsidy ensuring the retention of a much larger network than would be the case if market forces alone were allowed to prevail. Given the near impossibility of trying to allocate costs of running a railroad system accurately in such a complex industry and the desire of railroad managers to retain as large a network as possible, cross-subsidy has become established practice on most railroad networks across the world.

The commission, too, set minimum rates in an effort to prevent uncompetitive price reductions, and this would prove to be greatly troublesome to the rail companies, particularly after the Second World War. This measure was designed partly to prevent ruinous competition among railroads, but was also intended to protect the fledgling trucking industry against unfair pricing by the railroads. In the event, the legislation removed flexibility from the railroads in the face of the ever-expanding road-haulage industry and gave the truckers an advantage because they could simply undercut the rates of the railroads—which they had to publish—an almost identical situation to the UK, where the Big Four interwar companies were hamstrung in the same way.

The crucial omission in the Transportation Act that was eventually passed in 1920 was compulsion. Cummins had wanted the railroad companies to be forced to join together to create unified companies, but this notion was rejected by Congress, which decreed it should be voluntary. That effectively killed the plan, although the Interstate Commerce Commission was by law required to work up a scheme and, in so doing, frightened the companies into improving their behavior. The commission's plan went through numerous versions and eventually settled on a scheme, drawn up by an economist, William Z. Ripley, to consolidate the railroads into twenty-one companies. However, the Ripley plan was doomed from the outset by its voluntary nature, since those who might lose out through the consolidation were able to impose a veto. The large and profitable railroad companies did not want to be encumbered by having to take on the loss makers.

The Pennsylvania Railroad's reaction to the plan is a good illustration of the wider attitude of the railroads. The Pennsy, as it was known, was the leading railroad of the age and saw itself as a cut above the others, a view encapsulated by its calling itself the "Standard Railway of the World." There was no question of its allowing through any consolidation plan that did not confirm its primacy among the competing railroads of the East. The Pennsy was blessed, unlike most of the industry, with an articulate spokesman for its cause, Albert J. County, who was officially only a vice president but as its chief negotiator had the power to ensure that any consolidation would have to put the interests of his railroad first. He was "the rock upon which the plans of the planners and the dreams of the underdogs crashed."[3] Up to 1929, the Pennsy simply kept expanding by buying a series of railroads, including the New Haven and the Boston & Maine, which allowed it to rationalize services and consolidate its advantageous position. These acquisitions were paid for with shares, which was fine during the bull market of the mid-1920s but left the owners of the subsidiaries out of pocket after the stock market crash of 1929. As this example suggests, voluntary consolidations tended to work to the advantage of the larger railroad companies, who were able to benefit from economies of scale.

Having kept compulsory consolidation out of the legislation, the key measure that they opposed, the railroad companies were relatively pleased with the deal. Nevertheless, the discussions and wrangles over the ICC's consolidation plan lasted through much of the 1920s. Despite the uncertainty this created, these were, in many respects, good years for the rail industry. Ridership and freight carriage for the most part held up, and the railroads invested considerably in capital equipment, especially track improvements and locomotives. By 1930, nearly a quarter of locomotives were postwar models that were far more efficient than their predecessors. The manufacturers battled hard to resist the new technologies of electricity and diesel by offering improved models of steam engines. The railroads themselves were hesitant about making the change, since they had invested huge amounts of capital into steam technology, and, consequently, for the time being, the industry stuck with steam. There was no major expansion of electrification in the 1920s, and plans to double-track certain key routes, such as the western sections of the Pennsylvania and the Baltimore & Ohio, were delayed. Martin is in no doubt that the railroads suffered in this period from overregulation that limited their ability to renew themselves and prevented them from being adventurous in the choice of traction: "Developments like the diesel locomotive were delayed twenty years even though the steam

locomotive had passed its peak by 1914." As we have seen, there *were* significant enhancements to steam locomotive technology after 1914, allowing
faster and more efficient running, but Martin is right to say that diesels
should have been considered as an alternative far earlier. In fact, it was not
until the 1930s that diesel locomotives, which had numerous advantages
over steam, became widespread, spearheading the railroads' belated attempt
to modernize.

Before the decline of the railroads gathered pace in the 1930s, there was
time for one new pair of railroad barons to emerge, even as the debate in
the commission over consolidation continued. These were the Van Sweringen brothers, property developers from Cleveland, Ohio, who entered the
railroad business accidentally when they built a suburb called Shaker
Heights in their hometown and needed to provide a rail line to enable residents to reach downtown easily. Oris Paxton Van Sweringen and Mantis
James Van Sweringen, or the Vans, as they became known, were undoubtedly the strangest of the railroad barons. Born two years apart, the reclusive
bachelor brothers not only gave their very rare interviews together but also
shared a bedroom in a vast mansion called Daisy Hill. They were a mix of
extreme aggression and boldness in their business dealings, while in person they were modest and retiring. They were as inseparable in death as
they were in life, dying, only in their fifties, within a year of each other—
Mantis in December 1935 and Oris in November 1936. The Vans had
bought their first railroad, the New York, Chicago & St. Louis Railroad
(known as the Nickel Plate Road) from the New York Central purely to
provide a rapid-transit route from Shaker Heights to downtown Cleveland.
The Nickel Plate Road was an interesting example of a "nuisance" railroad,
a five-hundred-mile line built by speculators to take business away from
the Central's profitable Lake Shore route between Buffalo and Chicago.
Soon after its completion in 1882, it was bought at a good price by the Vanderbilts, as the investors had hoped, but following the outbreak of the First
World War, it was sold to the Van Sweringens out of fear that retaining it
would result in an antitrust prosecution. Although the Vans had originally
been interested only in a small part of the railroad, the acquisition inspired
them to build up a massive railroad empire that, at its height, before the
1929 Wall Street crash, had a paper value of $3 billion and stretched across

thirty thousand miles. Their holdings, controlled through a complex web of companies that made it uncertain as to precisely how much money they invested personally and how much consisted of what are now known as junk bonds, included the Erie Railroad, the largely coal-carrying Chesapeake & Ohio Railway, and the Pere Marquette Railway, which had a series of lines in the Great Lakes area of the Midwest. Since the commission was debating the future structure of the industry and therefore few railroads attempted any consolidation, the short-lived empire built up by the Vans was the only new major railroad company allowed by the ICC to be established during the 1920s. However, there were immediate doubts about its solvency, which were quickly confirmed once shares started plummeting during the crash. The Vans lost their fortune even more quickly than it had been built up, and they disappeared from public view, dying in apparent poverty.

There was a mixed reaction in the railroad industry to the danger posed by the automobile. The complacency of some executives was well summed up by a promoter of interurban railroads who was quoted as saying in 1916 that "the fad of automobile riding will gradually wear off and the time will soon be here when a very large part of the people will cease to think of automobile rides."[4] Others, though, seeing that their monopoly position was being challenged, sought to improve the service they offered passengers. This was particularly true on many longer-distance services, where there were marked improvements during the interwar period, but several companies with big commuting markets were also alert to the potential threat from the automobile. Although no major intercity lines were electrified in the 1920s, apart from some sections of the Pennsylvania, numerous suburban services were converted, but despite the obvious advantages, at times the catalyst of external pressure was needed for the change to be made. In Chicago, it was complaints from the city authorities over the nuisance caused by smoke from steam locomotives that made the Illinois Central electrify its services. In the East, the Philadelphia & Reading Railroad was forced to do so in order to speed up turnaround times in its Philadelphia station, which had limited capacity, while the Lackawanna followed suit partly for the same reason. Interestingly, although electrification greatly improved the passenger experience, since electric trains were cleaner and faster than their steam equivalents, this was rarely uppermost in the minds of the railroad managers making the decision. Rather, it was reducing costs and improving efficiency that motivated them to make the change. There was still, among many railroad managers, the notion that passengers were more trouble than they were worth. James J. Hill, builder of the Great Northern, characterized passenger services in bizarre terms, as "the equivalent of the male teat, neither useful nor ornamental."[5] Overall, while passengers at the time contributed around a quarter of total railroad revenue, the proportion varied widely from company to company, with the big railroads in the East being most dependent on fare income, while some midwestern railroads made little provision for troublesome humans. Hill's remark confirms the fact that, as mentioned before, generally for most railroads income from freight was higher than passenger revenue. This was true even in the 1920s, when passenger revenue was so high, and it goes a long way to explaining why the passenger business was allowed to wither away so quickly after the Second World War.

The hostility to passenger services, though by no means universal, was sufficiently prevalent to account for the general mood of complacency of the railroad companies about the rise of automobile travel. The year 1920 had seen the highest-ever number of passengers—1.2 billion, not including commuters—but by the end of the decade, total passenger mileage across all railroads had fallen by more than 40 percent, despite the population growing by one-eighth. At the time of the Wall Street crash of 1929, Americans were already traveling five times farther in their cars than by train. Although the railroads still had by far the biggest chunk of the business market and the prestige services continued to flourish, there was little attempt to speed up services overall: "The blue-ribbon extra-fare trains between the East Coast and Chicago revealed what passenger officials thought was most important: comfort, luxury and safety. Speed is the enemy of all of these, and it is the enemy of track maintenance as well [making it far more expensive]." Instead, the companies tended to focus on passenger care, trying to outdo each other in offering the most mollycoddling. Redcap porters would ensure that no passenger carried his or her baggage, and indeed on most major routes railroad travelers could avail themselves of a door-to-door service, neatly described by Martin: "The affluent Midwestern family whose son was leaving shortly for Yale College phoned the railroad depot the day before and had the expressman call in his van for the lad's trunks and suitcases. Father handed the man the railroad ticket and he duly punched the square indicating that the traveler's baggage—150 pounds were allowed [on a full-price ticket]—had been checked to destination."[6] In fact, it was even better than this implies. The luggage was not simply taken to the station in New Haven, but rather driven to the student's room at the college, where it would await his arrival. This door-to-door service was routinely provided for business travelers, too, who would inform the clerk at the hotel to arrange for the baggage to be taken to their next destination.

For the affluent customers, the prestige trains continued to vie with each other to provide the best service. The interwar period was the heyday of these services. The huge distances required to travel across the United States and the lack of any realistic alternative mode of travel for most journeys meant that the rich flocked onto trains, and the railroads made sure to cater to their every need. Even before 1914, the example of the Pennsylvania and New York Central in creating luxury trains was being followed elsewhere. In 1911, the Santa Fe launched the De Luxe, running once a week between Chicago and Los Angeles, a trip that took sixty-one hours. It was limited to just sixty passengers, who paid a supplement of twenty-five dollars (the equivalent of around eight hundred dollars today). The Santa Fe clearly tried to outdo anything the New York Central provided on the Twentieth Century Limited. Not only was nearly all the train's accommodation in individual rooms, and the passengers' every requirement attended to by a vast array of staff, ranging from a manicurist and barber to a librarian, but every "male passenger was presented with a pigskin wallet embossed with the train's title in gilt; and at the California border uniformed pages would swarm aboard with corsages for each lady."[7] Many luxury trains sought to develop distinctive aspects of their service to attract publicity and passengers. On its long trip between Chicago and Seattle, the Great Northern's Oriental Limited featured a 5:00 p.m. ritual when a steward, bearing a silver tea service and followed by a retinue of uniformed maids carrying sandwiches and patisseries, would walk down the length of the train, handing out these treats. Gyms, string quartets, swimsuit modeling, and Sunday services all featured on these trains. When it was relaunched in 1930, the North Coast Limited, which also ran between Chicago and Seattle but on the Northern Pacific's tracks, boasted an electrician solely required to look after the innovative art deco lightbulbs.

The major passenger flows were not, of course, just on the east-west axis. There were well-used long-distance passenger routes on both coasts. In the East, they stretched from the Northeast down to Florida, which was booming as a vacation destination, thanks partly to the railroad created by Henry Flagler. On the West Coast, the rapid expansion in the population of California, opened up by the transcontinentals, led to the creation of a range of successful services, especially in the key corridor between San Francisco and Los Angeles but also stretching right up to Washington State. One key route, used not so much by the rich but crucial to the internal settlement pattern of the United States, was Chicago–New Orleans. The efficiency of the service meant that Chicago was often the first place that African Americans, fleeing the Jim Crow laws of the South, ended up, seeking jobs in the burgeoning industries of the Midwest such as the stockyards of Chicago or the automobile plants of Detroit. And they brought with them their music, creating the renowned Chicago jazz and blues culture.

In their heyday, the prestige trains were major moneymakers, and after the crash and the Depression, the rail companies realized that modernization was essential for survival. Aviation, though still in its infancy, had begun to tempt a few courageous, affluent, and, given the early safety record, foolhardy travelers to venture into the skies. Just as the government had helped the nascent railroads with contracts to transport mail, they supported early commercial airlines with similar arrangements. The first post office airmail service started operating between New York City and Washington, DC, as early as 1918, and soon transcontinental flights were creaming off the lucrative mail business from the railroads. In 1925, private contractors were allowed to carry mail, just as the early railroad companies had done, and these flights started taking a few passengers as a sideline. There was at least one attempt by the railroads to merge the two modes with the launch of a joint venture by Transcontinental Air Transport, with two railroads, the Santa Fe and the Pennsylvania. They offered passengers a trip across America from coast to coast in forty-eight hours—cutting a day off the normal train service—traveling by rail at night, as nighttime flying was deemed too difficult, and by air during the day. By 1930, it became possible for the first time to fly all the way from coast to coast, but it was not until the advent of the DC-3—the Dakota—in 1936 that aircraft had sufficient capacity to allow the airlines to make a profit solely through carrying passengers rather than being covertly subsidized with a mail contract. Even with the introduction of the DC-3, aviation barely impinged on the railroads' long-distance market before the war, as in 1940 it still had barely 3 percent of the market.

Buses had begun to attract some passengers at the lower end of the market by the outbreak of the Second World War. The railroads, realizing the danger, began to operate numerous bus services themselves and acquired many of the small operators who proliferated in the 1920s. Greyhound buses started making transcontinental trips by 1927, and the national Greyhound network was created two years later. However, the road network was still poor, with large sections still unpaved, and the railroads remained competitive on key routes. For example, a journey between New York and Chicago by bus in the late 1920s took twice as long as the ride by rail and in far less comfortable conditions. Nevertheless, despite a downturn during the Depression, by the outbreak of the Second World War Greyhound Lines had become well established as a national carrier, serving nearly five thousand towns throughout the nation.

Trucks were already posing a more potent threat to freight traffic. The first trucks had appeared in 1904 but could not even begin to compete with the railroads until the technology was improved to make them more reliable and increase their payload. Moreover, cars and trucks initially posed no threat to the railroads simply because "there really was nowhere to drive them."[8] When a reckless doctor from Vermont, Nelson Jackson, accepted a bet to drive across the United States in 1903, it took him sixty-three days, as he spent much of the time repairing punctures and getting pulled out of potholes by helpful local farmers. The poor state of the roads was a direct result of the success of the railroads. Once it was clear, soon after the inaugural run of the Baltimore & Ohio, that the railroads were going to spread rapidly around the country, the turnpikes declined and there was no appetite to build any new roads. Throughout the nineteenth century, the more that the railroads established their dominance—in some places such as Colorado, they even bought up the old turnpikes to use as lines of route—the less appetite there was for spending any money on road building or even maintenance. In particular, any notion of establishing a national road system, an aspiration of numerous early-nineteenth-century luminaries, was quietly shelved.

In the twentieth century, however, the roads were about to get their revenge, although at first progress was slow. The first paved road outside cities was not built until the early 1900s, and, although urban streets improved, there was little progress during that decade on building intercity highways, despite the growing number of cars and their greater range. It was, initially, the states that took the initiative by creating well-funded highway departments to upgrade roads and construct new paved highways. At the federal level, little progress was made until 1912, when at last the federal government, under pressure from campaigners within the automotive industry, began to consider building a transcontinental road. In 1919, a military convoy traveled from coast to coast using the partly completed road known as the Lincoln Highway and took sixty days to make the journey. It was led by Lieutenant Colonel Dwight D. Eisenhower, who was so appalled at the poor condition of the roads that, when he was president in the 1950s, he launched the program to build the interstate network that would have such a devastating effect on the railroads (see next chapter). The thirty-three-hundred-mile Lincoln Highway, mostly called US Route 30, was not actually completed until 1923, but support for the project showed that the federal government was at last taking an interest in the issue, despite the fact that the Constitution, as mentioned in Chapter 1, notionally prevented federal funds from being spent on national infrastructure. Somehow in the rush to roads, this was forgotten, and in 1916 President Woodrow Wilson signed into law the Federal Aid Road Act, popularly known as the "Good Roads Bill," backed by a generous initial appropriation of $85 million in its first year, ostensibly to help farmers bring their produce to market.

A series of technological improvements further tilted the balance in favor of trucks. As well as the greater reliability of engines and added power allowing bigger payloads, the key development was the introduction of the heavy-duty pneumatic tire by both Goodyear and Dunlop in 1919 that reduced fuel consumption as well as the number of breakdowns caused by punctures. Trucking had the built-in advantage of flexibility, since trucks could go right to the door of farms and factories. Moreover, the industry was entirely unregulated until 1935, whereas the railroads were constrained by the rules imposed on them by the Interstate Commerce Commission, most important the requirement of a minimum charge per mile. This prevented the railroads from offering the same door-to-door price as the truckers, who cannily charged for the whole journey the amount the railroads required for the railroad leg. The railroads complained that the truckers were effectively subsidized, as the roads they drove on were state funded and the lack of regulation—and initially unionization—allowed them to operate without restraint. According to Martin, trucking was "a classic form of self-employment of men ill-suited for closely supervised work, who must work illegally long hours and drive at illegal speeds to pay for their or their employers' increasingly expensive rigs."[9] Although in numerical terms the trucks at first made only minimal inroads into the railroads' business, they targeted the high-value freight that was the most profitable part of the trade, leaving the railroads with the mineral and aggregate traffic that was least lucrative. The other section of the business that was quickly lost to the roads was the transportation of what was known as "less than carload" freight, small loads that were uneconomic on rail but easily carried by truck. House moves, too, soon transferred, helped by the fact that trucking the contents did not require everything to be crated, as required on the railroads. Overall, the truckers had the great advantage of being able to pick and choose which loads they wanted to carry, charging what they wanted, whereas the railroads were under a legal obligation to take whatever was offered at regulated prices.

The railroads thought, with some justification, that they were unfairly treated. As the author of a history of the Burlington suggests, "U.S. railroads are the only transportation mode that owns, maintains and operates its own infrastructure—and pays *ad valorem* taxes for the privilege."[10] This puts them at a great disadvantage when the going gets tough, as in the 1930s. Whereas trucking companies could quite easily simply take their excess vehicles off the road and therefore no longer contribute anything to the infrastructure, the railroads had far less flexibility. They had far greater fixed costs than their rivals, as they were responsible for the stations, tracks, and terminals, on which they had the added burden of having to pay taxes, whereas truckers had only the cost of their trucks and relatively small depots. As roads got better, the truckers' costs reduced, as they could travel faster, further increasing their competitive advantage.

The truckers had already profited from the Depression, reducing their prices to meet their impoverished customers' needs, something the railroads could not do. The railroads compounded their bad situation by pushing for a rate increase in the early 1930s that, surprisingly, the commission, once so obdurate, now granted. This was poor timing on the part of the railroads, another indication that they could not see the bigger picture. Even the regulation finally imposed on the truckers in 1935 ended up helping the industry by preventing cutthroat price competition between them and consequently allowing the industry as a whole to be more profitable. The highway network, too, was ever expanding, with 3 million miles—fifteen times the length of the railroad system—by the outbreak of the war, connecting every little village and hamlet that had been ignored by the iron road. As a result, when America entered the war following Pearl Harbor in December 1941, the trucks had 10 percent of the intercity freight business, a good toehold from which to expand, but a figure that shows the railroads were still dominant, even if they had lost much of their profitable trade. Despite all their difficulties and handicaps, the railroads retained a natural advantage for heavy loads and for long-distance transportation.

It was the automobile that would be the ultimate railroad killer, particularly of passenger services. The bald figures are instructive. From a total of 3.3 million cars—for a population of around 100 million during the First World War—by the end of the 1920s, that total had increased to 23 million, albeit for a larger population. Henry Ford was the main instigator, or culprit, depending on how one looks at it. His Model T, the first car specifically aimed at the middle class rather than the rich and cheaper since it was the first built using assembly-line methods, had cornered the market, with 15 million being produced by 1927, when it was superseded by later designs. Cars, of course, created much extra travel, so although their use expanded almost exponentially during the 1920s, the number of passengers traveling by rail largely held up, thanks to growing prosperity and the rising population.

Ironically, one of the reasons the railroads enjoyed such a boom in freight transportation in the 1920s was that they were carrying vast quantities of material for road building and for car manufacturing. Much of this would disappear once the roads improved, but they also carried huge quantities of iron ore, coal, and other minerals for the booming heavy industries. The months leading up to the Wall Street crash of 1929 were in many respects the apogee of the railroads in the United States, at least statistically. There were more than 20,000 daily passenger trains serving the 130 million population, a staggering 2.6 million freight cars (more than at any time in the railroads' history), and 57,500 locomotives, nearly all steam engines. The industry employed 1.6 million people, and although mileage had begun to decline from the peak of 1916, there were still nearly 230,000 route miles. Track miles, which include sidings and count both lines in double-tracked sections, had actually risen considerably in the period, demonstrating the level of investment undertaken by the railroads. Although most of the additions to the rail network were small branch lines serving a particular mine or factory, or creating useful connections, one remarkable new railroad came to be opened during the interwar years, with the completion in 1923 of the Alaska Railroad. Railroads had come late to the territory—which would become a state only in 1959—with construction not starting until the 1900s, stimulated by the Klondike gold rush, when several early efforts led to the bankruptcy of the companies that had built the lines. It was not until the federal government, seeing the value of a railroad in the mineral-rich territory, took over the lines in 1914 that work resumed and the railroad could be completed. In 1923, President Warren Harding drove in the traditional golden spike that completed the 470-mile line, from the sea at Seward to Fairbanks in the interior, which, unusually, was government run as part of the Department of the Interior (and survives today under the ownership of the State of Alaska, carrying both passengers, especially in the summer, and freight). As with many American towns, Anchorage, Alaska's biggest city, owes its existence to the railroad, since it was created when the federal government took over the line and realized it was the most convenient transfer point between ship and rail.

Despite the railroads' financial difficulties and the incursions into their market by the new modes of transportation, they still dominated transportation in the interwar period. An example of the scale of the passenger rail operation at this point was the success of the New York Central's Twentieth Century Limited, which, when launched in 1902, consisted of just one train with a handful of cars. Now, on the eve of the crash, the Central had a dedicated fleet of 122 coaches and 24 locomotives for the service, which typically ran as six or seven separate trains, each carrying a hundred or so passengers in luxurious conditions. Crucially for the company, the prestigious service was a vital part of its economics, earning revenues of $10 million annually.

The railroads were still booming when the Wall Street crash of October 1929 ended thoughts of growth and ensured that the 1930s would be an agonizing time for the railroads. Inevitably, the increased competition combined with the effects of the Great Depression that followed the crash plunged many railroad companies into the red. During the 1930s, companies responsible for more than a third of the overall mileage fell into bankruptcy, including such famous names as the Erie (yet again), the Missouri Pacific, the Rio Grande, and the Wabash. Even the major eastern lines, such as the Pennsylvania and New York Central, only just managed to stay afloat. As ever with railroads when times get tough, the government had to intervene, as they were still a far too important part of the infrastructure to be allowed to go to the wall. Under Franklin D. Roosevelt's New Deal, the Reconstruction Finance Corporation was created that was intended to bail out organizations deemed essential to the national interest, and railroads became the second-biggest beneficiaries after the banks.[11] In 1932, the initial payments were made, with the Baltimore & Ohio and the Van Sweringen group of companies being among the first recipients of this cash, which was used to reduce bank debts that the railroads could no longer service. Throughout the decade, hundreds of millions of dollars from the fund were used to pay off railroad debts.

The New Deal was, however, ultimately more helpful to the highways than the railroads. Highway construction had already been a great generator of jobs in the Keynesian mood of the 1930s, and in 1938 the Public Works Administration, created under the New Deal, agreed to fund construction of the Pennsylvania Turnpike, the nation's first superhighway. With a huge workforce of thirty thousand, it was completed just two years later and would be the model for the forty-eight-thousand-mile interstate system built between the 1950s and 1980s.

Despite the stringencies resulting from the Depression, the 1930s would see the major railroads embark on one last brave and flamboyant attempt to counter the threat from cars and planes in an effort to try to retain the passenger market. Technology had developed on the railroads, too, and they could now call on a formidable new weapon, the diesel locomotive. Even before the introduction of diesels, the railroad companies had started to realize that providing their rich customers with new wallets and putting on modeling shows was not all they wanted. More powerful steam locomotives, fewer station stops, and improvements to the track all enabled them to speed up their services. The country's most prestigious trains, the two rival New York–Chicago services, the Twentieth Century Limited and the Broadway Limited, finally cut the timing on the service from twenty to eighteen hours. However, because of the effects of the slump, other services were consolidated, which resulted in some expresses extending their times, as they had to call at more stations. In 1933, only forty-three daily US train services were timed to average more than sixty miles per hour on any part of their journey. America, which a generation before had boasted the world's most consistently fast services, was now falling behind Europe, where various countries were using modern steam technology or diesels to speed up their trains. Indeed, embarrassingly, it was Canada that could now claim to have the fastest expresses in North America. This was, though, about to change with the advent of the diesel in the United States the following year, which would prove to be a real game changer in terms of speed and would give the passenger rail services a new lease on life.

The rail companies' pre-1914 interest in electrification schemes suggested that they had begun to recognize the limitations of steam, but changing traction methods required courage, commitment, and deep pockets. As a result, few railroads continued with electrification programs in the uncertain climate following the First World War. The Pennsylvania was a key exception, embarking on an ambitious scheme to put up the wires on its lines to Philadelphia and later farther on to Harrisburg, as well as down to Washington, creating what was at the time one of the biggest electrified networks in the world. The other mainline long-distance railroads did not follow its example because of the cost and a reluctance to move away from steam. Electrifying the vast swaths of the sparsely populated Midwest or the virtually empty West was simply uneconomic.

Gas engines had been used as an experiment before the war by a few railroad companies, such as the Chicago, Burlington & Quincy, the Santa Fe, and the Union Pacific, which tried it on railcars with limited success. A more sophisticated version was used by the three-car trains of the Chicago Great Western on its Blue Bird service, running between the Twin Cities (St. Paul and Minneapolis) and Rochester, Minnesota, introduced in 1929, but these engines proved far less efficient than diesel. First developed by the eponymous German Rudolf Diesel, at the end of the nineteenth century, the first diesel locomotives used in regular service on a US railroad were switchers introduced by the Central Railroad of New Jersey in 1925. Although they were particularly useful for such yard work, and dozens more came into service in subsequent years, it was mainline services that would be revolutionized by their deployment. Their introduction stimulated a brief heady period when various companies tried to outdo each other in providing the most up-to-date trains with the best facilities and customer service.

It was a combination of new technology and forward-looking management that resulted in the first regular long-distance diesel service. The key technological advance was the use of light alloys in the engines by General Motors, which by generating a greatly improved power-to-weight ratio made them far more efficient. It was happenstance that the new engine caught the eye of Ralph Budd, the boss of the Chicago, Burlington & Quincy Railroad, at the 1933 Chicago World's Fair, and he realized its potential to revolutionize long-distance rail travel. Budd is one of the heroes of railroad history in the interwar period. In his previous job, at the helm of the Great Northern, he had overseen the construction of America's longest railroad tunnel, the 7.8-mile Cascade Tunnel (mentioned in Chapter 9) completed in 1929 on the main line through the Cascade Mountains in Washington State. It was built to shorten the route by reducing the height of the pass needed to cross the mountain range, therefore limiting the risk of delays in winter. To further boost capacity, the tunnel and the track running up to it were electrified because of the danger posed by smoke in confined spaces and the greater ability of electric locomotives to climb steep gradients. It was the type of investment that the more farsighted railroad managers focused on during the interwar period because the expenditure on improvements to the track and infrastructure paid off in terms of lower operating costs. Budd was one of the visionaries of the period, who, unlike many of his contemporaries, realized early the extent of the challenge to rail's monopoly from road transportation and complained, to no avail, about the fact that "the controlling ideas and policies of regulation which may have been entirely appropriate when railroads enjoyed a practical monopoly of overland transportation have now become obsolete and should be modified."[12] Sadly, it would be a long time before the regulators listened to this line of thought, which was articulated all too rarely by rail-industry advocates.

Budd, though, was keen to try to give the railroads the best possible chance of resisting the onslaught of the car. While many of his fellow managers were becoming increasingly doubtful about the possibility of ever making money out of passenger rail services, Budd launched a service based on diesel locomotives and excellent facilities that would serve as the benchmark for long-distance rail journeys. After seeing the General Motors diesel engine at the Chicago World's Fair, he commissioned a new type of streamlined diesel locomotive,[13] oddly enough from a company also called Budd. Dubbed the Pioneer Zephyr (Budd had just been reading Chaucer's *Canterbury Tales,* which refers to Zephyrus as the west wind and thus oddly started a trend of trains being called Zephyr), in May 1934 it made a record-breaking and much-publicized "Dawn to Dusk" run from Denver, Colorado, to Chicago, where its arrival coincided, quite appropriately, with the opening of the "Century of Progress" Exhibition at which the train was the centerpiece exhibit. The Zephyr covered the thousand-mile distance at an average of seventy-eight miles per hour in thirteen hours, just over half the normal timing of twenty-five hours, without stopping, an impossibility for steam locomotives. As with many such train-speed record attempts, there was much cheating, as other services were shunted into sidings and all 1,689 grade crossings were guarded by flagmen to stop car traffic well ahead of the train, which consisted of just one set of three cars. Even the stations were protected by local police and, oddly, Boy Scouts. Just to make sure that the train, which was carrying Budd as well as various reporters and dignitaries, caught the eye of the media, it also had a four-legged passenger, a burro inevitably called Zeph, a small donkey donated by a newspaper as a mascot. Best of all for Budd, the fuel for the run reportedly cost just $14.64 (at 4¢ per gallon).

Such a journey speed could not be replicated in normal service, but nevertheless the train was no mere publicity stunt. Rather, it set a trend, and running high-speed diesel services became the aspiration of rival rail companies, particularly on the long stretches through the West but also in New England. Within a couple of years, a whole family of Zephyrs, Cities, and Limiteds had emerged on various railroads, transforming the nature of passenger travel for those lucky enough to be able to afford it. The Burlington, spurred on by the ever-enthusiastic Budd, was the pioneer, introducing in quick succession the Twin Cities Zephyr between Chicago and Minneapolis–St. Paul, Minnesota, and the Mark Twain Zephyr down to St. Louis, Missouri, as well as consolidating the Denver Zephyr by introducing a twelve-car train that covered the route in a more easily achievable sixteen hours, still a great improvement on the original steam locomotive timing.

Other railroads soon followed suit, with a plethora of similar services being introduced within a couple of years of the inaugural Zephyr run. In a demonstration run, a six-car Union Pacific diesel broke the coast-to-coast record, set by a special steam train back in 1906, by no fewer than fourteen hours, crossing America from Los Angeles to New York in just fifty-seven hours and demonstrating the extent to which the railroad companies had failed to pay sufficient attention to cutting journey times. This was, however, only a publicity stunt to show the potential of diesel, and even with the new trains there was still no proper coast-to-coast service that did not involve changing trains—usually in Chicago, which had continued to flourish through its position as the main hub (Memphis, St. Louis, and New Orleans were the others) of the US railroad network and now boasted a half-dozen terminal stations.

The Union Pacific train was immediately put into service as The City of Portland between Chicago and Portland, Oregon, and the Milwaukee Road soon launched the Twin Cities Hiawatha, running between the same two cities as the Burlington's Twin Cities Zephyr but powered by new steam locomotives designed to run at a hundred miles per hour. Diesel, though, was now the fashion, and within a couple of years there were more than a dozen of these new diesel services, trying to outdo each other with the extra facilities and comfort they provided. Pullman joined in the craze by providing streamlined lightweight cars for several of these trains, but it was the decision of the Atchison, Topeka & Santa Fe Railroad to create an all-Pullman service that resulted in the service that could, justifiably, lay claim to being the most luxurious train in the world, *pace* the Orient Express. This was the Super Chief, which started running between Chicago and Los Angeles in 1936 in just under forty hours, a timetable that saved a full half day on its steam predecessor, the Santa Fe's old Chief, a prestigious steam train introduced a decade before. The Super Chief became the train of choice for movie stars and studio moguls for their trips between the coasts and undoubtedly set a new standard of comfort for its passengers: "Designed within by a group of eminent architects and stylists, its restaurant, observation lounge, bar and wide choice of overnight accommodation—every room richly panelled in wood veneers from the four quarters of the world—were very reasonable replicas of the hotel accommodation to which the Hollywood *haut monde* who frequented it were accustomed."[14]

These new streamliner services invariably offered all the accoutrements of the trains of the previous generation, but with modern extras such as air-conditioning and electric-razor outlets. The more spacious offered lounges, cocktail bars, and office facilities, and all provided meals that today would earn them a Michelin star or two, elegantly hosted by a dinner-jacketed maître d', as well as offering various sleeping-car options. There was, too, a great emphasis on making the trip itself into a pleasure rather than merely a trial to be endured, with a great emphasis on the smoke-free views afforded by the much larger windows.

The result of this feverish activity was that, for a short period in the late 1930s, the ten fastest regular train services in the world were all American streamliners. It was not so much the speed or the diesel-powered engines that caught the public's imagination, but rather their streamlining. They were, quite literally, beautiful behemoths, a source of pride and modernity in an era of economic struggle and austerity. The size and power of the elegant diesels seemed to epitomize American values and gave people something to celebrate.

Whereas the steam engine had conquered the West, the streamliners solidified the bonds holding the Union together. Even those people who were not able to ride on them could, at least, admire their shape and form and appreciate the speed with which they thundered through America's vast prairies and deserts. The papers were constantly hailing the latest development or extra service, as well as filling their gossip columns with the details of which celebrities graced particular trains. As a result of this extensive press coverage, streamlining became all the rage. Several railroads that did not introduce diesels nevertheless streamlined their steam locomotives, but while they looked very elegant, the improvement in fuel efficiency was minimal. But it was not just railroads. *Streamlining* became a byword for "modern," and all kinds of objects from cars and stoves to buses and ballpoint pens took on the look. Although the railroads had emulated, rather than invented, the streamlining designs with their eclectic mix of art deco and modernist features, they were responsible for spreading the message, as the trains were the most visible and ubiquitous embodiment of the style. It was, perhaps, the last time that the railroads, which had changed so much in American society, would exert a powerful influence on the fashion of the age.

The introduction of these new trains proved, too, to be good business. The favorable publicity they generated, and the lack of a realistic alternative mode of transportation on most of these long-distance routes, ensured that passengers flocked to them. Indeed, it was not long before they were unable to accommodate the demand, and the railroad companies' ability to respond was hampered by the very design that attracted the great numbers, since many of these trains were in fixed formations—which meant that additional cars could not be added at busy times. Nevertheless, the revenue they brought in was considerable: "A consultancy which analyzed the performance of 70 of the new high-speed diesel trains in 1938 found that all of them had stimulated new business and generated substantially more net revenue than their steam predecessors." Taken individually, many of these prestige trains were profitable, but their total income could not redress the losses being made by US passenger services as a whole. Traveling numbers declined rapidly in the early 1930s as a result of the Depression, and by the outbreak of the Second World War, losses on passenger services amounted to around $250 million annually. Worse, according to Geoffrey Freeman Allen, a chronicler of the history of luxury trains, the railroads were storing up trouble for themselves: "The more elaborately they furnished the trains and the more lavish the on-board service they presented, the more daunt-ing they would find both renewal and staffing costs in the post-war infla-tionary era."[15] Providing the epicurean meals was unsustainable for many companies, with the Pennsylvania, for example, losing $1 million per year on its dining service before the war and four times that much by 1949.

It was not only passengers who enjoyed privileges in special trains. Cer-tain shipments of freight were treated with almost the same care, notably the most valuable in terms of dollars per ounce, silk. This cargo was so pre-cious, valued at as much as $1.5 million per trainload—the equivalent of, say, $20 million today—that the trains were given priority, even over pres-tige passenger services. By ship and train, the fastest services reached New York just thirteen days after leaving Japan, the principal producer, and in January 1929 a train carrying solely silk covered the route between San Francisco and Chicago in just over two days, a good day and a half faster than the usual passenger services.

There was one other famous example showing that, when motivated, the railroad companies could get their act together and provide rapid ser-vices. The occasion was, ironically, the return to the United States in June 1927 of aviator Charles Lindbergh following his inaugural transatlantic flight. He arrived in Washington, DC, and most of the newsreel companies, eager to show the footage in the New York news theaters, arranged to fly their film there. However, the International News Reel Company beat all its rivals by using a special train commissioned from the Pennsylvania Rail-road equipped with a mobile film laboratory and pulled by a fast steam lo-comotive. Traveling at speeds of up to 110 mph, the 220-mile journey took only three hours, and the company beat its rivals by more than an hour, an all too brief triumph that entered into railroad folklore and was much boasted about by the Pennsy. The irony was that the film itself was fantastic propaganda for the nascent industry that would, within a generation, prove to be the nemesis of passenger rail in America.

Freight traffic, not so time dependent, remained steam hauled for far longer than passenger services. There have been suggestions that the rail-road companies would have been better off concentrating on investing in freight traffic rather than trying to save passenger services, but that misses the point. Until the Second World War, and even a bit beyond it, railroads were still the only viable way for large numbers of passengers to travel long distances. Moreover, the streamliners helped cheer up the mood of America after the Depression, which was no mean achievement.

It was only in 1941 that the first freight train was powered by diesel, and this time it was the Santa Fe that was the pioneer, though others, such as the Southern, the Great Northern, and the Milwaukee, soon followed. Given the obvious long-term advantages of diesel, the reluctance to change demonstrated again the railroad companies' hesitant attitude toward modernization. In fairness, it was not easy for them. At a time when they were beginning to be aware that their monopoly position was under threat, they had vast assets tied into steam technology and as a corollary required considerable investment to make the change to diesel. However, as we will see in the next chapter, once the conversion started, the steam locomotive disappeared remarkably quickly, becoming an endangered species within a decade and almost joining the dinosaurs within two.

At the other end of the scale from the big companies and the main lines, a vast web of railroads, many of which were loss making and vulnerable to closure, covered America during the interwar period. Even the big companies were not immune from abandoning sections deemed hopeless. The Santa Fe closed twenty-five miles of branch lines in three states as early as 1921 and another thirteen miles five years later, while the Baltimore & Ohio abandoned mileage in the midwestern states of Ohio and Indiana also during the 1920s. Overall, though, most of the losses were in the South and West.

The branch lines owned by what are sometimes called "mom-and-pop railroads" were the most vulnerable to closure. There were countless lines that ran just a few miles from a junction and survived by keeping costs down and services simple. Although the trains might be infrequent, they still provided a vital lifeline for the people on their route. Often there would be just one or two services per day in each direction, usually a mixed train carrying both passengers and freight. These lines' best hope of salvation was to be merged into a bigger railroad that then might quietly forget their existence but might, conversely, run the risk of sudden closure. These lines, often with exotic and romantic-sounding names, were the most vulnerable to the advent of competition from the short-distance truck carriers, and several fell into disuse during this period, with around twenty thousand miles being lost in the interwar years. Many of the casualties of the 1920s were basket cases that had long been loss making or probably should never have been built, such as "the Madison Southern Railway, operating in Florida, [which] had only one passenger car, and its passenger revenues for 1919 totaled $438." Amazingly, this railroad staggered on for three more years before closure. Even more amazingly, the fourteen-mile Kentwood & Eastern Railroad (showing unfulfilled Eastern rather than Western ambitions for a change) in Louisiana and Mississippi, which had no passenger car, "made a substantial amount of money each year from passenger revenues," presumably from people sitting in boxcars or the conductor's caboose, but this was not enough to prevent its closure in 1922.[16]

There was, of course, one group that was happy to sit in boxcars. There had been hoboes on the railroads ever since the American Civil War, but with the Depression the phenomenon increased exponentially. Moreover, it was not just adults but a vast horde of teenagers who were on the move, estimated by Errol Lincoln Uys to number a quarter of a million in the 1930s: "Often as young as thirteen, each one came from a different background, each left home to ride the rails for different reasons, and each had unique experiences."[17] They were part of an army, estimated at 1.5 million during the peak years of the early 1930s, who used the railroads to get around the country to seek work. They suffered a terrible toll. According to the Interstate Commerce Commission, in the decade to 1939 nearly twenty-five thousand trespassers—seven a day—were killed and the same number injured, often losing a limb, on railroad property. Although not all of these would have been hoboes, a great proportion undoubtedly were, as jumping on and off moving trains was a hazardous business,[18] belying the romantic notion of the life often presented in films and books. Hoboes, who have an annual convention every year in Britt, Iowa, distinguish themselves clearly from tramps and bums. Whereas hoboes travel and work, a tramp travels and begs, while a bum, who may or may not go on the road, simply drinks or takes drugs. The number was greatly reduced after the Second World War, partly by the greater affluence, but also by the conversion to diesels, which unlike steam locomotives do not have to stop for water, giving hoboes fewer opportunities to jump on and off trains. Hitchhiking for a while became their preferred mode of travel, and today greater security and containerization make jumping the rails far less common.

For the most part, the railroads prospered in the 1920s, and after the terrible downturn in the Depression began to recover as the war approached. The closures were, in fact, a minority, less than 10 percent of a very extensive network in the interwar years. The Interstate Commerce Commission was required to give permission for shutting a line and withheld it on numerous occasions. Moreover, with the war leading to a resurgence in railroad use, which enabled even the most moribund lines to suddenly get back in the black, most of these lines survived into the 1950s, when the branches started to be hacked off in great numbers.

Despite the growing competition, the regulatory difficulties, and their own failings, the railroad companies could point to a proud record of improvements in the interwar period. Although the railroads were undoubtedly slow to adapt to the changing environment, it would be wrong to suggest they remained impassive in the interwar period while the opposition were sharpening their knives. There were numerous technical improvements, such as centralized train control that allowed one dispatcher to set signals and switches across a large stretch of railroad, perhaps as much as 100 or 150 miles of track, a significant increase in efficiency. Safety, too, improved considerably. The number of accidents, both minor and major, fell dramatically in the 1930s as the result of the adoption of new technology. Whereas in the 1920s, there were several years in which there were more than a hundred rail passengers killed in accidents, during the 1930s the number of fatalities only once exceeded forty in a year. As George Douglas notes, "Railroad travel had once carried with it the threat of hazard and risk; now the typical American came to believe that train travel was by far the safest form of transportation." And it was, given that the death toll on the roads was mounting rapidly in this age before seat belts and strict drunk-driving legislation and that early aviation was uninsurable.

One calculation suggests that in the 1920s alone, the railroad companies spent as much on improving their lines as they had in the whole of their previous history. Indeed, the figures are impressive. Thanks to investment and better operating practices, the average daily mileage of a freight car went up by 50 percent between 1921 and 1940 (though only to 39 miles, which doesn't seem that impressive), but, more significantly, the annual ton mileage per employee almost doubled in that period. Writing in 1960, railroad historian John Stover, who produced these figures, concluded, "Critics of the railroads in recent years have often viewed the industry's management as being composed of old fogies, averse to change and still living in the nineteenth century. Actually, the twentieth century has been one continuous period of increased productivity."[19] It would not, however, be enough to save many from disaster in the aftermath of the war, a period in which the decline was rapid, painful, and, for passenger services, almost terminal.

11

A NARROW ESCAPE

The Second World War demonstrated that the railroads were still the backbone of the nation's transportation infrastructure. Aviation was still a minority activity, and the roads, despite the creation of the US highway system, were not only inadequate but also just too slow for the carriage of large quantities of men and matériel. Quite simply, trains ran faster than cars and trucks, with less manpower and more reliability. The internal combustion engine still had some way to go before it could be seen as the mainstay of national communication.

It was not just the military that used the railroads extensively during the war. The rationing of gasoline and the shortage of rubber for tires meant that long-distance journeys by car were no longer possible for the general public. Aviation was restricted to those helping the war effort. The middle class left their Fords and Chryslers in their front yards and went back, all too briefly, to the trains. The railroads not only satisfied the military's almost unlimited demand for transportation, but also became, once again, the lifeline of the entire national economy.

Hence, the railroads carried all but a handful of the troops heading for the ports, and virtually all the war matériel, becoming rather unlikely beneficiaries of the strictures of war. This time, though, the railroads were determined not to be humiliated by a government takeover. Realizing that they could not prevaricate as they had done in the First World War, the railroads cooperated far more effectively than previously and, benefiting from the considerable investment in equipment made in the interwar years, carried a much greater volume of both goods and passengers than in the earlier conflict. No longer were thousands of freight cars allowed to molder at railheads: the railroads worked together, rather than against each other, to ensure better coordination.

The logistics were made easier by the fact that ports on both the East and West Coasts were used, since the war was being fought both in Europe and in the Pacific, unlike in the First World War, when traffic was all eastbound. There was one similarity between the two conflicts, however. In both wars the railroads were dogged by severe industrial-relations troubles, as the labor unions found themselves in a strong position, given the huge demands placed on the railroads and the shortage of staff. Experienced railroad workers were in great demand—the number of people employed in the industry increased during the war from 1.1 million to 1.4 million—and with the railroad companies becoming profitable once again because of the increase in war traffic, the unions repeatedly put in wage demands. Skilled labor was in short supply, as not only were more people needed, but a quarter of existing railroad employees were called up to fight, including around 43,000 earmarked for the Military Railway Service, which built and repaired rail lines in areas of the conflict stretching from Sicily to the Philippines. President Roosevelt intervened twice on their behalf, forcing the railroads to agree to wage raises. On the second occasion, at the end of 1943, he took the management of the railroads into government control to avoid a strike for a three-week period during which he conceded to many of the unions' demands. However, even with these increased costs, the railroads remained highly profitable during this period. Neither freight rates nor fares were raised substantially during the war; it was the massive increase in volume carried that brought the railroads back into the black.

The conflict gave a remarkable boost to an industry that, at the outset of the war, had only partially recovered from the Depression. The raw figures are instructive. At the pit of the Depression in 1932, passengers traveled 16 billion miles on the trains. By 1940, that figure had risen only to 24 billion, but in 1943, the second full year of US participation in the war, the figure had quadrupled to 96 billion passenger miles. Freight showed a similar though not quite so marked growth, with the 1944 total of 737 billion ton miles being just about double the 1940 figure. There was new traffic, too. The railroads had never carried much oil, but as shipping was endangered by German U-boats, it became a highly profitable new business and the industry showed great flexibility by hastily cobbling together enough tanker cars. The economics of the railroads, many of which were still bankrupt at the start of the war, were transformed by this influx of business, showing yet again that railroads, with their high fixed costs, are invariably at the mercy of external factors. All significant railroads were profitable in 1942: "Railroads that only a few years before were being operated by trustees appointed by bankruptcy courts were paying handsome dividends."[1] Even the perennially ailing Erie, which had not produced a dividend since the 1870s, finally paid out to its long-suffering shareholders in 1943.

The railroads might have been profitable for the first time in more than a decade, but their safety standards, which, as we have seen, had improved greatly in the interwar period, slipped badly. The heavy use of the railroads for both military and civilian purposes, combined with the lack of investment, inevitably meant that they were being run down, and both punctuality and safety standards were compromised. On a mundane level, the trains were often delayed. This was noticed by the acerbic writer and critic H. L. Mencken, who traveled a couple of times a week between his home in Baltimore and New York and noticed that, for the first time, the trains were not always on time. Nor was the journey as comfortable. The Southern Pacific's timetable warned, "In our dining cars, we are rationed much as you are at home and we can't always get the supplies in our allotment." That meant just two meals a day were served, breakfast and then dinner, which could be taken anytime after 3:00 p.m., but diners were restricted to just one cup of coffee with their meal. And, of course, they were told "not to discuss what you see on passing trains," since, as the wartime propaganda posters stressed, careless talk might be overheard by enemy spies.[2]

Safety, though, was a more serious matter. The most tragic illustration of lax standards was an accident on the Pennsylvania Railroad at Frankford Junction, near Philadelphia, on September 6, 1943, when a train bound for New York's Penn Station derailed and hit a signaling gantry, killing seventy-nine passengers. Rumors that the wreck was the result of German sabotage were quickly proved to be groundless as the more believable but embarrassing truth emerged: the accident had been caused by poor maintenance, resulting in an axle-bearing failure. The list of survivors, who included a newspaper magnate and Lin Yutang, a famous Chinese writer, showed that the railroads were once again the transportation method of preference, indeed necessity, for all classes, since car use was so restricted.

Such disasters notwithstanding, it was, as Richard Saunders Jr. suggests, "the railroads' finest hour." The railroads regained their place at the heart of the nation's psyche. The most emotional memories of the war for many Americans involved the departure or arrival of trains filled with waving men and long waits in station cafés and on windswept platforms during which they experienced moments of hope and sometimes despair as, all too often, a loved one returned home maimed or, worse, in a wooden box. It was at railroad stations that "people said goodbyes to husbands, sons, daughters, brothers, and sisters, trying to be brave but hugging them harder than they ever hugged them before." The Second World War marked the last time that the railroads could truly be said to be at the heart of American life. As George Douglas puts it, "World War Two was a last hurrah for the railways."[3]

The decline of the US railroads after 1945 was at first so gradual that it was almost imperceptible. Instead of the expected postwar downturn in the economy, there was a boom, and railroads always do well when the economy is flourishing. The successful economy, however, only served to offset the underlying difficulties of the railroads and, in a way, by enabling more people to buy cars, exacerbated them. It was the passenger business that suffered worst initially, but later whole categories of freight also began to leach away at a frightening rate. The railroads had come out of the Second World War imbued with a sense of optimism. Not only had they regained the respect of the public, but they thought they would retain a vital role in the provision of passenger travel in the postwar period. They looked back on the success of the prestige diesel trains of the 1930s and thought that by just continuing to improve the service and speed up the timetable, they would retain a sizable proportion of the market.

The widespread conversion to diesel locomotives did indeed give the railroads a new lease on life, both by making the operation of services cheaper and by making journeys quicker and more pleasant. Diesel proved more popular than electrification, since it did not require massive new investment in the infrastructure. Once the higher price of the engines was covered—around twice the cost per horsepower—the savings in operating costs were considerable, since the diesels' greater efficiency meant they provided at least three times as much mileage from the same amount of fuel. Diesel locomotives, too, could be operated in twos or threes with just one engineer. Given that there was nothing left for the "fireman" to do, the savings would have been even greater had the railroad companies' management tackled the unions' insistence on retaining double manning of the locomotives. In fact, when the early Burlington Zephyrs had started running, there was only one driver in the cab, but in 1937 the Brotherhood of Locomotive Firemen and Enginemen decided to oppose this change strenuously. At the time, against the background of the Depression and the need for jobs, the public sided with the firemen, but according to Saunders, this was a crucial missed opportunity for the railroads: "The railroads themselves had little idea how important diesel was going to be. Steam men, who dominated railroad mechanical departments, assumed that the diesel's use would be limited to certain kinds of passenger trains and gimmicky ones at that."[4]

Although trying to retain firemen on diesels was ultimately indefensible, the unions had a good case in respect to their overall working conditions. The engineers were still expected to be on call at all times, with no extra pay, and be ready to drive a train safely for up to sixteen hours at a moment's notice. However, it was the issue of the firemen that came to a head in the late 1950s. North of the border, the Canadian Pacific had challenged the unions over double manning, and, after a brief strike, a royal commission was established that found in favor of the railroads. The two main railroads, the Canadian Pacific and the Canadian National, were allowed to stop hiring firemen, and several American companies wanted to follow suit. The unions were having none of it, however, and, as in Canada, a commission was established by the federal government to decide on the issue. It was headed by federal judge Simon Rifkind who, in his five-hundred-page report, produced "a reasoned set of recommendations that actually would have meant higher wages for most rail employees but at honest jobs of productive work." No new firemen would be hired, and, in part, the rigid structure of demarcations would have been broken. For the unions, though, these proposed measures were unpalatable, and they took the issue to court. Eventually, in April 1964, President Lyndon B. Johnson intervened and managed to convince the unions to postpone a threatened strike for two weeks. Johnson then summoned all the parties to the White House and showed them to the Cabinet Room, where they embarked on a marathon negotiating session—the equivalent of beer and sandwiches at No. 10 Downing Street, which in the 1960s and 1970s was the method of dealing with the unions preferred by the British prime minister, Harold Wilson. Eventually, the unions agreed to an end to the hiring of firemen, provided the existing ones would be allowed to continue working until they retired or left the industry. Nothing better illustrates the continued importance of the railroads as late as 1964 than the fact that the results of the successful negotiation were announced by a jubilant President Lyndon B. Johnson, who was so eager to inform the nation that he rushed to CBS's studios in a motorcade rather than wait for the cameras to come to the White House: "This settlement ends four and a half years of controversy. I tell you quite frankly there are few events that give me more faith in my country and more pride in the free collective bargaining process."[5] The fact that this statement came from a president from Texas shows the extent to which it is not only the role of the railroads that has changed in the intervening half century, as one could hardly imagine that more recent Texas president, George W. Bush, sorting out either the railroads or the unions.

The double-manning issue had, in fact, not really been resolved and would continue to burden the railroads with unnecessary expense for many years, since the deal announced by Johnson covered only three years and the unions were soon, once again, pressing for firemen to be retained. They were eventually phased out completely, though even today there is still an engineer and a conductor, who without a caboose now rides in the front, on every freight train. The conductor, in fact, still has a role, as there are many points in remote places that need to be operated manually or occasions where reversing movements are required. Even while firemen were retained, however, converting to diesel was still worthwhile for the railroads, since the plethora of cleaners and maintenance staff required to repair and run steam locomotives was no longer needed. Moreover, diesels could be used constantly, running 1,000 miles or more without needing any attention, whereas steam locomotives not only needed to be cleaned after every long trip, but also required hours to be fired up. Whereas a steam locomotive could be in productive use for around 150,000 miles a year at most, the best diesels could be used for almost double that mileage. One small detail encapsulates the extent of the savings from the shift to diesel: steam engines, as their name implies, need vast quantities of water, and when they were finally phased out, the railroads were able to dispense with the staggering amount of $50 million worth of water-supply equipment.

Nevertheless, the steam locomotive manufacturers tried to resist the inevitable. Even into the 1950s, bigger and better steam locomotives were being produced by the major manufacturers like Baldwin, but by 1960, all the main railroads had abandoned steam.[6] Once under way, the dieselization process was remarkably fast. Whereas at the end of the war, three-quarters of freight was still hauled by steam, by 1959 it was less than 1 percent. Diesel locomotives saved, at least temporarily, countless branch lines from closure, not only because they were cheaper to operate but also because, as they were lighter than steam engines, the track required less maintenance. The heavier and more powerful steam locomotives that had become standard on the main lines could not venture onto smaller branches as railroads cut back on maintenance to save money, and therefore it was the use of lighter diesel engines that extended the life of services on these lines. The introduction of diesel locomotives, therefore, together with other money-saving measures, notably cutbacks in passenger services, gave the railroad companies a final bit of breathing space, enabling productivity per employee to double between 1940 and 1960.

On the passenger side, improvements were still being made to the prestige passenger services in the immediate postwar period. Now "vista-domes" were added to the streamliners, special coaches with a glass-roofed upper deck that gave passengers an unparalleled panoramic view of the passing scenery. The ultimate development came in the early 1950s with "super-domes," with bigger and better viewing points, used by several railroads, principally on the long scenic trips through the Rockies and the western deserts. In order to attract leisure passengers, timetables were adjusted so that the train went through the most picturesque areas in daylight. The Baltimore & Ohio experimented with flashing a spotlight into the wilderness during nighttime hours to give the passengers in the upper deck something to see, but this daft idea was soon abandoned. A stranger—even rather surreal—experience could be had on the California Zephyr, where the coaches with their passengers on board were routinely put through a car washer to ensure that the windows were clean so that passengers could enjoy the view unrestricted by dirt.

These domeliners represented the apogee of train travel, making the journey itself fun, and stimulated the response of the airlines, who felt it was essential to provide similar levels of service. The first domeliner was introduced by that pioneering railroad man Ralph Budd of the Burlington, and soon about a dozen major American railroads were using them to attract passengers. The Great Northern's Empire Builder was the "supreme example" of the concept, according to Geoffrey Freeman Allen, as the railroad repeatedly spent millions of dollars on providing ever more luxurious train sets: "[On the] *Empire Builder*, the upper floor of the 'Super-Dome' seated 74 on settees angled towards the side-windows for comfortable viewing: the lower floor housed an enticing 35-seater lounge bar and writing room; an electrically powered dumb waiter made it simple to hoist drinks and snacks from the bar to passengers relaxing in the air-conditioned solarium above."[7] On the Twin Cities Hiawatha, drinkers in the "Tip-Top-Tap" lounge were advised of the next stop, as the name was illuminated on a display below the clock, whereas on the Santa Fe's Super Chief, passengers were kept up to date with news bulletins and stock reports and could write letters on special letterhead. And so on.

But it could not last. It was to prove a short-lived fad, an all too brief swan song for the railroads. For a while these trains made money, as they were frequently full and commanded premium fares, but the economics ultimately weighed against them. The airlines were gathering like paparazzi around a starlet, and their planes were becoming more efficient, faster, and bigger. Whereas a DC-3, still the workhorse of the skies in the late 1940s, could accommodate only 21 passengers and make four round-trips to the railroads' one, a decade or so later the Boeing 707 was carrying 176 and was able to make eight round-trips in the time it took a train to trundle across America's vastness. The choice between traveling overnight on a train from, say, New York to Chicago or hopping on a jet became a no-brainer, especially as airline fares plummeted.

With the rapid loss of their passenger market to the airlines in the 1960s, the railroads soon found the cost of providing an upmarket service on their long-distance services was unsustainable. Yet cutting out the creature comforts merely accelerated the decline in passenger numbers. To look after a maximum load of 323 passengers scattered royally in fifteen expensive cars, the Empire Builder required 25 service staff in addition to the locomotive crews and the conductor. Worse, under a national agreement with the unions dating back to the 1920s, locomotive staff were paid on a mileage basis, with a mere 100 miles constituting a full day's pay, whereas for the conductor and other on-board staff, it was 150 miles. These rules, drawn up when trains were far slower, proved crippling for the industry, but the unions steadfastly refused to recognize them as obsolete. It meant, for example, "it took eight crews to forward the *Burlington Zephyr* the 1,034 miles between Denver and Chicago, a feat done in 16.5 hours."[8] In other words, each crew member was receiving a full day's pay for a little more than two hours' work. Many staff had the choice of either collecting multiple wages for a day's work or simply performing a very short shift. It was easy money, but it was contributing to the death of America's passenger railroad.

The costs were so high that it was not uncommon for these luxury services to be killed off despite remaining popular and being well loaded. For example, according to Saunders, "The *California Zephyr* had an average occupancy rate of nearly 80 per cent (that would make any airline envious) right up to its last trip on March 22, 1970."[9] However, the economics just did not stack up in a world where railroads had lost their monopoly and the alternatives had become cheaper. Overall, passenger numbers were in steep decline. Whereas in 1944 there had been 600 million intercity passenger journeys, already by 1949 this had halved, as gasoline was no longer rationed, and by 1966 the number was just 105 million.

Commuter journeys, too, were falling, as cars became universal and jobs were less concentrated in downtown areas accessible by rail. By the late 1950s, all but a couple of railroads were losing money on their passenger services: the New Haven, centered around Boston and Connecticut, which had just about broken even but would soon go under and have to be taken over unwillingly by the Penn Central; and the Long Island Rail Road, the busiest commuter railroad in the country, which had gone bust in 1949 and was partly subsidized by the State of New York, which eventually took over the railroad in the mid-1960s. There was a similar pattern elsewhere—either the commuter networks were simply abandoned, or they were taken over by local city or state governments. The paradox was clear. As David P. Morgan, the editor of *Trains* magazine put it, commuter services were "a civic blessing" but "a corporate horror."[10] In other words, they lost the railroads a fortune but made life far more pleasant both for the passengers and for motorists who found the roads clearer. They saved city administrations a fortune, since, without them, more expensive roads and parking lots would have had to be built, but this basic fact was rarely taken into account in the rush to create the car-based economy.

Streetcar networks, which had started being pruned in the 1930s, were mostly closed down in the 1940s and 1950s. There were, however, a few exceptions, including the heritage systems in San Francisco and New Orleans and parts of the network in major cities such as Boston, Philadelphia, and Pittsburgh as a result of particular geographical circumstances such as tunnels running into hills that would have been difficult to turn into highways. The story of the closure of the Los Angeles network of streetcars and interurbans became a cause célèbre because it was widely seen as a conspiracy by the automobile industry, but the truth was more complex. The huge networks of "big red cars" of the Pacific Electric Railway that served the suburbs and the "big yellow cars" of the Los Angeles Railway that ran the streetcars in the central urban area both started struggling in the interwar period. Ridership had peaked in 1924 and then declined steadily, with a small recovery in the run-up to the war. There was much local debate about what to do with the system, and considerable hostility toward it was generated as car ownership rose and accidents between streetcars and automobiles became frequent. In 1940, the interurban Pacific Electric Railroad system was taken over by National City Lines, a subsidiary of the huge car manufacturer General Motors, and closed down. Four years later, the same company took over the Los Angeles Railroad and by the late 1950s had similarly abandoned the system. It was, therefore, easy to sense a conspiracy, especially as this was a nationwide phenomenon. Overall, between 1936 and 1950, National and another General Motors subsidiary, Pacific City Lines, took over more than one hundred streetcar systems in forty-five cities and converted them to buses provided by General Motors. The story in Los Angeles was one of the key cases used in a successful prosecution in 1949 of General Motors, along with Standard Oil and Firestone Tires, which had backed National City Lines, for breaking antitrust laws, and it featured as a subplot in the 1988 Steven Spielberg film *Who Framed Roger Rabbit?* General Motors and its codefendants were found guilty of conspiring to monopolize the sale of buses, gasoline products, and tires used by local transportation companies but not of forcing the replacement of electric-driven streetcars with buses. That was a key difference and rather dented a hole in the conspiracy theory.

Paul Mees, a strong supporter of public transportation, who has examined the story in detail, suggests that the streetcar systems were doomed anyway, since their problems stretched back to the end of the First World War. The number of passengers was falling rapidly just at the time when big sums of money were needed for reequipping them. Moreover, the local authorities responsible for the services were often lumbered with long-term franchise arrangements with private operators that they could not change and therefore found it difficult to raise fares or close down unprofitable lines or increase service levels on profitable ones. When buses, which were far cheaper to operate, were offered by General Motors to replace the decaying streetcars, the local authorities grabbed the chance to close down their burdensome streetcar systems. Of course, the very fact that General Motors bought up all these streetcar systems suggests that there was at least in part an ulterior motive, as the company stood to benefit from bus sales, but, as Mees suggests, without the type of intervention by local or national government that became commonplace in Europe, the streetcar systems were doomed: "Problems with privately operated, government-franchised urban public transport had arisen by this time all over the developed world. The solution virtually everywhere except the US was a public takeover upon the expiry of the franchise or even earlier."[11] In the United States, however, nationalization was seen as impractical and even unconstitutional by the federal government. It was, therefore, not so much General Motors and its fellow automotive industry companies that were at fault, but rather the strong American antipathy toward government involvement in the provision of services that led to the demise of the streetcar networks. Of course, the increase in traffic as the people took to their cars was another factor in their downfall, because the streetcars became embroiled in jams on the busy streets. However, when it came to the threat to all passenger rail services in the United States a few years later, as we see below, a public-sector solution was found at the instigation of the federal government.

It was not just the competition from the car and the airlines or the rigidity of the unions that was killing intercity passenger rail. Government policy, which had once so helped the railroads, was turning against them. The real killer was Eisenhower's curse, the creation of the interstate network of superhighways linking every town of significance in the United States. When Eisenhower became president in 1953, he had not forgotten his awful experience on his trip across the continent as a young officer, and he supported a bill to create the interstate network of superhighways that would not only ensure it was quicker to drive than take the train on most journeys but also, in effect, be a vast hidden subsidy to the trucking industry. Created by the Federal Aid Highway Act of 1956, the forty-six-thousand-mile system, officially named after Eisenhower, was built over a period of thirty-five years and cost in excess of $425 billion.[12] Federal funding was allowed because the system was seen as essential for military purposes and for use at times of national emergencies, and consequently the roads were engineered to very high standards, paid for by a national tax on fuel. It was the biggest construction project in American history and represented a crippling blow to the railroads, especially as road construction has continued to be supported through related highway-funding legislation also enacted by Eisenhower's administration in 1956.

Then there was the support given by many local authorities to the construction of airports. Every city wanted at least one, and occasionally two, and gave land and other help in kind, such as tax concessions. There was more covert help in the form of air traffic control services: "The tab for air traffic control was picked up by the federal government. Railroads installed their own signals at private expense and they paid taxes on their railroad stations," and, indeed, on all their other property, such as goods yards and even the track.[13] As if that was not bad enough, the railroads lost a major source of revenue in 1967 as a result of another government decision when the Post Office Department removed almost all mail cars, a long-established source of steady income, from passenger trains. There was even the St. Lawrence Seaway project that was funded by the Canadian and American governments, which opened up the Great Lakes to deepwater ships and seemed to threaten the viability of various railroad routes from eastern ports to the Midwest. In the event, the seaway soon proved to be built on a scale that was too small to accommodate big-enough ships, but nevertheless it was yet another project built by public cash that affected the privately owned railroads. The dice always seemed to be weighted against them.

The overall effect of all these factors was the gradual gnawing away at the profitability of the railroads. A microcosm of their problems can be gleaned from the story of the Elmira Branch, an unassuming minor line that ran between the shores of Lake Ontario in upstate New York and central Pennsylvania. It was part of the Pennsylvania Railroad and ran deep into New York Central territory, principally carrying coal but also a wider range of other goods. It remained, in the immediate postwar period, a busy railroad. Although its flourishing ice business had been killed off by refrigerated trains in the 1930s, milk was still carried in the 1950s, and there was considerable movement of agricultural produce, ranging from fresh fruit to flowers, in what were disparagingly called "cabbage trains." Processed food from various canneries and food plants, including a big Bird's Eye factory, was transported on the Elmira, along with a host of industrial products from companies big and small, several of whom had sidings connected with the line. There were junctions with a dozen other lines linking with five other railroads. It was not exciting, but it was profitable. Passenger trains had never played much of a role on the Elmira, being cut from four per day in the 1930s to just one in the 1950s, a night train with a through sleeper service linking Rochester, New York, to Washington, DC, that was discontinued at the beginning of 1956. That was, effectively, the beginning of the end: "Across the next decade, plants closed or shifted their business to trucks or converted from coal to oil; and shipper by shipper, the traffic fell away."[14] The last straw came in the form of Hurricane Agnes, a particularly violent storm that swept across the East Coast in the summer of 1972; it caused havoc to several rail lines and, in particular, damaged so many bridges and embankments on the Elmira that it was abandoned for through traffic, though a few sections linking with other railroads survived. Thus, in the space of barely a quarter of a century, a once thriving and profitable railroad was wiped off the map.

In a famous and remarkably prescient feature, published as early as April 1959, "Who Shot the Passenger Train?" in the magazine *Trains*, the editor, David P. Morgan, listed a series of reasons for its demise: "Man has yet to invent an overland passenger mode of transport with the train's unique combination of speed, safety, comfort, dependability, and economy. Yet the passenger train is a museum candidate today. Its native profitability has been frustrated by archaic regulation, obsolete labor contracts, unequal taxation and publicly sponsored competition." Morgan added, too, that railroad managers had failed to adopt sufficiently customer-friendly practices. He said that since 85 percent of the railroads' revenue came from freight, the only solution was to hive off the passenger trains and run them as a separate business. His words fell on deaf ears. Neither the railroads nor the politicians were ready at the time to take his advice, though eventually his idea was accepted by the government with the creation of Amtrak in 1971.

By the early 1960s, almost every major railroad was trying to close lines to passengers or reduce services, but they first had to petition the Interstate Commerce Commission, which did not always grant permission. There were, of course, covert ways of making services so unpalatable for any remaining passengers that closure was inevitable. There were a lot of tricks, both overt and underhanded, such as using old rolling stock, providing short trains with no catering or other facilities on board, demolishing station waiting rooms and restrooms, reducing the timetable to make it impossible to use the service efficiently, and so on. In Britain, during the same period, British Railways became a master of such practices.

The Lehigh Valley Railroad, principally an anthracite-carrying railroad but which also had at one time run the prestigious Black Diamond service between New York and Buffalo, was the first to petition the commission in 1958 when fewer than 350 people per day were using its service. Its last trains ran early in 1961, by which time two other major railroads, the Maine Central and the Minneapolis & St. Louis, had managed to abandon all their passenger services. A further eight railroads followed by the end of 1967, and then at the end of the decade the movement threatened to become a flood, as big names such as the Erie (which had now joined with the Lackawanna to form the Erie Lackawanna) and the Western Pacific sought to abandon passenger services. By then, passenger railroads were costing the railroads some $470 million per year in losses.

The railroads were so eager to get out of the passenger business that several of them simply stopped any trains that happened to be running when permission came through from the ICC, with the result, in the case of the Chicago, Aurora & Elgin, that the company's daily commuters were left stranded in town after services were cut in the middle of its final day in July 1957. Similarly, in January 1969, the Louisville & Nashville dumped its last fourteen passengers, who had the misfortune to be on its final Humming Bird service between Cincinnati and New Orleans, in Birmingham, Alabama, more than four hundred miles short of their destination and, after a delay, bused them the rest of the way. The Burlington tried the same trick, forcing its passengers to leave the train at a small town in Nebraska, but failed to notice that one passenger was a congressman—who promptly persuaded the commission to force railroads to give forty-eight hours' notice of any closure. Others, who had been allowed to end services in one state but not another, just stopped at the boundary, leaving passengers stranded. It was generally not long, of course, before the other state caved in. Such incidents were evidence of the railroads' desperation to quit the passenger business. Freight was quiescent and did not answer back. Passengers had, in the eyes of many railroad managers, always been a pain to deal with anyway. As Albro Martin sums it up, "Industries which have the bad fortune to deal directly with the public—especially where the public's total physical and mental welfare are one's responsibility for periods of from an hour to three or four days at a stretch—will always be fair game for public abuse."[15]

It was the failure of the biggest merger in corporate history up to that date that would finally trigger a response from government. In 1965, rumors of talks between two of the biggest railroad companies, the Pennsylvania and the New York Central, began to appear in the press, suggesting a measure of desperation on the part of both managements about the state of these behemoths' finances. They were prepared to bury their rivalry to save their railroads and in the process created the biggest railroad company America had ever seen, with more than twenty thousand route miles, the equivalent of the whole British network at its peak. After fraught negotiations and the meek acquiescence by Stuart Saunders, the chairman of the Pennsy, to various conditions imposed by President Johnson, the merger went through in February 1968. It started disastrously and got worse. The legacy forced on Saunders included not only taking on the ailing and loss-making New Haven Railroad as part of the deal, but also agreeing to union demands that there would be no redundancies and, remarkably, that the joint company would rehire five thousand previously laid-off workers, even though there were not necessarily any jobs for them.

As if that was not bad enough, the two companies proved to be simply incompatible. Despite years of ICC hearings into the merger, and endless negotiations, no one seemed to have thought through the practicalities: "It was a shotgun marriage that should never have happened."[16] The two companies were very different beasts. Whereas the Pennsy made its money from hauling raw materials such as steel, ore, and coal, the Central primarily concentrated on carrying merchandise and components to midwestern factories and car plants. The Pennsy focused on bulk, and delays to its services were less important than for the Central, whose customers were dependent on regular supplies. Even the computer systems were incompatible—one used punched tapes to input information (this was the 1960s!), the other punch cards—and therefore the two railroads could not communicate with each other. As on all railroads, most freight had to be channeled through at least one and often more classification yards, where railcars were sorted into trains for particular destinations. Within days of the merger, the yards were in chaos, as many trains had no waybills—the paperwork showing their provenance and destination—because of the computer failures and therefore were lost in the system. Clerks who had no knowledge of the layout of the other railroad simply sent out cars to a station they thought might be close to the destination. A shortage of serviceable locomotives added to the delays, and the poor management of staff often meant that crews were left hanging around doing nothing. Perishable goods predictably perished in the yards, and factories were left with shortages of parts. Eli Lilly, the pharmaceutical firm, reported that a car with frozen animal glands had arrived twenty-seven days late for the three-hundred-mile journey between its plants in Iowa and Indianapolis, and the contents had thawed, creating a stinking mess. In another case a hundred-car coal train was "lost" for ten days outside Syracuse, New York. Journeys that used to take a day now sometimes ran to five. The customers were in an uproar, bombarding the company for information but getting none. Indeed, little was done to appease them, and local trucking firms soon benefited from their custom. Worse, the top three executives—Saunders; Alfred Perelman, his counterpart on the Central; and the finance director, David Bevan—spent more time plotting against each other than running the company.

Possibly because he realized that the railroad business could not make any money, Saunders embarked on a massive round of acquisitions, resulting in the Penn Central owning an extraordinary 186 subsidiaries.[17] Moreover, he ran the company on the basis of what was kindly described as "creative accountancy" but was really outright fraud. He consistently overvalued assets and undervalued liabilities and boosted profits through paper deals to convince Wall Street that the company was profitable. It was in fact losing $1 million per day and started borrowing money at 10 percent interest, when even in the good times it was earning 5 percent: "Never, in recent times, had the books of a large corporation been so thoroughly cooked."[18] It could not last and it didn't. By the summer of 1970, the Penn Central executives halted their squabbling for just long enough to establish that they were reaching a point when there was not enough cash to pay the ninety-four thousand employees. Less than thirty months after the merger, on Sunday, July 26, 1970, the directors decided there was no alternative but to file for bankruptcy. It was the biggest corporate bankruptcy in Wall Street history until Enron thirty years later.

The press had a field day. Why, for example, did the Penn Central own five New York hotels and have a 25 percent stake in the New York Rangers ice hockey team? Or indeed, why did it own a charter airline company, Executive Jet Aviation, through a complex ownership structure made necessary by the fact it was illegal for a railroad to be involved in aviation? And best of all, what exactly went on during those "dates" for top executives that took place in parked sleeper cars in a remote part of New York's Penn Station, and who paid for them? It was all good fun, but it missed the central point. The lurid press coverage rather overshadowed the basic story that the railroads were not viable in the climate in which they were forced to operate, according to the authors of a book published soon after the collapse: "Here was the record-sized merger bringing together two badly disorganized, unprofitable companies in a discredited industry regulated by an unsympathetic federal agency, denounced by public and politicians for its poor performance record, and hemmed in by powerful unions clinging to archaic work rules." Furthermore, they added, there was "management blundering, corporate disloyalty, executive suite bickering, board-room slumbering, tight money, a national recession, inflation—and an unusually severe winter."[19] In effect, they concluded, even had the company been better managed and conditions for railroads been better, there was little anyone could have done to save the merged railroad. Bankruptcy, of course, did not mean the trains stopped running, and, as we will see below, a temporary public-sector solution was found to rescue the eastern railroads.

Meanwhile, other railroads, too, were falling down like flies hit by a spray of insecticide. The Jersey Central and the Boston & Maine had already gone bankrupt before the Penn Central collapsed. The Lehigh Valley declared bankruptcy two days after the Penn Central, and another major eastern railroad, the Reading, followed suit fifteen months later. Then came Hurricane Agnes in June 1972, which wrecked the economics of several more railroads.

First, though, the crisis in the passenger rail industry that had been brought to a head by the collapse of the Penn Central had put the government under pressure to find a solution, as it could not simply allow passenger rail to die. Rather ironically, given Americans' previous well-established hostility toward the railroad companies, in 1969 and 1970 the public clamor to keep the trains running had become louder and louder. It was in small-town America, where people did not have access to an airport but saw their passenger train clanking through every day, even though most never ventured onto it, that the pressure was most strongly expressed. The local congressman (or -woman) whose livelihood depended on their votes was easy to get on their side, and a momentum built up to save the train. Whereas these politicians might have been skeptical of the value of passenger rail services in the past, they realized that losing their hometown service was not going to look good at election time. Clearly, with the pace of closures accelerating and the Interstate Commerce Commission powerless on the sidelines in the face of these market forces, the end of all intercity passenger services appeared only a matter of time. America might not have liked the railroad companies, but they did like train travel, or at least the thought that it was available to them. A solution had to be found to prevent the death of a once great industry. And it could not be a private-sector one. The railroads, keen on concentrating on freight, would have none of it. They wanted out of the passenger rail business.

12

RENAISSANCE
WITHOUT PASSENGERS

There was only one way of saving passenger rail services, and that was government intervention. Out of the ashes of a once flourishing industry emerged Amtrak, that fantastic anomaly of modern American history, a nationally owned rail company. The federal government had, in fact, already become involved in subsidizing passenger services. After Lyndon Johnson, probably the last president who was a genuine enthusiast for rail, was reelected in 1964, he persuaded Congress to subsidize the Northeast Corridor Project, serving the major East Coast cities with new electric Metroliner trains on the New York–Washington route operated by the Pennsylvania and New Haven Railroads. The ultimate aim had been to create a 125-mph high-speed line between the two cities, but the merger of the three railroads and the subsequent collapse of the Penn Central meant that aspiration remains unfulfilled. Nevertheless, the Metroliners were a great success, tempting passengers out of cars and planes. The experiment was to prove important in the creation of Amtrak, since it showed that federally supported passenger rail could be successful.

Nevertheless, it was a difficult birth. There were fierce negotiations behind the scenes involving the railroads, Congress, the federal government, and the states. The plan to create Amtrak—*American train track,* which was initially going to be called by the awful name Railpax[1]—was first announced by the White House, now in the hands of the Republican Richard Nixon, in January 1970. Despite backroom deals involving considerable horse trading over what routes would be saved and which abandoned, in public there was not much debate, with the plan passing through both houses of Congress relatively easily. Although Nixon might have been tempted to veto such a bill, since creating a government monopoly business did not accord with his political instincts, the prospect that he might have to nationalize some of the big freight railroads ensured he signed it. The bill creating Amtrak was passed in the autumn of 1970, with the company due to come into being on May 1, 1971. When in the run-up to the starting date Amtrak's president, Roger Lewis, a former chief executive of a defense contractor with no railroad experience, announced that 110 of the 259 intercity routes covered by passenger services would be cut, there was a predictable outcry, and various last-minute attempts were made both in Congress and through the courts to derail the process. They all failed, however, and America gained its first-ever national rail service operating in all but a couple of the mainland states. Amtrak's network was "just a skeleton of a skeleton," as so many services had already been closed down by the private railroads with the permission of the Interstate Commerce Commission, and Amtrak was not even in a position to run all the promised routes on day one. Twenty railroads, all but six of those eligible, agreed to provide services for Amtrak. To join, they had to make a payment equivalent to a year's expected loss on passenger services and provide the rolling stock and other equipment necessary to run services. If that sounds onerous, there was a strong negative incentive to join because to refuse meant agreeing to continue to run their existing passenger trains for another four years. Since these services were invariably loss making, throwing in their lot with Amtrak seemed the least-worst option. The railroads would supply crews to operate the trains, but the on-board staff, such as catering staff and porters, were to be Amtrak employees. It was, as George Douglas puts it, "a typically American compromise—the kind of thing that makes no one totally happy."[2]

Amtrak was given an annual subsidy of just $40 million and a loan of $100 million to start with and then expected to become self-sufficient within five years. It was a Band-Aid solution that was not supposed to last, but in fact Amtrak has survived to this day, thanks to political support from some quarters and the reluctance of the federal government to allow rail passenger services to disappear. Amtrak was founded on a lie, a big lie, and has suffered ever since. Ostensibly, it was created as a "for-profit" company that might need a bit of a leg up initially with subsidy, but was then expected to stand on its own two feet. The stark truth is that for the United States to retain a passenger rail service, Amtrak or its successors would have to remain a publicly funded and subsidized company permanently, and even to recognize that reality is unpalatable for many American politicians. Jim McClellan, the key official in the railroad division of the Department of Transportation, admitted that promoting Amtrak as a conventional profit-seeking company was a great deception yet absolutely necessary to win over the politicians to the idea: "We did not put all our cards on the table. We bent the truth. That's politics."[3] In fact, profitability was always a pipe dream, as it is with most passenger railroads across the world, but the notion that getting into the black was always around the corner, let alone remotely feasible, would stymie the development of America's passenger rail service. Profitability was, after all, never a requirement for the road network.

Amtrak did not always live up to its first slogan, "We're making the trains worth traveling again." In the early days, its trains were run in all kinds of random liveries and in such a poor condition that at one point in the mid-1970s, "these rolling junk boxes were catching fire at the rate of one a day."[4] And in its efforts to be trendy, Amtrak made embarrassing mistakes, such as outfitting its female employees in hot pants. In the good times, such as the mid-1980s when airlines were doing badly or angering their passengers with lousy service and the economy was booming, it attracted extra passengers, but the complicated nature of railroad economics and the parsimony of the federal government toward Amtrak meant it could never respond adequately by putting on supplementary services or buying additional coaches. That is summed up by a bald statistic: the total government subsidy to Amtrak since its creation in 1971 amounts to less than one year's federal funding for the highways.

Amtrak's hopes of achieving profitability in the early days were made even less likely because of the age and condition of the equipment it inherited. Those lovely passenger cars introduced twenty or thirty years previously to carry passengers across the prairies and mountains of the West or down to Florida were now riddled with rust. The subsidies were nowhere near enough to cover operating expenses, let alone the need for new investment, but then salvation came in the form of a crisis, the oil-price hikes of the mid-1970s. Higher fuel prices pushed up the numbers traveling by train, and the Nixon administration was forced to increase Amtrak's subsidy to $650 million per year. By 2011, that had risen to $1.4 billion (though in real terms this represented a cut, since in 1971 money it was worth around $460 million). This is the result of the regular crises that, over the years, have on several occasions pushed Amtrak to the brink of collapse, usually during the administrations of Republican presidents elected on the basis that they would cut back its subsidies. In the event, like a damsel rescued from a burning castle, Amtrak is plucked to safety at the last moment with emergency funding but never any recognition of its long-term needs. Hence, cost cutting, paring back, reducing the number of trains, and scrimping on services such as meals have been the order of the day throughout its forty-year history. As a result, Amtrak has been dogged by tales of poor performance and service all through its history, though on some lines it has earned plaudits for its trains. Every time Amtrak needs new rolling stock, or wants to boost services, the federal government has stalled and tried to avoid putting in extra money. But then often it has relented, thanks to lobbying and the lack of an alternative. Amtrak has, too, to its credit, played a major role in saving and refurbishing some of the remarkable stations it inherited, such as Boston's South Station and Union Station in Washington, DC.

By the 1990s, Amtrak had been allowed to buy new coaches and even acquired a few sections of track in the Northeast corridor and Michigan, making it far easier to operate on those sections. However, hamstrung by federal control, the lack of funds for investment, and the harsh economics of the railroad, Amtrak has always been something of a Cinderella service. As an article in *Trains* magazine on Amtrak's fortieth anniversary suggested, "Despite oil price spikes in 2008 and 2011, sustained reliable funding for Amtrak seems as elusive as ever."[5]

The problem is that Amtrak is not really a national rail service in the European sense and provides a regular and frequent service only in the Northeast corridor, in California (where passenger numbers have increased dramatically), and between a few city pairs such as Chicago–Milwaukee and Chicago–St Louis. Elsewhere, with frequencies of one train per day or even just three per week, it is more akin to a rail-tour company than a conventional regular rail service. Indeed, some of those places may well just have a train at 4:00 a.m. in the morning, hardly conducive to attracting a high level of customers. Travel on these long-distance trains, some of which take more than two days to reach their destinations, is invariably more expensive than flying and therefore attracts only a limited market of older people with time on their hands and those who dislike taking to the air. The trains, too, run to far more lax schedules than the services they replaced, even though they often retain the traditional names like Sunset Limited and California Zephyr. The meal service offers fairly basic American food, served with none of the panache of the famous old prestige trains.

Amtrak's original remit excluded commuter services. Here too, though, government help was on the way, as in the 1970s several states recognized the need to subsidize these lines. In addition to New York's ownership of the Long Island Rail Road, the States of New Jersey, Massachusetts, and Pennsylvania also began to support their local services. In 1982, the law was changed to allow Amtrak to operate commuter services as a contractor on behalf of local transit authorities, and although it has recently lost some contracts to private operators, it still runs local services in several states.

With passenger rail services saved (sort of), the crisis for the freight railroads had to be addressed. Whereas the collapse in the passenger business was understandable given the advent of the car and the airplane, the losses mounting up in the railroads' freight business, the mainstay of their business for most of their history, were both less comprehensible and more threatening to their very survival. There was, indeed, a period in the 1970s when it was conceivable that the railroad business might have disappeared completely in America, apart perhaps from a handful of lines carrying coal or other minerals.

This crisis was the result of the harsh realities of railroad economics in the face of competition, but also because of errors made by railroad bosses and the failure of the regulator to realize that times had changed. The railroads lost whole chunks of their freight business in the decades after the Second World War. Virtually every category of freight was declining. Gasoline had gone over to pipelines, and livestock fared better in trucks, where it could be better looked after. According to Saunders, "While fresh vegetable was holding up, fresh fruit especially from Florida, was moving by truck—45 per cent in 1950, 72 per cent in 1963. Finished manufactured goods were shifting to trucks because of faster door-to-door service and gentler handling."[6]

The main response by the railroads was to moan, leading to this period being dubbed, rather unfairly since many of their complaints were valid, the "Crying Towel Years." They would argue that the odds were stacked against them by the government and all the factors outlined above and that they were unfairly treated. Their response was to cut back on services, close lines, and hope that sufficient savings could be made. They never were. The railroads started first to lose, then to hemorrhage, money. However, despite these losses, there was still a paradox. As Saunders suggests, "Freight transportation by rail in the 1970s was not like the horse and buggy," a technology that had had its day and could be superseded. Railroads, he contended, "were still the assembly line that connected a diverse, specialized, interdependent economy, and they were troubled—and no one knew what to do about it."[7] While the railroads were indeed losing various types of business, overall not only were they carrying more freight than ever before, but they were also becoming more efficient. They were cutting out loss-making mileage—with half the nation's network being closed between 1930 and 1980—and were gradually eating away at the labor practices that were so costly to them.

The constraints imposed on the railroads by overbearing regulation were highlighted by a prolonged fight between Southern Railway and the Interstate Commerce Commission over freight rates, known as the "Big John" case. In the early 1960s, the Southern invested millions of dollars on its track to enable it to support far bigger grain hoppers than previously. Rather than the twenty-five-ton limit of its old boxcars, its new "Big John" hoppers could hold one hundred tons each and were far easier to unload. Using them, the rate to carry grain between St. Louis and Gainesville, Georgia, fell from $10.50 per ton to less than $4.00, transforming the economy of cattle raising in the South: "For the first time, cattle in large numbers could be raised and fattened on cheap western grain in the mild climate of the South," demonstrating yet again the ability of the railroad to open new markets.[8] Indeed, food prices for many people would fall as a result. However, the commission did not like the arrangement, because rival Granger railroads that did not have the new equipment would be put out of business. Everyone was against the plan: the truckers who were undercut, the owners of barges still used on government-owned inland waterways, and of course the rival railroads. Far from complimenting the Southern on offering cheaper rates, the ICC refused to sanction them, and it took three rounds of court cases, and several years' battle, before, at last, in 1965, the way was cleared for the reductions. It was a landmark decision that paved the way for later deregulation.

The railroads also realized that consolidation and mergers would reduce costs and make them more efficient. The Chesapeake & Ohio, one of the more innovative big railroads, acquired both the Baltimore & Ohio and the Western Maryland in the early 1960s, while the Norfolk Western took on, among others, the Virginian and the Nickel Plate & Wabash, and eventually merged with the Southern in 1982. These mergers improved the financial position of the railroads concerned, but the industry as a whole was in a parlous state, not least because it was still constrained by regulation while facing unprecedented competition. Consequently, the decade of the 1970s was a time of great trauma for the industry and for the politicians who sought to find a solution that did not result in their closure but that, at the same time, did not cost the government huge amounts of money. Despite this being a period before environmentalism became fashionable, there was an awareness that closure of the railroads would have put an intolerable burden on the nation's highway system, since one train can take as many as 280 trucks off the road. The freight railroads therefore stuttered into the 1970s with no solution in sight, but it soon became obvious that the industry needed a complete overhaul if it was going to survive. The crisis came to a head in 1973 when, despite the freight railroads carrying more tonnage than ever before, several were already bankrupt or on the point of collapse. Penn Central, being run by a judge, threatened to stop all operations if it did not receive government aid by October 1. Yet, given the oil crisis, the railroads, which routinely use less than a quarter the amount of oil per ton mile than trucks, were proving their worth, while being unable to make a profit. The various bankrupt railroads were being kept solvent by temporary loans from the federal government, but the situation could not last. Numerous ideas were tossed into the debate, ranging from paring back the railroads to a small profitable rump—always the nirvana of governments restructuring railroads, but equally always unattainable, as each branch that is cut off reduces the carryings on the so-called profitable core—to creating a large public-sector national railroad company, a kind of American British Railways. This was far too socialistic for Nixon, or indeed Congress, who both desperately wanted a private-sector solution.

Inevitably, there was a compromise, and under the Regional Rail Reorganization Act of 1973 a huge conglomerate of seven bankrupt railroads, centered around the Penn Central and including the Erie, the Lackawanna, and the Lehigh Valley, was formed to maintain freight services in the key Northeast region. Called Conrail, at first it lost billions of dollars, and it needed another crucial legislative change to save American freight, the Staggers Act, named after its promoter, Harley Staggers, the Democratic congressman who steered it through Congress in 1980. The act finally deregulated the rail industry, repealing the legislation that had created the Interstate Commerce Commission nearly a century previously. It was fifty years too late, but was passed just in time to save the industry from collapse. At last, the railroads could set their own rates for carriage, which meant they could ensure that they were high enough to allow them to invest in improvements and earn their shareholders a reasonable rate of return. The carriage of coal, grain, cars, and intermodal containers—which could be used on both trucks and trains—grew rapidly, as the railroads were able to offer flexible and more attractive rates. The railroads were also allowed to close lines without seeking permission, which meant they could mothball unprofitable routes. The results were immediate. In 1981 Conrail made a small profit, and other railroads set about rationalizing their operations. Labor was shed, but the remaining workers were still well paid and unionized. Within ten years, the industry's costs had been halved, and most railroads were well on the road to regular profitability. There were hiccups on the way, however. Union Pacific, for example, suffered a Penn Central–style meltdown in 1997 when its merger with Southern Pacific proved to be an administrative nightmare. All the same, scenes that had attended the Penn Central debacle were reenacted, this time around Houston, its hub, with traffic getting lost, trains being held for days, desperate shippers searching for their railcars, and the company share price plummeting. It took two years to sort out and became so renowned as an example of incompetent management that it was even used as a joke on The Simpsons.

The measure of the turnaround in the industry can be gauged by the fact that in 1986, Conrail was privatized in what was the biggest-ever share placing in Wall Street history, worth $1.65 billion. From the sale of Conrail, which was later broken up largely into its old Pennsylvania and New York Central components and sold to Norfolk Southern and CSX, respectively, and a series of mergers, the industry sorted itself out into seven huge railroads, two of which are Canadian, called Class I and defined as having a turnover in excess of around $400 million; around thirty regional companies; and more than five hundred "mom-and-pop" railroads, short lines mostly serving one customer and feeding into the network, some of which are owned by bigger corporations. Although closures continue, there have been reopenings too, and overall more than a third of American rail mileage has survived, with 94,000 miles in use, more than eight times the size of the whole of the UK's system. The railroads carry an impressive 40 percent of American freight, measured in ton miles, a far higher percentage than in any other country. They have recovered enough to again be called the backbone of the nation's infrastructure, unheralded by the vast majority of Americans and for the most part invisible to them because of the lack of a truly national passenger rail network. People remember the passenger trains that they, or their parents, traveled on, but they do not see today's flourishing industry, since so many stations have now long since disappeared. The railroads are so invisible that to counter this in Seattle, a little viewing platform has been built where the Union Pacific and Burlington lines cross so that parents can take their children to look at the "choo-choos," which, of course, are almost all freight trains.[9]

The rail revolution instigated by the industry's financial crisis and the Staggers Act has not all been plain sailing. The fundamentals of railroad economics in the private sector are still harsh. The railroads have to tread a careful line between, on the one hand, investing for new capacity, which is essential to keep growing and to accommodate the new traffic seeking to use the railroad, which remains the most efficient long-distance carrier by far, and, on the other, keeping investors happy by paying sufficiently high dividends. Wall Street, just like the City of London, is addicted to short-term profits, and railroads are, by their very nature, long-term businesses that eat up billions in investment. The Union Pacific, the second biggest of the Class I railroads,[10] which now manages more than 32,000 route miles—three times the size of the whole UK network—has to spend, for example, around $1.7 billion annually just on maintaining and renewing its track and a similar amount in new investment. It is big business and always vulnerable to the vagaries of the economy, though actually the industry has ridden through the 2008 downturn and subsequent recession in remarkably good shape.

The railroad industry deserves credit for its ability to have exploited deregulation successfully. Other industries that have been deregulated, such as telecoms and aviation, have not enjoyed similar success, as unfettered competition and tearing up the rule book do not necessarily lead to profitability. The airlines, for example, had to be bailed out to the tune of $15 billion following 9/11 and have consistently needed to resort to Chapter 11 of the US Bankruptcy Code, which protects ailing companies from their creditors during economic downturns. The railroads, on the other hand, have consistently prospered since the Staggers Act. The current profitability of the US freight railroads has, however, come at a price for passenger rail. The freight railroads control the system, with the exception of the sections of track owned by Amtrak in the Northeast, and they are reluctant—to put it mildly—to accept more passenger services on their tracks. Moreover, freight trains generally have priority over passenger services. (America is one of the few countries in the world where this is the case.) Sitting in sidings while freight trains trundle by is not an attractive proposition for most passengers. The extent of freight's dominance is well illustrated by the refusal of CSX to allow the local commuter service extra trains to serve the Baltimore Orioles baseball stadium because it claimed there were not enough train paths. Yet the proximity to the railroad had precisely been one of the reasons for the location of the Orioles stadium when it was built in 1992. This is just a microcosm of the tension between the freight railroads, on the one hand, and the various local transit authorities and Amtrak, on the other. Each time a state or a transit authority seeks to boost train services, there are fierce negotiations over the extra cost and the capacity of the line. On several occasions, local authorities have had to fund improvements to the track in order to obtain train paths for their services. In truth, as already stated, for most of their history, most railroads have primarily been freight carriers, and it is that history that dictates the situation today.

Amtrak's decision to focus so much on long-distance, low-frequency trains was a mistake, although understandable because of political pressures from members of Congress who did not wish to lose their local trains. In fact, railroads function best in three markets—heavy freight, commuter networks, and passenger services between large cities spaced a couple or so hours apart—and there are many city pairs in the United States that would benefit enormously from a regular European-type train connection. Yet meeting such demand is very difficult for Amtrak. It is a government agency, and therefore not able to operate with commercial freedom. Worse, any new service requires subsidy at least in the short term—and perhaps forever—and therefore there is a great reluctance by both state and federal governments to sanction any such initiative. Moreover, in the present structure, there is no way for private investors who might be willing to part-fund a scheme to be involved in passenger rail.

In the 1990s, ambitious plans to connect the country with a network of high-speed trains were announced, and as a result Amtrak launched its Acela Express service between Washington and New York in December 2000. However, these ambitions have largely foundered under the twin difficulties of cost and the hostility of the freight railroads, although the Acela services, operated with new high-speed trains, have proved popular and profitable. While the Acela is sometimes referred to as America's only high-speed service, it does not really qualify as such since by European or Asian standards it actually runs quite slowly. Although the trains are capable of running as fast as 165 mph, well above the normally accepted high-speed definition of 125 mph, the fastest services average only about 80 mph, because they have to share tracks with conventional trains and there is not enough money to upgrade much of the nineteenth-century infrastructure. Moreover, the cost of buying the equipment was greatly inflated because of the particularly onerous safety rules, which require far higher crashworthiness standards than elsewhere. This is because American railroad safety has continued to be governed by the idea of reducing the damage resulting from accidents rather than trying to prevent them completely, the philosophy that prevails in Europe.

Moreover, Amtrak, always losing money on its long-distance trains, and forever starved of sufficient funds, has never had the resources or the political backing to develop a truly efficient railroad on its key northeastern network. The fact that in 2010 domestic aviation carried 677 million people whereas Amtrak proudly announced it had passed the 30 million mark for the first time reveals the size of the task facing the railroads in their efforts to claim a share of the intercity business, but is also evidence of their potential for growth. There are many lost opportunities even where there is a railroad. For example, the 128-mile route between San Diego and Los Angeles has more than twenty round-trip flights a day because the dozen daily trains take just under three hours, an average speed of not much over 40 mph. A faster and more frequent rail service would undoubtedly take the planes out of the air, given the hassle of air travel, just as in England, where, for example, there are no direct flights between London and Birmingham, the same distance apart, but which benefit from more than one hundred trains per day in each direction.

Barack Obama's $9 billion stimulus package for what was rather misleadingly called "high-speed rail" in 2009 was designed to address this issue by stimulating train travel on various routes, either with improvements to existing lines or in other cases the construction of new high-speed lines. It has had a rocky ride, a reflection yet again of American ambivalence toward the railroads. Originally intended to create ten high-speed corridors and fund a variety of other rail projects, nearly all the money has now been focused on improving services on a half-dozen existing links, such as Seattle–Portland and Chicago–St. Louis, but the biggest chunk of money has been allocated to the development of the controversial nearly $100 billion California high-speed rail scheme linking Los Angeles and San Francisco and eventually intended to connect several other major cities. Strong initial support for California's ambitious high-speed plans turned into a strong majority against the scheme once the local media started highlighting the proposed cost (originally quoted at $35 billion), the timetable (completion will now not be until midcentury), and the need to demolish hundreds of homes on the route.

Hostility toward the very idea of rail, often presented as an alien socialist concept by right-wing politicians oblivious to the history of their own country and the railroads' role in creating it, is never far below the surface. This is evidenced by the fact that Republican administrations in Florida, Wisconsin, and Ohio have rejected being involved in the stimulus package, sending back $2 billion in funding to the federal government because they did not want to be burdened by the long-term costs of running railroads. Partly, this response was inevitable. The Obama plan was a hodgepodge of schemes and ideas with the understandable but misconceived aim of stimulating the economy with a classic Keynesian package of measures rather than as a way of reviving passenger rail in the United States.

Commuter rail and indeed streetcars, now called "light rail," have enjoyed a revival, as public money has paid for much-needed investment in new trains and improved infrastructure. In many cities, it soon became obvious that allowing suburban services, often well patronized, to die was a mistake, given the congestion on the roads, and large-scale closures essentially ended by the early 1970s. Already, more-enlightened cities were expanding or coordinating their systems. Northern Illinois, centered on Chicago, is illustrative of the way that commuter rail and public transportation services have generally enjoyed a revival in several forward-looking cities. The creation of the Regional Transportation Authority in 1973, which was approved in a highly controversial and narrow vote, enabled a wide variety of local commuter services to be coordinated under a new brand name, Metra. The authority took over the commuter services of the bankrupt Rock Island in 1980 and subsequently the local routes of the Milwaukee Road when it went bust and the Illinois Central's electric line. Add in services run on a contract basis by the Burlington Northern and the Union Pacific, as well as the Chicago L and several other lines, and the result has been the creation of a busy commuter network carrying more than three hundred thousand people on an average weekday. This type of initiative was replicated across the country, and as George Douglas, writing in 1992, suggested, "with this infusion of public aid, suburban train service in the major cities where it once flourished— New York, Boston, Chicago and Philadelphia—is probably a good deal better than it was thirty years ago."[11] Investment has continued in suburban rail, and several unlikely cities such as Dallas and Albuquerque have modest rail systems; many more are under construction in a host of major cities, often reusing long-abandoned lines.

The opening of the BART (Bay Area Rapid Transit) system in the San Francisco area in 1972 marked a renewal of interest in metro lines in the United States. Although it has been riven with funding problems and technical difficulties, it has built up into a system with more than one hundred route miles and nearly four hundred thousand daily users. Other cities such as Washington, Los Angeles, and Miami have followed suit with new heavy-rail rapid-transit systems. Streetcars have made a comeback, too. The first modern light-rail system in the United States was opened in 1981 in San Diego, and several cities followed in the 1980s, including Sacramento, Denver, and Portland. As well as its heritage cable system, San Francisco boasts modern streetcars, too. Increasing numbers of cities started looking at reviving streetcars, and in the first decade of the 2000s, more than a dozen new systems began operation. Despite the success of most schemes, new projects invariably arouse opposition, both on grounds of cost and, surprisingly, sometimes even environmental concerns.

These concerns demonstrate the way that rail remains ever controversial. Even when there is support for rail initiatives, obstacles seem to be placed in its way almost casually and with little regard for the consequences. When a 2008 collision in Los Angeles—caused by a commuter train driver being distracted by his cell phone—killed twenty-five people, the government moved swiftly to mandate that all trains should have "positive train control," an electronic signaling system that will automatically stop or slow down a train to prevent a crash if the engineer misses a red signal. Although the system may ultimately benefit the railroads marginally by making it possible to run extra trains, effectively they are being asked to pay several billion dollars—the final bill is expected to total $10 billion—to improve the safety of an industry that is already far less dangerous than any other form of land transportation. Commuter railroads, funded largely by local authorities, will in particular struggle to find the sums to pay for the installation of the equipment, for which a comprehensive risk analysis has not been produced. There have been in fact few accidents in the past that would have been prevented by this technology, yet again it appears that the government has been prepared to burden the railroads with an unfunded mandate because most politicians do not seem to understand railroads.

It is not only the government that hampers progress for the railroads. Many schemes to increase the use of some routes, or indeed reinstate working on lines, have been opposed by well-organized local interests. Ed Burkhardt, the president of Rail World, a company that owns several short lines, suggests it is a lack of historical understanding that results in the breadth of opposition: "It's a completely spoiled population that has no concept of how this country got rich. If you want to build a new railroad line anywhere in this country, you will be up against huge opposition."[12]

The ferocity with which Americans have turned against their trains can only be explained by the depth of their original love affair with them. The railroads were initially bound up deeply with the American psyche, as they were seen as the cradle of enterprise and the harbinger of progress. The relationship, though, quickly soured when the railroad barons created a climate of antipathy that seemed to gel with a suspicion that mass collective travel was not right for Americans (except, oddly, in planes!). Sarah H. Gordon probably best encapsulates the way that the affection for railroads was, so easily and so finally, transferred to the automobile. Although, in part, it was the policies of the railroad companies that raised the hackles of Americans, in truth it was their very collective nature, something that could not be remedied, that was at the root of the disenchantment:

> As railroads centralized their services, focusing on major routes between cities, the automobile provided transport that could potentially go anywhere. . . . [T]he automobile met the needs of all those fairgoers, picnickers, politicians, and others who found it more difficult to arrange for special fares and excursion trains. The train required more conformity of behavior than ever before. Sitting quietly with arms and legs inside the car, no stopping en route, no rowdiness, no drinking, for many added up to no fun and precious little individuality. The car, if nothing else, held out the promise of adventure that the railroad had offered about a hundred years before.[13]

The car remains, for most Americans, the default form of transportation. Rail is seen as a poor man's option that needs support from taxpayers, always an unpopular notion. It is easy to criticize the railroads as subsidy junkies that are a drain on government finances. However, that is more a result of presentation than substance. The modern big freight railroads have none of the self-promotion skills of their forebears and their Phoebe Snow–type publicity antics. On the contrary, the amazing boost in efficiency since the 1980s and the important role they play in carrying freight are little known to the average American, who imagines that roads are the dominant mode even for long-distance traffic, which is far from the case.

Indeed, the $1.4 billion in taxpayer subsidies that Amtrak received in 2011 has to be viewed in the context of support for roads. Depending on what factors are included, it is even possible to suggest that the cost of roads in terms of infrastructure, pollution, climate change, maintenance, road accidents, policing, and so on is greater per mile than the support given to Amtrak. Yet road spending, as in the UK, is generally viewed as investment, while spending on rail is considered subsidy. This is a long-standing gripe of rail supporters. In 1959, the Interstate Commerce Commission calculated that between 1921 and 1959, $140 billion of public money had been provided for streets and highways. Yet between 1950 and 1956, at a time when the railroads were struggling, railroads paid $1.1 billion in federal, state, and local government taxes, amounting to 11 percent of their revenue. However, the railroads themselves invest far more in their own businesses than other industries, typically around 18 percent of revenue.[14]

The paradox is that, in many respects, there is a residual affection for the railroads. On a visit to the Lancaster Quilt & Textile Museum, in Pennsylvania, I was struck by an exhibition dedicated to how Christmas had been celebrated throughout the twentieth century. There was a room for each decade, and whereas everything from the style of the trees and the baubles hung on them to the wrapping paper on the presents and the style of the greetings cards changed as time wore on, there was one ever-present gift that seemed to delight the children over the whole period: a train set. Translating that nostalgia into support for railroads in the twenty-first century is a challenge.

Although it may seem hard to be optimistic for America's passenger railroads in the face of such widespread ignorance and, at times, sheer hostility, there is in fact plenty of potential. The railroads need to be seen as modern. Amtrak's long-distance trains, evoking the nostalgia of a long-gone era, are not, in fact, a good advertisement for the railroads. They require subsidy and are effectively a tourist attraction rather than an integral part of the nation's infrastructure. Few, apart from rail fans and those with a flying phobia, would notice their abandonment. As mentioned above, the railroads are strong in three major markets, and transporting people thousands of miles slowly across a continent by rail is neither cost-effective nor particularly environmentally sustainable.

Running frequent fast services between city pairs such as New York and Washington, or Dallas and Houston, is precisely where the railroads have a key advantage and can operate on a commercial basis, although probably not if they have to bear the full costs of providing the infrastructure that their rivals on the roads do not. There is plenty of scope to exploit these opportunities, but that requires strong political direction backed by not inconsiderable sums of money. While the high cost estimates for improvements—a feature of railroads in the UK, too—understandably give ammunition to rail's opponents, there is no doubt that America would benefit enormously from a better passenger rail network. One suggestion would be to allow private companies to develop property around new rail facilities, the basis of how much rail construction is funded in Japan.

It is very likely that as the oil starts to run out and becomes very much more expensive, Americans will rue the day that they allowed their passenger rail services to decline to the point of near extinction. All that money begrudged over the years to Amtrak will not be seen as canny business but rather as a missed opportunity. Rail's energy efficiency and its comfortable travel are advantages that no other mode offers. Railroads are enjoying a revival across the world in the form of metros, light rail, suburban services, and high-speed lines for intercity travel, as well as retaining a large share of the market for freight in several countries. Perhaps nothing better illustrates the reinvention of rail in the twenty-first century than the fact that Saudi Arabia, the world's biggest oil producer, is building major new lines for both freight and people across the country. Nearby Dubai, that town built in the desert on the basis of the ubiquity of the car, has opened two metro lines stretching forty miles and has plans for two more.

Can America join in this rail renaissance? In a way, it has already done so. Its freight railroads are very successful and profitable and have ridden out the recent recession in a remarkably healthy state. American railroads carry more freight than any other system in the world apart from Russia. Warren Buffett, the legendary investor and stock market player, who bought the Burlington Northern Santa Fe Railway in 2009 for $26 billion, does not back losers. He is a philanthropist, too, and stated clearly that the environmental advantages of rail were one of the reasons that prompted his investment. The railroads' construction of new tracks to carry coal from the

Powder River Basin in Wyoming is another major success story, as production has expanded dramatically because of the relatively "clean" nature of the coal mandated by the Clean Air Act of 1970. The area now provides 40 percent of America's total needs, serving more than forty power stations from Texas to Ontario, Canada. Starting with a single-track line built in the 1970s, the railroads have invested more than $2 billion to build or refurbish hundreds of miles of track to serve the mines. Although there have been problems in meeting the demand, consolidation of the railroads involved— it is now a joint operation between Union Pacific and Burlington Northern Santa Fe—has resulted in a smooth-running operation that runs up to eighty trains per day on the track heading east out of the area. Each train consists of between 125 and 150 cars, making it the line with the heaviest annual load in the world. Again, it is a success story that has attracted little attention in the wider public. The huge double-stack container trains that run from the Pacific Coast to Chicago and beyond, and which necessitated many parts of the old transcontinental lines being double-tracked, and the coal traffic from the Appalachians to the East Coast are other success stories of the freight railroads.

In terms of suburban and commuter rail, numerous cities have recognized their importance as a way of reducing congestion. There is, too, a hidden benefit, one that is rarely discussed. It is noticeable that New Yorkers, who have by far the best public transportation system in America, are fitter and healthier than Americans elsewhere, thanks to their high use of railroads and their consequent readiness to walk. New York's Metropolitan Transit Authority is struggling to keep up with rising demand and is spending $3 billion on extending the Long Island Rail Road from its present cramped terminal in Penn Station to Grand Central and on to Queens.

Every American who travels to Europe and sees the way that the railroads have survived and flourished in the twenty-first century is a potential convert to rail. Amtrak's recent surge in passenger numbers at a time of great economic difficulty suggests there is much latent demand. Where there is a reasonable service, such as in the Northeast or on some lines out of Chicago, young people, perhaps less hooked on cars than their parents, are being attracted onto trains because traveling on them means they can still use their cell phones, laptops, and other electronic devices. The railroads have a 40 percent share of the New York–Boston rail-air market, and it could be much more if the trains were faster. Or indeed, if gas prices rise even further.

The harsh truth, however, is that America will not get a national railroad network, high-speed or otherwise, without a more radical and comprehensive strategy than was contained in the stimulus package, which was an attempt to please everyone and ended up being ineffective. Nevertheless, much can and should be done. The less newsworthy or dramatic development of suburban rail systems and light-rail networks may be a better way of initially getting more people quickly onto the railroads than the big-ticket, high-speed rail schemes promoted by a government eager to attract the headlines. The fact that the stimulus package is concentrating on a few key corridors is the right way to go, but it would be better to do a few cheaper ones rather than throw vast amounts of money at schemes like California's high-speed rail project that are unlikely to see the light of day for a generation or more, if ever. America could enjoy a new age of the train. Environmental conditions may again make flying difficult or expensive. Cars are losing their allure and are unsuitable for many long journeys. America needs to relearn the joys of railroads that have served them so well in the past and, indeed, continue to do so today, albeit invisibly.

Notes

CHAPTER 1. THE RAILROADS WIN OUT

1. The British sections of this chapter are based partly on my earlier book *Fire & Steam*.

2. Often spelled "waggonways."

3. Jack Simmons and Gordon Biddle, *The Oxford Companion to British Railway History* (Oxford University Press, 1997), 567.

4. As with most of these early developments, their precise origin is subject to debate.

5. George Rogers Taylor, *The Transportation Revolution, 1815–1860* (1951; reprint, Harper Torchbooks, 1968), 56.

6. Ibid., 57.

7. Ibid., 63; Thomas Crump, *A Brief History of the Age of Steam* (Robinson, 2007), 83.

8. Taylor, *Transportation Revolution*, 55.

9. Ibid., 15.

10. Ibid., 21.

11. Technically, West Virginia did not exist at that time, as it was still part of Virginia.

12. It eventually became part of Highway 40.

13. Ibid., 26, 29.

14. Albro Martin, *Railroads Triumphant* (Oxford University Press, 1992), 8; Taylor, *Transportation Revolution*, 28.

15. Francis T. Evans, "Roads, Railways, and Canals: Technical Choices in 19th-Century Britain," *Technology and Culture* 22 (1981).

16. It can still be seen in the Conservatoire National des Arts et Métiers in Paris.

17. They were not yet chartered as cities.

18. *Rocket* was then merely a description of a firework rather than a spaceship, though some had been used for military purposes, too.

19. Now, rather oddly, called Jim Thorpe, after the celebrated Native American–European American athlete.

20. Quoted in Dee Brown, *Hear That Lonesome Whistle Blow: Railroads in the West* (1977; reprint, Touchstone, 1994), 22. There are other claimants for this feat, notably John Stevens, the early railroad enthusiast who laid out a circular track in his garden and built a small steam engine, the sixteen-foot-long Steam Waggon, to run on it, but in reality it was little more than a toy.

21. Sarah H. Gordon, *Passage to Union: How the Railroads Transformed American Life, 1829–1929* (Elephant Paperbacks, 1997), 27.

22. Officially known as the South Carolina Railroad.

23. John F. Stover, *American Railroads* (University of Chicago Press, 1961), 15; Stewart H. Holbrook, *The Story of American Railroads* (Bonanza Books, 1947), 23.

24. Most accounts suggest he was black, but this may well be motivated by racism.

25. George H. Douglas, *All Aboard: The Railroad in American Life* (Paragon House, 1992), 26.

26. Hamburg is now a completely moribund place.

27. John Latrobe, quoted on the website www.eyewitnesstohistory.com/tom thumb.htm. There is a full-scale model of the locomotive in the Smithsonian Museum in Washington, DC.

28. Holbrook, *Story of American Railroads,* 23.

29. This figure comes from the very comprehensive website www.oldrailhistory .com, which includes some very basic railroads not counted by official sources but whose inclusion it justifies with a definition available on the site. The variation is small, however, and the figure of 987 miles given for the end of 1835 can be taken as the best estimate.

CHAPTER 2. A PASSIONATE AFFAIR

1. *Bloodgood v. Mohawk & H.R.R.,* 18 Wend. 9, 48 (N.Y. Ct. Err. 1837).

2. Quoted in George H. Douglas, *All Aboard: The Railroad in American Life* (Paragon House, 1992), 37, 75.

3. Ibid., 75, 76.

4. Sarah H. Gordon, *Passage to Union: How the Railroads Transformed American Life, 1829–1929* (Elephant Paperbacks, 1997), 19.

5. Douglas, *All Aboard,* 77.

6. As a back-of-the-envelope calculation, say enough to support 150 miles of line, or say a subsidy of 2.5 percent, given there were around 4,000 miles by then.

7. Stewart H. Holbrook, *The Story of American Railroads* (Bonanza Books, 1947), 40–41.

8. James A. Ward, *Railroads and the Character of America, 1820–1887* (University of Tennessee Press, 1986), 28.

9. Charles Caldwell, "Thoughts on the Moral and Other Indirect Influences of the Rail-Roads," *New England Magazine* 2 (January–June 1832): 299.

10. Ward, *Railroads and the Character of America,* 75, 80, 57 (emphasis in the original).

11. Ibid., 57, 93.

12. The term *booster spirit* was first mentioned by Daniel Boorstin.

13. Even modern trains struggle up anything greater than 1–2 percent.

14. *Navvies* is an abbreviation of *navigators,* for these men were the direct descendants of the workers who had built the canals. They are described in a wonderfully thorough and evocative book, *The Railway Navvies* by Terry Coleman (Hutchinson, 1965).

15. Theodore Kornweibel Jr., *Railroads in the African American Experience* (Johns Hopkins University Press, 2010), 11.

16. Ibid., 18.

17. Ibid., 15; William D. Middleton, George M. Smerk, and Roberta L. Diehl, eds., *Encyclopedia of North American Railroads* (Indiana University Press, 2007), 454.

18. Even today there are still nearly two hundred thousand such crossings that result in accidents that cause a couple of hundred deaths annually.

19. Dee Brown, *Hear That Lonesome Whistle Blow: Railroads in the West* (1977; reprint, Touchstone, 1994), 24; Holbrook, *Story of American Railroads,* 31.

20. Ward, *Railroads and the Character of America,* 31.

21. Quoted in Charlton Ogburn, *Railroads: The Great American Adventure* (National Geographic Society, 1977), 16.

22. Jim Harter, *World Railways of the Nineteenth Century: A Pictorial History in Victorian Engravings* (Johns Hopkins University Press, 2005), 248.

23. Holbrook, *Story of American Railroads,* 35.

24. George Rogers Taylor, *The Transportation Revolution, 1815–1860* (1951; reprint, Harper Torchbooks, 1968), 53–54.

25. Mark Aldrich, *Death Rode the Rails* (Johns Hopkins University Press, 2006), 13, 14.

26. John F. Stover, *American Railroads* (University of Chicago Press, 1961), 18.

27. According to US Census figures, though some historians question the accuracy of this statistic.

28. We even find a particularly incongruous *& Eastern* in Chapter 10.

29. George Rogers Taylor and Irene D. Neu, *The American Railroad Network, 1861–1890* (1956; reprint, University of Illinois Press, 2003), xi.

30. Douglas, *All Aboard*, 28.

CHAPTER 3. THE RAILROADS TAKE HOLD

1. Andrew Dow, *Dow's Dictionary of Railway Quotations* (Johns Hopkins University Press, 2006), 6.

2. George H. Douglas, *All Aboard: The Railroad in American Life* (Paragon House, 1992), 31.

3. Ibid., 72, 35.

4. In American literature it is sometimes referred to as the world's first trunk railroad, which is very far from accurate, since several European countries already boasted substantial main lines.

5. Stewart H. Holbrook, *The Story of American Railroads* (Bonanza Books, 1947), 60.

6. There was, however, a 1946 book by Edward Hungerford, *Men of Erie*, published by Random House.

7. See my earlier book *Blood, Iron, and Gold* (PublicAffairs, 2010) for a description of the struggle to create a railroad through the Western Ghats.

8. The origin of the name is unclear. It is also uncertain whether the animosity between the two groups, which flared up in various parts of the United States on canal and railroad projects, was based on religion—the Corkonians as Catholic, the Fardowners as Protestant.

9. Holbrook, *Story of American Railroads*, 61.

10. Ibid., 62, 63.

11. H. Roger Grant, *Erie Lackawanna: Death of an American Railroad* (Stanford University Press, 1994), 1.

12. Ironically, in recent times China has built many hundreds of miles of its high-speed rail network using a similar system of a raised railroad on piles.

13. Initially, it was four feet and eight inches, but the half inch was soon added.

14. Mark Reutter, introduction to *The American Railroad Network, 1861–1890*, by George Rogers Taylor and Irene D. Neu (1956; reprint, University of Illinois Press, 2003), xii.

15. Ibid.

16. Albro Martin, *Railroads Triumphant* (Oxford University Press, 1992), 46.

17. Holbrook, *Story of American Railroads,* 61.

18. Now Harriman, New York.

19. The word *order* refers, here, to a signaling instruction.

20. Holbrook, *Story of American Railroads,* 68.

21. A railroad term for drivers and other crew who ride in the coaches as passengers.

22. Martin, *Railroads Triumphant,* 260; Holbrook, *Story of American Railroads,* 82.

23. Holbrook, *Story of American Railroads,* 84.

24. Originally called the Chicago and Aurora Railroad.

25. There is, however, a through line running alongside Union Station.

26. Holbrook, *Story of American Railroads,* 139.

27. The lack of direct rail links between Chicago's various stations was fine for the first century or so while the railroads were effectively a transportation monopoly, but eventually it was to cost them dearly. (The legacy of this competition remains. In 2010, when I traveled around America by rail, I arrived from Pittsburgh in a train that terminated at Chicago's Union Station, and when the next day I headed off west for Seattle, the service left from the other side of the same building on entirely separate tracks, as even today there is no through-passenger service.)

28. John F. Stover, *American Railroads* (University of Chicago Press, 1961), 20.

29. Charles Dickens, *American Notes* (Bernhard Tauchnitz, 1842). All these quotes taken from pages 69–74. Available online at Google Books.

30. Quoted in Stover, *American Railroads,* 33.

31. Robert Louis Stevenson, *Across the Plains* (1879; reprint, Bibliobazaar, 2006), 10.

32. Holbrook, *Story of American Railroads,* 37.

33. Sarah H. Gordon, *Passage to Union: How the Railroads Transformed American Life, 1829–1929* (Elephant Paperbacks, 1997), 68.

34. Douglas, *All Aboard,* 57; Gordon, *Passage to Union,* 69.

35. Douglas, *All Aboard,* 58.

36. Tyrone Power, *Impressions of America,* www.gutenberg.org/catalog/world /readfile?fk_files=514357&pageno=53.

37. Holbrook, *Story of American Railroads,* 77.

38. Douglas, *All Aboard,* 67.

39. Anthony Burton, *On the Rails* (Aurum, 2004), 89; *New York Tribune* quoted in Holbrook, *Story of American Railroads,* 35.

40. James A. Ward, *Railroads and the Character of America, 1820–1887* (University of Tennessee Press, 1986), 66.

41. Charlton Ogburn, *Railroads: The Great American Adventure* (National Geographic Society, 1977), 17.

42. In a bizarre coincidence, one of the worst railroad disasters in postwar US railroad history occurred in September 1993 when a barge hit a bridge at Big Bayou Canot, near Mobile, Alabama, pushing the rails out of alignment and subsequently derailing an Amtrak train, which plunged into the creek, killing forty-seven people.

CHAPTER 4. THE BATTLE LINES

1. Quoted in James A. Ward, *Railroads and the Character of America, 1820–1887* (University of Tennessee Press, 1986), 45.

2. Sarah H. Gordon, *Passage to Union: How the Railroads Transformed American Life, 1829–1929* (Elephant Paperbacks, 1997), 75.

3. Ward, *Railroads and the Character of America,* 55.

4. See my earlier book *Engines of War: How Wars Were Won and Lost on the Railways* (Atlantic, 2010) for a detailed analysis.

5. Albro Martin, *Railroads Triumphant* (Oxford University Press, 1992), 15.

6. Gordon, *Passage to Union,* 138.

7. Martin, *Railroads Triumphant,* 52; John F. Stover, *American Railroads* (University of Chicago Press, 1961), 55.

8. Gordon, *Passage to Union,* 136.

9. Ibid.

10. Ibid., 137.

11. John Westwood, *Railways at War* (Osprey, 1980), 24, 21.

12. They would not, in fact, escape direct nationalization in the next major conflict, the First World War, as we will see in Chapter 9.

13. Joseph Hankey, "The Railroad War," *Trains* (March 2011): 32.

14. This was the first of two major battles at this location. To add to the confusion, they are known as the Battles of Manassas by the Confederates, who tended to name battles after towns or villages, in contrast to the Unionists, who used creeks or rivers.

15. Ibid., 27.

16. Ibid., 24.

17. Stover, *American Railroads,* 55.

18. Martinsburg later became part of West Virginia, which separated from secessionist Virginia in 1863.

19. George H. Douglas, *All Aboard: The Railroad in American Life* (Paragon House, 1992), 107.

20. James M. McPherson, *Battle Cry of Freedom: The American Civil War* (Penguin Books, 1990), 527.

21. Quoted in Charlton Ogburn, *Railroads: The Great American Adventure* (National Geographic Society, 1977), 24.

22. Quoted in Thomas Weber, *The Northern Railroads in the Civil War, 1861–1865* (1952; reprint, Indiana University Press, 1999), 144.

23. George Edgar Turner, *Victory Rode the Rails: The Strategic Place of the Railroads in the Civil War* (Bobbs-Merrill, 1953), 201.

24. Stover, *American Railroads,* 61.

25. John Buchan, *A Book of Escapes and Hurried Journeys* (Thomas Nelson and Sons, 1925), and available online (http://gaslight.mtroyal.ab.ca/gaslight/escapemn .htm). This account is based on the one in my previous book *Engines of War.*

26. Douglas, *All Aboard,* 113.

27. Stewart H. Holbrook, *The Story of American Railroads* (Bonanza Books, 1947), 122, 126.

28. John Elwood Clark, *Railroads in the Civil War: The Impact of Management on Victory and Defeat* (Louisiana State University Press, 2001), 97.

29. Some reports suggest 20,000.

30. McPherson, *Battle Cry of Freedom,* 675.

31. Westwood, *Railways at War,* 47.

32. Quoted in Weber, *Northern Railroads in the Civil War,* 199.

33. Ibid., 225.

34. Stover, *American Railroads,* 56.

35. Some recent estimates suggest that the figure may be as high as 750,000.

36. Gordon, *Passage to Union,* 146.

37. Quoted in Ogburn, *Railroads,* 23; Slason Thompson quoted in Weber, *Northern Railroads in the Civil War,* 3.

CHAPTER 5. HARNESSING THE ELEPHANT

1. Thomas Weber, *The Northern Railroads in the Civil War, 1861–1865* (1952; reprint, Indiana University Press, 1999), 43.

2. Theodore Kornweibel Jr., *Railroads in the African American Experience* (Johns Hopkins University Press, 2010), 26.

3. Dorothy R. Alder, *British Investment in American Railways, 1834–1898* (University Press of Virginia, 1970), 83.

4. David Haward Bain, *Empire Express: Building the First Transcontinental Railroad* (Viking Penguin, 1999), 17.

5. Clifford Krainik, "National Vision, Local Enterprise: John Plumbe Jr. and the Advent of Photography in Washington, DC," *Washington History* 9, no. 2 (1997–1998): 5; Dee Brown, *Hear That Lonesome Whistle Blow: Railroads in the West* (1977; reprint, Touchstone, 1994), 28.

6. Brown, *Hear That Lonesome Whistle Blow*, 32.

7. Oscar Lewis, *The Big Four* (Alfred A. Knopf, 1938), 3, 23.

8. Bain, *Empire Express*, 137.

9. Lewis, *The Big Four*, 62.

10. John F. Stover, *American Railroads* (University of Chicago Press, 1961), 75, 76.

11. Anthony Burton, *On the Rails* (Aurum, 2004), 94; Brown, *Hear That Lonesome Whistle Blow*, 13.

12. Brown, *Hear That Lonesome Whistle Blow*, 52.

13. Ibid., 58.

14. Bain, *Empire Express*, 157.

15. Brown, *Hear That Lonesome Whistle Blow*, 64, 65.

16. Stephen E. Ambrose, *Nothing Like It in the World* (Simon & Schuster, 2000), 217.

17. Henry Stanley quoted in ibid., 219; Charles Savage quoted in Brown, *Hear That Lonesome Whistle Blow*, 122.

18. According to Dodge's autobiography, quoted in Ambrose, *Nothing Like It in the World*, 220.

19. A small town exists today on the site.

20. Brown, *Hear That Lonesome Whistle Blow*, 102, 100.

21. Bain, *Empire Express*, 191.

22. Brown, *Hear That Lonesome Whistle Blow*, 85.

23. Ibid., 85.

24. Ibid., 101.

25. Ibid., 125.

26. Stewart H. Holbrook, *The Story of American Railroads* (Bonanza Books, 1947), 170.

27. It is an irony of Whitney's dream of Asian trade that today one of the main functions of the railroad lines crossing the western United States is to carry containers full of goods from China.

28. Albro Martin, *Railroads Triumphant* (Oxford University Press, 1992), 29.

29. James A. Ward, *Railroads and the Character of America, 1820–1887* (University of Tennessee Press, 1986), 99.

30. Amtrak ran its Sunset Limited service between Los Angeles and Jacksonville, Florida, from 1993 to 2005, when the track east of New Orleans was wrecked by Hurricane Katrina. In Canada, too, there have been various coast-to-coast services.

31. Richard White, *Railroaded: The Transcontinentals and the Making of Modern America* (W. W. Norton, 2011), xxi.

32. George H. Douglas, *All Aboard: The Railroad in American Life* (Paragon House, 1992), 115.

33. Keith L. Bryant Jr., introduction to *Encyclopedia of North American Railroads*, edited by William D. Middleton, George M. Smerk, and Roberta L. Diehl (Indiana University Press, 2007), 10.

CHAPTER 6. RAILROADS TO EVERYWHERE

1. Sarah H. Gordon, *Passage to Union: How the Railroads Transformed American Life, 1829–1929* (Elephant Paperbacks, 1997), 166.

2. N. J. Bell and James Arthur Ward, *Southern Railroad Man: N. J. Bell's Recollections of the Civil War Era* (Northern Illinois University Press, 2006).

3. Gordon, *Passage to Union*, 168.

4. This term comes from the Northerners' custom of carrying their personal effects in a carpetbag.

5. Gordon, *Passage to Union*, 174, 173.

6. Theodore Kornweibel Jr., *Railroads in the African American Experience* (Johns Hopkins University Press, 2010), 43, 44.

7. Ibid., 45, 44; J. C. Powell, *American Siberia; or, Fourteen Years' Experience in a Southern Convict Camp*, Reprint Series in Criminology, Law Enforcement, and Social Problems, no. 105 (1891; reprint, Patterson Smith, 1970).

8. Gordon, *Passage to Union*, 166.

9. *New York Times*, January 21, 1863, referring to the Erie Gauge War of the 1850s, described in Chapter 3.

10. It was actually the Burlington & Missouri River Railroad until it amalgamated with the Chicago, Burlington & Quincy in 1872.

11. Quoted in George H. Douglas, *All Aboard: The Railroad in American Life* (Paragon House, 1992), 170, from *Handbook for Immigrants to the United States*, published by the American Social Service Association.

12. Quoted in Dee Brown, *Hear That Lonesome Whistle Blow: Railroads in the West* (1977; reprint, Touchstone, 1994), 250.

13. Douglas, *All Aboard*, 159; Richard White, *Railroaded: The Transcontinentals and the Making of Modern America* (W. W. Norton, 2011), xxiv.

14. Stewart H. Holbrook, *The Story of American Railroads* (Bonanza Books, 1947), 213.

15. In railroad terms, a washout denotes the erosion of the track bed by flowing water, as a result of heavy rain or flooding.

16. William D. Middleton, George M. Smerk, and Roberta L. Diehl, eds., *Encyclopedia of North American Railroads* (Indiana University Press, 2007), 729.

17. A Ponzi scheme pays returns out of sums invested by other investors and therefore makes no genuine profit. It is named after Charles Ponzi, one of the first perpetrators of this type of fraud.

18. John F. Stover, *American Railroads* (University of Chicago Press, 1961), 76.

19. Ibid., 78.

20. The Great Northern's premier passenger service was named Great Northern in Hill's honor, a name that today's Chicago–Seattle Amtrak retains.

21. Ibid., 79.

22. Douglas, *All Aboard,* 160.

23. Gordon, *Passage to Union,* 158.

CHAPTER 7. GETTING BETTER ALL THE TIME

1. Several sources suggest 1836 or 1837, but this seems unlikely, as the first section of line only started operating in 1837 and through-running between Philadelphia and Chambersburg began in 1839.

2. William D. Middleton, George M. Smerk, and Roberta L. Diehl, eds., *Encyclopedia of North American Railroads* (Indiana University Press, 2007), 847.

3. *Baedeker's* quoted in Albro Martin, *Railroads Triumphant* (Oxford University Press, 1992), 51; "London parson" quoted in Dee Brown, *Hear That Lonesome Whistle Blow: Railroads in the West* (1977; reprint, Touchstone, 1994), 141.

4. Geoffrey Freeman Allen, *Luxury Trains of the World* (Bison Books, 1979), 13.

5. The Pullman conductor was not the same person as the overall train conductor.

6. Theodore Kornweibel Jr., *Railroads in the African American Experience* (Johns Hopkins University Press, 2010), 115.

7. Ibid.

8. Allen, *Luxury Trains of the World,* 16.

9. Ibid., 15.

10. This practice of ordering food by telegraph, incidentally, became very widespread in India right through the twentieth century, though there the meals were eaten on the train.

11. Allen, *Luxury Trains of the World*, 13.

12. Both quotes in Mark Aldrich, *Death Rode the Rails: American Railroad Accidents and Safety, 1828–1965* (Johns Hopkins University Press, 2006), 21.

13. As recently as June 2011, as I was writing this chapter, five people on a train were killed by a truck whose driver had presumably dozed off, slamming into the middle of an Amtrak train in Nevada.

14. Allen, *Luxury Trains of the World*, 15, 24.

15. I was amazed on my visit to Chicago in October 2010 to discover numerous such "diamond" crossings still exist, though now, happily, protected by sophisticated signaling.

16. George H. Douglas, *All Aboard: The Railroad in American Life* (Paragon House, 1992), 74.

17. Aldrich, *Death Rode the Rails*, 35.

18. Dick Nelson in Brown, *Hear That Lonesome Whistle Blow*, 175.

19. Stewart H. Holbrook, *The Story of American Railroads* (Bonanza Books, 1947), 291, 295, 297.

20. Appendix in B. A. Botkin and Alvin F. Harlow, eds., *A Treasury of Railroad Folklore* (Crown, 1953), 510.

21. Middleton, Smerk, and Diehl, *Encyclopedia of North American Railroads*, 340.

22. The Dalton legend traveled far, since, as a child in the 1960s, I read a French comic called *Spirou* (Squirrel) that featured a regular comic strip about *les frères Dalton*, a group of cowboy gangsters who were portrayed as invariably stupid and inept.

23. Sarah H. Gordon, *Passage to Union: How the Railroads Transformed American Life, 1829–1929* (Elephant Paperbacks, 1997), 155.

24. Holbrook, *Story of American Railroads*, 373; Gordon, *Passage to Union*, 164.

25. Brown, *Hear That Lonesome Whistle Blow*, 172.

26. Douglas, *All Aboard*, 179; Brown, *Hear That Lonesome Whistle Blow*, 137. The latter remark was made by Robert R. Young, president of the Chesapeake & Ohio Railroad, in the late 1940s, as he was pushing for a true transcontinental service.

27. Douglas, *All Aboard*, 181.

28. Robert Louis Stevenson, *The Amateur Emigrant* (1895; reprint, Carroll & Graf, 2002), 117.

29. Ibid., 139.

30. Brown, *Hear That Lonesome Whistle Blow*, 244.

31. Stevenson, *Amateur Emigrant,* 139. Even today Amtrak seems occasionally to delight in failing to give adequate warning, as when during my 2010 tour I was nearly left at a tiny station in Mississippi when seeking refreshments and not warned about the imminent departure, even though the crew had said we would be stopping for a while.

32. For a time, after the introduction of dining cars on the Santa Fe, Harvey provided the catering.

33. Gordon, *Passage to Union,* 224.

34. Oliver Jensen, *Railroads in America* (American Heritage, 1975), 246.

35. Middleton, Smerk, and Diehl, *Encyclopedia of North American Railroads,* 309.

36. Gordon, *Passage to Union,* 226; Kornweibel, *Railroads in the African American Experience,* 242.

CHAPTER 8. THE END OF THE AFFAIR

1. Richard White, *Railroaded: The Transcontinentals and the Making of Modern America* (W. W. Norton, 2011), xxii; James A. Ward, *Railroads and the Character of America, 1820–1887* (University of Tennessee Press, 1986), 131.

2. Sarah H. Gordon, *Passage to Union: How the Railroads Transformed American Life, 1829–1929* (Elephant Paperbacks, 1997), 8.

3. Stewart H. Holbrook, *The Story of American Railroads* (Bonanza Books, 1947), 354.

4. Ibid., 356.

5. Congress did not standardize time until 1918.

6. Ibid., 359.

7. Gordon, *Passage to Union,* 202.

8. Ibid., 212, 8.

9. The records are listed in ibid., 180.

10. Ibid., 181.

11. Ibid., 184, 285.

12. Ibid., 286.

13. Oliver Jensen, *Railroads in America* (American Heritage, 1975), 246.

14. Miami was known at the time as Fort Dallas.

15. William D. Middleton, George M. Smerk, and Roberta L. Diehl, eds., *Encyclopedia of North American Railroads* (Indiana University Press, 2007), 996.

16. Estimates vary between twenty-three and twenty-six.

17. Alfred D. Chandler Jr., *Railroads: The Nation's First Big Business* (Harcourt, Brace & World, 1965), 23.

18. Ibid., 98.

19. Ibid., 107.

20. Ibid., 129.

21. George H. Douglas, *All Aboard: The Railroad in American Life* (Paragon House, 1992), 206.

22. Robert Sobel, *Panic on Wall Street: A History of American Financial Disasters* (Macmillan, 1968), 180.

23. Widely cited but not properly sourced.

24. Chandler, *Railroads,* 130.

25. White, *Railroaded,* 440.

26. Ibid., 441.

27. John F. Stover, *American Railroads* (University of Chicago Press, 1961), 119.

28. David Mountfield, *The Railway Barons* (Osprey, 1979), 133.

29. They had to cross the isthmus by mule until the opening of the Panama Railway in 1855.

30. Holbrook, *Story of American Railroads,* 87.

31. Not to be confused with the Erie Gauge War, described in Chapter 3.

32. Leslie A. White, *Modern Capitalist Culture* (Left Coast Press, 2008), 195.

33. Douglas, *All Aboard,* 152.

34. Mountfield, *Railway Barons,* 146.

35. See Appendix B in Andrew Dow, *Dow's Dictionary of Railway Quotations* (Johns Hopkins University Press, 2006), 287, for the background to this quotation.

36. Mountfield, *Railway Barons,* 179, 182; Middleton, Smerk, and Diehl, *Encyclopedia of North American Railroads,* 719.

37. Middleton, Smerk, and Diehl, *Encyclopedia of North American Railroads,* 511; Douglas, *All Aboard,* 204.

38. Middleton, Smerk, and Diehl, *Encyclopedia of North American Railroads,* 513.

39. Ibid., 11.

40. Stover, *American Railroads,* 120.

41. Ibid., 121.

42. Henry George, "What the Railroad Will Bring Us," *Overland Monthly* (October 1868): 38.

43. Richard Saunders Jr., *Main Lines: Rebirth of the North American Railroads, 1970–2002* (Northern Illinois University Press, 2003), 30.

44. Stover, *American Railroads,* 129.

45. *Wabash, St. Louis & Pacific Railway Company v. Illinois,* 118 U.S. 557 (1886).

46. The *Chicago Inter-Ocean,* January 2, 1887, quoted in Gabriel Kolko, *Railroads and Regulation, 1877–1916* (Princeton University Press, 1965), 41.

CHAPTER 9. ALL KINDS OF TRAIN

1. John F. Stover, *American Railroads* (University of Chicago Press, 1961), 137.

2. Albro Martin, *Enterprise Denied: Origins of the Decline of American Railroads* (Columbia University Press, 1971), 17.

3. With the odd exception, such as the Western Pacific from Salt Lake City to Oakland, California.

4. Albro Martin, *Railroads Triumphant* (Oxford University Press, 1992), 342; Martin, *Enterprise Denied,* 128.

5. Martin, *Enterprise Denied,* 23.

6. Geoffrey Freeman Allen, *Luxury Trains of the World* (Bison Books, 1979), 76.

7. Martin, *Enterprise Denied,* 26.

8. She was actually briefly revived in both the late 1940s and early 1960s on trains running from Hoboken.

9. George H. Douglas, *All Aboard: The Railroad in American Life* (Paragon House, 1992), 232; Sarah H. Gordon, *Passage to Union: How the Railroads Transformed American Life, 1829–1929* (Elephant Paperbacks, 1997), 308.

10. There are a very small number of exceptions where towns have passed ordinances preventing trains from sounding their horns in an effort to give their residents a better night's sleep.

11. Martin, *Enterprise Denied,* 26.

12. Ibid., 361.

13. Douglas, *All Aboard,* 241.

14. Ibid., 247.

15. Ibid., 248, 249.

16. Robert C. Post, *Urban Mass Transit* (Johns Hopkins University Press, 2010), 50, 58.

17. Ibid., 58.

18. George W. Hilton and John F. Due, *The Electric Urban Railways in America* (Stanford University Press, 1960), 12, 25.

19. Post, *Urban Mass Transit,* 61; Paul Mees, *Transport for Suburbia: Beyond the Automobile Age* (Earthscan, 2010), 17.

20. Hilton and Due, *Electric Urban Railways in America,* 3.

21. Ibid., 23, 24.

22. Ibid., 3.

23. William D. Middleton, George M. Smerk, and Roberta L. Diehl, eds., *Encyclopedia of North American Railroads* (Indiana University Press, 2007), 411.

24. Martin, *Enterprise Denied,* 61.

25. Different sources offer alternative figures, such as 258,000 in Albro Martin's *Enterprise Denied* and 259,000 in Richard Saunders Jr.'s *Merging Lines: American Railroads, 1900–1970* (Northern Illinois University Press, 2001).

26. Martin, *Enterprise Denied*, 337; Saunders, *Merging Lines*, 36; Rea quoted in Douglas, *All Aboard*, 321.

27. Martin, *Railroads Triumphant*, 355.

28. Saunders, *Merging Lines*, 36.

CHAPTER 10. THE ROOTS OF DECLINE

1. Parts of this chapter are based on my earlier book *Blood, Iron, and Gold* (PublicAffairs, 2010).

2. Richard Saunders Jr., *Merging Lines: American Railroads, 1900–1970* (Northern Illinois University Press, 2001), 42, 45.

3. Ibid., 55.

4. Geoffrey Freeman Allen, *Railways of the Twentieth Century* (Winchmore, 1983), 70.

5. Widely quoted, including in ibid., 69.

6. Albro Martin, *Railroads Triumphant* (Oxford University Press, 1992), 121, 120.

7. Allen, *Railways of the Twentieth Century*, 9.

8. George H. Douglas, *All Aboard: The Railroad in American Life* (Paragon House, 1992), 317.

9. Martin, *Railroads Triumphant*, 359.

10. Lawrence H. Kaufman, *Leaders Count: The Story of BNSF Railway* (BNSF Railway, 2005), 74.

11. Technically, the Reconstruction Finance Corporation was created by his predecessor, Herbert Hoover, but Roosevelt greatly extended its scope and the amount of money it had at its disposal. The scheme bears an uncanny resemblance to the "quantitative easing" that has become almost routine following the banking crisis of 2008.

12. Ibid.

13. For the most part, these were technically diesel-electrics. In other words, the diesel combustion engine was used to run an electric motor that then powered the locomotive.

14. Allen, *Railways of the Twentieth Century*, 76.

15. Ibid., 76, 77.

16. Sarah H. Gordon, *Passage to Union: How the Railroads Transformed American Life, 1829–1929* (Elephant Paperbacks, 1997), 345.

17. Errol Lincoln Uys, *Riding the Rails* (Routledge, 2003), 11.

18. Welsh poet and vagabond W. H. Davies, author of *The Autobiography of a Super-Tramp* and a frequent rider of the rails in the United States and Canada in the decades on the cusp of the nineteenth and twentieth centuries, was one such victim when he fell under a train in Ontario, crushing his foot and resulting in the loss of his leg below the knee.

19. John F. Stover, *American Railroads* (University of Chicago Press, 1961), 225–226.

CHAPTER 11. A NARROW ESCAPE

1. George H. Douglas, *All Aboard: The Railroad in American Life* (Paragon House, 1992), 383.

2. Quoted in Richard Saunders Jr., *Merging Lines: American Railroads, 1900–1970* (Northern Illinois University Press, 2001), 77.

3. Ibid.; Douglas, *All Aboard*, 382.

4. Saunders, *Merging Lines*, 73.

5. Ibid., 153, 155.

6. A few trains powered by steam locomotives were run by the Grand Trunk Western in 1961.

7. Geoffrey Freeman Allen, *Luxury Trains of the World* (Bison Books, 1979), 101.

8. Saunders, *Merging Lines*, 108.

9. Ibid.

10. David Morgan, "Who Shot the Passenger Train?," *Trains* (April 1959).

11. Paul Mees, *Transport for Suburbia: Beyond the Automobile Age* (Earthscan, 2010), 17.

12. In today's money, but a precise figure is difficult to arrive at, as local road improvements were at times included in the contracts.

13. Saunders, *Merging Lines*, 107.

14. Ibid., 102.

15. Albro Martin, *Enterprise Denied: Origins of the Decline of American Railroads* (Columbia University Press, 1971), 367.

16. Rush Loving Jr., *The Men Who Loved Trains: The Story of Men Who Battled Greed to Save an Ailing Industry* (Indiana University Press, 2006), 57.

17. The Penn Central was not the only railroad that tried to set itself up as a conglomerate—bizarrely, the Illinois Central at one time owned El Paso Mexican foods.

18. Loving Jr., *Men Who Loved Trains*, 68.

19. Joseph R. Daughen and Peter Binzen, *The Wreck of the Penn Central* (Little, Brown, 1971), 339.

CHAPTER 12. RENAISSANCE WITHOUT PASSENGERS

1. Amtrak's official name is the National Railroad Passenger Corporation.

2. Richard Saunders Jr., *Main Lines: Rebirth of the North American Railroads, 1970–2002* (Northern Illinois University Press, 2003), 59; George H. Douglas, *All Aboard: The Railroad in American Life* (Paragon House, 1992), 393.

3. Don Phillips, "The Road to Rescue," *Classic Trains* (Summer 2011): 28.

4. Saunders, *Main Lines*, 59.

5. Bob Johnston, "Amtrak's Critical Turns," *Trains* (July 2011): 27.

6. Saunders, *Main Lines*, 36.

7. Ibid., 3, 21.

8. Richard Saunders Jr., *Merging Lines: American Railroads, 1900–1970* (Northern Illinois University Press, 2001), 294.

9. Others have popped up too, notably at Folkston, Georgia.

10. The Burlington Northern and Santa Fe Railway is just 150 miles longer.

11. Douglas, *All Aboard*, 255.

12. Dan Machalaba, "What to Do About NIMBYs," *Trains* (September 2010): 42–49.

13. Sarah H. Gordon, *Passage to Union: How the Railroads Transformed American Life, 1829–1929* (Elephant Paperbacks, 1997), 280.

14. John F. Stover, *American Railroads* (University of Chicago Press, 1961), 217.

A Note on Sources

Compiling a concise bibliography out of the wealth of American railroad literature is as difficult as making the choices over the content of this book. So this list is by no means comprehensive, but merely reflects my sources, prejudices, and preferences and is highly selective, as I have only included those that I found particularly useful. There are many other books that I have quoted, and the references can be found in the Notes. Nevertheless, this brief bibliography will give a few sources for further reading. I would, too, be dishonest if I did not confess to using at times that wonderful resource Wikipedia, which has definitely improved in terms of accuracy over the years, even if there are, inevitably, some errors. However, books are not infallible, either, as I have discovered when coming across conflicting sources.

First, the general books. Of course, one of the reasons I was stimulated into writing this one was the lack of a recent concise book on American railroads. Two of the best are more than a half century old. Stewart H. Holbrook's work *The Story of American Railroads* (Bonanza Books, 1947) is idiosyncratic, lengthy, anecdotal, and fun. John F. Stover's *American Railroads* (University of Chicago Press, 1961) is rather the opposite, sober and full of hard facts. Charlton Ogburn, *Railroads: The Great American Adventure* (National Geographic Society, 1977), is an eccentric pictorial account with a lot of good anecdotes, and *High Iron: A Book of Trains* (Bonanza Books, 1938) is an evocative tome by the legendary railroad writer Lucius Beebe. *Railroads Triumphant* by Albro Martin (Oxford University Press, 1992) has plenty of good history but is rather marred by the bad-tempered tone and the incoherent structure. The best of the more recent ones is probably George H. Douglas, *All Aboard: The Railroad in American Life* (Paragon House, 1992), a solid and well-written book. These general books cover the early years of the railroads, while *The Transportation Revolution, 1815–1860* (1951; reprint, Harper Torchbooks, 1968) by George Rogers Taylor puts the development of the railroads into a wider perspective.

There are numerous coffee table–type books that are dominated by pictures, and I can't really recommend any because of the lack of narrative and the rather random selection of material. The *Encyclopedia of North American Railroads* (Indiana University Press, 2007) edited by William D. Middleton, George M. Smerk, and Roberta L. Diehl, on the other hand, is thorough and informative, though as with all such books it is sometimes not as comprehensive as you expect when you are after that little nugget of information.

My focus on social history led me to two thoughtful but very different books. James A. Ward, *Railroads and the Character of America, 1820–1887* (University of Tennessee Press, 1986), examines the psychology that led to the widespread support for the railroads, while Sarah H. Gordon's *Passage to Union: How the Railroads Transformed American Life, 1829–1929* (Elephant Paperbacks, 1997) is a thorough analysis of their impact for that period and is the best sociological assessment I came across.

On the Civil War, the vast literature rarely examines the role of railroads. Two classic exceptions are Thomas Weber, *The Northern Railroads in the Civil War, 1861–1865* (1952; reprint, Indiana University Press, 1999), and George Edgar Turner, *Victory Rode the Rails: The Strategic Place of the Railroads in the Civil War* (Bobbs-Merrill, 1953). *The American Railroad Network, 1861–1890* (1956; reprint, University of Illinois Press, 2003) by George Rogers Taylor and Irene D. Neu provides an excellent perspective on how much railroads had progressed by the end of the Civil War. This is an area, I suggest, that could do with a lot more mining, and I did come across a nice ghostwritten "memoir," *Reflections of a Civil War Locomotive Engineer* by Diana Bailey Harris, based on contemporary letters (self-published, 2011).

The literature on the transcontinentals is so great that it is almost a whole category of its own and rather reflects the imbalance in American railroad history, which places far too much importance on this story in relation to the rest. I therefore confine myself to just a couple of mentions. The best standard works I found are David Haward Bain's *Empire Express* (Viking Penguin, 1999) and Wesley S. Griswold, *A Work of Giants* (Frederick Muller, 1962), but there are countless more good books. A fascinating recent addition, which questions much of the conventional thinking and many of the myths on the building of the first transcontinental, is *Railroaded* by Richard White (W. W. Norton, 2011).

Dee Brown's *Hear That Lonesome Whistle Blow* (1977; reprint, Touchstone, 1994) is a classic account of how the railroads conquered the West, and *Last Train to Paradise* by Les Standiford (Three Rivers, 2002) is a detailed roller-coaster account of the crazy Florida Keys scheme by Henry Flagler. One other little gem I came across is Robert Louis Stevenson's account of slumming it across America by train, *The Amateur Emigrant* (originally published posthumously, in 1895, but widely available, including with Carroll & Graf, 2002). Albro Martin, *Enterprise Denied: Origins of the Decline of American Railroads* (Columbia University Press, 1971), is excellent on the creation of the Interstate Commerce Commission and its role in stymieing railroad investment. The old and dry *Railroads and Regulation, 1877–1916* by Gabriel Kolko (Princeton University Press, 1965) proved to be a gem as a reliable account of the period. Geoffrey Freeman Allen's *Luxury Trains of the World* (Bison Books, 1979) has superb detail on the heyday of great American trains, as does his *Railways of the Twentieth Century* (Winchmore, 1983).

For more modern times, the two books by Richard Saunders Jr. are superb accounts of the railroads in the twentieth century: *Merging Lines* (Northern Illinois University Press, 2001), which covers the period 1900–1970, and its sequel, *Main Lines* (Northern Illinois University Press, 2003). Alfred Runte's rather angry *Allies of the Earth* (Truman State University Press, 2006) is an evocative study of how America allowed its passenger rail services to wither away, while Joseph Vranich's *Derailed* (St. Martin's Press, 1997) highlights Amtrak's failings.

I made extensive use of several histories of particular railroads, notably Joseph R. Daughen and Peter Binzen, *The Wreck of the Penn Central* (Little, Brown, 1971), written soon after the collapse, which gives it a nice immediacy; Lawrence H. Kaufman, *Leaders Count*, published by the Burlington Santa Fe itself in 2005 and therefore rather hagiographic; and H. Roger Grant, *Erie Lackawanna* (Stanford University Press, 1994). Another good account of the postwar crisis in the rail industry is Rush Loving Jr., *The Men Who Loved Trains* (Indiana University Press, 2006).

On specific aspects of the story, George W. Hilton and John F. Due, *The Electric Urban Railways in America* (Stanford University Press, 1960), provides an almost encyclopedic account of the tragic story of the interurbans, a tale that is often neglected in railroad history; Mark Aldrich's book on safety, *Death Rode the Rails* (Johns Hopkins University Press, 2006), includes a lot of data on accident rates, as well as offering a coherent narrative; and Robert C. Post tells the story of city transportation technologies in *Urban Mass Transit* (Johns Hopkins University Press, 2010).

Finally, if I were to award a prize for the best book on a railroad topic, it would have to go to Theodore Kornweibel Jr.'s *Railroads in the African American Experience* (Johns Hopkins University Press, 2010), which is groundbreaking, comprehensive, beautifully illustrated, and superbly written and highlights an area that has been widely neglected.

Index

PAUL BIGLAND

Christian Wolmar is a writer, broadcaster, and railway and transport expert. He has written for major British newspapers for many years and has contributed to many other publications, including the *New York Times* and *Newsday*. His most recent books are *Blood, Iron, and Gold* and *Engines of War*.

PublicAffairs is a publishing house founded in 1997. It is a tribute to the standards, values, and flair of three persons who have served as mentors to countless reporters, writers, editors, and book people of all kinds, including me.

I. F. STONE, proprietor of *I. F. Stone's Weekly*, combined a commitment to the First Amendment with entrepreneurial zeal and reporting skill and became one of the great independent journalists in American history. At the age of eighty, Izzy published *The Trial of Socrates*, which was a national bestseller. He wrote the book after he taught himself ancient Greek.

BENJAMIN C. BRADLEE was for nearly thirty years the charismatic editorial leader of *The Washington Post*. It was Ben who gave the *Post* the range and courage to pursue such historic issues as Watergate. He supported his reporters with a tenacity that made them fearless and it is no accident that so many became authors of influential, best-selling books.

ROBERT L. BERNSTEIN, the chief executive of Random House for more than a quarter century, guided one of the nation's premier publishing houses. Bob was personally responsible for many books of political dissent and argument that challenged tyranny around the globe. He is also the founder and longtime chair of Human Rights Watch, one of the most respected human rights organizations in the world.

•   •   •

For fifty years, the banner of Public Affairs Press was carried by its owner Morris B. Schnapper, who published Gandhi, Nasser, Toynbee, Truman, and about 1,500 other authors. In 1983, Schnapper was described by *The Washington Post* as "a redoubtable gadfly." His legacy will endure in the books to come.

Peter Osnos, *Founder and Editor-at-Large*